Fingering the Jagged Grain

Keith E. Byerman

Fingering the Jagged Grain

Tradition and Form
in Recent Black Fiction

The University of Georgia Press   Athens and London

5753

© 1985 by the University of Georgia Press
Athens, Georgia 30602
All rights reserved

Designed by Sandra Strother Hudson
Set in Mergenthaler Linotron 202 Meridien
The paper in this book meets the guidelines for
permanence and durability of the Committee on
Production Guidelines for Book Longevity of the
Council on Library Resources.

Printed in the United States of America

89 88 87 86 85   5 4 3 2 1

Library of Congress Cataloging in Publication Data

Byerman, Keith Eldon, 1948–
    Fingering the jagged grain.

    Bibliography: p.
    Includes index.
    1. American fiction—Afro-American authors—
History and criticism.   2. American fiction—
20th century—History and criticism.   3. Afro-Americans
in literature.   I. Title.
PS153.N5B9   1986   813'.54'09896   85-1102
ISBN 0-8203-0789-0 (alk. paper)

Portions of this book are based on the following
previously published articles by Keith Byerman:
"Black Vortex: The Gothic Structure of Eva's Man,"
MELUS 7 (Winter 1980–81): 93–100;
and "Intense Behaviors: The Use of the Grotesque
in *Eva's Man* and *The Bluest Eye*," *College Language
Association Journal* 25 (1982): 447–57.

The blues is an impulse to keep the painful details and episodes of a brutal experience alive in one's aching consciousness, to finger its jagged grain, and to transcend it, not by the consolation of philosophy but by squeezing from it a near-tragic, near-comic lyricism.

—*Ralph Ellison*

For, while the tale of how we suffer, and how we are delighted, and how we may triumph is never new, it must always be heard. There isn't any other tale to tell, it's the only light we've got in all this darkness.

—*James Baldwin*

Contents

vii

Acknowledgments

I WOULD LIKE TO THANK Michael King, Wayne Lesser, Ramon Saldivar, and Gay Wilentz for their willingness to read and comment on various chapters of this work. I also appreciate the responses of scholars at a number of conferences who offered valuable suggestions on presentations based on excerpts from this book. The University of Texas was gracious enough to provide a University Research Institute Summer Research Award at a crucial time in my writing and to provide a Special Research Award to pay for typing and editorial assistance. Suzanne and Ira Kennedy were good typists and good friends throughout. The University of Georgia Press editorial staff, and especially Karen Orchard and Ellen Harris, have been diligent and helpful in getting this study into print. Finally, I thank Mary-Margaret Byerman, who typed, edited, commented, sustained, and cared enough to help make certain that this work was done right.

Fingering the Jagged Grain

Introduction

Making a Way of No Way: Folklore, Ideology, and the Shape of Recent Black Fiction

IN THE CONTEXT of the civil rights and black power movements, black writing exploded on the literary scene in the mid-1960s. As part of the black arts movement, it gave expression to the anger, frustration, and cultural-political ideas of a group of young writers. Though much of the work was versified polemic, it profoundly changed the conventional literary wisdom by insisting on a black perception of the world and of literary activities. A new aesthetic emerged that emphasized revolutionary usefulness as a principal measure of artistic merit.[1]

Starting in the late 1960s, a related but different kind of writing began to emerge. This work, primarily in fiction, has taken seriously the call to use black cultural materials in devising an aesthetic. In fact, it has made much greater use of black cultural history than have the black aestheticists. At the same time, however, these newer authors have recognized the importance of literary forms and traditions. A number of them have commented publicly on the influence of modern European and white American writers on their styles and fictional devices.[2] Significantly, they also have shown the impact on their work of Ralph Ellison, Jean Toomer, and Zora Neale Hurston—precisely those writers sometimes attacked for being insufficiently "black." Thus, the fictionists to be examined here, including Ernest Gaines, Toni Morrison, Alice Walker, Ishmael Reed, and others somewhat less well known, have shaped a technically sophisticated body of literature by combining the methods of modern fiction making with the materials of folk culture. More basically, I wish to argue that this culture has determined the nature of the aesthetic.

1

The narratives produced address the significant political and moral issues of black American life through the vehicle of good storytelling. These writers deal with one of the fundamental concerns of art: the right and necessity of imagination and expression. Their racial heritage gives a special poignance to these issues because, as Robert Stepto has pointed out, the informing motifs of black life are literacy and freedom.[3] Implicitly, then, for black writers, questions of art are questions of power. But this does not necessarily lead to any particular ideological stance (as it did for the Black Arts artists and critics) beyond affirmations of life, of voice, and of freedom in the broadest sense of these terms. Because recent authors have discovered in their cultural history both the same affirmations and appropriate expressive forms, they have incorporated in their work the themes, values, and structures of that culture.

Black American culture is that dialectic which W. E. B. Du Bois called "double-consciousness,"[4] the awareness of being both black and American, of having ties to Africa but living in a land of slavery and oppression controlled by nonblacks. Refusal to accept dehumanizing conditions required both an awareness of the nature of the oppressor, accompanied by strategies for dealing with him, and a cultural life and group identity independent of that Other.[5] These two needs produced a folk life emphasizing both faith and rebellion, integrity and trickster behavior, accompanied by mother-wit and stubborn hope. Characterized by a desire for freedom, it also recognizes that the struggle is long and the enemy formidable. It is, in other words, a double-faced culture, looking to the outside to measure the opposition and to the inside to gain sustenance for both the specific historical struggle and the universal pains and pleasures of human life.

Black folk culture is used in this study in a very broad sense to mean both the history of the black masses and the primarily oral forms of expression that have developed over that history. These forms comprise blues; jazz; spirituals; sermons; toasts; the dozens; cautionary tales; trickster tales; legends; memorates; rural and urban speech patterns; folk beliefs such as voodoo, conjure, and "superstition"; and folk characters such as Brer Rabbit, Stagolee, John Henry, the loup garou, flying Africans, the conjure woman, the good-time woman, and the aunt.[6]

Contemporary black writers have mined this vein of cultural material not merely to give color to their narratives, as has frequently been the case in American literature, but, more important, to create the very shapes of their writing. Folk culture gives them access to their racial history, not only as a content of struggles for freedom, literacy, and dignity, but also as a form of dialectical experience, practice, and belief. Black folk forms generally have a call-and-response structure that relates performer and audience;[7] corresponding to this structure is a thematics of individual and community, oppression and freedom, black and white, silence and voice, trickster and tricked, order and chaos. The folklore presents a complex of strategies for living with such polarities, which can be destructive but also powerfully creative.

This material has varied uses in fiction, some of which have been suggested by Hennig Cohen: "Folklore in American literature has been put to work in a number of ways—among them, to advance, to characterize, to provide structure, and to defend, explain, and raise questions about the nature of society."[8] The concerns of the present study are the structural and thematic significances of Afro-American cultural materials for recent black fiction.[9] Just as folklore has an inherently dialectical form, so the narratives using it take on this characteristic. By "dialectic" I mean the pattern of dynamic oppositions within the context of a whole.[10] Reality is a totality, with interrelated parts, that changes according to circumstance and that leaves nothing in isolation. As an example, race relations in America imply a relationship of blacks and whites that both joins and separates them and that exists in tension precisely because each group defines itself in terms of the other. White supremacy, in this sense, needs blacks in order to have any meaning. Moreover, this relation is a constantly shifting one that changes both its configuration and perceptions of that configuration.

More precisely, folklore serves in the literature as the antithesis of closed, oppressive systems. Closed systems may be political, economic, cultural, religious, racial, sexual, aesthetic, or philosophical; they may be black or white, male or female, psychological or physical. They seek to suppress individuality, community, imagination, voice, freedom, or even life itself by imposing a homogeneous order on a heterogeneous reality. The fiction usually establishes the reality of this order, frequently through its effects on the central character, and then offers an alternative through some aspect of the folk culture.

Folk history and lore oppose systems of order by means that can be summarized in Jacques Derrida's term *differance*. Differance implies both a "differing from" and a "deferral of."[11] In the case of recent black fiction, folk material is made to differ from oppressive orders by being historical, changing, disreputable, and performative. By definition, it is a body of wisdom, wit, and story accumulated over time. As such, it can be made to contradict the representations of the past and of reality offered by apologists for oppression. This folk material stands as a group memory which contains among other things the human costs necessary for the powerful to attain their positions. As Janheinz Jahn has said of the spirituals, they served as both "plaint and complaint" for the slaves who created them.[12] The fiction also captures the constant change that marks a folk culture and which distinguishes it from systems which attempt to justify themselves as permanent and natural. Folk characters display fluid identities, folk tales and songs are given in different versions, and folk values are adapted to changing circumstances; in all the writers, improvisation continually occurs. Folklore in these texts assumes no originary presence or absolute that fixes its content or form. By implication, it challenges the claims of authority based on original purity (as in white supremacy) or on unchanging reality (as in capitalism or sexism).

Folk tales, especially, call into question conventional notions of moral propriety. By using variations on Brer Rabbit and John the Slave, authors can show that survival often necessitates practicing deception rather than openness. The behavior of such figures, like that of various "bad niggers,"[13] refutes the contentions that doing good, as defined by those in power, aids one in either this life or the next, and that, conversely, playing tricks or doing evil produces punishment. They deny the validity of sacrifice and suffering as natural human conditions and thereby resist any system that demands sacrifice and suffering for its perpetuation.

A key aspect of the folk culture for contemporary writers is the idea of performance. In music, narrations, preaching, and dozens-playing, for example, the material derives its value not only from its content but also from its presentation. As Jahn has noted, the "I" of the story is often very prominent.[14] But this does not mean that any simple, straightforward equation can be made between the performer and the first-person experiences rendered by him or her. Any number of roles can be adopted by the blues singer or the storyteller. He has as many faces as the shape-shifters who

4

constitute characters in many of the fictions. What we have then is a difference from the concept of *positive identity*, a fixed identity that can be manipulated because the one identified has been categorized and thus brought into the system.[15] Role playing denies such permanence and external control, in part by suggesting that the fixed identity, like the system that produces it, is only one among several possibilities.

Performance also defers presence by emphasizing its existence as a form of discourse. It is never reality, only a variation on it. Masking, role playing, "signifying," and other forms of black performance all create a distance from certainty; they are always appearance, but they deny this status in the very process of enacting it, and so prevent the possibility of knowing the reality behind them, if such a thing in fact exists. Both the content of cultural materials, in trickster tales and folk wisdom, and the style in the double meanings of the spirituals and the sexual metaphors of the blues, implicitly stress this putting off of both origin and presence. Such ambiguity contradicts the one-dimensional demands of controlling systems.[16] Both language and identity retain a variety of possibilities that cannot be contained or manipulated easily. They emphasize play, imagination, freedom, and creativity, qualities that are sufficiently unpredictable to be anathema to a mechanistic order.

The lack of certainty includes the sense of identity. These writers reject the Black Arts notion that blackness and humanity are fixed, clearly definable qualities. Instead, identity becomes a process, a continual creation partly in negation of those forces that deny individuality and self-determination and partly in affirmation of the disorderly, vital history they see as the black experience. Thus, the black self in recent fiction grows out of a *negative dialectics* in making an identity from this tension.[17] It must be understood that "negative" here implies neither that the self or the culture is somehow a poor imitation of white society nor that either is a simplistic reaction to that society. Instead, it suggests that Afro-American culture and identity have emerged in the context of a dominant white social structure, that in this social structure black and white are bound together by their common history, and that neither can be properly understood in isolation from the other. Moreover, that negation constitutes an affirmation to the extent that black culture rejects dehumanization. The novels and stories become the record of both personal and group suffering and joy and, even

5

further, show that individual and community, suffering and joy are themselves inseparable realities. Folk material, as a literary device, keeps alive the memory of this complex condition in opposition to systems that suppress such history in the name of racial superiority or revolution or the greater good. By incorporating blues, badman tales, sermons, and other materials, black authors remind their readers that life cannot be reduced to a smoothly running machine and that human beings are more than cogs in that machine.

A language much enhanced by folk elements is a noteworthy characteristic of this body of fiction. Urban and rural black speech patterns possess a metaphoric colorfulness not readily apparent in standard English; "talking that talk" makes many of the narratives, especially those of Ernest Gaines, Alice Walker, Toni Cade Bambara, and Toni Morrison, much more vivid than they would be otherwise. But, more important, the verbal artistry so apparent in black culture creates a motif of the fiction: language itself. In one sense, much of contemporary writing in general is about nothing other than the power and limits of expression.[18] Just as important for black writers, the word has a place in black cultural history. In Africa, *nommo* (the word) creates reality; it gives meaning to otherwise meaningless objects. In voodoo, the conjurer knows the secret language of spells which can bring about love or death.[19] In slavery, spirituals often gave information about secret meetings, while Brer Rabbit tales seemed harmless to whites but carried subversive messages for putatively powerless blacks.[20] Language, then, has always been a source of power in black life, and its ramifications continue to be explored in black literature. A recurrent theme is the conflict between those who use words to constrict, objectify, and dehumanize, and those who insist on the ambiguous, ironic, liberating aspects of language. In the struggle for discursive power, the fictions take the form of quests for voice, for authority over the narration itself.[21] To be able to render the experience, to give it, in effect, a name, is to bring it into being and, by extension, to bring oneself into being as the narrator. If the story, as is frequently the case here, concerns the struggle for the definition of black life, then the narrative serves to expose the arbitrary semiotics of oppression and claims, by its very existence, a victory for the black voice. Moreover, the tradition of trickster behavior, of masking, and of performance incorporated in the fiction emphasizes the free play of sign systems and gives special value to the liberating qualities of a semantically multivalent language.

Black culture has further consequences for the form of contemporary black writing in that the theme of black negation of oppression is itself a version of the call-and-response pattern of most black verbal art. In traditional black church services, the preacher depends on the expressed reactions of the congregation to judge the direction and success of his sermon. He is not a solo performer in isolation from his audience, but one part of a communal experience. Likewise, the dozens, an insult ritual, requires a crowd to inform the two combatants of the quality of their exchanges.[22] Within these forms, then, cooperative, creative, changeable expression is encouraged. In the fiction, the claims of the dominant order to a logocentric, absolute control are countered and "contextualized" by some form of folk expression.[23] The "call" to order by those who dominate receives a response from the folk realm, often in the form of a voice which refuses to forget or to be silenced. Thus, domination through discourse, through the definition of reality, is resisted by an alternative discourse.[24]

Moreover, this call-and-response pattern leads not to resolution and progress in terms of plot but instead to some form of return. The story moves not by the successful ending of conflict but by a repetition of it in another version. *The Autobiography of Miss Jane Pittman,* for example, does not show Jane's gaining of wisdom or identity; rather, it plays variations on the paradigmatic story of a rebel's resistance to the "rules" of the racist South. Only names, times, and situations change. This pattern reflects the idea of the "cut," a technique in black music: "The 'cut' overtly insists on the repetitive nature of the music, by abruptly skipping it back to another beginning which we have already heard."[25] Such a device marks a difference from European cultural notions of progress and resolution; it puts off, past the conclusion of the black literary text, the goal for which the quest was begun or the realization of a completed and understood self. It envisions instead a world of organic process in which repetition and change are the only constants. The repeated event marks both certain constants in life (such as communion, struggle, creation, and death) and the changes in the mode of these constants brought about by history. Thus, in

7

Jane Pittman, each generation of rebels has a purpose different from preceding ones, both because the oppressors change and because the earlier resistance forced such change.

Since the tale remains much the same, the role of the teller becomes very important. Jahn has said of the blues performer that he expresses the experiences of the community in his music. He provides a personal version of a common condition, and this linking of the individual and the community makes him effective.[26] Just so, the authors discussed below make use of central characters and narrators who are part of or in confrontation with the folk and who in their repetitions create paradigms from personal experiences, and in their themes of love and trouble resemble the blues artist. The tellers become a part of the story not only by participating but also by convincing the audience through various devices of the value of the tale. In other words, they must be successful performers. They may hold readers through their innocence, their sophistication, their air of bewilderment or wisdom, or their intensity to and sometimes beyond the point of madness. The tale does not have to be told in any particular way, but it must display a sense of style that is at once shared and distinctive.[27]

Thus, the fiction does not operate in terms of a simplistically dualistic conflict that shows the triumph of the good-hearted folk over the evil racists, capitalists, or sexists. Such a resolution, first, would compromise the folk material by ignoring the historical context out of which it emerges. That context reveals that the struggle for expression and freedom is perpetual, that oppression takes many forms, and that it seems ingrained in the human condition. Further, the writers recognize that resistance to oppression is intrinsically related to that oppression. For example, black culture itself exists in part because whites have chosen to make the arbitrary sign of skin color into an ontological distinction. Thus, the expressive achievements of blacks—spirituals, blues, literature—are inextricably interwoven with the continual suppression of these achievements. Finally, the folk culture provides strategies for endurance and improvement, not for domination. The lesson of the lore is "making a way of no way," making the best of conditions rather than presuming to dictate them. According to the experiential wisdom itself, the quest for control, given human greed and fallibility, leads inevitably to the same resistance that created the wisdom. Domination generates insubordination and trickster behavior, not submission. Just so, the writers tend to produce open-ended stories which do not force a resolution on conflicts which are, both in literary and historical terms, inherently unresolvable. In this sense, as in others discussed above, folklore shapes the inner form of contemporary black narrative.

The foregoing discussion attempts to suggest the larger patterns of the work of a number of contemporary authors. But I do not intend to imply that a mold exists by which black novels and stories are shaped. The authors included here vary widely in the uses and kinds of folk materials they include and in the ways they treat the underlying dialectic of oppression and resistance. They were, in fact, selected as much for their differences as their similarities. In some cases, they are antagonistic: Alice Walker's increasingly apparent feminist values conflict directly with the view of Ishmael Reed that black women, perhaps unconsciously, conspire with their white oppressors in emasculating black men. In addition, the quest for a black voice has produced a chorus; styles and techniques, as well as attitudes, cover the spectrum of literary possibilities.

In recognition of this dialectic of unity and diversity, the present study is organized into four parts. The first focuses on Ralph Ellison's *Invisible Man* as a paradigmatic work for more recent writers. Even though not all the authors under consideration would acknowledge Ellison's importance, he in fact produced over thirty years ago a work which displays the same concern for both literary excellence and folk material. While the pioneering efforts of Jean Toomer, Charles Chestnutt, and Zora Neale Hurston in the use of folk culture cannot be ignored, the author of *Invisible Man* created the literary space in which fictionists with a modern (and especially modernist) literary sensibility, an awareness of the totalitarian potential of oppressive systems, and an appreciation of the value of folk experience could operate successfully.

The second part examines authors—James Alan McPherson, Ernest Gaines, Toni Cade Bambara, and Alice Walker—who use the traditional devices of fiction, such as chronological plot development, reliable narration, round characters, and "realistic" situations and actions. Even when the situations seem extreme, as is often the case with Walker's work, she uses her considerable skills to convince us that such lives and circumstances are possible in the realm of black experience.

The third part looks at two writers, Gayl Jones and Toni Morrison, whose interests in spiritual and psychological realities cause them to exceed the boundaries of realism. Both focus on the nonrational elements of human life: madness, death, sexuality, and, in Morrison's case, the fantastic. Jones's narrators border on insanity, while Morrison, through omniscient voices, creates worlds of violent accidents, bizarre characters, and folk magic. Their writing contains gothic elements in the sense that they deal with obsession, with ghosts, with violence that has a sexual character, and with the grotesque.

The last part—on Ishmael Reed, Leon Forrest, and Clarence Major—concentrates on the experimentalist element in contemporary black fiction. Though these writers differ in the techniques they employ and the degree of literary radicalism they display, they share an overt concern for the limits and possibilities of fiction writing. None of them accepts the realistic assumptions of the traditionalists; each sees as problematic the process of telling a story. Reed uses parody to demonstrate the arbitrariness of genres. Forrest creates extreme effects with stream-of-consciousness narratives, rhetorical intensity, and richness of cultural allusion. Major toys with fictional devices—plot, character, narrative voice, style—in revealing the imprisoning impact of conventional story making.

The writers included have been selected primarily because of their artistic skills. Some are well known, while others have been inexplicably ignored by critics. What should also be acknowledged is that this study does not presume to cover the field of contemporary black fiction. Several excellent writers of the past fifteen years have been omitted, the casualties of a need to balance breadth of coverage with depth of analysis. Such significant talents as David Bradley, Ronald Fair, Paule Marshall, Kristen Hunter, John Edgar Wideman, Charles Wright, and Henry Van Dyke deserve and, I am confident, will receive much critical attention in the future. My task, as I see it, is to help open this critical territory, not to prescribe its boundaries.

One

History Against History: A Dialectical Pattern *in* Invisible Man

WHAT MAKES *Invisible Man* a crucial text for contemporary black fictionists is its combining of traditional Afro-American themes and devices with the stylistic and structural methods of modernist literature. Like Frederick Douglass, W. E. B. Du Bois, Zora Neale Hurston, and Richard Wright before him, Ralph Ellison addresses the problematic of black identity in a society that has consistently denied the validity of that identity. Like them, he seeks in the folk experience some nurturing resource for his struggling, oppressed characters. But more than any of them, he finds in modern writing, including Joyce, Faulkner, and Hemingway, a means by which to symbolize these concerns. He quite consciously adopts the techniques of stream-of-consciousness, surrealism, literary allusion, and either lavishness or economy of style, depending on the particular effect he wishes to create. Furthermore, the theme of identity is given a twentieth-century Western gloss in the use of Freudian, Marxist, and existentialist notions of self that are expounded upon in the novel. In doing all this, Ellison provides a wealth of possibilities for the contemporary black writer.

But if his contribution were limited to bringing black fiction into the modern Western canon, his influences would be relatively small, for he would essentially be teaching others how to be imitative of white literary masters.[1] An examination of certain structural patterns in *Invisible Man*, however, suggests that Ellison is doing what blacks have consistently done with American culture: laying claim to certain aspects of it that can be used

11

in the ongoing creation of a truly Afro-American cultural life. In this case, modernist devices aid in rendering a narrative whose dialectical structure follows the call-and-response pattern of traditional black expression. It is through this underlying narrative order that Ellison provides those who come after him with a literary paradigm that enables them to be fully contemporary and yet true to their cultural heritage.

A fruitful way to delineate this paradigm is to examine the patterning of history in the text. Two kinds of history are involved: history as an abstract, ideological view of man's position and possibilities in the world; and history as what Theodor Adorno calls the "concrete particular," the specific events involving individuals and groups over time.[2] The first involves an imposition of meaning on the past, present, and future that may necessitate distorting or ignoring the social reality. The second emphasizes specific, discontinuous reality to the point of denying the possibility of meaning. *Invisible Man* repeatedly sets up the opposition of these two perspectives. In the three sequences to be discussed—college experiences, life in New York, and the Brotherhood—an ideological position is taken that defines the situation of blacks in a certain way, usually for the purpose of manipulation. Shortly thereafter, an experience occurs that negates the ideology; this negation occurs by accident and is embodied by a disreputable figure. But the negation is truly dialectical in that the ideology contains the seeds of its own opposite, while the negative position itself can only have meaning in the context of the ideology. Moreover, the dialectic is non-Hegelian in that the meeting of thesis and antithesis results not in synthesis but in disruption. The narrator is plunged into a violent surrealistic experience that explodes the opposition he has witnessed. Only after this nightmare does a new statement occur. This statement involves an exploration of history related to social action; implicit in each version of it is a new ideology and thus the next dialectical stage.

Such an approach makes possible a reconsideration of the whole question of identity and suggests the ambiguity implicit in the theme of invisibility. It also makes possible a linking of two aspects of the text that have been given increasing critical attention: politics and folklore.[3] Moreover, it demonstrates the role of the artistic intelligence in shaping a text without imposing a closure that would become another ideology.

I

THE FIRST SEQUENCE involves Mr. Norton, Jim Trueblood, the Golden Day bar and Homer Barbee. While Norton is often seen as a wealthy hypocrite, it might be useful to take him and his philosophy seriously for a moment. The point at which to start is one that Norton himself suggests: Ralph Waldo Emerson and fate. In his 1852 essay entitled "Fate," the Concord sage argues that only through the recognition of destiny and necessity can the individual hope to achieve significance: "The right use of Fate is to bring up our conduct to the loftiness of nature."[4] In his first reference to the topic, Norton indicates that he has achieved this condition; he repeatedly comments that his fate is a pleasant one. He makes his comments in the context of describing for the narrator his participation with the founder in creating the college and the satisfaction he has gained in seeing a dream realized. Fate here obviously means the choices one makes in life and the consequences of these choices. Norton feels that he has in fact made the "right use of Fate."

But at this simplest level, the narrator experiences a degree of doubt about Norton's self-satisfaction:

> As I drove, faded and yellowed pictures of the school's early days displayed in the library flashed across the screen of my mind, coming fitfully and fragmentarily to life—photographs of men and women in wagons drawn by mule teams and oxen, dressed in black, dusty clothing, people who seemed almost without individuality, a black mob that seemed to be waiting, looking with blank faces, and among them the inevitable collection of white men and women in smiles, clear of features, striking, elegant and confident.[5]

Although the narrator almost immediately puts this image out of his mind, its appearance in the form of a historical artifact offers an empirical challenge to Norton's definition of the past. The whites pictured display a sense of pleasant fate in their confidence and elegance. These are people who know what they want and are certain of getting it. This "inevitable collection" fits Emerson's description of "the instinctive and heroic races as proud believers in Destiny."[6] The other figures in the photographs are diametrically opposed. They are not even figures, but a "black mob" with "blank faces," who, not in tune with fate, are waiting and looking for

13

something. The image implies that the whites have confidence in part because they refuse to see the reality around them. Furthermore, the use of "inevitable" in reference to the group of whites suggests that they have imposed themselves on blacks.

With this in mind, we can see that Norton's development of his idea is ominous, for he now moves to include the narrator and all other blacks in his fate. "I had a feeling that your people were somehow connected with my destiny. That what happened to you was connected with what would happen to me. . . . I mean that upon you depends the outcome of the years I have spent in helping your school. That has been my real life's work, not my banking or my researches, but my first-hand organizing of human life" (*Invisible Man*, 32–33). Norton defines himself by his relationship to blacks; working for them has been his "real life's work." In return, he expects blacks, including the narrator, to define themselves in relation to him. He does this precisely by laying on them the responsibility for his fate; like the whites in the photograph, he makes himself an inevitability. His characterization of his work—"first-hand organizing of human life"—indicates his dialectical relationship with blacks: he will be their fate and they will be his. Emerson indicates the effects of such work: "An expense of ends to means is fate;—organization tyrannizing over character."[7] What is for Emerson a law of nature is for Norton a principle of social relationships. His association with blacks, an unequal one, is simply a matter of the great order of things. They become his fate in determining the relative success or failure of one of his projects in life; he becomes theirs in attempting, in God-like fashion, to structure their very existence. Moreover, as Emerson says, this structuring means the loss of individual identity. Norton knows this: "*You* are important because if you fail *I* have failed by one individual, one defective cog" (*Invisible Man*, 35).

Clearly, Norton sees himself as grounded in nineteenth-century American liberalism. He completes his being by assuming responsibility for those less fortunate than himself. But the very generosity of that position reveals its foundation in self-interest. He takes as his right the definition of what blacks should be, and that definition grows out of his bourgeois sensibility. Naming the relationship Fate enables him to put a commodity value on his beneficence. In exchange for playing God, he receives the privilege of structuring black life to fit the machine of his universe. The black contribution to this relationship is in a willingness to become cogs in that machine. Again, Emerson clarifies the situation: "For though Fate is immense, so is Power, which is the other fact in the dual world, immense. If Fate follows and limits Power, Power attends and antagonizes Fate."[8] Because he retains the power, Norton is willing to grant to blacks the role of fate.

But another kind of fate operates in this section, and it leads directly to the negation represented by Jim Trueblood. Norton describes not only his relationship with blacks but also another, more intimate and more important relationship: that with his daughter. Critics have often seen this part of the conversation as revelatory of Norton's latent incestuous feelings.[9] While this position has some validity, the incident can be read on other levels as well. The Norton who would dominate and define black life himself worships at this dead girl's altar. He uses the language of sentimentality to speak of her. In this very act, however, he succeeds in making her abstract and nonhuman: "She was rare, a perfect creation, a work of purest art" (*Invisible Man*, 33). This act of reification makes it possible for him to evade responsibility for her death. Though he says, "I have never forgiven myself" (*Invisible Man*, 34), the assertion that she was "too pure and too good and too beautiful" for this world allows him to consign her to a cruel fate and not to his own negligence. Furthermore, this denial of experience leads to a rationalization of the exploitation of blacks. Norton wants the school to be a living monument to his daughter. He justifies the burden he has laid on the narrator in the name of the white woman.

Significantly, the exploitative implications of Norton's ideology remain unstated. His sincerity must be assumed in order to realize the full impact of his encounter with Jim Trueblood. If he is merely lying, then the shock of the next scene loses credibility. For Trueblood forces him to recognize another aspect of fate altogether. Unlike the abstract, mechanized, and sentimental depiction made by Norton, the destiny described by Trueblood is painfully, even brutally, personal. In contrast to Norton's control, Trueblood is a man who cannot help but lose control; economic conditions create the situation and the unconscious urgings of a dream culminate in the act of incest. Thus Norton's view of fate as a rational force that aids those who choose to do right is contradicted by Trueblood's story of the irrational. But even more, the violation of moral order, the surrender to the irrational represented by incest, does not lead to the destruction of the evildoer. In point of fact Trueblood has prospered under the stigma of his sin. Norton's own "fated" efforts to inspire black uplift are seriously compromised by the narrative of a man who has succeeded by defying the primary taboo of civilization.

The nature of the act also negates Norton's position. It is not necessary to impute incestuous desires to the millionaire in order to see the impact the sharecropper's experience has. In contrast to the "too pure" white girl, Matty Lou is clearly seen by her father in all her emerging womanhood: "But I'm realizin' that she's a woman now, when I feels her turn and squirm against me and throw her arm across my neck, up where the cover didn't reach and I was cold. She said somethin' I couldn't understand, like a woman says when she wants to tease and please a man. I knowed then she was grown and I wondered how many times it'd done happened and was it that doggone boy" (*Invisible Man*, 44). Trueblood's world is filled with passionate human beings, not cogs or artworks. Moreover, unlike Norton's daughter, Matty Lou has connections with the past: Trueblood thinks of her in terms of a former girlfriend and of her own mother. Placing her in such a social and historical context complicates the meaning of the experience and thus makes any reductive judgment absurd. A ghost of Norton's own design haunts him; Trueblood is daily confronted with the concrete ambiguous reality of Matty Lou and their shared past.

The shock that Norton experiences is twofold. There is the shock to his system of morality when a man so completely defies the universe and yet prospers. The very naturalness with which Trueblood speaks of his daughter's desirable humanity verges on moral chaos in Norton's scheme of things. Even if he were capable of such thoughts, they are so sublimated by social conditioning and psychological defenses that they could never be brought to consciousness. To even suggest such a possibility represents to Norton the potential destruction of his universe. Even though he gives Trueblood money, Norton feels primarily threatened and puzzled, not pornographically entertained by the story of incest.

That payment, however, is important to the negation that Trueblood represents. Significantly, the offer of money first comes at the beginning of the encounter, before the tale has been told. Norton's first reaction of horror to the fact of incest is accompanied by an apparent belief that money can right the universe. But it also reestablishes his normal relationship with blacks,

16

which is one of giving payment, in the guise of charity, in exchange for some service. And while the incest story provides sensationalism, it also offers a validation of the racist underpinnings of Norton's ideology. The tale of black desire, dream, and sin affirms and reveals, in the white man's mind, the sense of racial difference that is the foundation of his charity. Trueblood's narrative "proves" that blacks are in fact more animallike, less moral, and more sexual than whites could ever be. Because he will not allow himself to think of his own daughter in human, much less incestuous terms, Norton feels himself inherently different from and superior to the storyteller.

Moreover, what is true for Trueblood must also be true for Bledsoe and the Founder and all other blacks. Whatever these people may think of themselves, Trueblood's story reassures Norton that they are ultimately incapable of real civilization. His money only encourages them to pursue a false dream of financial success and political power, and thus it provides him ultimate control over them. His help to them poses no threat to himself because their inherent limitations make it impossible for them to acquire real power. Trueblood's story is in fact, then, the threat to blacks that Bledsoe later claims it to be. This is verified by the fact that Norton's monetary gesture is identical to that of local whites. We find then that Trueblood serves to negate Norton's definition of fate, of human relationships, and of his charity toward blacks.

But this negation is disturbing in that it occurs through Trueblood's apparent affirmation of the white stereotype of blacks. To paraphrase a folk admonition, it occurs because the black man tells his business to a white man. The response to this problem is that *telling* is Trueblood's business; the narrator describes him as "one who told the old stories with a sense of humor and a magic that made them come alive" (*Invisible Man,* 36). In this context, he has found that the story of his troubles provides income for his family; it is not insignificant that he tells his tale to Norton only after the white man has offered to help him. He remarks that he has told the story a number of times.[10] The evidence suggests that Trueblood is in fact a very shrewd manipulator of the situation who wears the mask of a naïf. Behind the mask are hints of the folkloric John the Slave and the badman. The teller presents himself as an innocent, caught in adverse circumstances and victimized after the fact by the black college officials, who turns to whites for assistance. Trueblood claims that white aid surprised him in its extent; he receives not only protection but also work and money in exchange for telling the story.

Having established his character in these preliminary comments, he moves on to what he knows his audience wants to hear. "He cleared his throat, his eyes gleaming and his voice taking on a deep, incantatory quality, as though he had told the story many, many times" (*Invisible Man,* 42). He knows from his previous recitations and from Norton's initial response that he is dispensing a forbidden knowledge, and he adopts the appropriate attitude. He delays gratification and thus increases anticipation by giving very precise, apparently minor, details about his past and his attitudes. In doing so, he establishes his control over both the material and the audience; they will know what he wants them to know when he is ready to tell it. In the process of building suspense, he clearly establishes the conditions that motivate the incest; all are beyond his control. He must sleep with the girl because of poor housing and economic conditions; she, reaching adulthood, instinctively responds to a man sleeping with her. Thus, what happens will have the air of inevitability, and this reduces moral responsibility.

With character and situation established, Trueblood describes the dream. Worth noting is that the dream presents the black man as an instinctive rebel. "And I'm so tired and restless to git to the man, I goes through the front door! I knows it's wrong, but I can't help it" (*Invisible Man,* 44). He further violates social custom when he finds himself in the bedroom of a white woman. Moreover, she embraces him and slowly draws him to the bed. Trueblood seems to be playing games here with white racism. Since all this occurs in a dream, he takes no responsibility, but he still arouses and exposes the fears of whites. In a kind of comic social telescoping, the black man granted a little social equality (the front door) is immediately on the verge of having intercourse with the white woman. But in an important twist, she wants to be taken; he is the one resisting. The images of the pure Southern woman and the black rapist are both challenged from within the safe confines of a dream. Thus, Trueblood toys with white miscegenist fears and by doing so proves himself superior to them. Like John the Slave, he can play his joke without fear of reprisal.

Even in describing the act of incest, which he sees as immoral, he offers a defiant image. At the moment he discovers that both he and Matty Lou want to continue the act, he recalls an incident of outlawry:

> I guess I felt then, at that time—and although I been sorry since—just 'bout like that fellow did down in Birmingham. That one what locked hisself in his house and shot at them police until they set fire to the house and burned him up. I was lost. The more wringlin' and twistin' we done tryin' to git away, the more we wanted to stay. So like that fellow, I stayed, I had to fight it on out to the end. He mighta died, but I suspects now that he got a heapa satisfaction before he went. (*Invisible Man*, 47)

The comparison suggests the role of the bad man, such as Stagolee, who has no concerns other than his immediate desires. Neither social convention nor death itself has any influence on his behavior. At this moment in the story, Trueblood finds satisfaction in his violation of taboo; in point of fact, he never entirely repudiates this moment. Even when he feels his wife has the right to punish him, he turns away just enough to keep her from killing him. Ostracized by the community, he accepts isolation only long enough to shape his experience into a song; he then returns to take responsibility for his family and to tell his story to whoever is willing to pay.

He accepts payment, then, not for a self-demeaning confession, but for a well-wrought tale that ponders a moral dilemma. Like the blues, Trueblood's narrative tells the experience of finding something both illicit and achingly desirable. A boastfulness of sorts exists in talking of being caught in the most illicit of all acts and living to tell about it. Not only has he overcome his family and community, but God himself has apparently approved by allowing him to prosper. What distinguishes his story from Norton's is not its validation of either good or evil, black or white; rather it is that it remains open. Trueblood does not resolve the dilemma he experienced; he simply captures it all in an artistic form. Norton, on the other hand, has described a closed universe in which experience is reduced to didactic statement, emotion abstracted into sentimentality, and human beings reduced to cogs. He expresses an ideology that seeks to move outside human history; Trueblood articulates a concrete world of human experience and possibility within history.

Norton responds to Trueblood's story with money and shock: the money because he thinks his prejudices have been verified, the shock because that verification may itself reveal the chaotic underside of his social order. This dialectical condition does not resolve itself immediately; instead we are led to the chaos of the Golden Day tavern, where the most sane man is also the most mad. This scene is important in that it places Norton and the narrator in the midst of a group they should identify with: educated, ambitious, middle-class blacks. Trueblood can be dismissed perhaps as an uncivilized, uneducated peasant; the men at the Golden Day are clearly the ones Norton claimed as his fate. Their experience has been the inverse of Trueblood's: by trying to rise in the world, rather than submit to fate, they have ended up in an asylum. By striving to be civilized, they have managed to be locked up, released only to purchase liquor and sex. Thus, the scene confuses reason and irrationality, order and chaos. The very presence of Norton, the man in control, causes a riot; appropriately, he receives a head injury and is revived with alcohol. But at the same time, he finds a doctor who makes a sophisticated diagnosis of his condition and attempts to tell him the truth about black-white relationships. He clearly both validates and refutes the Emersonian ideology Norton had earlier expressed. He proves that blacks do have the intelligence and desire to make themselves what they want to be. His training proves that the benevolence of men such as Norton can be fruitful. But that very intelligence enabled him to penetrate to the manipulative underpinnings of Norton's system; for applying his intelligence this way, he is declared paranoid and his ability shelved. The very qualities that made achievement possible rob that achievement of significance.

Norton's position is thus brought into doubt by its success. When he attempts to recover from the shock of Trueblood's story, he finds himself instead thrown into a chaos where sanity and insanity, success and failure are indistinguishable. What we have is neither Norton's closed universe nor Trueblood's open one, but rather an explosion in which there is neither order nor possibility.

Homer A. Barbee's speech attempts a resolution of the tension between Norton's ideology and Trueblood's history. The speech enacts a ritual in which history becomes mythic legitimation of the college's ideology. The Founder is linked to Christ and Moses as a man of power, humility, and strength of character. Ellison has noted that this section was written in the context of his reading of Raglan's *The Hero* and that it follows some of the patterns of that work.[11] The Founder is shown enduring pain and threats to his life before his triumph. Barbee encourages his audience to experience vicariously those moments and thus to share in his vision. He also validates the position of President Bledsoe by recalling the actual passing on of authority from one generation to the next. Thus the speech seems clearly intended to manipulate the historical record so as to reinforce an ideology of accommodation, humility, and progress. The discovery that Barbee is in fact blind seems an ironic commentary on the realization of the Founder's vision.

But another set of possibilities is at work that renders the speech more ambiguous. Blind Homer recounting the Founder's history is blind only to the present, not the past. He twice indicates that he has not visited the campus since the Founder's death; his interpretation of the present must depend upon the information given him by others, especially Bledsoe. Barbee himself, then, may well be manipulated into believing that the dream has been realized.

Moreover, elements of the tale itself seem inconsistent with the ideology. "I'm sure you have heard of his precarious infancy, his precious life almost destroyed by an insane cousin who splashed the babe with lye and shriveled his seed and how, a mere babe, he lay nine days in a deathlike coma and then suddenly and miraculously recovered" (*Invisible Man*, 92). While the intent is clearly to put the child in the tradition of wondrously saved infants, such as Jesus and Moses, the information about the "shriveled seed" is more ambiguous. It may well be evidence of the great difficulties that the Founder overcame; but it also has the obvious implication of the loss of manhood involved in the ideology of humility. If we take this second interpretation as something embedded in Barbee's speech rather than imposed by the ironic perspective of the narrator, then we have a case of concrete history warning against the ideology that would contain and manipulate it. It suggests to the audience of young men the potential for emasculation in the vision.

Other evidence reinforces the dialectical nature of the speech. In the midst of a description of the Founder's kindly, patient, humble leadership, Barbee makes this statement: "And your parents followed this remarkable man across the black sea of prejudice, safely out of the land of ignorance, through the storms of fear and anger, shouting, LET MY PEOPLE GO! when it was necessary, whispering it during those times when whispering was

21

wisest. And he was heard" (*Invisible Man*, 93). The metaphors of escape do not suggest at all a policy of accommodation to the existing racial conditions, as for example is found in Booker T. Washington's advice to "cast down your buckets where you are."[12] The rhetoric is closer to that of runaway slaves, and the shouting suggests the polemics of Frederick Douglass. The whispering is indicated as a strategic practice, not as standard policy.

The cost of shouting is implied in the sequence of events which Barbee next presents. We learn that the Founder has enemies who plot against him. But a mysterious figure warns him of ambush; dismissing it as a hallucination, he is shortly thereafter caught in the trap. Ignoring the admonition of the mysterious figure leads to near-fatal results; the optimistic, rational determination of the Founder is clearly mistaken. This event calls into question the rejection of the nonrational and unexplainable that is a part of the education that the college offers.

The nonrational must not only be given its due, according to the story; it might be the only means of survival. The Founder's life is saved by a man thought insane, but who has knowledge of the folk arts of healing and who initiates him "deep into the black art of escape" (*Invisible Man*, 94). Part of that black art is the willingness to defend oneself: "And you left him on the morning, hidden in a wagonload of cotton, in the very center of the fleece, where you breathed the hot air through the barrel of the emergency shotgun; the cartridges, which thank God it was unnecessary to use, held fanwise and ready between the spread fingers of your hand" (*Invisible Man*, 95).

Much of the mysterious and potentially violent character of the Founder's story can be explained as necessary to the creation of the myth. If he is to be properly recognized as the creator of a social order and its ideological underpinnings, then a degree of mystification must go on in order to make him an exemplary figure. (In this context, it is significant that he is never given a name, but only a title.) But the very process of recounting the history involves the speaker in the ambiguities of language and historical reality. The man who exemplifies openness and humility only survives by his engaging in "black arts" (with both racial and demonic implications) and his willingness to kill to save himself. If he is an exemplary figure, then it is not at all clear what he exemplifies: he seems as much a model of

22

rebellion and opposition as of submission and cooperation. He resembles the narrator's grandfather, who called himself a spy in his own country.

If history does not entirely uphold the ideology, then the impositions of language will be made to do so. Barbee asserts the meaning of the story:

> Sing out their long black songs of blood and bones:
> Meaning HOPE!
> Of hardship and pain:
> Meaning FAITH!
> Of humbleness and absurdity:
> Meaning ENDURANCE!
> Of ceaseless struggle in darkness, meaning:
> TRIUMPH . . .

(Invisible Man, 97)

By forcefully insisting that the negative features of black experience necessarily have positive meanings, Barbee reduces the significance of the history he has recounted. He imposes a definition on black identity that undercuts any alternatives to the social order he is defending. But that imposition is necessary precisely because the historical experience itself is so rich and ambiguous in meaning.

II

WITH THE COMPLETION of Barbee's speech the pattern of ideology, historical negation, explosion, and attempted synthesis is completed. But the pattern is not a closed one, for the speech is the necessary context for a new statement of ideology. If Barbee's speech gives ritual validation to the college's order, Bledsoe's confrontation with the narrator precisely defines the ahistorical character of his ideology. His interpretation of reality differs from Norton's in that it claims no philosophical or sentimental foundations. It is firmly grounded in present-minded cynicism and opportunism. Like Norton's position, it assumes a fixed relationship between blacks and whites, but, whereas Norton created a justification for the exploitation of blacks, Bledsoe seeks to manipulate whites so as to gain power for himself. This necessitates the creation of masks that project the values that Barbee announced at the end of his speech, but which hide the very antithesis of

23

those values. The encounter between the narrator and Bledsoe can be seen as a very precise education in the difference.

The surprising element in all this is the fact that Bledsoe feels it necessary to reveal so much. With such comments as, "Why, the dumbest black bastard in the cotton patch knows that the only way to please a white man is to tell him a lie" (*Invisible Man*, 107), he destroys the impression left by Barbee's sermon. Such destruction is the necessary first step, since the narrator has in fact identified with the articulated values of Norton. As the insane doctor told him, he truly believes that "white is right." In order for education to take place, he must be moved from a white frame of reference to a black one. But clearly that step is not a great one, as Bledsoe indicates when he calls the narrator a "nigger." It has the same connotation of scorn and dehumanization that it would have if spoken by a southern white. Thus both Norton and Bledsoe see blacks as objects to be manipulated; the difference is that Bledsoe sees men like Norton in the same way. "The only ones I even pretend to please are *big* white folk, and even those I control more than they control me" (*Invisible Man*, 110). He establishes this control by telling them what he ascertains they really want to know; he penetrates the mask of white sentiment and reads the real thought. But for this to be successful, he must never allow his own mask to be removed nor even allow it to be recognized as a mask. Even this possibility does not appear to intimidate him. When the narrator threatens to tell what he had learned, Bledsoe is only momentarily taken aback and quickly responds: "You're a black educated fool, son. These white folk have newspapers, magazines, radios, spokesmen to get their ideas across. If they want to tell the world a lie, they can tell it so well that it becomes the truth; and if I tell them that you're lying, they'll tell the world even if you prove you're telling the truth. Because it's the kind of lie they want to hear" (*Invisible Man*, 110). No grounds exist on which to resist Bledsoe's definition of reality. Even the threat of exposure causes no concern since whites simply cannot believe in the idea of black manipulation. The nature of the mask is to deny its own existence.

The problem with this ideology is that the masking and manipulation become ends in themselves. They generate no new possibilities; the universe they describe is closed. "I don't even insist that it was worth it, but now I'm here and I mean to stay—after you win the game, you take the prize and you keep it, protect it; there's nothing else to do" (*Invisible Man*, 111). Trapped within his own system, Bledsoe can use his power only to perpetuate it, not to gain any other personal or social end. His willingness to tell all to the character he is about to destroy becomes a way of claiming his identity. The need to destroy after the confession is dictated by the fact that the narrator has a countervision, as indicated by his insistence that an objective truth outside Bledsoe's manipulation does exist. Moreover, the confession, by exposing the masquerade, gives the narrator a perspective outside the ideology. Even if forced to adopt certain behavior within the system, he will remain implicitly critical of it by the sheer fact of his knowledge. While incapable at the moment of using that intelligence, he would continue to be an unpredictable element in a system reliant on predictability. But even his expulsion must be done systematically so as not to disturb the operation. By playing on the narrator's admiration of power and his commitment to the ideals of the Founder, Bledsoe can successfully make him disappear without appearing to do so. Exile in New York will be seen by the boy and Norton (if he should care) as perfectly consistent with the values of the institution.

The negation of Bledsoe is the New York cartman, who also wears masks but whose maskings are precisely designed to preserve, not abolish, the past. He claims kinship with the narrator because of their common southern heritage, which he demonstrates through the blues, folkloric references, and verbal play. In his performance he reveals the ambiguity of historical reality, including his own identity: he names himself variously Peter Wheatstraw, Blue, and "seventhsonofaseventhsonbawnwithacauloverbotheyesand-raisedonblackcatboneshighjohntheconquerorandgreasygreens" (*Invisible Man*, 134). Such masks do not conceal true identity as in Bledsoe's case, but in fact reveal the insufficiency of a unitary concept of identity. Each name suggest both a connection with a concrete folk past and a set of desirable personal characteristics, such as luck, courage, and daring.

His song, the "Boogie-Woogie Blues," offers a similar multiplicity of meaning. Unlike Bledsoe's iron leg chain, which is smooth and shows no effects of either time or suffering, the cartman's song follows the blues pattern of containing while not denying the painful aspects of experience. His story of a woman with "feet like a monkey / Legs like a frog" (*Invisible Man*, 131) whom he cannot help but love clearly recognizes the unattractive features in reality and yet embraces them. He makes no attempt to resolve this duality of experience; rather he articulates it in artistic form.

The job of the cartman reinforces his negative role. He carries away blueprints, not of projects completed but of those conceived but never undertaken. His response to the narrator at one point in their exchange makes clear his understanding of the situation:

> "Yeah, this ain't all neither. I got a coupla loads. There's a day's work right here in this stuff. Folks is always making plans and changing 'em."
>
> "Yes, that's right," I said, thinking of my letters, "but that's a mistake. You have to stick to the plan."
>
> He looked at me, suddenly grave. "You kinda young, daddy-o," he said. (*Invisible Man*, 133).

It is not the narrator's youth that is the crucial issue, but his willingness to accept the versions of reality offered by Norton and Bledsoe. The need to have a plan that structures reality for a single purpose and to remain committed to that plan even if, as Bledsoe discovered, it no longer has any inherent value demonstrates a totalizing ideological impulse that the cartman rejects in both statement and practice.

The narrator's response in this scene reinforces the negative dialectical purpose of the cartman: "And suddenly I felt uncomfortable. Somehow he was like one of the vets from the Golden Day" (*Invisible Man*, 132). The vets cannot simply be dismissed as madmen because their comments are true to a level of experience outside the realities defined by Norton and Bledsoe. "I'd known the stuff from childhood, but had forgotten it; had learned it back of school" (*Invisible Man*, 134). Trueblood and the cartman artistically undermine ideology by presenting a reality that is multifaceted, ambivalent, and historically concrete. They cast doubt on the official education the narrator has received, not by imposing an alien vision but by appealing to what the narrator attempts to forget.

The need to remember is made clear in the explosive, surreal scene of the middle portion of the book. Bledsoe's claims about the need for power and control have literal significance when the narrator is subjected to shock treatment in a hospital after his factory accident. The sense of the present is distorted by the various machines, doctors, and lights that are brought to bear on his case. He has no sense of his location or even his body except when it is subjected to painful treatments. The doctors seem to view him simply as a machine to be made functional: " 'Hush, goddamit,' one of the faces ordered. 'We're trying to get you started again' " (*Invisible Man*, 177). Just as he was a cog in Norton's machine and an element of Bledsoe's power setup, so now he is a malfunctioning industrial tool.

He experiences great pain; he "contains" it through memories of his southern past. His grandmother's songs and his boyhood jingles enable him to endure both the physical discomfort and the icy, mechanical attitudes of the doctors. The pernicious import of the latter becomes apparent as the physicians debate the appropriate treatment: " 'And what's more,' the voice went on triumphantly, 'the patient is both physically and neurally whole.' 'But what of his psychology?' 'Absolutely of no importance!' the voice said" (*Invisible Man*, 180). Since the narrator is one of the "primitive instances," they see no need to take into account his thinking or quality of being. This indifference to identity is premised on an ideological position larger than the individual: "I listened with growing uneasiness to the conversation fuzzing away to a whisper. Their simplest words seemed to refer to something else, as did many of the notions that unfurled through my head. I wasn't sure whether they were talking about me or someone else. Some of it sounded like a discussion of history" (*Invisible Man*, 179–80). The narrator himself becomes convinced of his lack of identity. He loses the capacity to become angry, and he begins to feel himself a part of the machine: "Where did my body end and the crystal and white world begin?" (*Invisible Man*, 233). This conviction grows when he is asked questions; he fails to recall any personal information. He does not know his own name, his mother's name, his birthplace.

What prevents his total loss of identity is his cultural history. When asked who his mother is, he thinks of a response from playing the dozens, the Afro-American ritual of insult. When asked about Buckeye the Rabbit, he recalls not only a children's song but also the distinction between that folklore figure and Brer Rabbit. The questions seemed designed to demonstrate the loss of identity and the creation of a psychological blank slate, but they have quite the opposite effect: "He pointed to the question, word by word. I laughed, deep, deep inside me, giddy with the delight of self-discovery and the desire to hide it" (*Invisible Man*, 183–84). The reference triggers not only memory but also the need to mask that memory. The cultural information contains within it the means of its own survival. The rabbit is the trickster figure, who gets what he wants by pretending not to want it and who keeps what he has by pretending not to have it.

Having defeated the machine and doctors, at least in part, makes the narrator feel quilty. Still caught up in the need to cooperate in a system, to stick to a plan, he cannot make use of the knowledge he has gained:

> Left alone, I lay fretting over my identity. I suspected that I was really playing a game with myself and that they were taking part. A kind of combat. Actually they knew as well as I, and I for some reason preferred not to face it. It was irritating, and it made me feel sly and alert. I would solve the mystery the next instant. I imagined myself whirling about in my mind like an old man attempting to catch a small boy in some mischief, thinking, Who am I? It was no good. I felt like a clown. Nor was I up to being both criminal and detective—though why criminal I didn't know. (*Invisible Man*, 184)

He is apprehensive about the implications of his actions; he finds in himself the impulse to break the rules, and he is disturbed by the satisfaction he has in doing that. He tries to brand it immature behavior, the actions of "a small boy in some mischief," and thus dismiss it. He calls himself a clown, apparently trying to suggest the foolishness of his thinking. But the clown succeeds precisely by being a master manipulator of appearances: he turns the criminal act of deceit to the purposes of humor and profit. His duplicity calls into question the nature of surface reality, of the conventions of social behavior. And the better he is at doing this, the more he is rewarded by that very society. Thus, the extent to which he identifies with Buckeye the Rabbit, mischievous boys, and clowns, and hides that identification is the extent to which he is in fact a criminal. Rather than being a name or function to be given or taken away by Norton, Bledsoe, doctors, or the Brotherhood, his identity is his retention of the ambivalent, nonidentical, concrete, and subversive history that is repeatedly and painfully brought back to him.

Some indication of the potential of that history is found in the final scene of this sequence, the narrator's eviction speech. A brief, though much-remarked, episode establishes the framework for the scene. The narrator stops one day to buy a yam. The pleasure he derives from eating it gives him a sense of exhilaration: "I walked along, munching the yam, just as suddenly overcome by an intense feeling of freedom—simply because I

was eating while walking along the street" (*Invisible Man,* 200). His statement is important in the light of another made at the hospital: "When I
discover who I am, I'll be free" (*Invisible Man,* 185). The act of participating
in and enjoying an element of his heritage has given him his freedom.
Again he labels what he learns as childish, but then he turns it to a complex
assertion: "I yam what I am!" (*Invisible Man,* 201). The play of language
connects his past with his identity. Not just a symbol of his being, the yam
constitutes a concrete part of that being. Yams eaten in boyhood have literally made the narrator who he is. The subject and object in this encounter
give meaning to each other in their connection to a particular history.

But the verbal play also generates another possibility. "I yam what I
am!" restates the self-definition of the Old Testament YHWH. God, the self-
created, has no name because any label would restrict his possibilities, and
as omnipotent, omniscient, omnipresent being, he recognizes no limitations. The narrator's version simultaneously establishes his humanity and
his God-like potential. The "yam" places him within a particular history
and thus within humanity. It also denies while it asserts his possible divinity. The pun indicates that the statement does not take itself seriously;
the narrator does not believe himself God's equal. But the content does
imply a quality shared with God: a negation of all restrictive definitions of
his being. In the act of recognizing his history and thus his humanity, he
discovers the divine possibilities in himself. He cannot be reified by the
identities that Norton, Bledsoe, and the doctors attempt to impose. He even
is offered the knowledge that not all aspects of being are beneficial, as
indicated by the frostbitten end of the yam. What remains to be learned is
that it is only in constant negation of all positive ahistorical ideologies and
identities that he can hope to find his true being.

The narrator begins to assert his reality in a speech that recalls Barbee's
in its linking of history and ideology. The boy who learned the importance
of control and power from Bledsoe now becomes the man who can manipulate a crowd through the power of his voice. This newfound power comes
by establishing a connection between historical reality in the form of old
people and their accumulated artifacts and the need to engage in social-
political action. Before the full impact of the eviction scene is rendered, a
voice in the crowd insists that they only need a leader in order to do what
must be done. The narrator, after gathering the social and emotional infor-

mation he needs, will take on that role. But what he finds first is the disturbing quality of the scene: "Now I recognized a self-consciousness about them, as though they, we, were ashamed to witness the eviction, as though we were all unwilling intruders upon some shameful event; and thus we were careful not to touch or stare too hard at the effects that lined the curb; for we were witnesses of what we did not wish to see, though curious, fascinated, despite our shame, and through it all the old female, mind-plunging crying" (*Invisible Man*, 205). The shame is not that the "effects" are inherently obscene; rather it is that their displacement from their context of human experience, their appearance in the cold light of day on the street, reveals their triviality and insignificance. The members of the crowd see exposed the artifacts of their own accumulated history, and they fear that their lives are similarly merely scattered objects with no meaning. Outside the specific human structure of signification, meanings for both the people and the objects are lost.

Of course, this shame and fear exist precisely because of the dialectical nature of the scene. The crowd feels the shame and fear because private, individual experience has been made public. They cannot know the personal significance for "the old female" of the items which the narrator lists; what shames them is the violation of that personal significance, the making of private matters public. And, of course, their very presence defines this as a public event. The nature of the history revealed is precisely that its significance must remain private.

Unless, ironically, it can be converted to public action. The narrator sees, as Barbee did, that history can be opportunity for leadership if properly controlled. The crowd becomes outraged at the marshal's behavior toward the old woman, and the narrator steps in at the crucial moment. His first impulse is to call for law and organization in a chaotic situation. What is noteworthy about his performance is precisely his consciousness of it as a performance. He feels encouraged when he finds the crowd willing to listen to him, but then when they dislike what he says, he ponders the situation: "Oh God, this wasn't it at all. Poor technique and not at all what I intended" (*Invisible Man*, 209). The concern for technique suggests a speaker much more interested in style than in substance, a man in fact defining himself purely in terms of style. The discomforts of a few moments before are brought under control so as to be manipulated for personal recognition.

30

While the narrator has no particular ideology to advance at this point, he has an opportunity to exercise power for its own sake, much as Bledsoe did. The speech works through its rhetorical logic, without any clear direction; the narrator develops whatever the crowd responds to. When they tire of his recounting of history, he turns to the immediate issue of eviction. But even here, he plays with language: "Dispossessed? . . . 'Dispossessed!' 'Dispossessed,' eighty-seven years and dispossessed of what? They ain't *got* nothing, they caint *get* nothing, they never *had* nothing. So who was dispossessed?" (*Invisible Man*, 211).

The extent to which his rhetoric is pacifying rather than provocative is indicated by the marshal's encouraging him to continue. But the narrator primarily wants to please the crowd, and so he gives an ironic twist to his law-and-order language by arguing for resistance as the true spirit of the law. But the crowd reacts more strongly than he anticipated; they overwhelm the marshal just as the vets in the Golden Day overwhelmed Supercargo, their supervisor. The rhetoric of order produces chaos. But it is a mark of the narrator's manipulative skills that he can regain control, though only to the extent of directing, not dissipating, the crowd's energy. He finds that sufficient: "It was like a holiday. I didn't want it to stop" (*Invisible Man*, 214). Like Barbee, the narrator finds that the material of history has potential for the exercise of power; unlike his predecessor, however, he has no end to which to direct that power.

III

THE FINAL IDEOLOGY of the novel, represented by the Brotherhood, offers him direction in the name of history. But in fact this organization moves in the realm of abstraction rather than concrete experience. The first thing that the narrator learns from Brother Jack is that he must ignore mere history:

> "But you mustn't waste your emotions on individuals, they don't count."
> "*Who* doesn't count?" I said.
> "Those old ones," he said grimly. "It's sad, yes. But they're already dead, defunct. History has passed them by. Unfortunate, but there's nothing to do about them." (*Invisible Man*, 220–21)

The ideology has moved beyond the realm of Norton, who saw blacks as cogs, and of Bledsoe, who wanted to manipulate for personal gain, to a new stance where the narrator is a center of power that can be used for vast social purposes. In a character who was attentive to Norton and admiring of Bledsoe, a position as "the new Booker T. Washington" obviously has its appeal. "It was unbelievable, yet strangely exciting and I had the sense of being present at the creation of important events, as though a curtain had been parted and I was being allowed to glimpse how the country operated" (*Invisible Man*, 232).

But if the possibilities for power have increased, so have the costs of such power. Not only must the narrator turn away from the old people at the eviction in order to see the larger meaning of history, but he must also deny his own past and identity. He must put aside whatever he has learned in college in order to be properly educated in sociology, economics, and history; what he knows can only be what the Brotherhood considers knowledge. Moreover, he must forget his connection with his family and leave the home of Mary Rambo, his nurturing connection with his southern past. Most important, he must surrender his identity and take on the one designated by the organization. This action coalesces the ideological demands of Norton and Bledsoe. The new identity makes it possible for the narrator to become a cog in the machine of Brotherhood; individual ambitions will interfere with the program of the organization. Moreover, since the Brotherhood has revolutionary designs, its members can be effective only by masking their true identities. Like Bledsoe, their power can only be exercised if their real intentions are successfully hidden.

The Brotherhood represents as closed a system as that of either Norton or Bledsoe. Identity and history will be denied. In the name of materialism and historical realism, neither the materials of history nor the realities of human experience will be permitted to intrude upon the truth of Brotherhood. But it is also evident that those realities must be constantly and consciously repressed. The drunk at an organization party cannot be reasoned out of his condition, so he must be forcefully evicted from the presence of reason. The old people are not dead, but stubbornly and intrusively alive; it is the consciousness of them that must be killed if the machinery of Brotherhood is to continue functioning. The education of the narrator must proceed so that he will no longer be aware of the complexities of experience, but only the intricacies of the theoretical machine. The various encounters in the Brotherhood section—with the Committee, with Brother Tarp, with Ras, with Clifton—represent the conflict between attempted rational control by the Brotherhood and repeated challenges to that control by the "irrational" events of experience. The dialectic at work is not that of social classes, as claimed by the Brotherhood, but rather that of abstract History and concrete history.

Consistent with the global designs of the Brotherhood, resistance to it takes a variety of forms. Ras, the black nationalist, offers a direct challenge, but one limited because it too is a closed system, one built on race rather than economics. Rinehart provides a more fundamental alternative because he denies the possibility of system and thus represents the claims of chaotic experience over those of authoritarian theory. He multiplies rather than denies identity. As both priest and pimp, he encompasses the spectrum of reality in a way the universal, abstract system of the Brotherhood never could. But the price of such freedom and possibility is the loss of all but appearance. The variety of identities can only work if each one remains isolated from the others; only if, in other words, the versions of the self have neither past nor connection. He is as much locked into disorder as the Brotherhood is into order.

But a third possibility exists, one at the very center of the Brotherhood. In Tarp, the narrator finds a figure who accepts the principles of the organization, but who also retains ties to his personal and cultural past. Tarp gives the narrator a piece of leg chain which, unlike the smooth one on Bledsoe's desk, has been scarred and torn. According to the old man's story, it got into that condition because of his desperate and painful escape from a chain gang. Like the artifacts of the evicted, this piece of metal in its very being asserts a truth of black history that ideologues consistently deny. Moreover, Tarp points out the portrait of Frederick Douglass that hangs in the narrator's Harlem office. Significantly, Douglass represents not only resistance to an oppressive order but also the importance of subtlety in making that fight. In his first narrative Douglass refused to specify the means of his escape, arguing that such information would only aid the enemy.[13] Like his predecessor, Tarp fights for principles, but he knows the value of disguise, even and perhaps especially in the presence of so-called friends such as the Brothers.

33

Caught between the dehumanizing order of the Brotherhood and the negations of the black alternatives, the narrator finds himself, as before, in an explosive situation. This time the explosion takes the form of a riot. As in the previous cases of the Golden Day and the hospital machine, this scene blends in surrealistic fashion reason and irrationality, order and chaos, History and history. The riot itself is an unplanned ritual of purgation, as the undirected explosion of frustration takes the form of both festive celebration and serious, deliberate ceremony. The celebration can be seen in the costumes that result from breaking into stores: "I saw a little hard man come out of the crowd carrying several boxes. He wore three hats upon his head, and several pairs of suspenders flopped about his shoulders, and now as he came toward us I saw that he wore a pair of gleaming new rubber hip boots. His pockets bulged and over his shoulder he carried a cloth sack that swung heavily behind him" (*Invisible Man*, 407). This impromptu Saint Nicholas, like the original, carries gifts that could not be acquired except on this special occasion. Moreover, we learn that the sack is a cotton-field bag brought from the South. Thus, Dupre makes creative and unselfish use of an artifact of the past. Another celebratory act is a parade:

> And I saw a crowd of men running up pulling a Borden's milk wagon, on top of which, surrounded by a row of railroad flares, a huge woman in a gingham pinafore sat drinking beer from a barrel which sat before her. The men would run furiously a few paces and stop, . . . shouting and laughing and drinking from a jug, as she on top threw back her head and shouted passionately in a full-throated voice of blues singer's timbre:
>
>> If it hadn't been for the referee,
>> Joe Louis woulda killed
>> Jim Jefferie
>> Free beer!!
>
> —sloshing the dipper of beer around.
> We stepped aside, amazed, as she bowed graciously from side to side like a tipsy fat lady in a circus parade, the dipper like a gravy spoon in her enormous hand. Then she laughed and drank deeply while reaching over nonchalantly with her free hand to send quart after quart of milk crashing into the street. And all the time the men running with the wagon over the debris. (*Invisible Man*, 411)

34

This bacchanalian excess clearly expresses the release of frustration and pent-up emotion. It shows the loosening of inhibition and the resultant inebriation and waste. It is the populist version of Rinehart's nihilism. But it is related to Rinehart in another way, its style. There is a distinct rhythm in the running and stopping of the men, and the woman, though tipsy and fat, still moves graciously and nonchalantly. As the ritual earth mother, dispensing her milk and urban honey, she acts flawlessly. The instinctive sense of drama and style indicates, in the midst of chaos, desire for an order that is vital and human, as opposed to one that is repressive, manipulative, and dehumanizing. In contrast to the vets at the Golden Day, who were guilt-ridden even in their debauchery, this riot seems liberating and creative.

The more serious part of the disorder also carries with it a sense of order and even responsibility. The men of one tenement very carefully evacuate all the people from it and then very deliberately set it on fire. The narrator, whose sense of reason has been trained to resist such behavior, finds it admirable: "It didn't occur to me to interfere, or to question. . . . They had a plan" (*Invisible Man*, 412). Moreover, he finds himself renewed by participation: "And now I was seized with a fierce sense of exaltation. They've done it, I thought. They organized it and carried it through alone; the decision their own and their own action. Capable of their own action" (*Invisible Man*, 414).

The possibility of action that emerges from a concrete historical and social condition rather than from ideological conviction makes the narrator aware of a different approach to reality. Dupre and Scofield respond to their immediate situation, and their actions serve a valuable cleansing purpose, even if they appear to be destructive. Norton and the Brotherhood can afford to build abstract structures partially because they control them. Dupre, Scofield, and their families, who are locked into concrete structures, can only create lives for themselves by destroying those enclosures.

But there is another level of action in this episode. Just as society found it useful to allow the vets to vent their hostilities at the Golden Day and just as the doctors manipulated the psychic condition of the narrator, so the Brotherhood finds the riot useful, and in fact may have even fomented it for its own purposes:

35

> Could this be the answer, could this be what the committee had planned, the answer to why they'd surrendered our influence to Ras? Suddenly I heard the hoarse explosion of a shotgun, and looked past Scofield's glinting pistol to the huddled form from the roof. It was suicide, without guns it was suicide, and not even the pawnshops here had guns for sale; and yet I knew with a shattering dread that the uproar which for the moment marked primarily the crash of men against things—against stores, markets—could swiftly become the crash of men against men and with most of the guns and numbers on the other side. I could see it now, see it clearly and in growing magnitude. It was not suicide, but murder. The committee had planned it. And I had helped, had been a tool. A tool just at the very moment I had thought myself free. By pretending to agree I *had* indeed agreed, had made myself responsible for that huddled form lighted by flame and gunfire in the street, and all the others whom now the night was making ripe for death. (*Invisible Man,* 417–18)

Thus there is reason behind the chaos; more precisely, the reason creates the chaos. On a far larger scale than either the Golden Day or the plant hospital, we see how the logic of the ideology explodes itself. This case, however, is more pernicious because the explosion is perhaps deliberate rather than a byproduct. But as in the earlier scenes, the effects here exceed intentions. Dupre and the fat lady, however momentarily, have achieved a sense of freedom and full humanity. They have, through destruction and waste, created something important by taking control of their own destinies. This very human experience, outside the pattern of any ideology, opens the lives that the patterns would close.

The proper relation between chaos and order is the problem the narrator faces in completing the structure of his story. If he duplicates Barbee's speech or his own at the eviction by simply bringing together history and ideology, then he makes possible the closure he wants to avoid. If, in other words, he finishes off his tale by providing himself with the rationale to leave his very concrete hole, then he justifies his reemergence into the world of ideology, with the probability of being locked into one even more dehumanizing than that of the Brotherhood. This is the meaning of his nightmare. He has been castrated by Norton and Bledsoe and Jack, but he can deal with this because he has tried to define his manhood in their terms. He can be more truly himself because they have cut away parts that really were theirs rather his. This does not reduce the pain, but it does

36

make it tolerable. "The real terror, though, is the final image of the dream: And high above me now the bridge seemed to move off to where I could not see, striding like a robot, an iron man, whose iron legs clanged doomfully as it moved. And then I struggled up, full of sorrow and pain, shouting, 'No, no we must stop him!' " (*Invisible Man*, 431). The bridge is made an iron man by the narrator's testicles, and thus is the future of the narrator himself. Through all of his experiences he retained some saving grace, a sense of history or humanity that qualified his commitment to ideology. But the development beyond the Brotherhood, which so nearly succeeded in making him an unthinking machine, will be the perfection of the mechanism, the destruction of all human qualities. Since power has been so appealing to him, the temptation upon emergence will be to seek ultimate power.

The alternative is not silence and impotence. Rather, it is the bringing of abstract History into concrete history through the telling of the tale. Combining the storytelling of Trueblood, the blues performance of the cartman, and the principled tricksterism of Tarp makes possible a narrative that is not closed, that does not impose a new ideology. By showing the human costs of closed, oppressive systems, he brings into question the validity of such systems. The means of doing this, however, is not nihilism, which as an antisystem can be just as oppressive. Rather he offers us the multivalent and open order of art. The telling of these experiences turns them into concrete history. The artistic rendering of that history only strengthens its open character. By using a variety of techniques—surrealism, storytellers, folk rhythms, extended symbolic patterns—Ellison provides meaning to the various experiences without destroying their distinct character. Each can work on a number of levels, can have a multiplicity of identities, without reducing the story to chaos. The narrator, whose history is these various experiences, thus can have reality without being forced into a one-dimensional identity. The novel *Invisible Man*, in its richness of language and symbolic meaning, tells us of the eternal conflict between oppressive structures and liberating history. By doing so, it enacts the meaningful freedom it describes.

Just as Trueblood knew how to manipulate his audience to create the maximum effect, so the narrator uses a variety of techniques to hold our attention. He offers us sex and politics and humor, three key ingredients to a good tale. He presents himself as a naïf and thus can retain our sympathy even when we question his actions. He creates an aura of suspense, intrigue, and action without becoming mechanical in the telling. Moreover, like Trueblood, he gives the audience what it wants, but he does so in his own way. And like Tarp, he refuses to forget the suffering he has experienced. He imitates the cartman in that the pattern of the story is the pattern of the blues. The key to that pattern is that the painful, complex experience must be made to seem as real as possible while the sense of the artfulness is maintained. As Ellison has said elsewhere: "The blues is an impulse to keep the painful details and episodes of a brutal experience alive in one's aching consciousness, to finger its jagged grain, and to transcend it, not by the consolation of philosophy but by squeezing from it a near-tragic, near-comic lyricism. As a form, the blues is an autobiographical chronicle of personal catastrophe expressed lyrically."[14]

We know on the first page of the text that we are being told a story, because the narrator from his position in present time tells us so. The existence of the prologue foregrounds the artfulness by emphasizing the fact of structure. The story proper then recounts various painful episodes, but the techniques call attention to themselves as shifts from realism to surrealism and as commentaries on the various experiences are offered. Also, the repetition inherent in blues form is apparent. Characters and incidents replicate others; themes are taken up, then submerged, only to reappear later. While none of the characters and scenes are identical, and thus resist abstraction and allegory, the existence of similarities suggests that there are patterns of meaning in experience. James Baldwin's comment in "Sonny's Blues," though it simplifies the meaning of the blues more than Ellison does, nonetheless seems pertinent: "For, while the tale of how we suffer, and how we are delighted, and how we may triumph is never new, it always must be heard. There isn't any other tale to tell, it's the only light we've got in all this darkness."[15] For the story to be constantly retold, the teller must always find new possibilities in it; otherwise it ceases to be a story of life. Repetition can never be reduced to identity. Though Jim Trueblood repeated his tale to every white man, he was always shaping and refining it, adjusting it for greater impact and increased control. Within and between the layers of the story in *Invisible Man* new meanings constantly open. Thus the telling of the story becomes a way of resisting closure. Even when the narrator attempts to explain his meanings, as he does in the epilogue, his comments are tested against the scenes he has presented. The concrete experiences, not the abstractions from them, are the test of meaning. And because those experiences work on a number of levels, the tale refuses to be reduced to a system.

The narrator resembles Rinehart in his emphasis on style and on multiplicity of possibility. The narrative presents a variety of styles, as in the cases of Trueblood, Barbee, the cartman, Tarp, and Ras the Exhorter-Destroyer; each is given the full play of a certain kind of rhetoric. The narrator's own range of styles is wide. He makes a number of speeches, each distinguished by the conditions under which it is given; he engages in verbal combat with Bledsoe, Ras, and the committee, during which he blends a certain folk intelligence with common sense, often to no good end; and he recounts the story in both realistic exposition and in the surreal language of dreams. This spectrum of styles undercuts any single definition of the experiences described. Just as the different roles performed by Rinehart defy any simple definition of his identity, so the variety of styles in the narrative defy a reductive interpretation of the reality presented.

This defiance also applies to the narrator's identity. Like Rinehart, he remains a figure somewhat obscured; but in his case it is because he does not tell us his name. In a way, the two are diametrically opposed: Rinehart is nothing but a name, while the narrator is everything except a name. The effect of the narrator's namelessness is to force us to create an identity for him through his experiences and his words. He will not be tagged and thus dispensed with. Names in the story have significance, which is often explained in the text. Trueblood has engaged in incest. Tobit (two-bits) is worthless, while Jack is a one-eyed dealer of fates. To have a name in this story is to be categorized, even though often complexly so. Like YHWH, whom he echoes in the "I yam who I am" statement, the narrator will not be limited in his possibilities. He is defined by his concrete being within his fictional work, not by his label. Thus in telling his story he forces us into his history for our knowledge. Each incident recounted forces a redefinition of his identity, and because each has multiple levels of meaning, he cannot be reified.

Thus, the narrative itself becomes the alternative to a closed system.

Because both language and experience are multiple in meaning, the text remains open. The accomplishment of the narrator is not in preparing to emerge from his hole, but in staying there to tell his story. He achieves a negative dialectic by telling the history of History; the telling combines the order of narrative structure with the chaos of the concrete particular. He joins the specificity of experimental identity with the meaningfulness of art. Narrative art becomes the negative of ideological reification; it becomes the way in which true identity can be achieved. The art of *Invisible Man* allows the narrator his identity in nonidentity; it reveals him to us in all his glorious invisibility.

Two

Negotiations: The Quest for a Middle Way in the Fiction of James Alan McPherson and Ernest Gaines

Both Ernest Gaines and James Alan McPherson have explicitly denied the role of a black literary tradition in their work.[1] Yet this very denial of literary fathers, also made by James Baldwin, Ralph Ellison, and Amiri Baraka (LeRoi Jones), has itself become a part of the tradition. Each generation of Afro-American writers seems to need to create a space for itself by claiming kin to no black predecessor or by citing the influence of European and white American artists, such as Joyce, Hemingway, or Turgenev. By defining their background in such a way, Gaines and McPherson, as well as others, can use a variety of techniques to render Afro-American experience without being seen as limited to a particular racial tradition. In fact, however, this very process of adapting nonblack forms to black materials is one of the most important links to Ellison in particular and to black experience in general. From Phillis Wheatley's early verses through the moralistic style of the slave narratives and Wright's naturalism to Ellison's symbolic and experimental novel, black writers have consistently turned European and white American forms and techniques to their own purposes, just as blacks in general have changed the religious and social institutions of the dominant culture to meet their special needs. Thus Gaines and McPherson, in defining their work in one tradition, have replicated one closer to home.

Within their fictions, they come closest to Ellison in their concern for the relationship of these two intertwined but not identical cultures. Like the older writer, they see the threat that a white system of oppression, in its economic, political, and cultural manifestations, poses for blacks. Also like him, they see that the black folk culture provides ways to resist that threat. To a large extent Gaines and McPherson, like Ellison, structure their narratives by moving characters between the black and white worlds. These characters, often narrators, thus embody the dialectic that pushes the narrative forward. But, as in *Invisible Man,* these fictions do not resolve the central tensions; instead, characters are left on the edge of some new possibility, without a clear indication of the point at which they have arrived.

James Alan McPherson's two short-story collections, *Hue and Cry* (1969) and *Elbow Room* (1977), present characters who have been uprooted from a traditional life and who seek, through communication with another, some means of establishing lost connections. Either the speaker or a central character is a present-minded person of middle-class aspirations who would prefer not to deal with a painful or ambiguous past but who cannot avoid doing so. Since McPherson consistently concludes that communication is either impossible or ineffectual, the narratives frequently end with cries of pain and despair. The stories selected are those which make the most extensive use of folk materials, but in their portrayals of those who desperately need to tell their suffering and those who seek to avoid such stories, they are typical of the collections.

"A Matter of Vocabulary," the first story in *Hue and Cry,* illustrates the pattern and tone of the collection. It is the story of Thomas Brown, a thirteen-year-old black boy who must negotiate between unacceptable conventions (religion, work, race) imposed on him and certain anticonventional experiences that prove painful for him. He must come to terms with everything alone, since he had been taught in the Catholic school "that in complete silence lay his safety from being slapped or hit on the flat of the hand with a wooden ruler."[2] His lonely journey is structured as movement between the poles of convention and anticonvention.

The first pairing is deacons and drunks. Interrupted while playing in the church, Thomas sees the deacons steal money from the Sunday-school collections. But he rather than they feels guilt: "Thomas had stood up and looked at them; all three of them, big-bellied, severe and religiously righteous" (*Hue and Cry,* 3). Their severity necessitates the boy's first lie about his behavior, and their hypocritical self-righteousness makes it impossible for him to attend church again. The narrative clarifies the double meaning of their warning to him: "Ain't no use tryin' to hide in God's House" (*Hue and Cry*, 3). Those without power or influence can be made to look guilty whatever their behavior, while those who appear pious can commit their petty crimes with impunity.

Though Thomas continues to feel guilt for his lie throughout the story, he does not return to the church. Instead, each Sunday morning he visits the neighborhood drunks, who are "sleeping or waiting in misery for the bars to open on Monday morning" (*Hue and Cry*, 4). They are versions of the street-corner men that Elliot Liebow and Roger Abrahams have described as part of the urban black community.[3] As such they dispense the bittersweet wisdom of their experiences; they can tell Thomas about aspects of life that he cannot learn elsewhere. But his motivations for being a listener are complex. On the one hand, his association with them is a way of accepting his guilt; feeling himself damned for playing in the church sanctuary, he seeks the fellowship of those that the community has condemned. On the other hand, they satisfy his need for an adult male figure, since "his own father had been that way" (*Hue and Cry*, 4). Having discovered the flaws of the church fathers, he turns to those who are at least open about their failings: "He felt good toward the men, being almost one of them, and liked to listen to them curse and threaten each other lazily in the hot Georgia sun" (*Hue and Cry*, 4).

As fathers, they show him possibilities for his life that he could not learn in more conventional ways. One of these possibilities is defiance of convention itself: he watches Leroy, "who wet the dirt behind the old house where they sat with no shame in his face and always shook himself in the direction of the Baptist Church, two blocks down the street" (*Hue and Cry*, 6). But because they are more concerned with their bitterness than with Thomas's well-being, their influence can be pernicious. Told by them never to marry " 'cause a bitch ain't shit, man. . . . A bitch'll take all yo' money and then throw you out *in the street*," the boy is so troubled that "after a few weeks of this he found himself very afraid of girls" (*Hue and Cry*, 4). The refusal to take responsibility for their own condition limits their usefulness as father figures for Thomas.

When his Sunday activity is finally discovered, he is battered by another flood of condemnatory words, this time from his mother. Though "she was a very warm person and sometimes she hugged him or touched him on the face when he least expected it," she could be "severe" (*Hue and Cry*, 8). She recites to him the Baptist dogma she has learned over the years about the promise of heaven and the threat of hell. To emphasize the abstract nature of her sermon, a number of words are capitalized: "Then they gonna call the Roll with everybody's name on it and the sheeps are gonna be divided from the goats, the Good on the Right and the Bad on the left" (*Hue and Cry*, 7). Even when Thomas asks if such division applies to his missing father and thus draws tears from his mother, she uses the language of her ideology rather than addressing the concrete emotional concerns of her son. Despite the fact that her consideration for her son is greater than that of the deacons, her use of an identical phrase—"You can't hide from God"—that was earlier discredited reveals the coercive character of her belief. Moreover, her righteousness, like that of the deacons, has a price: "But to please her, and to make her know that he was really sorry and that he would really try to go back to church, and to make certain in her mind that he genuinely wanted to have a place on the Right on Judgment Day, he helped her cook dinner and then washed the dishes afterwards" (*Hue and Cry*, 8–9).

The irrelevance of her faith is made clear when we learn that a major problem facing Thomas at the time of his mother's sermonizing is his racial identity. He discovers his difference from others when, in trying to be the polite child he has been taught to be, he speaks to people on the street, only to have them ignore him. He finally correlates this rudeness with skin color but cannot discover the logic of the prejudice. His potential for self-hatred is manifested in his connection of racial identity and excremental functions: "He began to consider whether only people like him had to go to the toilet and whether or not this thing was the cause of his complexion; and whether the other people could know about the bathroom merely by looking at his skin, and did not speak because they knew he did it" (*Hue and Cry*, 5–6). Because he will not speak, no one corrects his conclusion; moreover, his experience encourages him to believe he is little more than social detritus. His identification with the drunks is ambiguous: they teach resistance but also failure. The deacons make him feel hopelessly guilty without themselves taking responsibility; his mother's belief does not penetrate to the level of his real insecurities.

The one who does penetrate, though also without helping, is Mrs. Quick, whom Thomas believes is a conjure and root woman. He is certain that she knows everything about him, and because of this, her words do have an effect: "Upon the last word in this pronouncement she had locked her eyes on his and seemed to look right into his soul. It was as if she knew that he was doomed to stand on the Left Side on that Day, no matter what good he still might do in life. He had said nothing, but her eyes looked so deep into his own that he had no other choice but to hold his head down" (*Hue and Cry*, 13). Her power over him is based on her knowledge of the world. Moreover, her ability to see him truly (she tells us, for example, that he is left-handed, a fact which he associates with being on God's left side) means that he cannot find safety in either silence or lies. She speaks the only completely true words he had heard, and he is terrified by them.

He has no words himself to express this terror, and retreats into silence and superficial goodness. In working at the supermarket all of his concerns—racial identity, morality, and fatherlessness—are brought together. In some sense, they seem to be resolved: he is honest, hardworking, and appreciative of his wages; while blacks are limited in the jobs they can hold in the store, he has risen to a position of some small responsibility. The owner patronizes him and encourages him to be a member of the company's family. In his job he achieves a degree of invisibility that enables him to observe and make judgments on others, including whites. Because he is intelligent and proficient, he also feels himself superior to his superintendent, a white woman. Miss Hester is made uncomfortable by his silence, "because she could not know what he was thinking" (*Hue and Cry*, 19). Like the deacons and his mother, she finds security but not truth in words. She is reassured when told that he is thinking about school, even though in truth he is considering how unattractive and unpleasant she is. Unaware of his actual thoughts, she repeatedly calls him a good boy.

By masking he attains a degree of safety, in traditional trickster fashion. However, he soon discovers that he has been deceiving himself. This revelation comes when his brother Eddie has a confrontation with the owner and quits his job. The apparent cause is an error Eddie makes in delivering groceries, but he actually quits only after whites question his right to language:

> "The people who got the wrong bags might bring them back," Eddie said. His nose was still sweating in the cool room. "Evidently somebody took my cart by mistake."
>
> "*Evidently! Evidently!*" said Miss Sarah Feinberg. "Miss Hester, you should

please listen to *that! Evidently.* You let them go to school and they think they
know everything. *Evidently,* you say?" (*Hue and Cry,* 26)

Miss Feinberg's response is a modern, urban version of the slave master's
prohibition against black literacy. Even though he knows that his family
will suffer because of his rebellion, Eddie must act when he sees the true
threat against him. He later tells Thomas that his revenge will come after he
learns "all the big words in the world," so that "when I go back in there
I'm gonna be talking so big that fat old Miss Sarah won't even be able to
understand me" (*Hue and Cry,* 29).

In contrast, Thomas remains at the grocery. He understands and sym-
pathizes with Eddie, but he too desperately needs security to follow his
brother's lead. He feels safe in the store, even though he has seen the tentative nature of that safety. He also realizes the price that he must pay:

> He did not want to think about his brother or his mother or the money, or
> even the good feeling he got when Milton Feinberg saw them buying the
> Saturday night groceries. If Big Funk did not come, then perhaps he could
> catch another glimpse of Do-funny before he left the store. The Rich Old
> Lady would not come again until next week. He decided that it would be
> necessary to record the faces and bodies of new people as they wandered,
> selectively, with their shopping carts beyond the big window glass. He liked
> it very much now that none of them ever looked up and saw him watching.
> That way he did not ever have to feel embarrassed or guilty. That way he
> would never have to feel compelled to nod his head or move his mouth or
> eyes, or make any indication of a greeting to them. That way he would
> never have to feel bad when they did not speak back. (*Hue and Cry,* 28)

Security costs permanent silence, false names, and invisibility; it costs, in
other words, the total loss of human contact and communication. And for
this price, he receives a false father, self-hatred, and a sense of doom.

Another folk figure arrives at the end of the story to provide a true word
for Thomas. The Barefoot Lady is notorious in the neighborhood; whenever she is drunk, she rummages through the garbage cans and stands
outside the back door of the funeral parlor, screaming her love for Mr.
Jones, the mortician. Early in the story, Thomas offers her food and tries to
understand the reason for her cry, but "he had no word to place it" (*Hue
and Cry,* 16). At the end, she returns and screams again. This time, Thom-

as's accumulated suffering gives him an insight and, most important, a word:

> And then he knew why the Barefoot Lady came to that place almost every night to cry where there was no one alive in the building to hear or care about her sound. He felt what she must feel. And he knew now why the causes of the sound had always bothered him and would always bother him. There was a word in his mind now, a big word, that made good sense of her sound and the burning feeling thing he felt inside himself. It was all very clear, and now he understood that the Barefoot Lady came in the night not because she really loved Mr. Jones or because he had once buried someone for her for free, or even because she liked the blue-and-white lighted sign. She came always in the night to scream because she, like himself, was in misery, and did not know what else to do. (*Hue and Cry,* 30)

Thomas is given a voice, a word, a means of expression. But the word is not a saving one; nothing in his world has changed. The problems of racism, religious doubt, and fatherlessness will continue to plague him, and, unlike Eddie's multisyllabic vocabulary, Thomas's words do not even offer the hope of vengeance. What they do offer is what the blues traditionally have offered: a sense of shared suffering, a communication of misery that brings at least a momentary order to the experience. For Thomas, the discovery of the ordering possibilities of expression is the message of his initiation.

Ralph Ellison has said of the blues that "they at once express both the agony of life and the possibility of conquering it through sheer toughness of spirit."[4] The agony of life comes through most clearly in "A Matter of Vocabulary"; toughness of spirit is much in evidence in "A Solo Song: For Doc," the most anthologized of McPherson's stories. In tone, theme, and narrative structure, the story fits the tradition of black performance. It simultaneously celebrates and mourns a man and a way of life in recalling Doc Craft's experiences as a waiter on passenger trains. Thematically, it insists on the importance of a younger generation's remembering the style and perseverance of an older one, even if times have changed. Structurally, the narrator tells the story of a legendary figure, similar to John Henry or Stagolee, who displays reckless courage against insurmountable odds. The emphasis is not on the outcome but on the demonstration of manhood. In addition, the narrative uses the call-and-response structure common to

47

such black folk forms as sermons, gospel music, and jazz. In this case, the narrator constantly reminds us of his younger audience, a young black man who does not share the values of the teller or of Doc. The narrative derives much of its energy from this sense of a necessary resistance to itself.

The structure is reinforced by the content of the story. Doc combines the efficient characteristics of John Henry with the trickster ones of John the Slave. The name Doc Craft, given him by other waiters, is indicative of this combination:

> His real name was Leroy Johnson, I think, but when Danny Jackson saw how cool and neat he was in his moves, and how he handled the plates, he began to call him "the Doctor." Then the Sheik, coming down from his high one day after missing the lunch and dinner service, saw how Doc had taken over his station and collected fat tips from his tables by telling the passengers that the Sheik had had to get off back along the line because of a heart attack. The Sheik liked that because he saw that Doc understood crackers and how they liked nothing better than knowing that a nigger had died on the job, giving them service. . . . "Yeah," says the Sheik, who did not say much. "You're a crafty motherfucker but I like you." (*Hue and Cry*, 47–48)

One thing that makes Doc a legendary figure is his perfection of style in the service he provides. The demeaning, menial nature of the work is counteracted precisely by turning it into an art. That artfulness can become a source of power:

> What did he like about the road? He liked what I liked: the money, owning the car, running it, telling the soldiers what to do, hustling a bigger tip from some old maid by looking under her dress and laughing at her, having all the girls at the Haverville Hotel waiting for us to come in for a stopover, the power we had to beat them up or lay them if we wanted. (*Hue and Cry*, 53)

Thus, a job which seems to be an exploitation of blacks becomes, by a reversal common to trickster stories, a means of exploiting the exploiters.

But if Doc's story were only one of craftiness, even if directed against an oppressor, then the narrator's tale would be an interesting but not ultimately serious one. That seriousness comes in the ordeal, that part of the story which links Doc to John Henry. This part reveals the underlying dialectic that provides the meaning the narrator seeks to communicate to his young audience. Like John Henry, Doc is tested against a man-made system; the important difference is that while the steel driver must battle a steam-powered machine, Doc faces a structure of words, the rule book of the railroad company. The fact that both men are defeated is overshadowed by the skill and courage they display in the contest.

When the railroad company realizes that money will be made in freight rather than passenger service, it decides to get rid of the older, unionized waiters. Doc, as the best of these, is an important symbol of what the company must destroy in order to achieve its economic ends. Initially, it works through the contract that it had itself offered the waiters: "Those fat company lawyers took the contract apart and went through all their books. They took the seniority clause apart word by word, trying to figure a way to get at Doc. But they had written it airtight back in the days when the company *needed* waiters, and there was nothing in it about compulsory retirement. Not a word" (*Hue and Cry,* 60). The company is defeated in its first effort by its own text. By assuming the permanence of certain conditions, they display a flaw which can work to the advantage of the weak but wily.

But the rule book is different, for it grows out of the recognition of change. The book was created to regularize the service blacks provided, but "*we* know the service and they had to write the book the way we gave the service and at first there was nothing for the Old School men to learn" (*Hue and Cry,* 57). But the company sees in this flexible text a method of achieving the ends it desires. "So they began changing the rules, and sending us notes about the service. Little changes at first, like how the initials on the doily should always face the customer, and how the silver should be taken off the tables between meals" (*Hue and Cry,* 57). Though they know the reasons behind such changes, the waiters have difficulty adjusting, because "we were getting old and set in our old service" (*Hue and Cry,* 57). In other words, the loss of that very craftiness and adaptability that created the style in the first place causes problems under the changed circumstances.

The narrator explains that the company sent its best inspector to test Doc on the rules. Such a detail both shows the determination of the company to defeat him and enhances the legendary quality of the tale: "He was the Waiter's Waiter, out there by himself, hustling the biggest tip he would ever get in his life. Or losing it" (*Hue and Cry,* 64). The antagonistic nature of the contest is reinforced by two further details. The first is the character of the inspector; he is known as the Unexpected Inspector because of his ability

49

to turn up anywhere any time to examine the waiter's abilities. The narrator knows that this is the great test, "because Jerry is the kind of man who lies in bed all night, scheming. I knew he had a plan" (*Hue and Cry*, 65). The other detail is the provision of a different kind of waiter against which Doc can be measured. In comparison to Doc's pride in his work and his refusal to be a mere menial, Uncle T. Boone is sycophantic, so much so that even the inspector hates him. Though Boone is told to shut up when he claims that the loss of humility among the waiters is the cause of reduced employment, he is correct, though not in the way he intends. The men of the Old School have rejected any idea of their inferiority, and to that extent, the company seeks to force them into their "place" as dependent, irresponsible beings. Boone symbolizes all that Doc and the narrator reject and thus also all that they must resist.

The contest, then, is between two men who are the best at what they do, and it is played for very high stakes. The narrator reports every nuance of this legendary conflict: "Then he got the silver crumb knife from the Pantry and gathered all the cracker crumbs, even the ones Jerry had managed to get in between the salt and pepper shakers" (*Hue and Cry*, 67). The service is flawless: "When Doc poured that pot of hot tea into that glass of crushed ice, it was like he was pouring it through his own fingers; it was like he and the tray and the pot and the glass and all of it was the same body" (*Hue and Cry*, 67–68).

Despite such artistry, Doc is defeated by the words of the book. A trivial change in the required performance has escaped his attention, but not that of the inspector. Even though the service impressed even Jerry as the best possible, he still savors his victory. The Waiter's Waiter has been reminded that he is, after all, a black man serving at the pleasure of the white company. Dismissed from his job, Doc dies a few months later. He has been robbed of the one thing that gave his existence meaning, the dignity of his art.

The value of the service as art is what the narrator tries to explain to the young man through his artful story. He senses that a tradition is being lost that gave significance to the experiences of men like Doc. The young man must be made to understand that the human element in the work is more important than the mechanical mastery of the rule book, repeatedly called the "black bible" by the narrator. This phrase suggests the storyteller's fear that the service will come to be equated with the book, and those that come after will accede to the company's view that these men are automatons with no human value. The point is not to compel the listener to imitate Doc, because this would only lock him into an archaic system; rather, the object is to encourage him to think negationally and creatively about the rules he seems to believe in.

The narrator doubts his success: "And I wonder why I should keep talking to you when you could never see what I see or understand what I understand or know the real difference between my school and yours" (*Hue and Cry,* 72–73). But the telling, not the understanding, is crucial. As long as the story is told, Doc's pride and his courage remain alive to contradict the mechanistic and racist implications of the book. Moreover, the verbal artistry of the story reenacts the physical art of Doc and thereby carries on the resistance to the words and word manipulators that defeated Doc.

In "Gold Coast," McPherson reverses the perspective of "A Solo Song" by providing us with a narrator who shares the conventional values of Thomas and the young listener of the earlier stories. Also like them, he is confronted with a challenge to those values. This point of view allows us to see how a conventional mind justifies its participation in dehumanization in the process of telling the story. Ultimately, the narrator defeats himself because the telling of concrete human experiences contradicts his self-justifications and condemns him. A story of a cry not heeded, "Gold Coast" also describes the ways the cry's significance is evaded.

The narrator, Robert, presents himself as an ambitious young man with a highly developed sense of irony. He takes a job as a janitor's assistant in part out of sheer caprice: "I had never been a janitor before and I did not really have to be one and that is why I did it" (*Hue and Cry,* 77). Moreover, he derives perverse pleasure from shocking the refined sensibilities of his middle-class acquaintances. Finally, the job does not threaten his literary ambitions since "it is possible to be a janitor without really becoming one" (*Hue and Cry,* 77). Thus, like the young man in "A Solo Song," he does not take seriously his situation.

This comfortable attitude is disturbed when he finds himself between opposed forces who do take matters seriously. On the one hand is James Sullivan, the aging building superintendent who "had been in that building thirty years and had its whole history recorded in the little folds of his mind, as his own life was recorded in the wrinkles of his face. All he had to show for his time there was a berserk dog, a wife almost as mad as the dog, three cats, bursitis, acute myopia, and a drinking problem" (*Hue and Cry*, 79–80). Sullivan, like the Barefoot Lady and the narrator of "A Solo Song," has a past of struggle and suffering that begs for articulation. Moreover, he wants to tell of both the good and the bad of his life. Robert's posture as a disinterested observer leads him to disregard the human experience behind the stories:

> These were his memories, and I would obediently put aside my garbage cans and laugh with him over the hundred or so colorful, insignificant little details which made up a whole lifetime of living in the basement of Harvard. And although they were of little value to me then, I knew that they were the reflections of a lifetime and the happiest moments he would ever have, being sold to me cheap, . . . for as little time and interest as I wanted to spend. It was a buyer's market. (*Hue and Cry*, 82)

Rather than ponder the material so freely offered to him, Robert prefers to seek out the stories of the wealthy tenants of the building. Even here, Sullivan's experience rather than his own intelligence gives some meaning to those lives. His explanations of the contents of a Jewish resident's garbage, for example, while superficially anti-Semitic, reveal more about insecurity and the desire for assimilation than any of Robert's researches could have done. Further, that experience has given Sullivan a strong resistance to middle- and upper-class values that runs counter to the narrator's own desires.

That which Sullivan opposes is embodied by Miss O'Hara:

> I never found out just why Miss O'Hara hated the Sullivans with such a passion. Perhaps it was because they were so unkempt and she was so superciliously clean. Perhaps it was because Miss O'Hara had a great deal of Irish pride and they were stereotyped Irish. Perhaps it was because she merely had no reason to like them. She was a fanatic about cleanliness and put out her little bit of garbage wrapped very neatly in yesterday's *Christian Science Monitor* and tied in a bow with a fresh piece of string. (*Hue and Cry*, 87)

She seeks to enroll Robert in her campaign to rid the building of Sullivan, and his own ambitions and values are aligned with hers, even if not so actively engaged. He will not enter the Sullivan apartment because of the disorder, but he does feel a condescending sympathy for the old man. He refuses to commit himself to either side, and his vacillation is the subject of the story.

Such neutrality is not easy to maintain, even for one who sees it as aesthetic distancing. The concrete human element keeps intruding itself in ways that deny Robert the pleasure of neatly ordering his experience. On the one hand, Miss O'Hara's prejudice is reinforced by Robert's white girlfriend, who finds Sullivan distasteful and bothersome. "His conversations, she thought, were useless, repetitious, and promised nothing of value to me. . . . She was not at all cold, but she had been taught how to tolerate the old-poor and perhaps toss them a greeting in passing. But nothing more" (*Hue and Cry*, 90).

This patronizing manner complements the narrator's own attitude, but it is undercut by the pretenses of Robert and Jean's own interracial relationship. They can easily dismiss Sullivan's dislike of it, but the pressures of the larger society cannot be disregarded. The most forceful demonstration of social pressure occurs during a game the two of them play, entitled "Social Forces," "the object of which was to see which side could break us first":

> The last round was played while taking her home in a subway car, on a hot August night, when one side of the car was black and tense and hating and the other side was white and of the same mind. There was not enough room on either side for the two of us to sit and we would not separate; and so we stood, holding on to a steel post through all the stops, feeling all the eyes, between the two sides of the car and the two sides of the world. We aged. And, getting off finally at the stop which was no longer ours, we looked at each other, again expectantly, and there was nothing left to say. (*Hue and Cry*, 95)

Neither Jean's sophistication nor Robert's aestheticism is adequate to such a human reality. And the creation of the game in the first place suggests complex, ambiguous motivations for the relationship. Each of them exploited the other for reasons that they refused to articulate.

For the purpose of the story, this episode has forced on Robert an awareness of the painfulness of experience that could sensitize him to Sullivan. From this point on, his choices and actions take on a moral quality; no longer innocent of human suffering, he must take responsibility for it. But

53

even though the old man intrudes more than ever, desiring communication and understanding, Robert remains distant: "I began to avoid the old man. . . . I began to consider moving out" (*Hue and Cry*, 95–96). At this very time, Miss O'Hara wins an important battle by forcing the removal of Sullivan's dog, one of the few comforts in his otherwise unpleasant life. The event triggers Robert's first invitation to the Sullivans' apartment. His initial repulsion is softened somewhat by the other man's assertion of a shared sense of loss. This opening makes it possible for the narrator to deal with the troubles in his own life:

> And even though he was drunk and dirty and it was very late at night, I believed him and liked him anyway because having him there was much better than being alone. After he had gone I could sleep and I was not lonely in sleep; and it did not really matter how late I was at work the next morning, because when I really thought about it all, I discovered that nothing really matters except not being old and being alive and having potential to dream about, and not being alone. (*Hue and Cry*, 99)

Robert accepts the relationship with Sullivan not out of any human sympathy, but because the presence of the old man strengthens the sense of their difference, and to that extent Robert supplies the needs of his own ego by feeding off the other man's life-experiences and wisdom.

One of the barriers to the young man's identification with the older one is the feeling that the conversations and remembrances are useless. As the narrator makes clear, nothing in Sullivan's life improves: his wife continues to be sick and belligerent, his grief over the dog only intensifies, and Miss O'Hara gains support in her campaign to have him dismissed. Even when Robert does make sympathetic gestures, they are fruitless because of Sullivan's hopelessness. This despair more than anything leads to the final break; young and resilient, Robert cannot tolerate the idea that suffering and death are inevitable and pervasive. He refuses to learn from the concrete, personal history that Sullivan keeps forcing on his consciousness: "There were girls outside and I knew that I could have one now because that desperate look had finally gone somewhere deep inside. I was young and now I did not want to be bothered" (*Hue and Cry*, 102).

The only escape is leaving the building. In doing so, Robert believes that he has left behind the burden of Sullivan's life. He finds, however, that he is haunted by the experience and the man:

I saw him once in the Square walking along very slowly with two shopping bags, and they seemed very heavy. As I came up behind him I saw him put them down and exercise his arms while the crowd moved in two streams around him. I had an instant impulse to offer help and I was close enough to touch him before I stopped. I will never know why I stopped. After a few seconds of standing behind him and knowing that he was not aware of anything at all except the two heavy bags waiting to be lifted after his arms were sufficiently rested, I moved back into the stream of people which passed on the left of him. I never looked back. (*Hue and Cry,* 104)

Of course, in one sense the last statement is not true; the narrating of the story is his way of looking back, perhaps to assuage his guilt, perhaps to find the answer to why he stopped behind the old man. The existence of the narrative is his confession that he has committed a sin in refusing the burden of human sympathy. He reenacts Sullivan's behavior in compelling the listener to hear his tale of suffering. His words do not relieve the pain of what has been experienced; rather they keep up the battle against the Miss O'Haras who would toss out in neat packages what they consider to be human garbage.

In *Elbow Room,* McPherson brings into the foreground concern for the *way* of telling, in contrast to the emphasis in *Hue and Cry* on the *need* for telling. He repeatedly poses as a problem the adequacy of narrative techniques to the materials that make up the narrative. For example, in "A Sense of Story," a judge seeks to create a meaningful order out of the transcripts of a case. He assumes that inherent in the record is a pattern waiting to be discerned. In "Problems of Art," a white lawyer makes out of the information given him a story about his client that provides a successful defense. Only later does he learn that a crucial missing fact falsifies the defense. The significant question is whether it is at all possible to derive order and meaning from the facts of experience. And such a question is not merely academic: in "A Sense of Story," a man's life depends on which story the judge decides fits the facts. "The Story of a Dead Man," "The Story of a Scar," and "Elbow Room" are representative dramatizations of this quest for narrative truth.

The narrator of "The Story of a Dead Man" is an older version of the young men of *Hue and Cry*. He has successfully entered the black middle class through hard work, education, and the disguising of his southern background. The narrative is his effort to make sense of his relationship with his cousin Billy Renfro. To create order, he must sort through a chaos of lies, rumors, and innuendo. The order that results must carefully balance loyalty to his family ties with preservation of his middle-class reputation. The material with which he works presents a twofold difficulty: on the one hand, Billy is a legendary figure, much like the "bad nigger" of folklore; on the other, he is clearly the narrator's double. "He and I are one with the same ancestors, and whatever fires rage in him I must look to find smolderings of within myself."[5] Here, then, is the narrator's problem: how to construct a story that resolves the opposition of a chaotic, vital, folk self and an ordered, sterile, conventional self. The Billys of the world should be dead (hence the title), but they retain a hold on more "modern" men who can neither accept nor reject them.

This ambivalence appears in the narrator's direct address to his audience. His posture is defensive, but he alternates between defenses of Billy from unknown enemies and defenses of himself from Billy. A few pages after he says, "I bother to refute these rumors because the man is my cousin, and I am honor-bound to love him as I know he really is" (*Elbow Room*, 24), he also says, "But it is certainly not true, as Billy has gossiped among the family, that when he arrived I refused to see him at my office" (*Elbow Room*, 32). The narrator, in his insecurity, must constantly move between affirmation of the past and justification of a present that seeks escape from the past.

The desire for rejection is clarified when the stories about Billy are told. In these examples of profanity, imprisonment, and violence, Billy is patterned after the arrogant, socially defiant bad man of black lore. "From the late nineteenth century black lore was filled with tales, toasts, and songs of hard, merciless toughs and killers confronting and generally vanquishing their adversaries without hesitation and without remorse."[6] The stories that the narrator recounts reinforce such an image of Billy. He gets revenge on a redneck storekeeper who had refused to wait on him; he goes to prison for stabbing a man; he loses an eye during domestic violence. In the course of his work as a repossessor of cars, he has fought a number of gun battles. Moreover, the narrator has a difficult time separating legend from fact, because "the man is an accomplished liar" (*Elbow Room*, 23). Billy seems determined to make himself into a mythic figure, and the narrator seems determined to supplant that fiction with one of his own.

The image he wants to create of his cousin must be seen in the context of the image he presents of himself. He tells us that though they share the same first name, he took the formal William, leaving the nickname to the other child. And though Billy tried to teach him the ways of the folk culture, the lessons had limited effect: "I followed as much of his advice, given the stricter circumstances of my home, as was discreet" (*Elbow Room*, 26). He also stayed with his aunt "while Billy gallivanted." Early in life, he comes to see discretion and self-righteousness as virtues, and he retains these attitudes as he matures. When he visits Billy in prison, with the "Dead Man Blues" being sung in the background, he sermonizes on the value of conventional behavior: "I tried my best to communicate to him some sense of the broader options available to the man in possession of salable knowledge. I mapped out my future in blocks of years, stepladders of subgoals, ending with an affirmation of my ultimate ambition to settle into the good life in Los Angeles" (*Elbow Room*, 29). Billy dismisses this extended effort at inspiration with a request for a sandwich and soda. "Then he laughed, a strange uncaring demon laughter. The sound bragged of his urge to self-destruct. Ah, Billy! He just would not do! He listened only to the beating of his own heart" (*Elbow Room*, 30). What the narrator does not realize is that the beating of the heart is the element left out of his own design.

His subsequent behavior substantiates this in the very process of fulfilling his dream:

> In contrast to him, I moved westward, but only as far as Chicago, and settled in against this city's soul-killing winter winds. I purged from my speech all traces of the South and warmed myself by the fire of my thirty-year plan. Employment was available in the credit reference section of the Melrose Department Store, and there I established, though slowly, a reputation for efficiency and tact. Because I got along, I began moving up. In my second year in Chicago, I found and courted Chelseia Raymond, a family-backed, efficiency-minded girl. She was the kind of woman I needed to make my children safe. (*Elbow Room*, 31–32)

In contrast to Billy's employment in a direct, violent job, William hides himself in an abstract world of numbers; and in contrast to Billy's dangerous love affairs, William seeks out a safe, "efficiency-minded" wife. He denies as completely as possible the concrete, chaotic, vital world of his past. In doing so, he must submit himself to the soul-killing of the city and to reification as an efficient cog in the store's merchandising machine.

His carefully constructed world is threatened by the intrusion of Billy. William tries to carry off the convergence of the two worlds by, in effect, disguising Billy as himself. In place of the black, death-haunted suit, William dresses his cousin in one of his own gray pinstripes. To hide the missing eye, Billy wears the other's blue sunshades. At dinner, William successfully keeps the conversation away from a too-close examination of Billy's life. His deception fails, however, when his father-in-law, sensing a common heritage, begins to recall his own past, in all its unsanitized detail. "Billy seemed to have induced some unhealthy chemical reaction in Mr. Raymond. He and Billy seemed locked in some unholy union" (*Elbow Room*, 38). The union is against all the order that William worships, and it makes it clear that the life-giving disorder is just below the surface.

Billy strips off the shades and the suit and then tells a wild, violent, but effective story of the actual reason for his lost eye. In the process he destroys all conventional distinctions between truth and fiction and between good and evil; he also disrupts a mechanical, chronological sense of time. Though the events of this story concern an automobile repossession that supposedly occurred years earlier, at the end Billy dramatically tosses onto the table a set of blood-flecked keys. Then he and Mr. Raymond burst into "wild, almost hysterical laughter" (*Elbow Room*, 42). In the folk world Billy represents, ritual time is the true time. His life is the repeated facing and defying of death, and in that ritual he affirms life.

In the conclusion, the narrator tries to reconstruct his world. He claims that Billy is always welcome in his house, though not to tell stories: "Chelseia agrees, and says our family unit will likely be the place where Billy finds ultimate reconstruction, once he has put aside his wanderings. I say it is just a matter of time. We are, after all, the same age. Yet I have already charted my course. I have settled into Chicago, against the winter whippings of this city's winds. He can do the same" (*Elbow Room*, 42–43). But such assertions are rendered meaningless by the narrative power of Billy's story. William's comments are those of a man resigned and perhaps doomed, and not those of one who could successfully engage a Billy Renfro. He himself resembles the dead man of the title. But in the process of narration, and in the need for narration, William creates a possibility for himself. First, in recounting both Billy's life and his own encounter with it, he ritualizes time by recapitulating experience; in this way he frees himself of a progressive notion of reality that denies the validity of the past. Second, the vividness of his recreations of Billy's tales puts the lie to his implicit claim that his life is better than his cousin's. In the very process of making his case, he refutes it. Finally, he creates an order that is capable of presenting a disorder. In doing so, he gives value to the life-affirming principle that Billy symbolizes. In his attempt to defend a conventional, mechanistic order, he unites folk and aesthetic qualities that are the most powerful resistance to that order. In trying to be most completely William, he most effectively becomes Billy.

"The Story of a Scar" is a tale of a narrator who moves between his own stereotyped sense of poor black life and the personal and painful experience of the woman who tells him her story. He tries to neutralize the effect of her history by forcing it into a sociological category, but her narrative ability repeatedly forces him to consider the concrete human situation. What drives *his* narration is the tension between her need to remember both the pain and joy and his need, despite his own blackness, to deny any connection with the reality she describes.

A combination of pomposity and intrusiveness is evident in the narrator's opening question to the woman: "As a concerned person, and as your brother, I ask you, without meaning to offend, how did you get that scar on the side of your face?" (*Elbow Room*, 97). Since we have been informed that the question, though formally phrased, is only the result of idle curiosity, we have reason to doubt the reliability of this narrator. We are to see him ironically, and the woman immediately reinforces this impression, as her response exposes his insincerity and verbal posturing: " 'I ask *you*,' she said, 'as a nosy person with no connections in your family, how come your nose is all bandaged up?' " (*Elbow Room*, 97).

He evades the "signifying"[7] implications of her comment by pigeonholing her:

> [The scar] was as real as the honey-blond wig she wore, as real as her purple pantsuit. I studied her approvingly. Such women have a natural leaning toward the abstract expression of themselves. Their styles have private meanings, advertise secret distillations of their souls. Their figures, and their disfigurations, make meaningful statements. Subjectively, this woman was

59

the true sister of the man who knows how to look while driving a purple Cadillac. Such craftsmen must be approached with subtlety if they are to be deciphered. (*Elbow Room*, 98–99)

His attitude is that of the social scientist examining some exotic phenomenon. He is a bemused observer, condescending toward one he considers an inferior.

When he asks his "subtle" question about her scar, she makes it clear what she thinks of him: "Black guys like you with them funny eyeglasses are a real trip. You got to know everything. You sit in corners and watch people. . . . I read you the minute you walk in here" (*Elbow Room*, 99). When he tries to reestablish surface intimacy with her "as [her] brother," she gives a "dozens" response: "How can you be my brother when your mama's a man?" (*Elbow Room*, 99). Their shared laughter breaks down the barriers that his sophisticated posturing could not.

Only after such a ritual of recognition can her story, which is a kind of women's blues, be told. But the assumed identification of speaker and audience repeatedly breaks down as the young man seeks a clear-cut pattern of motivation and meaning. He wants a simple answer, while she feels compelled to provide the full, ambiguous story. One reason for the narrator's intrusions may be that he resembles Billy Crawford, a central figure in her story: "And the more I look at you the more I can see you just like him. He had that same way of sittin' with his legs crossed, squeezin' his sex juices up to his brains" (*Elbow Room*, 100). Moreover, Billy had the same tendency to categorize and thereby dismiss people.

Despite his arrogance, according to her tale, she finds herself falling in love with him as he teaches her both social graces and self-respect. He can provide a way out of a life of irresponsibility and insecurity. But the price she pays for her new life is the loss of her old friends and her enjoyment of life. Made aware of this by her more experienced friend Red Bone, she begins to reconsider. While she does not reject Billy, "I begin to watch [him] with a different kind of eye" (*Elbow Room*, 104). She draws away from him toward a man more clearly in accord with her self-image: "He was a strong talker, a easy walker, that dude was a *woman* stalker!" (*Elbow Room*, 105).

At this moment, the narrator, "overwhelmed suddenly by the burden of insight," breaks in:

60

> "I *know* the man of whom you speak. There is no time for this gutter-patter
> and indirection. Please, for my sake and for your own, avoid stuffing the
> shoes of the small with mythic homilies. This man was a bum, a hustler and
> a small-time punk. He broke up your romance with Billy, then he lived off
> you, cheated on you, and cut you when you confronted him." So pathetic
> and gross seemed her elevation of the fellow that I abandoned all sense of
> caution. "Is your mind so *dead,*" I continued, "did his switchblade slice so
> *deep,* do you have so little *respect* for yourself, or at least for the idea of
> *proportion* in this sad world, that you'd sit here and *praise* this brute!?"
> (*Elbow Room,* 105)

Again, the narrator judges on the basis of stereotypes rather than experience. Moreover, he assumes that her weakness is a failure in storytelling,
that she engages in "gutter-patter and indirection" because she does not
know how to express her experience. Impatient for a meaning that validates his own view of the world, he violates her sense of narrative.

Her comment condemns and reveals his superficiality and reductiveness:
" 'You know everything,' she said in a soft tone, much unlike her own. 'A
black mama birthed you, let you suck her titty, cleaned your dirty drawers,
and you still look at us through paper and movie plots' " (*Elbow Room,*
105–6). The superiority of the narrator is shown to be just as false as his
knowledge. She becomes more and more angry as he refuses to recognize
his ignorance. Like Billy Crawford, he insists that his "objective" reading of
the world is truer than the actual experience of it.

She proceeds to show him the tragic consequences of such arrogance.
"Now her voice became deep and full, as if aided suddenly by some intri-
cately controlled well-spring of pain. Something aristocratic and old and
frighteningly wise seemed to have awakened in her face":

> "Now this is the way it happened," she fired at me, her eyes wide and
> rolling. "I want you to *write* it on whatever part of your brain that ain't
> already covered with page print. I want you to *remember* it every time you
> stare at a scarred-up sister on the street, and *choke* on it before you can work
> up spit to condemn her." (*Elbow Room,* 106)

The events justify this castigation, because it was the rationalist Billy
Crawford who cut her in a fit of jealousy. What makes this revelation so
important is less its exposing of the narrator's ignorance than its questioning of the way of thinking that the narrator shares with the assailant. To the

woman, Billy's way of thinking about the world correlates with his violence: "He didn't say more on the subject, but later that evenin', after the movie, he said, 'I was in the war for two years. It made me a disciplined man, and I hope I don't ever have to lose my temper.' I didn't say nothin', but the cold way he said it was like a window shade flappin' up from in front of his true nature, and I was scared" (*Elbow Room*, 109). The threat is obviously very calculated, the result of a cold-bloodedly rationalistic manner. Seeing others as objects and not as self-determining beings, he has no qualms about destroying them when they violate his sense of order.

The lesson for the narrator is clear: his attitude toward the woman and others like her is a sign of a failed humanity rather than a superior one. In contrast to "The Story of a Dead Man," the lesson here is learned. Though deeply troubled, the narrator yields to the criticism: "And then I remembered the most important question, without which the entire exchange would have been wasted. I turned to the woman, now drawn together in the red plastic chair, as if struggling to sleep in a cold bed. 'Sister,' I said, careful to maintain a casual air. 'Sister . . . what is your name?'" (*Elbow Room*, 112). Although trying to sustain his distance, the narrator can no longer objectify this woman. She has become an individual, with a specific, very real history; asking her name signifies the discovery of this particularity. The narrator has learned the lesson of her blues through his inability to remain an indifferent audience.

In addition, his narrative of her story, told in the past tense, adds a new meaning to the tale. The narrative is itself the record of the wound he has received, since for him her story is a parable of his own arrogance. His retelling is the tracing of the scar she has left on his sense of himself.

In the title story of *Elbow Room*, the narrator questions, in the process of narrating, the possibility of imposing order on experience. Two voices, the "editor" and the "narrator," repeatedly interrupt the story to debate the structure and underlying aesthetic of the narration. They constitute, in effect, a metafictional subplot analogous to the thematic and structural concerns of the main story. In this secondary story, the editor is the voice of reason and convention, in conflict with a narrator who claims to be "the open enemy of conventional narrative categories" (*Elbow Room*, 215). Because the narrator takes this stance, the editor "felt compelled to clarify slightly, not to censor but to impose at least the illusion of order" (*Elbow*

Room, 215). Clearly, the editor is another of McPherson's conventional characters confronted with the disorder of experience.

For the narrator, the issue is aesthetic in a basic way. More fundamental than a final draft is his concern for the adequacy of *any* narrative order to render experience. In the main story, the narrator himself is the one who assumes the priority of certain categories and who presumes to distance himself from reality. A secondary character, he constantly labels and debates the principal figures, a black woman and the white man who marries her. In them he looks for evidence of the failure of their individuality and signs of their surrender to the hostility and pressure of society. The touchstone of his analysis is their propensity for the construction of stories. In the case of Virginia, this is the ability to narrate effectively the events of her life. For Paul, it is a matter of self-construction; the narrator sees him building and then tearing down self-definitions. As a white man in love with a black woman, he must deal not only with the pressures of family and society, but also with his impulse to endlessly examine his own motives. As a black man, the narrator frequently challenges his assumptions and seeks to find that ulterior motive that will force Paul back into the category of racist white man: "The thing that illuminated him, that provided the core of his mystery, might have been simple guilt, or outright lust, or a passion to dominate, or a need to submit to a fearful-seeming object. All such motives enter into the convention of love" (*Elbow Room,* 222).

Such reduction, however, is not adequate to the complexity of Paul's character. Each imposition is refuted: " 'This is real life,' he said, 'not the movies' " (*Elbow Room,* 226). Nonetheless, the narrator assumes a superior wisdom: "He really did not understand. I think he still believed he was a free agent. . . . He looked confused, hurt, almost on the edge of anger. I felt bad for having intruded into his story, but there was a point I wanted very much for him to see" (*Elbow Room,* 227). Paul's "story" is his effort to give coherence to his relationship with Virginia. He fights the racist objections of his father to the marriage, but he is still in the process of deciding what he is fighting for and not just against. Contrary to the opinion of the narrator, the character believes in his power to shape and give meaning to his life.

To the narrator, "story" has additional connotations. It is the conflict, with ironic potential, between Paul's belief and those racial and social rules

that the narrator believes eliminate any true free agency. He is simply waiting for this tragic drama to play itself out. Even if reality is not a movie, it
has a scriptlike pattern that destines both interracial marriage and self-
realization to ultimate failure.

At another level, the narrator has chosen not merely to observe Paul's
story but to intrude upon it. Not satisfied to wait for the inevitable, he tries
to force his knowledge on the others, in part because he likes them and
seeks to ease their pain, but also because he is not totally certain of that
knowledge. He will make the story fit his meaning by making himself a
character. By doing so, he enters the contingent world, where figures like
Paul and Virginia believe that reality has possibilities that cannot be contained within fixed patterns. By becoming an actor in his own play, the
narrator creates the potential for his own education, even more than the
education of his characters.

Virginia, the vehicle of his learning, has a reputation as a storyteller:
"Virginia Valentine was a country raconteur with a stock of stories flavored
by international experience. Telling them, she spoke with her whole presence in very complicated ways. She was unique. She was a classic kind of
narrator. Virginia Valentine was a magic woman" (*Elbow Room*, 221). She
is an urban, cosmopolitan version of the folk yarnspinner capable of mes-
merizing listeners through words. Moreover, characterizing her as a magic
woman makes possible a definition of narrative as a means of conjuring up
mysteries rather than tidying up experience. What is open to him, then, is
both a new sense of experience and a new sense of story.

Virginia uses her skills in part to protect Paul during his conflicts with the
world, the narrator, and himself. She reassures him about his ongoing argument with his father; she comforts him when people begin to call him
"nigger"; and she throws the narrator out of the house when he becomes
condescending about Paul's racial innocence. This latter action she justifies
through a parable:

> In Calcutta you see crippled beggars out in the street, and people just walk
> around them. Now a Westerner would say that's cruel, but them fucking
> Indians so damn complicated they probably look at that same beggar and see
> a reincarnated raja that lived in us a thousand years ago, ate too much of
> them hot spices, and died of gout. *Shit!* He don't *need* nothing else! So they
> don't worry about how he looks now. But patience is a Christmas-morning

64

thing. You have to accept what's under the tree and keep on believing there's a Santa Claus. Both you *and* that nigger of mine have to learn that. (*Elbow Room*, 230)

Virginia is a voice, not of reason, but of humane sense. She does not deny the existence of suffering, and she does not try to neutralize it through philosophical or aesthetic theorizing. She advises acceptance of life's difficulties, but still asserts the value of the imagination—believing in Santa Claus. She sees the world as one of both pain and possibility; by maintaining rather than resolving this tension, she can sustain both herself and Paul.

Virginia also teaches the narrator the aesthetic meaning of this tension. As her relationship with Paul develops and comes to include a pregnancy, her narrative style begins to change: "I saw Virginia Frost losing control of her stories. As her belly grew, her recollections began to lose their structure. The richness was still there, but her accounts became more anecdotal than like stories. They lacked clarity and order. . . . She had inside her an epic adventure, multinational in scope, but the passion needed to give it permanent shape was obviously fading" (*Elbow Room*, 234–35). A new aesthetic emerges which emphasizes immediacy over permanence and lifelike disorder over fixed structures. While the narrator sees this technique as flawed, his own story takes on more and more of the same qualities. The relationship between Virginia's storytelling and her marriage is never clarified, and the narrator frequently shifts from an observer-participant to an outside, almost omniscient voice. Moreover, stories not directly related are woven into the narrative of Paul and Virginia. The editor keeps intruding to question the narrator on his material, but he seldom receives a satisfactory answer. The narrative makes demands that resist an externally imposed structure, and the narrator can do little other than let the story take its own shape.

At the end, the narrator tells us that the couple have had their baby and have reconciled with Paul's family. He describes one of the photographs he has received in the mail:

The third picture was of Virginia and Paul standing on either side of an elderly couple. Virginia was smiling triumphantly, wearing her mug's cap. The old man looked solemn. The woman, with purple-white hair, was holding the baby. Paul stood a little apart from the others, his arms crossed. His beard was gone and he looked defiant. There was a familiar intensity about his face. On the back of this picture someone had written: "He will be a *classic* kind of nigger." (*Elbow Room*, 241)

The note recalls Virginia's comments on race, but it also is in counterpoint with a last, angry exchange between Paul and the narrator, who had again been claiming that Paul knew nothing of what it was like to be black. The white man resentfully made one final assertion: "And I know what a *nigger* is, too. It's what you are when you begin thinking of yourself as a work of art!" (*Elbow Room*, 240).

The narrator cannot refute this definition, for he has in fact reified himself in his relationship with Paul. He has assumed a distance and standard that deny his own humanity. In the process of making Paul into a tragic figure, he has made himself into the all-knowing Black Man, symbol of all Paul cannot know. He is in sharp contrast to the "classic nigger" that the baby will become, because he has parents who resist reifying categories.

The narrator's recognition of his own flaws is the source of his narrative. Faced with the failure of a categorizing art, he himself resists the demands of the editor. He seeks a truer aesthetic that will unite experience and imagination, that will allow the story to find its own order, even if he cannot be certain what that order is: "It was from the beginning not my story. I lack the insight to narrate its complexities" (*Elbow Room*, 241).

Since the editor cannot comprehend the idea of an inner form, the process of education continues. What the narrator learned from Virginia and Paul he must pass on, not in philosophic and aesthetic exposition but in the narrative process itself. He must give life to the word, if he is to be true to his humanity and his art.

McPherson's stories are quests for a language that not merely reflects experience but actually embodies it. The model is the folk storyteller, who, in the telling, reproduces the intensity of both joy and pain for the listener. Most often, this listener is unaware of his need for such an experience. By shifting the point of view in the later stories from the teller to the listener, McPherson dramatizes the movement from an unquestioning, often self-righteous attitude toward life to an uncertain, dialectical way of thinking and perceiving. The now-enlightened characters must live with the tension between the desire for an ordered, fixed meaning and the recognition of a disordered but vital world. These narrators must shape stories without distorting the reality they are articulating. As artists, they must always be negotiating this danger-filled middle way.

The fiction of Ernest Gaines is much more solidly situated in the folk community than the primarily urban stories of McPherson. For that reason, perhaps, Gaines's attitude toward folk material is more complex. Like McPherson, he sees in such material and characters the possibility for resistance to the oppressive conventions of the dominant culture. But he also insists that the folk community itself, with its well-established mores, can become an imprisoning force. The most successful of his characters are those who negotiate their way amid the forces of racist repression; folk parochialism that is in fact an acceptance of that repression; and open resistance, which often leads to death. These characters survive by accommodating themselves to the existing system without sacrificing their dignity and by living on the psychological edge of the folk community, near enough to absorb the genuine wisdom of that experience but not so close as to fear change and resistance. The stories and novels are structured so that these characters in the middle confront on the one hand those who defend "the rules," the status quo both maintained within the black world and imposed on it from the outside, and on the other hand those rebels and nonbelievers who are willing to die in order to break out of the limitations of the system. Either choice as an absolute becomes a death wish, and the task of the middle character is to find a life-affirming way to exist. In Gaines's fiction, as in McPherson's, this way is not fixed or patterned; it is continually improvised. The books always conclude with such characters on the edge of some testing experience, having gained certain insights but waiting to turn those into concrete action. Success in action is not guaranteed; the books end with the same contingency as they began. The difference is in the characters' willingness to confront the world even against the odds.

In *Catherine Carmier* (1964), Gaines's first published novel, he creates two characters who must, each in a different way, move between conflicting forces. The three worlds of the novel—black, black Creole, and white—create a variety of cross-tensions that cannot be avoided. For Jackson Bradley, the initial conflict is between the traditional world of his Aunt Charlotte and the larger, more insecure world of the North. He has returned to the rural Louisiana community from California; Charlotte expects him to stay and teach in the local school. Though he feels isolated and uprooted in the North, his education and experience there make it impossible to live in this southern backwater. He is thus similar to McPherson's middle-class young men who lack a sense of the past and who are troubled by those who have one. He believes in reason and cosmopolitanism and therefore cannot accept religious faith and parochialism. He must find a way to reject Charlotte's world without causing her more pain than necessary.

His situation is further complicated when he finds his love for Catherine reawakened. The daughter of the Creole Raoul Carmier, she has been taught to despise the blacks of the community. Despite her father's prejudice, she loved Jackson when she was younger, and she later had a child by another black man. Raoul, out of love and desperation, has tried to isolate her, and she, out of love also, has accepted that confinement. But this acquiescence breaks down in the presence of Jackson as Catherine is forced to choose between her two loves, which are in effect two worlds. Raoul represents the old order in his attachment to the land, to his family, and to his Creole heritage. Jackson represents freedom, opportunity, and escape from an oppressive society.

But the opposition is even more complex than such polarities suggest. Raoul's rule-bound world has in large part been created to resist the ever-impinging economic domination of the Cajuns, who have taken more and more of the land from blacks and Creoles. Like John Henry of the folk songs, Raoul counteracts the dehumanization of the new mechanical age through sheer physical effort. He refuses any compromise or accommodation, knowing all the time that his exertions are doomed. He clings so tightly to Catherine because she too cares for the land and because she sees his struggle as heroic. Ironically, his battle against dehumanization has robbed him of much of his humanity. He has little use for his neighbors; for his other daughter, Lillian; or for his wife, who out of loneliness and frustration had an affair with a black man, an affair that produced the family's only male child. We learn late in the book that Raoul was responsible for this child's death, which occurred some years before the present time of the narrative. In his imprisonment of Catherine and killing of Marky, he has in effect destroyed his own future in the struggle to save it.

Similarly, Jackson, though he seems free, has created his own prison through despair and self-doubt. The very openness of his future makes it impossible for him to move into it. He cannot accept an order based on emotion and faith, but in its place he would impose a rational system that would ultimately be just as rigid as Raoul's. He is admirable in his refusal to accommodate himself to the rules of racial segregation, but his action is private; he cannot bring himself to open resistance: "Already he had heard that they were asking whether or not he was a Freedom Rider. What a joke. He a Freedom Rider? And what would he try to integrate, this stupid grocery store? He felt like laughing in their stupid faces."[8]

He has no place here, either in affirmation of or resistance to this southern life. He seeks to take Catherine away, but he has no place to take her. His love for her is desperately egocentric; like Raoul, he needs her to affirm the value of his existence. And also like Raoul, he would imprison her in his ego. In choosing between them, Catherine, who loves them both, must choose her life's cage.

But both Catherine and Jackson are presented with alternatives in the form of minor characters. Madame Bayonne, the first of these characters, situates herself at the edge of the black community. Fully knowledgeable about its members, she maintains a critical attitude toward them. Her career as a teacher with a strong sense of the outside world has conditioned her to a certain distance from the community. The children believe she is a witch. She combines, in sum, the wisdom of the folk and the critical perception of the larger society.

Because she is both inside and outside, she offers Jackson an alternative to both his own alienation and the blind faith of Raoul and Charlotte. In their conversations about Charlotte and the Carmiers, she constantly reminds him of the human consequences of actions and decisions. She tells him the history of the community and explains why it is the way it is. By showing him the human reality of this life, she suggests a way of living in it without submitting to it. She has lived her life on the edge, both caring about and criticizing the community; she has willingly paid the price of a reputation for eccentricity in order to maintain this freedom.

Della, the mother, has resisted Raoul's bitterness and isolation by loving him despite himself. But she is not a totally self-sacrificing woman: her affair and her love for the resultant child show her to be one who will not accept reification. The black lover and the black son are both symbols of her larger resistance to Creole social rules, as well as to her need for love.

She has paid for this rebellion with years of neglect and hostility. Nonetheless, she has aided Catherine in both of her affairs with Jackson.

Moreover, when Jackson and Raoul finally have their fistfight, Della is the one who explains to the younger man the implications of his victory:

> No, you right, you not a hero. But he's a proud man, and after what happened tonight, he won't ever be able to raise his head in front of her like he done before. So that means she'll have to leave. He'll see to that. And then I get my chance—a chance I been waiting for for twenty years. No, I'm not proud to see my man get beaten. No woman wants that. But what happened here tonight is best for everybody. If y'all hadn't fought out there, and if he hadn't got beaten, he wouldn't 'a' never let her go. (*Catherine Carmier*, 247)

The fight has produced a more natural order. The husband and wife and the two lovers will be paired so as to produce an equilibrium. Another equilibrium is created with her remark that Jackson in effect became her son Marky. As such, his defeat of Raoul was the just punishment for the twenty-year-old killing. For Della, then, order has been restored.

But Jackson must also learn patience. Catherine will not come to him immediately; there must be time for the relationships to sort themselves out and for a reconciliation to the new order. For Della, who has suffered and kept faith for twenty years, and who is in tune with the slow rhythms of the land and the folk, there is no doubt that love will come in its own time. But for Jackson, who has no experience of either faith or suffering and who lives by the chronology of the modern, rational world, no such confidence is possible. Della offers him the wisdom of experience, but he is left to decide whether he can accept it. Catherine must undergo a transition to a new reality; if she succeeds, she can come only to a Jackson who has learned endurance and faith. Thus both must reject the confinements of the old world, but in the name of the values of that world.

Of Love and Dust (1967) more thoroughly dramatizes the process of negotiation by making the narrator the character in the middle. He is caught between the system of rules created by landowning whites and enforced by Cajuns and the defiance of Marcus, whose rebellion eventually leads to his death. As a man who works hard and has benefited somewhat from the plantation system, Jim Kelly sees little to be gained from open resistance; in fact, he tends to see such resistance as a threat to those blacks who have adjusted to the white-dominated economic and political structure. On the other hand, he is keenly aware of the indignities that that system inflicts on blacks. Because he sees himself as a man of intelligence and not action, he vacillates between self-criticism for tolerating injustice and criticism of those who can act without thought of the consequences. He has lost faith in everything—repeatedly he talks about God's absence—but he has suffered enough himself to be sensitive to the suffering of others. In fact, he is a blues performer, both literally and figuratively. He plays a blues guitar and, in several passages, he describes in blues idiom the loss of Billie Jean, who left him for a more glamorous life. More important, his narrative itself echoes the blues, telling as it does a story of love and trouble, of the Man and the Bad Nigger,[9] of passion and violence, and of fate and individual struggle. The narrative is also a composition structurally, as Kelly puts together with his own information episodes told to him by others. The result is a folk narrative with multiple voices, unified by the central storyteller, who is himself a folk performer.

Kelly tells an intense story of murder, interracial love, revenge, and intrigue. Marcus, who has been charged with murder, is bonded out on work release to Marshall Hebert, who owns the plantation where the narrator works. The latter becomes involved when Marcus's godmother asks Kelly to look after her godson. He reluctantly agrees, though he sees the young man as wild and incorrigible.

The plan of Hebert and his Cajun overseer, Sidney Bonbon, is to break Marcus, much as troublesome slaves had been broken in earlier times. Kelly unwillingly aids this effort by driving the tractor that moves at a constant, rapid pace, too fast for the inexperienced Marcus. Nothing can be done to make the work easier, for Bonbon is constantly there, mounted on his horse directly behind the workers. Kelly does what he can, offering advice on what clothes to wear and how to treat blisters and sunburn and in general how to adjust to the intolerable circumstance.

But Marcus refuses to adjust. He refuses to wear anything other than city clothes and shoes; he spends nights drinking and whoring rather than sleeping; and he remains angry and arrogant. He plots both escape and revenge, and he calls Kelly a "white-mouth" for warning him against rash behavior and for reminding him that he did in fact kill a man. The rashness is evident when he tries to seduce Pauline, Bonbon's black mistress. When this fails, he crosses racial boundaries himself to have an affair with the overseer's wife, Louise, who cooperates so that she might get even for Bonbon's infidelities.

The complexity of the rules under which racial oppression operates in the novel is illustrated by these two affairs. While both are technically illegal under southern law, Bonbon's relationship with Pauline has the tacit approval of social custom, just as under slavery a white man is assumed to have the right to use sexually any black woman he wants. The woman, having no social or legal standing, can do nothing but submit. What complicates this affair is that Bonbon comes to love Pauline and she him. Such a situation violates the rules, for it implicitly undermines the social order based on white control.

The other affair is carried on in sharp contrast to Bonbon and Pauline's. Though Marcus and Louise each initially exploit the other for purposes of revenge, they soon fall in love. However, the slightest hint of the black man's meeting with the white woman would lead to his death, probably at the hands of a lynch mob. His action is inherently political, striking as it does at the heart of racist ideology by treating the white woman as something other than the taboo object the ideology has made her.

The difference can be seen in the attitudes of the two characters who witness these parallel love affairs. Aunt Caroline, who lives next door to Pauline, finds the openness of Bonbon's behavior distasteful; it offends her sense of morality, but she must at least admire his loyalty and perseverance. She must make the best of the situation, for she can do nothing to change it. Aunt Margaret, on the other hand, is not only offended but also terrified by Marcus and Louise. The white woman forces her to make the secret meetings possible, and, although she attempts to warn off Marcus and to protect Louise's child, she can do nothing to stop activities she believes threaten everyone. What frightens her is the belief that the two enjoy their activities and love each other; such a result means that they may lose whatever sense of self-preservation remains.

Kelly, as the collector and recorder of these stories, shares her concern. He sees Marcus as a man totally self-centered; even when he moves from anger to love, he lets his feelings determine his actions and does not care about the effects on others. Like Stagolee and Dupree of folk legend, he delights in defying convention and is indifferent to the consequences of his behavior. Early in the narrative, Kelly dislikes him for this reason; keeping his promise to Miss Julie does not necessarily mean tolerating Marcus's actions. However, as the story progresses, the refusal to break under the pressures becomes a source of admiration. Even if Marcus acts selfishly and irrationally, he does so with a courage that cannot be denied.

The only possible result, of course, is death for the defiant one. Appropriately, it comes at the very moment Marcus believes he and Louise have managed to escape, with the help of the owner. But Hebert, who hates both Marcus and Bonbon, arranges matters so that the Cajun will kill the black. With Marcus dead, Louise goes insane; Bonbon, found innocent of murder, leaves with Pauline to avoid the wrath of his wife's family.

Before he goes, Bonbon talks to Kelly about their common entrapment in the mechanism of exploitation: "Me and you—what we is? We little people, Geam. They make us do what they want us to do, and they don't tell us nothing. We don't have nothing to say 'bout it, do we, Geam?"[10] Kelly goes a step further when he recognizes that even Marcus's rebellion serves the purposes of the oppressive system: "And what had Marcus done that was so wrong? Yes, he had killed—yes, yes—but didn't they give him the right to kill? I had been thinking about this in the field all evening and I had said to myself, 'Yes, yes; it's not Marcus, it's them. Marcus was just the tool. Like Hotwater was the tool—put there for Marcus to kill' " (*Of Love and Dust*, 269). With oppression and exploitation so pervasive, it is little wonder that the impulse of the black community is toward resignation and self-effacing caution.

But Kelly, inspired by Marcus's courage and granted insights into the social order, refuses to be submissive. When he too is forced to leave the plantation because he knows too much, he rejects Hebert's letter of recommendation. Such a gesture seems small, but it does announce his determination to move outside dependency on the manipulators of the social-economic machine. He may work for white men in the future, but he has ceased to be willing to sacrifice his integrity to their power.

But his most effective act of resistance is remembering. Aunt Margaret, in a final conversation, explains the necessity and importance of forgetting:

> "You see, you won't forget," she said.
> "I can't, Aunt Margaret."
> "That's why you got to go," she said. "You'll just keep reminding him [Hebert]."
> "You forgot, already, Aunt Margaret?" I asked her.
> "Yes," she said. (*Of Love and Dust*, 279)

The narrative, by its very existence, rejects this attitude. It keeps alive Marcus's rebellious efforts, which, when linked to the badmen of folklore, grant him heroic, legendary status. But the deeper significance is in remembering why the rebellion failed. By assigning responsibility and dramatizing the mechanism of oppression, Kelly provides a critical perspective for the audience of his narrative. Thus, while the story may be one of failure and suffering, the storytelling in itself opens new possibilities for resistance.

Bloodline (1968), Gaines's collection of short stories, takes a different approach to fixed orders. Here, through first-person narrators of varying sophistication, he describes central absences, things lost or not yet obtained, which characters try to bring into presence. But, given Gaines's narratives of process rather than resolution, the presence must be always deferred. The narrators come to understand that the quest, rather than the object of the quest, is of greatest importance.

The first story in the collection, "A Long Day in November," would seem to contradict the formulation just articulated. At the end of the story, which comes at the end of the day, the narrator, a six-year-old boy, is warmly and safely in his bed, listening to the lovemaking of his parents. All these elements—ended story, ended day, warmth, lovemaking—are signs of resolution, of a presence obtained. But closer analysis suggests that, while an equilibrium has been achieved that is satisfactory to the naïve narrator, it does not mark a true resolution of the story's conflicts.

The narrative picks up the conflict at a middle point, when Amy leaves her husband, taking away their child Sonny and returning to her mother's home. She does this because she feels that Eddie cares more for his car than for his family. She considers his attention to the automobile a sign of his lack of manhood. To him, the car symbolizes freedom and a certain status in the community. Sonny is caught in the middle, with no comprehension of the significance of the fight. For him the conflict comes out of nowhere: he communicates no sense of a history of contention, and he has no doubts about his father's manhood. As narrator, he serves a defamiliarizing function by robbing readers of their normal adult manner of reading about domestic conflict.[11] By being very concrete, but not interpretive, he allows the full expression of the perspectives of the combatants. But *because* he cannot interpret, the reader must engage in an evaluation of those perspectives. Moreover, since these stances are often presented euphemistically, precisely because of the presence of the narrator, the reader must make the connection between the verbal sign and the underlying meaning. Thus, the storytelling and -reading is a basic pattern of reading signs.

The story itself is about reading signs. Even before the automobile becomes central, an example is provided by Sonny himself. He is distressed by his parents' separation, but he cannot articulate that distress. One effect of it is that he does not prepare his lessons. The combination of domestic disruption and lack of preparation creates so much stress that he urinates on himself in front of the class. While he cannot explain his behavior, his teacher reads it to mean trouble at home, while his classmates see it as a lack of maturity. Moreover, the reader sees in it an analogue to his father's immaturity, thus reinforcing the theme of a quest for manhood.

The automobile is, of course, the key symbol. Eddie at first does not realize its full symbolic significance; he seeks the return of Amy through the intervention of the minister and through the advice of his friends, but none of them is effective. Only when he visits the conjure woman, a renowned reader of signs, does he find out what he must do. The car must be sacrificed if he is to restore domestic tranquility. Selling or abandoning it is not sufficient; only total destruction is permissible.

The ritual which follows suggests that the entire community is involved in what seemed to be a private dispute. With everyone present, the burning of the car, as a purging of Eddie's immaturity and irresponsibility, reenacts the initiation rites necessary for the perpetuation of all cultures. It also means, of course, the end of Eddie's freedom and individuality, as he is now socially, emotionally, and physically tethered to the family and the community. And for this, he is labeled an adult. His mother-in-law, his constant antagonist, comments, "He's a man after all."[12]

Taking the ritual for reality, Amy returns home. But she requires of Eddie one final gesture to signify his role in the family and the community. She insists that he beat her as an indication of his control over her, and "because I don't want you to be the laughingstock of the plantation" (*Bloodline*, 75). The burning showed what he was willing to give up for love and responsibility; the beating shows his assumption of that responsibility. He is compelled to use force to demonstrate his control.

But the ritual lacks substance; Eddie performs it only because Amy, over

75

whom he supposedly demonstrates control, demands he do it. As in the burning, he does only what he is told to do. Like his son, he must be taught the meaning of manhood by a woman. And both are rewarded at the end by a return to the womb: Eddie to the body of his wife and Sonny to the warm, dark comfort of his bed. This connection at the conclusion of the story suggests an important irony in that the achievement of symbolic manhood coincides with infancy. Eddie has performed the public and private rituals that signify his manliness, but he has not been transformed by them into an adult. Even the responsibilities he is about to undertake, such as aiding in Sonny's education, are done only at the behest of his wife.

Amy, thus, is a conservative trickster. Against his will, she makes Eddie accept the forms of socially responsible behavior and places on him the mask of domination so that the family as a whole will achieve respectability in the community. Meanwhile, she in fact remains the one in control, training her husband and her son to be men according to her definition. If either were to become in reality what they are in appearance, then her position would be untenable. Thus, the presence—manhood—that is continually sought must never be obtained.

The situation in "The Sky Is Gray" is more difficult because the woman must rapidly educate her eight-year-old son in the tenets of manhood and integrity. With her husband gone, this poverty-stricken mother must teach her children the principles of survival in case she might die. This task gives her some of the qualities of the moral hard man; she is unsentimental, silent, uncompromising, and principled. The tension in the story results from James, the son-narrator, trying to understand the world as his mother presents it.

One of the first lessons comes when she forces him to kill two small redbirds he has caught in a trap. When he resists, she beats him until he stabs them. Since they contain so little meat, he has trouble comprehending the lesson. Because his mother will not explain, he is baffled until his aunt tells him that his mother has taught him that survival overrides sentiment. The mother's silence is significant; by not telling, she forces James to seek out answers rather than have them handed to him. As important to survival as food is the use of his intelligence. The world is filled with signs and rituals; he must learn to read them through the application of mother-wit.

When James develops a toothache, the opportunity arises for a more complex education, since they must enter the world of whites. The first lesson in Bayonne does not involve the mother at all; what it does do is reveal James's potential for an appropriate education. In the dentist's office, an argument begins between a young, educated man and a minister of the Old School. The young man, though much like Jackson of *Catherine Carmier* in his alienation and pessimism, does insist on the rejection of the old values of humility and accommodation. Black manhood, he insists, will come only from reason and an unrelenting honesty about the realities of the world. He argues that words unaccompanied by actions are meaningless: " 'Citizens have certain rights,' the boy says. 'Name me one right that you have. One right, granted by the Constitution, that you can exercise in Bayonne' " (*Bloodline*, 101). The minister takes all this as an assault on his faith and, after a number of objections based on Christian dogma, he strikes the young man out of frustration and fear. The frustration comes from being unable to defeat the young man's logic, while the fear comes, as it usually does in Gaines's fiction, from the belief that such open resistance to white ideology can only bring harm to the entire black community. Even though the young man admits his despair, he is still admired by James: "When I grow up I want to be just like him. I want clothes like that and I want to keep a book with me, too" (*Bloodline*, 100). In admiring reason and literacy, he is siding with those who resist the closed system of Bayonne. Again, the lesson is that the use of the mind is a key to integrity.

How that lesson can be applied in the everyday world of Bayonne is indicated by his mother. After the dentist closes for lunch without seeing James, they must wander the streets in the bitter cold, unable to enter any of the white-owned restaurants. When James cannot stand the cold any longer, they go into a hardware store. His mother positions him beside a hot stove and then asks to look at ax handles. While examining them, she constantly watches her son; when he is sufficiently warm, they leave without buying anything. Since they had virtually no money to begin with, she acted with a degree of deception, though to obtain an important end.

But more than this, the scene, when paired with another shortly after, reveals her attitude toward whites. Cold again, they go into a diner in the black section of town, where James again stands by the stove. He soon announces that he is warm, but his mother responds, "Got to pay them something for they heat" (*Bloodline*, 109). Such a thought never was expressed in the white store. Apparently an ironic Golden Rule motivates her actions: exploit those who exploit you, but deal fairly with those of kind intentions.

The most complex application of this lesson comes in the last scene of the story. An elderly white woman who has watched the two of them walk up and down the street invites them in to have something to eat. But the mother resists, unwilling to accept charity and by implication dependence on whites.

> "Just a minute," the old lady says. Mama stops. "The boy'll have to work for it. It isn't free."
> "We don't take no handout," Mama says.
> "I'm not handing out anything," the old lady says. "I need my garbage moved to the front. Ernest has a bad cold and can't go out there."
> "James'll move it for you," Mama says.
> "Not unless you eat," the old lady says. "I'm old, but I have my pride, too, you know." (*Bloodline*, 113)

An act of kindness must be carefully negotiated. Mama must retain her dignity while not offending this white woman; even altruism must be tentative in the racially charged atmosphere of Bayonne. Each woman goes outside the boundaries of the conventions—Mama by asserting pride, the white woman by recognizing it—but they must do so in terms of the conventions. Such behavior is necessary because the social conditions made explicit in earlier scenes have created layers of distrust and misunderstanding on both sides. Since direct communication of desires and intentions is impossible, a certain etiquette is essential to guarantee integrity on both sides.

To show the artificiality of the arrangements, James insists that the garbage cans are empty. "I tell myself I ain't go'n be nobody's fool, and I'm go'n look inside this can to see just what I been hauling" (*Bloodline*, 115). He is prevented from doing so by the white woman and thus does not reveal the emptiness of the performance in which he has participated. But the performance is empty only in a literal sense. By carrying those cans, James has learned another lesson in his education; the form of certain behavior is at least as important as the content, especially in matters of race relations. When the system insists on objectifying both sides, then the means of overcoming it is through creative manipulation of its rules. Such acting must always be a balancing act, teetering between abject submission and open resistance.

Its contingent character is evidenced when the elderly woman tries to give the mother more salt pork than her quarter will buy. Her gesture is not accepted because it is seen as a reversion to condescending charity. This error of kindness is withdrawn in line with the principle of mutual dignity. The mother then comments quite sincerely, "Your kindness will never be forgotten" (*Bloodline*, 117). The kindness is not in the physical objects given, but in the recognition of a common humanity.

The possibility that James has been successfully educated is suggested at the conclusion of the story:

> The sleet's coming down heavy, heavy now, and I turn up my coat collar to keep my neck warm. My mama tells me turn it right back down.
>   "You not a bum," she says. "You a man." (*Bloodline*, 117)

The lack of verbs in her final statement is crucial. In the structure of black dialect, Gaines finds an ambiguity appropriate to his perspective. The statement can be both indicative and imperative, present and future. It is not limited to the clichéd resolution of the story of successful initiation that implies that manhood is a clearly defined presence finally and absolutely attained. Manhood is already implicit in that James sees the value of what is taught him; it is possible to the extent that he comes to know when he must bear the brunt of the storm with dignity. He must display courage and, by implication, defiance, in refusing to consider life's storms to be stronger than he is. When he has mastered the subtle differences between bum and man, then he will become the latter.

The painful nature of the quest for manhood is the subject of "Three Men." Proctor Lewis, the nineteen-year-old narrator, believes himself to have gained that status through acts of violence, including the stabbing of which he is accused in this story. Further verification for him comes in his outsmarting of whites; he knows that he will avoid prison by turning himself in and then by being bonded on work-release to Roger Medlow, a wealthy plantation owner. The story develops by demonstrating the absence of manhood and its actual status as a neverending process.

In his cell, his opposed possibilities are represented by Hattie Brown, a homosexual, and Munford Bazille, an older more experienced version of Proctor himself. Hattie articulates all the conventions of bourgeois society in talk of decent people and acceptance of the status quo. Symbolically, he is those blacks who have submitted to the system, who have emasculated themselves at the bidding of those who rule the society. Proctor repeatedly refers to him as a woman, implying that he is inherently incapable of manhood.

Bazille tells a folk tale that points out the difference between Hattie and himself:

> It start in the cradle when they send that preacher there to christen you. At the same time he's doing that mumbo-jumbo stuff, he's low'ing his mouth to your little nipper to suck out your manhood. I know, he tried it on me. Here, I'm laying in his arms in my little white blanket and he suppose to be christening me. My mammy there, my pappy there; uncle, aunt, grandmammy, grandpappy; my nan-nane, my pa-ran—all of them standing there with they head bowed. This preacher going, "Mumbo-jumbo, mumbo-jumbo," but all the time he's low'ing his mouth to my little private. Nobody else don't see him but I catch him, and I haul 'way back and hit him right smack in the eye. I ain't no more than three months old but I give him a good one. "Get your goddam mouth away from my pecker, you no-teef, rotten, egg-sucking sonofabitch. Get away from here, you sister-jumper, God-calling, pulpit-spitting, mother-huncher. Get away from here, you chicken-eating, catfish-eating, gin-drinking sonofabitch. Get away, goddam it, get away." (*Bloodline*, 140)

He makes a distinction between those who not only have lost or distorted their own masculinity but who would deprive others of it and those who resist emasculation, even if it means defying those at the respected center of the society. He makes himself one of the disruptive figures, like Jim Trueblood of *Invisible Man*, the drunks in McPherson's "A Matter of Vocabulary," and Marcus in *Of Love and Dust*. He seems to define manhood in terms of open defiance and violence, thus reinforcing Proctor's self-image.

But his point is more subtle:

> But they don't stop there, they stay after you. If they miss you in the cradle, they catch you some other time. And when they catch you, they draw it out of you or they make you a beast—make you use it in a brutish way. You use it on a woman without caring for her, you use it on children, you use if on

other men, you use it on yourself. Then when you get so disgusted with
everything round you, you kill. And if your back is strong, like your back is
strong, they get you out so you can kill again. (*Bloodline*, 140–41)

Even the "bad nigger" can be used by the system: "They need us. Because
without us, they don't know what they is. . . . With us around, they can
see us and they know what they ain't" (*Bloodline*, 137–38). The Munford
Brazilles are created and encouraged so that the original guilt, the initial
violence of oppression, can be evaded.

But the evasions and oppression only work if the Hattie Browns and
Munford Brazilles refuse to learn the true source of their behaviors. With
knowledge comes something else—a sense of responsibility. Once the
black man knows why he acts as he does, he can choose to accept individual responsibility and thereby move out of the cycle of violence. Paradoxically, for Proctor, going to prison may be the route to manhood and
freedom, if he knows why he goes:

> "So you don't go to the pen for killing the nigger, you go for yourself. You
> go to sweat out all the crud you got in your system. You go, saying, 'Go fuck
> yourself, Roger Medlow, I want to be a man, and by God I will be a man. For
> once in my life I will be a man.' "
> "And a month after you been in the pen, Medlow tell them to kill you for
> being a smart aleck. How much of a man you is then?"
> "At least you been a man a month—where if you let him get you out you
> won't be a man a second. He won't 'low it." (*Bloodline*, 141)

The Hemingwayesque call for courage in the face of death is quite deliberate. Gaines presents an extreme case so as to force on his narrator a basic
moral choice. The story cuts through all the subtleties of the earlier novels
and stories to demonstrate the underlying tension in black life: to accept
the definition of self given by the prevailing social order so as to live is in
effect to choose death-in-life, but to defy that same order in the name of
self-definition is often to choose death itself. Most of Gaines's work is not
so explicitly dualistic, but he frequently presents characters who are willing
and even eager to die for the cause in which they believe.

Proctor is not initially such a character. He cannot accept Bazille's interpretation of his fate, preferring to believe that he can manage his life
within the old framework. But after the old man leaves, Proctor's time is
spent in contemplation of his condition; this thinking is in and of itself a

new process for him and one that he finds deeply troubling: "I have to stop thinking. That's how you go crazy—thinking" (*Bloodline,* 149). When a fourteen-year-old who has been beaten by the white officers is thrown into the cell, Proctor has the opportunity to articulate his thoughts. In the process, he comes to understand the necessities of his own manhood: "I knowed I was going to the pen now. I knowed I was going, I knowed I was going. Even if Medlow came to get me, I wasn't leaving with him. I was go'n do like Munford said. I was going there and I was go'n sweat it and I was go'n take it. I didn't want have to pull cover over my head every time a white man did something to a black boy—I wanted to stand" (*Bloodline,* 152).

The scene marks the change in Proctor from "bad nigger" to "moral hard man."[13] From being totally self-absorbed and incapable of seeing his real relationships to others and to the society as a whole, he comes to an understanding of the life-affirming value of resistance. By seeing Bazille in himself and himself in the fourteen-year-old, he transcends his egocentrism and perceives the larger pattern of oppression. His refusal to fit into that pattern becomes his identity and his manhood. As a result, he begins to play the role of father that Bazille has played for him. He tells the boy his probable fate, but he also washes his wounds. More important, he involves the boy in his own fate:

> "If Medlow come to get me, I'm not going," I said to the boy. "That means that T. J. and his boys coming, too. They go'n beat me because they think I'm a smart aleck trying to show them up. Now you listen to me, and listen good. Every time they come for me I want you to start praying. I want you to pray till they bring me back in this cell. And I don't want you praying like a woman, I want you to pray like a man. . . . That's the only way I'll be able to take those beatings—with you praying." (*Bloodline,* 153)

Even though Proctor himself does not believe in God or prayer, he sees the necessity of inspiring in the boy belief in something. Being forced to consider the suffering of another, the boy is caught in a web of responsibility and human relationships that destroys his isolation. Under such conditions, a community of responsible human beings is created that, by its very existence, resists resignation to the racist order.

At the end, Proctor is not at all certain that his nascent manhood and community are enough: "Was I going to be able to take the beatings night after night? I had seen what T. J. could do to your back. I had seen it on this kid and I had seen it on other people. Was I going to be able to take it? I don't know, I thought to myself. I'll just have to wait and see" (*Bloodline*, 155). He does not doubt his choice; he only questions his ability to pay the price of that choice. He wonders not whether he will resist but whether he has the courage to make that resistance successful. In a sense, the question is moot because the choice itself has made the qualitative difference; he no longer accepts victimization as an inevitable and natural product of the system. By choosing suffering consciously, he in fact becomes self-determining, for he is turning a tool of oppression into a test of himself and thus into a tool of resistance. He, not the oppressor, chooses his method of suffering; in this choice he frees himself psychologically from outside control. In effect, he makes himself one of the folk figures pursuing freedom in the context of enslavement and thus becomes part of the negative dialectic that is black culture.

The central figure of "Bloodline," Copper Laurent, seeks to overcome the dialectic to bring about a new presence but in the very process enacts the dialectic. Copper's quest, as narrated by Felix, a seventy-year-old plantation worker, is to lay absolute claim to his origins. Black son of Walter Laurent and nephew of Frank, the present owner, he is the only direct descendant of the family line. He uses this information to demand from Frank his heritage, but the uncle refuses in the name of the rules which govern black-white social, legal, and economic relationships. In his rejection of the social realities of southern life, Copper is another of Gaines's alienated young men. But he differs from Jackson, Marcus, and others in that he has a revolutionary sensibility. He calls himself General and he constantly talks of an army of blacks at his command. Felix sees in this delusions of grandeur that endanger the community.

The irony of the story is the utter rightness of Copper's claim. In his assertiveness, his arrogance, his forceful character, he is more a Laurent than the sickly, self-doubting Frank. But these family qualities are accompanied by the traditional Laurentian feeling of superiority over and indifference to the blacks on the plantation. He attacks and humiliates those men sent to bring him to the Big House. He treats with disdain any of those who have accommodated themselves to the existing conditions. Like his white father, he only respects those who make a public display of their courage.

What he ignores, and what Felix insists on, is that the maligned black community is itself the source of his resistance. Even though at seventy he is no longer required to work, Felix does so out of a sense of pride and the value of labor: "So I came up to the yard now just to keep the old hands busy. Because once the hands had stopped, the man wasn't no more" (*Bloodline*, 163). In other words, he works for his own sake and not out of any sense of duty to whites. Moreover, he and 'Malia, Copper's aunt, are the only blacks who can say what they want to Frank. They question his orders, and he feels compelled to justify himself. Moreover, Felix can even speak the unspeakable:

> "I'll tell him you sent for him," I said. "Who I'm suppose to say?"
> "You forgot my name, Felix?"
> "No sir. I just thought you might want me to say his uncle, though."
> (*Bloodline*, 166)

Such candor is possible only if the conventions of white supremacy have in reality been subverted. They have been broken down by the endurance and sustained dignity of 'Malia and Felix. By remaining within the system and playing by rules in which they do not believe, they have been able to neutralize the effects of that system.

Through such subversion, they have kept alive the very black pride that makes Copper's demands political rather than merely selfishly personal. Because of them, he knows the connection between his own experience and that of all disinherited blacks, the ones that constitute his "army." His problem is that he sees the army as an abstraction, not as the concrete reality of the black community he scorns. In the end he must fail because his absolute demands cannot be adapted to the historical conditions. As arrogant General, he retreats rather than risk engaging the enemy under such circumstances.

But the narrator cannot so easily dismiss Copper, for he knows the contingent nature of history. Though subversion has worked in the past, it cannot bring ultimate victory because it needs the very system that it opposes. And while the representatives of that system may falter, as Frank has, the system itself has remarkable resiliency. It not only absorbs the Coppers by labeling them madmen, but it can also regenerate itself through them. Such regeneration is on the horizon of this story in the form of the white niece who will in all probability inherit the land and turn it over to the Cajuns, who feel none of Frank's noblesse oblige toward the blacks. Caught within history, Felix and 'Malia cannot escape its dynamic. Unless they can find new strength and new strategies, they will be cast aside. For this reason, they need the promise of Copper: "Tell my aunt I've gone. But tell her I'll come back. And tell her when I do, she'll never have to go through your back door again" (*Bloodline,* 217). Whether the promise can be fulfilled is irrelevant; its statement renews faith in the ongoing struggle. The concreteness of the promise shows a potential for responsibility on Copper's part that may bring his radicalism within history.

In the final story of the collection, "Just like a Tree," Gaines attempts to define as a presence and positive identity that fictional space occupied by the black folk. Aunt Fe is the product of this attempt, but the method of narration opposes the idea of presence. Multiple voices describe this old woman's last evening, but her own voice is not among them. Thus, each of the voices gives us a "difference from" and not an "identity with" the character at the center. No voice is privileged, and so none can give an absolute version of Fe; moreover, the sum of the versions, which is the narrative, is not a complete picture, in part precisely because Fe is silent. What was in the earlier stories the quest of the characters becomes here the quest of the reader for the truth at the heart of the black experience.

One starting point in the search for meaning is the fact of silence. Two characters, both crucial to the plot, never speak directly; these two are Fe and her grandnephew Emmanuel. Emmanuel motivates the action of the story. Because he is a civil rights activist, the family fears that all of its members, including Fe, might be harmed by angry whites. She is to be taken to the North and safety by one of her daughters, despite her own desire to stay where she is. All the speakers record their observations at her home the night before she is to leave. Since she remains silent, these voices are our only source of information.

They suggest that Fe is a space occupied by certain characteristics rather than an integrated identity. The children find here an old-fashioned and thus exotic life. The white woman recalls nurturing comfort in the midst of

85

a life otherwise uncertain and sterile. Aunt Lou knows her as the lifelong companion. To all, she manifests religious faith and self-sacrifice. In other words, each character defines her in terms of some positive value that satisfies a need of her own. In this sense she has no being except as an extension of others, and paradoxically, this nonbeing is described as her being.

Fe affirms all and negates nothing. But in a conversation with Emmanuel recorded by Etienne, we see another possibility open. Fe herself has kept alive the memory of violence against blacks, specifically against their family. Emmanuel recalls being told the story:

> "Just the two of us were sitting here beside the fire when you told me that. I was so angry I felt like killing. But it was you who told me get killing out of my mind. It was you who told me I would only bring harm to myself and sadness to the others if I killed. Do you remember that, Aunt Fe?"
>
> She nods, still looking in the fire.
>
> "You were right. We cannot raise our arms. Because it would mean death for ourselves, as well as for the others. But we will do something else—and that's what we will do."

A moment later she gives him her blessing: " 'Good-bye, Emmanuel,' she say. She look at him a long time. 'God be with you' " (*Bloodline,* 246–47).

By keeping alive the tale of suffering, Fe has helped create the conditions for nonviolent resistance. The heart of Gaines's history-bound narratives is this internal dialectic of the black community. The traditional folk figures remember; through tales, personal experience, folk wisdom, and religious faith, they conserve the concrete history of the race. They pass along this accumulated intelligence to those young and courageous enough to seek the end of suffering and injustice. These rebels most often fail because of the sheer strength of the opposition, but their attempts enter into the folk history, to be kept alive for the next generation. The relationship, of course, is not neat and mechanical. The aunts and fathers often fear the rebellion of the sons because they have come to value conservation more than change. And the sons often disdain the wisdom of their elders, seeing in it compromise and irrationality. But in Gaines's fictional worlds, both the refusal to change and the refusal to heed the folk wisdom bring sterility and death.

In "Just like a Tree," Aunt Fe's teaching of Emmanuel has made possible rebellion; but that fact means that it threatens her own existence. Too old and improperly constituted to be a rebel, she seems capable of no action and thus will be taken away to safety. But she rejects escape; she has no desire to be taken from the place she has created and which has created her. In a final act of resistance, she wills her own death rather than submit to the actions of the cautious. Thus the end of the story, when she dies on the morning of her planned departure, should not be read only as a sentimental coincidence. Rather, like the tree of the title, she *will* not be moved. Dying is her refusal to surrender to the same violent forces that lynched her father years before. But in the typical style of the folk, it lends itself to ambiguity. It does appear as sentimental coincidence, and thus she appears as the stereotypical black mammy who cannot live outside the idyllic world of the South. In her final act, Fe wears the mask that she has always worn, but it hides a very different face. Thus, the presence and the origin dissolve, and the absence becomes the reality.

In *The Autobiography of Miss Jane Pittman* (1971), Gaines extends and modifies the concerns of "Just like a Tree." Jane, like Fe, is old and respected at the time of the narration. But, unlike Fe, she tells her own story and tells of her whole life. At 108 when she speaks, she has, unlike the earlier narrators, undergone a full range of experiences in the world of the folk. But she has not thereby gained a fixed wisdom; she is not a fully defined presence. Like Fe, she has a sense of incompletion, of an absence that compels an openness to change.

As perhaps the ultimate "aunt" figure in Gaines's fiction, Jane would appear to be at the heart of the folk community. But she is a center that constantly decenters itself. Repeatedly, she places herself at the edge of the community and not at its heart. In the process, she forces a reconsideration of the nature of that community, much as Fe did. Jane presents herself not as the center, but as the character in the middle, negotiating between the conservative and radical positions in the black community and between black and white societies. This stance gives the book a dynamic form; ultimately, it means that the novel resists closure. Even the frame of Jane's narrative is not closed; the history teacher who records her story is present only at the beginning. As we shall see, this leaves an important gap at the end which forces open the narrative.

The book takes its shape in part from slave narratives in its movement from slavery to freedom. But it shows this as a constant and repeated movement; as the form of enslavement changes, so must the form of freedom. Also present are the same devices for coping with oppression that appeared in the antebellum narratives: accommodation and acceptance, rebellion and flight, and a middle ground which might best be called strategic resistance. This last is characterized by a refusal to accept the imposed definitions of black life, but a simultaneous refusal to rebel openly. Such a position requires both a moral seriousness within the black community and a willingness to engage in trickster behavior in relations with the white community. The story of Jane Pittman is the story of this middle stance.

From the beginning she asserts herself as one who will not quietly submit. When the plantation on which she is a slave is visited by northern soldiers, she is given the name Jane by one of them. She gladly accepts it as a replacement for her slave name. The fact that it is given to her by a white man becomes irrelevant when she earns it by enduring beatings from her mistress for no longer responding to "Ticey." The name becomes hers through an act of resistance and negation; she gives it a concrete meaning and thus makes it part of an emerging black identity in a way that could not have been intended by the Yankee soldier. Her behavior is condemned by many of the slaves as childish and foolish.

Her position outside the conservative center of the folk community is reinforced by her decision to leave the plantation when emancipation is proclaimed. In making this choice, she pits herself against the older wisdom, which questions the pursuit of an elusive freedom at the risk of security and safety. In Jane's young mind, freedom, symbolized by Ohio, is worth any risk. The degree of risk becomes fatally clear when the departing group is attacked and massacred by white patrollers. Jane can save only herself and Ned, the son of Big Laura, the leader of the group and the first of a series of rebels in the book. The scene itself establishes the basic pattern of the book: an act of resistance is led by a heroic figure, who is ultimately killed by the forces she or he opposes; in the aftermath, Jane remains to preserve whatever gains have been made, including the legend of the hero, and to prepare a new generation of rebels. In the role as preserver and nurturer, Jane describes her relationships with the forces being opposed, including white society, conservative blacks, and nature. The relationships are not entirely antagonistic; unlike the rebels, Jane humanizes them by presenting them as concrete particulars.[14] In this manner, the book avoids becoming an overt ideological statement. The specificity also places Jane's narrative within its history and thereby gives each of the episodes of resistance its own character while placing it within the larger pattern. Jane is the folk figure who records this interconnection of individual experience and historical form.

In her marriage to Joe Pittman, we see an important variation of the central event. Joe's resistance is not political; even when he is financially exploited by Colonel Dye in his effort to leave the plantation, he chooses to pay rather than fight. Joe seeks instead an economic freedom that comes by pitting himself against nature. He acquires a reputation as the best horse breaker in the Texas-Louisiana area, and he will not be stopped from riding wild horses even by Jane's fear for his life: "Now, little mama, man come here to die, didn't he? That's the contract he signed when he was born—'I hereby degree that one of these days I'm go'n laydown these old bones.' Now, all he can do while he's here is do something and do that thing good."[15]

Like Raoul in *Catherine Carmier,* he is a John Henry figure who makes his identity by challenging forces greater than himself. He defines his manhood by his victories over the uncontrolled energies of nature. Not even a "death horse" can deter him: "He was the devil far as I was concerned, but Joe stood there grinning at him. Joe said he had given them more trouble than all the other horses put together. He was stronger and faster than any horse he had ever seen. Run for days and wouldn't get tired. Leap over a canal that a regular horse wouldn't even try. After they had been after him about a week some of the men started saying he was a ghost" (*Miss Jane Pittman,* 90–91).

Recognizing the elemental and death-dealing power of the animal, Jane seeks to counteract it with the power of voodoo. But in her very attempt to foil destiny by sprinkling powder around the corral, she releases the horse and thus sets in motion the action leading to Joe's death. As Jane foresaw, the stallion was deadly, and Joe met his inevitable fate. His resistance was futile, but heroic.

Such an interpretation, however, denies human responsibility at the same time it praises human heroism. Joe's action seems the result of an inherent character trait and not the effect of choice; moreover, both the horse and the voodoo practices move the episode outside the realm of human control. But Jane's actions must be more closely examined. In her very efforts to save Joe, she causes his death. The voodoo does not work, and Joe's death occurs not under the controlled conditions of horse breaking, but in the uncontrolled conditions of darkness and underbrush caused by Jane's actions. Moreover, Joe consciously chooses to put himself in that situation. The underlying point, then, is that human actions can make a difference, even in the face of overwhelming force. Jane's position is one not of passive observation but of active engagement in the history she is recording. As verification, she keeps alive the memory of Joe Pittman in the name she carries.

The story of Ned, who combines his mother's love of freedom with the instinctive courage of Joe, reinforces the theme of human responsibility. In this case, Jane finds herself between Ned, who openly works for black education and civil rights, and Albert Cluveau, the Cajun hired to assassinate him. Raised by Jane and repeatedly told the story of his mother, Ned shows very early signs of rebellion. Compelled to leave Louisiana because of his politics, he goes to Kansas to get an education. Years later, he returns, having changed his name to Ned Douglass, to start a school in which to teach basic literacy and the principles of his namesake, Frederick Douglass. He publicly rejects the accommodationist philosophy of Booker T. Washington and insists that blacks stand up for their rights: " 'This earth is yours and don't let that man out there take it from you,' he said. 'It's yours because your people's bones lays in it; it's yours because their sweat and their blood done drenched this earth' " (*Miss Jane Pittman*, 107).

At the same time that she is encouraging Ned, Jane develops a relationship with Albert Cluveau. Though white and racist, he enjoys fishing with her, drinking her coffee, and running small errands for her. But his obsession is the killing he does for a living: "Sometimes I got him off talking about killing. I would make him talk about fishing and raising crop. He could talk about anything. Because most of the people round here either fished or farmed for a living anyhow. But in the end killing always came back in Albert Cluveau's mind. He wasn't bragging about it, but he wasn't sorry either. It was just conversation" (*Miss Jane Pittman*, 103).

When he is assigned the assassination of Ned, he first refuses and then warns Jane. He is a man locked into the forces of oppression who cannot escape despite his own desires. When Ned ignores Jane's admonitions, Albert has no choice but to fulfill his contract: "Cluveau hollered for him to stop and get down on his knees, but he kept running on Cluveau with nothing but his fist. Cluveau shot him in the leg—the white people had told Cluveau to make Ned crawl before killing him. When Cluveau shot him, he fell to one knee, then got back up. Cluveau shot again. This time he tored off half his chest" (*Miss Jane Pittman*, 115). In this encounter, Ned dies on his own terms; like Big Laura and Joe Pittman, he refuses to be a victim of the force he opposes. And like them he is remembered: "Even the rain couldn't wash the blood away. For years and years, even after they had graveled the road, you could still see little black spots where the blood had dripped" (*Miss Jane Pittman*, 115–16).

In contrast to Ned's nobility, Cluveau becomes pathetic. Trapped between his racism and his humanity, he feels a deep, superstitious guilt. He avoids Jane and then comes to believe that she has put a curse on him. While she denies this, his belief in the power of voodoo leads to madness that takes the form of her desire for his punishment: that he will hear the chariots of hell coming for him before he dies. In his insanity, he hears them for years before his death. Either Jane is disingenuous in telling the tale and is hiding her dark powers from a rationalistic and perhaps Christian audience, or else she has simply stimulated Cluveau's conscience and let it do the rest. Her very ambiguity gives her a degree of power despite her apparent inability to change circumstances. Whatever the source of her power, she effectively exacts punishment when the white legal system refuses to act. She uses folk wisdom and practice in response to the violence of the system. The oppressors' very act of destroying resistance inspires new forms of resistance within the oppressed community.

Much of the narrative after Ned's death is devoted to examination of the "rules" of the system, including those that apply to black-white love, race and politics, and the control of nature. In each case, the destructive effects of those rules are demonstrated not through argument but through specific examples in this fictional history. Alternatives are also presented, as in Jane's habit of talking to trees, not out of madness but out of respect: "But when you talk to an oak tree that's been here all these years, and knows more than you'll ever know, it's not craziness; it's just the nobility you respect" (*Miss Jane Pittman*, 146). In this behavior she follows an African tradition which holds that the spirits of ancestors reside in natural objects;

91

symbolically, her action demonstrates her respect for that which has endured over time.

The structural role of the black community itself is seen in the sections on religion in its more institutional forms. In "The Travels of Miss Jane Pittman," the narrator presents a folk allegory of the religious experience.

> And I moved down into the water, and all around me alligators snapped at my legs. I looked and—snakes—hundreds and hundreds of them swimming toward me. But I kept moving with the sack on my back, and with every step the water got deeper. When it came up to my neck I looked up to see how far I had to go—and there was Albert Cluveau. He was sitting on the horse that had killed Joe Pittman, he was holding the gun that had killed Ned. I looked back over my shoulder, and there was Joe and Ned on the other bank beckoning for me to come back to them. But I would not turn back. I would go on, because the load I was carrying on my back was heavier than the weight of death. When I got near the bank Albert Cluveau raised the gun to shoot me. But when he saw I was 'termined to finish crossing he disappeared, too. As soon as I put my feet on solid ground the Savior was there. (*Miss Jane Pittman*, 135)

This brief narrative functions as an initiation ritual; by telling it to the church, Jane justifies her full entry into that central institution of the black community. It is noteworthy for its recognition of Jane's personal responsibility in the major events of her life. The deceptive images of Joe and Ned suggest the deception she has practiced in evading responsibility for what happened to them.

In entering the church, Jane enters a world of fixed values and potentially a world of oppression. Her ambivalence about religious structures as opposed to religious experience is evident when she is first given the position of church mother and then deprived of it when she comes to prefer listening to baseball games to attending Sunday services.

But the full impact of religious ideology and its relation to white oppression is shown in the story of Jimmy Aaron, the last of the book's rebels. Because they tend to read the world as allegory, the old people constantly search for a sign of God's blessing on them. In Jimmy they believe that they have found one. He is presumed from birth to be The One, the new Moses to lead them out of the spiritual wilderness. Out of this belief comes a repression of all of Jimmy's natural development: they refuse to allow him to play with others, to experiment sexually, or to doubt his religious calling. They act, in other words, to make him what they believe him to be.

But, as has been the case throughout the book, systematic oppression breeds resistance. Jimmy returns from years of education in New Orleans, and he returns in part to be The One. His leadership, though, is to be political rather than religious. Once the church realizes this, they refuse to listen to him; it is Jane who must become his defender. In the process, she begins to doubt the potential for civil rights activity in the community: "They sleeping out there. Look around you, Jimmy; look at this place. Travel over this parish. Do you hear anything rumbling? No. Things must rumble before they move. The nigger, Jimmy, must one day wake up and push that black guilt off his back. Must tell himself I had it on too long. But I won't be here when that happen, I'm afraid" (*Miss Jane Pittman*, 227).

The people are crucial to Jimmy's efforts, for unlike Ned he needs them to participate directly in the resistance. He and Jane both know the consequences of such action: the blacks on the Samson plantation are old and poor, with no place to go if Robert Samson chooses to throw them off his land, as he has already done with some. Nonetheless, Jane, despite her great age, remains convinced that she at least must act.

When Jimmy is killed before the demonstration, Jane faces a dilemma. Her pattern has been to slip into the background on such occasions, and she is given the opportunity to do so here:

> "Go back home," he said.
> "You mean get off, don't you?" I said.
> "I mean go on back home," he said.
>
> (*Miss Jane Pittman*, 243)

However, this time she is the one who resists: "Me and Robert looked at each other there a long time, then I went by him" (*Miss Jane Pittman*, 244). In this moment that closes the narrative, she negates those forces that have killed Big Laura, Ned, and Jimmy by linking their rebellion with her own understanding of all that Robert Samson represents. The nurturing aunt and the rebel are joined in her, not as positive identity subject to ideology and repression but as the elusive folk, whose meaning is negation. Appropriately, the conclusion offers not resolution, but the opening to new experience. Jane walks past Samson to go to Bayonne and the suffering and triumph to be found there. She acts on faith, with no guarantee of success.

Consistent with this tone, the structure of the novel follows the pattern of the folk narrative. It is presented in dialect, with repetitions, apparent digressions, and a series of stories linked by the character of the teller more than the tight structure of plot. In essence then, Gaines has used the folk form to present the meaning of the black folk experience. Jane Pittman embodies the history of those who had no one to record their stories.

However, there is a crucial gap in the narrative that adds another level to the folk theme and structure. The opening scene of the novel, which is a rather conventional frame explaining how the narrative came to be, is said to be set some time after the events of the narrative itself. What is not explained is how Jane could return to the Samson plantation and tell her story, when Robert Samson threatened to evict those who protested. The question is not merely speculative, given the theme of folk resistance. Jane's return ought to be impossible, but the very existence of the narrative means that it has happened. The silence of the text on this point is intriguing, for it suggests some sort of trickster behavior on the part of the narrator, in that, even though a feeble old woman, she has conquered the powerful Samson, through means not made clear to the reader. Moreover, the frame narrator conspires in this silence and thereby places *his* narrative in the folk tradition. This suggests that not only political action but narrative itself must take the form of resistance. If the reader is given all the information the story has to offer, then the text becomes a closed, fully rationalized object. But the creation of mystery and ambiguity compels acts of attention and thus resists reduction.

The Autobiography of Miss Jane Pittman is Gaines's fullest expression of the folk experience; in the novel that follows, *In My Father's House* (1979), he in some ways starts over again. He returns to the primal conflict of father and son, in which the son is alienated and rootless while the father is imprisoned by convention. The difference is that it is now the father who must journey to self-knowledge.

In this new story, resistance itself has become the convention. Philip Martin, the central character, has gained reputation and respect among both blacks and whites as a civil rights leader. His problem is that protest has become so routine that the black middle class has become cynical about its effectiveness and the more radical elements question the participation of whites. Martin, who established himself a decade earlier, cannot adapt his techniques to the changing circumstances. He still has the power, through his white associates, to compel action but not belief or enthusiasm. He is a man comfortable in the present but about to be bypassed by history.

He is forced out of this present by the interjection of a force that is simultaneously past and future. Robert X, an illegitimate son unknown to his present world, suddenly appears. He seems very much a burned-out case:

> He was too thin, too hungry-looking. She didn't like the little twisted knots of hair on his face that passed for a beard. He looked sick. His jaws were too sunken-in for someone his age. His deep-set bloodshot eyes wandered too much. He could have just been released from the state pen. He definitely looked like somebody who had been shut in. They probably had let him go because they figured they had punished him enough already and knew he would die soon.[16]

This ghost seems less interested in claiming his heritage than in haunting the father he holds responsible for his condition. The prison of Robert's life has been his resentment of Martin for abandoning his mother and himself. He has made this psychological jail a physical one by spending his time in a tiny room in his mother's house.

Robert serves primarily as a function of Martin's character. He is that absent part against which Martin has shaped his present self. But bringing the two sides together does not make possible a unitary self. Instead, it multiplies the difficulties, for the past is imprisoning rather than liberating. Martin instinctively accepts and becomes obsessed with this son, but he also tries to maintain his position in the present, represented by another son figure, Jonathan, the assistant minister. While Robert wants to destroy him by forcing him into the past, Jonathan seeks to supplant him by pushing the movement into the future.

Unable to sustain this tension, Martin ultimately chooses Robert and in the process compromises the movement. Ironically, both sons win: Martin begins a journey into the past and is replaced as leader by Jonathan. But choosing the past does not free him; the chains of middle-class respectabili-

95

ty are replaced by chains of guilt. Martin feels compelled to go back to uncover the truth of the past and in effect undo what he has done.

The quest begins with a conversation between Martin and Robert. After the son accuses the father of unmanning him by abandoning the mother, Martin tries to explain himself:

> I couldn't bit more leave that room, that woman I didn't care nothing in the world for, than I can right now carry this car here on my back. I was paralyzed. Paralyzed. Yes, I had a mouth, but I didn't have a voice. I had legs, but I couldn't move. I had arms, but I couldn't lift them up to you. It took a man to do these things, and I wasn't a man. I was just some other brutish animal who could cheat, steal, rob, kill—but not stand. Not be responsible. Not protect you or your mother. They had branded that in us from the time of slavery. That's what kept me on that bed. Not 'cause I didn't want to get up. I wanted to get up more than anything in the world. But I had to break the rules, rules we had lived by for so long, and I wasn't strong enough to break them then. (*In My Father's House,* 102)

He explains later that he gained his manhood by praying and by devoting himself to breaking the rules in the name of a higher law. But the triumvirate of masculine identity—fatherhood, God, law—is exactly what Robert has suffered for and now rejects.

The suffering and negation exceed Martin's comprehension, and he must have comprehension if he is to maintain his sense of himself. His desperate need for positive identity drives him to another abandonment—of the movement and the family of his present life. His former paralysis becomes obsessive motion, and the racist rules are replaced by the equally coercive conventions of a modern mind that insists that reality have an orderly and rational structure.

Given the new system of rules at work, Martin cannot find understanding in the rural folk community. He first journeys there, but he cannot articulate to his nanane or the others the nature of his problem. In fact, his reputation as a modern leader blocks access to the past. The only thing he can get from them is guidance into the urban community. In a symbolically appropriate night trip to Baton Rouge, he searches for the friend of his youth, Chippo Simon.

Along the way, he meets several people. One is another son figure who feels the same alienation as Robert, but who has converted his frustration

into suicidal revolutionary action. Despite Martin's appeals for the reconciliation of fathers and sons, Billy knows that connections are no longer
possible. Each son—Billy, Robert, Jonathan—rejects the father and thus
the past; in this apparently necessary process, they lose any hope for a
meaningful direction of the future.

On the way to Chippo's, Martin meets in a brief period fathers, sons,
mothers, and lovers. Each is an opportunity to examine from a different
perspective the lost connection between generations. Each one serves to
reaffirm the quester's view that the division creates a desperate circumstance. Each conversation makes it more urgent for Martin to learn the
truth of his son and thereby save them both.

In Chippo, Martin discovers his alter ego. A man of wild ways and habits
of dissipation, he is all that the minister would have become if he had not
found God and political action. Chippo has become a legendary figure, an
urban "bad nigger." Thus, in one sense, when Chippo reveals information
about Johanna, Robert, and the other children, it is Martin revealing the
past to himself. But the folk side is not immediately liberating; Martin
wants to return to Robert in order to correct his mistake of the past. He
assumes that history is an account book and that he can cancel out the
suffering by placing in it Robert's true name, Etienne. Unlike Chippo, who
knows, as do all of Gaines's folk characters, that time is organic and unrepeatable, Martin believes it is a mechanism that can be tinkered with and
modified to cancel his guilt.

To reinforce Chippo's point, Martin's wife Alma brings the information
that Robert-Etienne has committed suicide. Left without the opportunity to
tinker, Martin falls into self-destructive despair. He wants to give up his
present life for the wanton one of the past; immediately he wants to drink
and copulate himself into oblivion. But Chippo, whose life he would be
imitating, will not permit such behavior. Instead, he implies, Martin must
accept all of his history, both the past and the present, and himself in that
history, as a man who must live with his guilt, his suffering, and his joy. His
identity is not fixed as either the failed father of the plantation or the successful leader of the city; it is a process that contains both of those as well as
whatever he makes himself in the future. Having been deprived of the
ahistorical structure of his political life and of the equally life-denying self-
destruction when that life crumbled, Martin is left in a confused state: "I'm

97

lost, Alma. I'm lost" (*In My Father's House,* 214). No longer residing in the house of any system—racial, religious, or parental—he must construct a shelter closer to the reality of his experience.

In *A Gathering of Old Men* (1983), Gaines returns to the territory and narrative techniques of his earlier works. He tells the story of a group of old black men who, though denied dignity all their lives, have a final opportunity to assert their manhood. The chance comes when a Cajun field boss, Beau Boutan, is killed in front of the shack of Mathu, the only man in the community to have consistently stood up to both the Cajuns and the whites. As soon as word spreads of Boutan's death, the black men begin arriving on the scene, each carrying a recently fired shotgun that could have been the murder weapon. Much of the novel is devoted to the "confessions" of these men, each of whom tells the sheriff why he had sufficient motive for the crime. These voices, plus a few others, are, as in "Just like a Tree," the bearers of the narrative. In effect, Gaines again creates a communal history of black life in rural Louisiana.

That history is violent, oppressive, and dehumanizing. The story told by Uncle Billy, the oldest of the men, is typical:

> "What they did my boy," the old man said, staring blankly at Mapes, his head bobbing again. His swollen bottom lip trembled nervously. "The way they beat him. They beat him till they beat him crazy, and we had to send him to Jackson. He don't even know me and his mama no more. We take him candy, we take him cake, he eat it like a hog eating corn. Don't offer none to them other crazy people. Don't offer none to nobody—me, his mama, or them other crazy people. Just put his head in the cake and eat it like a hog eating corn."[17]

Though the beating that caused this behavior occurred years earlier, the pain clearly remains just as acute as when the violence took place. A perpetual present has been created, because the anguish is lived with daily. Billy does not simply relive that original violence; he lives the history generated out of that act. In this sense, the assault continues every moment of his life. Mapes, the sheriff, fails to understand this:

> "When did all this happen, Uncle Billy?"
> "Years back, when he come home from that war."
> "What war?"
> "That war with Hitler and them Japs."

"You've been holding a grudge against Fix [Boutan's father] all that time, Uncle Billy?"

"I don't hold no grudge. My Bible tells me not to hold no grudge."

(*Gathering*, 80)

Grudge implies a desire for revenge for some original violation. But each trip to Jackson is another act of violence, another assault on the humanity of Billy and his wife. To kill Beau Boutan is not to seek revenge on his father for the treatment of Billy's son; it is to exact justice for continuing criminal behavior. Killing Beau does not balance the books, according to some talionic code; such a principle would implicitly suggest that Billy's suffering could be canceled. The murder neutralizes nothing; it is simply a refusal to allow the crimes of the racists to be erased. Each story told by the old men serves a similar purpose: to expose the marks that have been made on them throughout their lives and to attempt, for the only time in their lives, to get recognition of their own definitions of reality. The "ink" for their self-marking is the blood of Beau Boutan; the script written by each is, like Uncle Billy's, the story of his own bleeding.

One aspect of this bleeding is the lack of manhood each of them has felt throughout his life. Though they have been repeatedly assaulted, physically and mentally, they have been incapable of resistance to such treatment. In some instances their ineffectiveness has sexual connotations; "Rooster" tells about his fears: "Used to call me Little Red Rooster all the time. People even said him [Mathu] and Beulah had fooled around some behind my back. I never asked him, I never asked her—I was too scared" (*Gathering*, 181). But the more important self-incrimination is their passivity in the face of cruelty and violence; they have been unable and, perhaps, unwilling to do anything to save their wives, children, and brothers: "And what did I do about them killing my boy like that? What could a poor old nigger do but go up to the white folks and fall down on his knees? But, no, no pity coming there. Some went so far to say my boy shoulda been glad he died in the 'lectric chair 'stead at the end of a rope. They said at least he was treated like a white man. And it was best we just forget all about it and him" (*Gathering*, 102).

As in Gaines's earlier works, folk memory has a paradoxical effect: it keeps alive the sense of injustice and suffering, but, precisely for that reason, it makes resistance to these things more difficult. Though aware of the

99

probable futility of action, these men cannot free themselves of guilt over their inaction. The killing of Boutan becomes an opportunity to purge that guilt by claiming responsibility for an action that they had all committed in their minds many times. Even if they did not actually do it, they had the motive and desire to do so, and thus their claims are psychologically true even if not factual. The confessions are ritual forms by which they assert their manhood. Ironically, they are able to do this because they have little of their lives left; as old men, they see this as a final grand gesture. If they have failed to live as men, at least they can die as such.

It is important in this context to know that they expect to die. Part of the folk knowledge is that Fix Boutan always responds violently to assertive behavior by blacks; the killing of his son should bring about something approaching a race riot. But at this point Gaines introduces, as he frequently does, the complex relationship of cyclical folk history to linear history. The blacks are denied their apocalyptic moment, not because of cowardice on either side, but because of the very amelioration of racial conditions that they have always hoped for. The sheriff is the first to recognize what has happened:

> "Because, you see, me, you, and all the rest of them were thinking about Fix thirty years ago. Thirty years ago Fix woulda been here, woulda hanged Mathu on the nearest tree, and all the rest of you brave people woulda been still hiding under the bed. But something happened the last ten, fifteen years. Salt and Pepper got together. Now, it's nobody's fault but yours," Mapes said, looking round at all of us. "Nobody's fault but yours. Y'all did it. Y'all wasn't satisfied Salt played at LSU on one side of town, and Pepper played for Southern on the other side of town—no, y'all wanted them to play together. Y'all prayed and prayed and prayed for them to play together. Well, they did—and that's what happened. Salt went back and talked to his daddy. Gil—that white boy who stopped by here—that's Salt. Y'all know him, you seen him on television enough. Went back and told his daddy he needed Pepper and Pepper needed him. Told his daddy he wouldn't go along with his daddy to lynch Mathu. Told his daddy, even, if the name Boutan got in the papers, he would never be All-American. But y'all the ones did it," Mapes said. He was moving around the yard. He was looking us all in the face. Stop a second and look at one, then move, and stop and look at another one awhile. "Y'all the one—you cut your own throats. You told God you wanted Salt and Pepper to get together, and God did it for you. At the same time, you wanted God to keep Fix the way Fix was thirty years ago so

100

one day you would get a chance to shoot him. Well, God couldn't do both. (*Gathering*, 170–71)

The interdependence of the folk and racist worldviews is clearly stated here. The folk need the evil of the oppressor in order to define themselves and to validate their own goodness. They create their lives and culture within these parameters. The boundaries become justifications for their flaws and limitations. But this dialectical situation is inherently dynamic; the folk, despite their fatalism, do have an impact on that history they often believe themselves to be only victims of. They hope and dream, in order to continue, but if the hopes and dreams are realized, even partially, then the terms by which they have been defined and have defined themselves change, bringing about uncertainty and instability. These people have grown old desiring equality and hating Fix; when something like equality occurs, Fix ceases to be a satanic figure and becomes instead simply another old man living in a world he too does not understand.

In terms of the novel, this means that apocalypse becomes farce. The old men get their fight, but it is with a group of drunken Cajuns that Fix has dissociated himself from. On both sides everyone is frightened and militarily incompetent. The only exceptions are Charlie and Luke Will. The latter is the Cajun leader, who refuses to believe that the world has changed. Charlie is the weakest of the old black men, one who has for fifty years absorbed the humiliation and abuse heaped on him by the Boutans and others. Finally, when he can absorb no more, he kills Beau but, in his usual manner, runs away after begging Mathu to take the blame. However, his refusal to be beaten both expresses and generates his latent manhood, and he returns late in the story to add his own true narrative to the fictions told about the killing. Appropriately, Luke Will and Charlie are the only ones killed at the end, and, again appropriately, they die because they are not willing to hide:

> I heard Lou hollering to him to stay down, but Charlie wasn't listening to anybody. He was headed straight toward that tractor. And he hadn't made more than two, three, maybe four steps when I heard the first shot. I saw him staggering but he didn't go down; I saw him shooting but not sighting. I saw Lou out there waving his hands, telling everybody to stop, stop, stop. He was running all over the place, saying stop, stop, stop. I saw Charlie still going toward that tractor, but he wasn't shooting now, just falling, slowly, slowly, slowly till he had hit the ground. (*Gathering*, 209)

101

The scene is reminiscent of the assassination of Ned Douglass in *The Auto-biography of Miss Jane Pittman*, with the important difference that Charlie is willing to kill as well as die. Each is a strong, heroic figure rebelling against an oppressive system. Ned fights with principles because to do otherwise is suicide; Charlie fights with guns precisely because Ned's principles have triumphed: Luke Will is the final convulsion of an old order now dead. Charlie, because he has achieved manhood through violence, must also die as a part of that order. Nonetheless, his manhood is authentic and desired by the others:

> He kept on looking at us, but after a while you could tell he wasn't seeing us no more. I leaned over and touched him, hoping that some of that stuff he had found back there in the swamps might rub off on me. After I touched him, the rest of the men did the same. Then the women, even Candy. Then Glo told her grandchildren they must touch him, too. (*Gathering*, 209–10)

This ritual embodies the African belief in the ongoing presence of the dead and the hope that such presence can aid the living. But it also signifies an appropriation of Charlie into the community as one whose manhood has been achieved; because he, the weakest of them, became strong, so they all can be strong. They will need such strength in the new world Mapes described. The old world, symbolized by Charlie's courageous and violent death, is passed. The community itself becomes the figure in the middle; it comprises old people who must begin a new life without the conventional wisdom of the past, and children, who must have some knowledge of the past in order to make sense of the future. The community, like Jane Pittman and others, has discovered the possibility of self-definition. Like these others, it must apply its experience in order to improvise the future.

Such a conclusion suggests a more profoundly organic sensibility than that of McPherson, who seems more willing to leave his characters in a state of despair or guilt. Gaines ends with renewal, though not necessarily with any sense that the future will be easier. In both cases, some folk experience leads to some insight, either for the character or for the reader's apprehension of the character. Such insight makes possible an awareness of the need to oppose some systematic restriction on life and individuality and expression; whether this awareness leads to action is often beside the point. Frequently, the telling of the experience is the only end. The telling serves to preserve the fictional history, to order it in a nonoppressive manner, and to give a voice to a speaker whose experience has itself often been the suppression of voice. Gaines and McPherson concentrate on the emergence of a black male identity that has sufficient flexibility to survive and prosper in a world seemingly bent on destroying it.

Three

Women's Blues: The Fiction of Toni Cade Bambara and Alice Walker

As WRITERS, Toni Cade Bambara and Alice Walker focus on the female side of the issues raised by McPherson and Gaines. They tell stories of the initiations of black girls into womanhood, defining in the process the complex meaning of being black and female in a culture that has denigrated both qualities. As in the case of the male authors, they differ from each other, Bambara being primarily a short-story writer concentrating on the northern urban experience while Walker, best known for her novels, emphasizes the rural and southern aspects of black life. Also like Gaines and McPherson, they are essentially traditional in their use of fictional forms, choosing as they do to represent the world in realistic terms. Those terms are frequently harsh and unconventional, but they remain within mimetic boundaries. Through such realism they present the experiences of black women, who are shown to suffer in the world but who also discover ways to endure and prosper, the latter usually in spiritual or psychological rather than material ways. The principal source of strength is the knowledge, gained through folk wisdom, that suffering seems the destiny of women and that survival is a valid revenge for the pain. Moreover, "living to tell about it" becomes a means of control, since the remembering refutes any claim that suffering and exploitation can be justified. The realistic structures of their fiction lend verisimilitude to the tales of racial and sexual oppression and triumph.

The thematic emphasis here is intentional; both writers tend toward

104

feminist ideology, either in depicting the mistreatment of women or in asserting a superior female sensibility, gained largely through painful experience. Frequently, Walker and Bambara integrate this ideological position with folk values so that each enhances the other. Political concepts give direction and force to an often fatalistic folk wisdom; the realities of the folk link ideology to a concrete history. But this conjunction does not always work, since the folk worldview implicitly assumes that endurance rather than political power is its objective. It insists not on overcoming the enemy so much as outwitting and outliving him. These authors, in their more polemical moments, seek the means of supplanting the oppressor. The very language and structure of their folk sources, however, render their work more ambiguous than they seem to intend. Their occasionally ahistorical politics come into dialectical conflict with their historically conditioned cultural materials. Such a conflict makes for uneasy fictional structures where apparent resolution hides the absence of the very thing claimed. Despite themselves then, these fictions remain open rather than closed.

Toni Cade Bambara's stories focus on the ways gender roles, ideology, family, and community condition the experiences of black women. She portrays initiation as a painful but frequently rewarding ritual. Like McPherson, she seeks to take her characters from a state of certainty to a state of doubt, but unlike him, she does not so clearly define the conventions of that certainty. She implies that the realm of woman is more organic and less overtly confrontational than that of man. Nonetheless, a dialectic is clearly at work, one that is in some ways more complex since it adds to generational, racial, and cultural oppositions the polarity of male-female. While Bambara says that she is "much more concerned with the caring that lies beneath the antagonisms between black men and black women,"[1] she does repeatedly examine the nature of those antagonisms. Moreover, like Gaines and McPherson, she finds in folk material the means for her characters to resist fixed, dehumanizing identities, whether sexual, racial, or cultural. And also like these male writers, she tends to leave her characters at the edge of some new experience rather than with a sense of the completion of action and thus the resolution of oppositions.

"My Man Bovanne," the initial story in *Gorilla, My Love* (1972), links sexual and ideological conflicts. It tells the story of Hazel, a middle-aged black woman whose behavior scandalizes her ideologically correct children:

> "And you going to be standing there with your boobs out and that wig on your head and that hem up to your ass. And people'll say, 'Ain't that the horny bitch that was grindin with the blind dude?'
>
> "And then there's the drinkin. Mama, you know you can't drink cause next thing you know you be laughin loud and carryin on," and he grab another finger for the loudness. "And then there's the dancin. You been tattooed on the man for four records straight and slow draggin even on the fast numbers. How you think that look for a woman your age?"[2]

The children, in their ideological purity, seek to eliminate the individuality and freedom of the mother. They implicitly fix the definitions of *mother* and *black* so as to satisfy the necessities of their political efforts. They justify those efforts in the name of "the people," and thus public recognition of the "grass roots," as Hazel calls herself, is mandatory. But the reality of those grass roots must be suppressed if the ideological system is to function efficiently. They rationalize such suppression as necessary to the struggle against the oppressor, the white social structure. Paradoxically, the children must control the mother because they see her as fitting the white society's stereotype of the licentious, irresponsible black woman. In the place of that image they would impose the image of the serious, puritanical mother. As Hazel understands, either imposition is a form of repression: "Felt just like the police got hold to me" (*Gorilla, My Love,* 6).

This repression extends to efforts at masking, both literally and verbally. The very concept of grass roots is falsified: "Me and Sister Taylor and the woman who does heads at Mamies and the man from the barber shop, we all there on account of we grass roots. And I ain't never been souther than Brooklyn Battery and no more country than the window box on my fire escape. And just yesterday my kids tellin me to take them countrified rags off my head and be cool. And now can't get Black enough to suit them" (*Gorilla, My Love,* 4).

The ideology requires a denial of black history in the name of Black History. Cultural unity requires all blacks to be southern and African and thus simplistically connected to a heritage of oppression and violence. But Hazel's insistence in her narrative on concrete history refutes such a reductive view.

106

Similarly, her inappropriate behavior is part of a larger pattern. Elo, the daughter, finds blind Bovanne repulsive: " 'Dancin with that tom,' say Elo to Joe Lee, who leanin on the folks' freezer. 'His feet can smell a cracker a mile away and go into their shuffle number post haste. And them eyes. He could be a little considerate and put on some shades. Who wants to look into them blown-out fuses that—' " (*Gorilla, My Love,* 6).

By refusing to hide his flaws, his imperfect humanity, Bovanne, like Hazel, makes the ideologues uncomfortable. Unmasked reality too clearly reminds them of the concrete experiences of human suffering that cannot be masked and thus not neatly absorbed into the more abstract Black Suffering that is part of their system. The eyes of Bovanne are a concrete particular that cannot be reified and manipulated for political purposes.

The crucial question, which Hazel evades in her narrative, is the origin of this conflict of generations. She has brought up these children, it may be answered, in the folk wisdom of her own experience. Their rejection and repression of that wisdom implies a desire for a positive identity and presence not possible in that experience. Hazel herself, with wig and short dress, wears a complex of disguises that hides some reality and signifies a created role difficult to distinguish from the white stereotype. This suggests that she is caught up in and conditioned by the history her children want to transcend. They prefer a less ambiguous status for themselves.

But transcendence is not possible. As has been pointed out, the ideology is itself a form of posturing; as such it reflects a fear that whites may be right about blacks, that the race may well be nothing more than toms and goodtime women.

These two forms of masking differ in that Hazel accepts rather than denies history. Hers is necessary for the more important activities of life. It makes possible the enacting rather than the mere proclamation of black pride:

> Bein cute, but you got to let men play out they little show, blind or not. So he chat on bout how tired he is and how he appreciates me takin him in hand this way. And I'm thinkin I'll have him change the lock on my door first thing. Then I'll give the man a nice warm bath with jasmine leaves in the water and a little Epsom salt on the sponge to do his back. And then a good rubdown with rose water and olive oil. Then a cup of lemon tea with a taste in it. And a little talcum, some of that fancy stuff Nisi mother sent over

last Christmas. And then a massage, a good face massage round the forehead which is the worryin part. Cause you gots to take care of the older folks. And let them know they still needed to run the mimeo machine and keep the spark plugs clean and fix the mailboxes for folks who might help us get the breakfast program goin, and the school for the little kids and the campaign and all. Cause old folks is the nation. That what Nisi was saying and I mean to do my part. (*Gorilla, My Love*, 9–10)

The possibility of change must be found within the historically determined community; it cannot be imposed from outside. The struggle for a better life is inextricably interwoven with the concrete, sensuous joy of lived experience. Each makes the other possible. This forms the dialectic which the children evade and which Hazel both sees and lives.

"Mississippi Ham Rider" develops a variation on this theme. In this version the narrator, an outsider, confronts folk experience. Employed by a white-owned record company to locate and sign blues performers, she has the same tendency as Hazel's children to see the folks as oddities. And again, the folk figure adopts masks to fit the desired image. But neither this evasion nor the masking can ultimately hide the deeply disturbing reality revealed to the narrator.

The first intimation of a threatening experience comes not from Ham himself, who is initially dismissed as "a salty stud," but from those who form part of his community:

The waitress had wiped the counter menacingly and was leaning up against the pie display with her hands on her hips. I was trying to figure out whether I should follow Rider, put Neil on his trail, or try to scrounge up a story from the townsfolk. The waitress was tapping her foot. And the cook, a surly-looking bastard in white cap, was peeping over the edge of the kitchen counter, his head kind of cocked to the side so that the sweat beaded around his nostril. I was trying to get myself together, untangle my legs from the stool and get out of there. It was obvious that these particular sinister folks were not going to fill my dossier with anything printable. But before I even reached the door I was in the third person absentular. "So what's this high-yaller Northern bitch doin' hittin' on evil ole Ham?" (*Gorilla, My Love*, 47–48)

On the one hand, the tone of the passage suggests the conventional city slicker's superior attitude toward country bumpkins. The narrator finds herself in an uncomfortable situation, and she blames the narrowmindedness of the others for that. On the other hand, the question asked is exactly the one that must be addressed.

We learn from the narrator's conversations with Neil, the white song collector, that the exploitation of black musicians has a long history and, further, that their own activities are simply another stage of that misuse: "But old man Lyons, dearheart, wants him in the flesh to allow the poor folkway-starved sophisticates to, through a outrageous process of osmosis, which in no way should suggest miscegenation, to absorb their native—" (*Gorilla, My Love,* 50).

The narrator clearly shares this cynical attitude about the meaning of their work. The whites are fools who are looking for nothing more than an updated minstrel show, but, as Neil recounts his attempts to recruit the musicians, it becomes apparent that he considers blacks uncivilizable aborigines: "Along with the numerous tapes of chats and songfests, Neil had collected from the Delta and the Carolines a volume of tales that didn't go into the album catalogues, things he was saving for some sensational book he'd never write. The payoffs, bribes, bargains and deals, interviews in jail cells, drug wards, wino bins. Things apart from the usual folksy atrocity story" (*Gorilla, My Love,* 53). With her flippant, dismissive tone, the narrator aligns herself with the exploiters, with the added fillip that she approves of the blues artists making as much as they can on the deal: "One good exploitative act deserved another" (*Gorilla, My Love,* 54). She accepts the bourgeois view that greed motivates human behavior; she prefers to take an observer's stance and merely watch the exploitations play themselves out: "It was grotesque no matter how you cut it. I wished I was in films instead. Ole Ham Rider beseiged by well-dressed coffee drinkers wanting his opinion on Miles Davis and Malcolm X was worth a few feet of film. And the quaint introduction some bearded fool in tight-across-the-groin pants would give would justify more footage" (*Gorilla, My Love,* 54).

But as was the case with McPherson's middle-class characters, this role as disinterested outsider cannot be sustained. In the final scene, a series of dislocations of the narrator occurs. She cannot find a comfortable sitting position, and when the food is served, she cannot identify some of the dishes, even though they are associated with what she knows at home. Moreover, Ham's sense of humor seems lost on her, just as it does on Neil. But understanding begins to be important to her. She opens to the possibility that there are levels of experience that her superficial perspective cannot accommodate. Ham refuses, for example, to do the expected songs: " 'I don't sing no cotton songs, sister,' he said, picking up a knife. 'And I ain't never worked in the fields or shucked corn. And I don't sing no nappy-head church songs neither. And no sad numbers about losing my woman and losing my mind. I ain't never lost no woman and that's the truth" (*Gorilla, My Love*, 55–56). To Neil's question about what kind of songs he does sing, Ham replies, "My kind."

The narrator unexpectedly faces an intelligent, self-conscious individuality. Ham Rider knows what whites expect of him, but he will only deal in the truth of his own experience as a performer. But even this she tries to homogenize with her cultural biases: "He was impressive, the way a good demolition site can be, the way horror movies from the thirties are now. I was tempted to ask him how many people he had killed in his lifetime, thinking I had at last gotten hold of his vein of humor. But I sat and waited for him to sing. I was sure that on the first job he'd turn the place out and maybe do somebody in, just for the fun that was in it" (*Gorilla, My Love*, 56). Ham has been comfortably labelled a throwback, a creature of a different time and place magically brought to life for her enjoyment.

But this attitude does not hold: "And then a really weird thing came over me. I wanted to ask him a lot of dumb things about the South, about what he thought of the sit-ins and all" (*Gorilla, My Love*, 56). In this moment, the narrator understands that the man sitting before her is not an object out of time, but a man very much within human history. She sees him suddenly as someone who can teach her something important about herself and her heritage. To gain this knowledge she is willing to drop her own posturing, to risk asking "dumb things" in order to gain valuable answers.

But this opportunity passes, not by her choice but because of that very history she needs explained: "But he had already taken on a legendary air and was simply not of these times. I cursed Mr. Lyons' fairy-tale mentality and quietly indulged in fabricating figures from whole cloth" (*Gorilla, My Love*, 56). Ham dons the mask that he must always wear to protect his truest self from the whites who, as always, use him for their own purpose. What disturbs the narrator is that she is considered part of that outside world, one who cannot be trusted with the folk secrets.

110

"He looked up at Neil and then he did smile. I wouldn't ever want him to smile at me" (*Gorilla, My Love,* 57). That smile is filled with irony. It presents the face of blacks who have had to accommodate themselves to the expectations of the white world if they were to obtain what that world offered. But it also contains the knowledge, distrust, and hatred that accompany being forced into such a performance. It is the trickster's strategic grin joined to the badman's reckless leer; but both are given shape by the bittersweet experience of the human being behind the mask. For the narrator, this is the true terror of that smile.

"The Johnson Girls" shifts the focus from two generations to one, but it still is concerned with creating a community through folk materials. The narrator learns the value of shared experiences of love and suffering and, in the process, moves from a state of certainty about herself and her world to a state of openness to new and perhaps more painful realities. This initiation, which is emotional rather than intellectual, makes it possible for her to be integrated into the community of black women. In the beginning of the story, she, like other young adults in *Gorilla, My Love,* disdains the lore and wisdom of older members of the community. She dismisses the teachings of Great Ma Drew, a conjure woman: " 'See now, when I was comin up,' she say, bammin the cards down, 'the older women would gather together to train you young girls in the ways of menfolks.' I yawn cause I'm sick of this speech and in a hurry to get back upstairs with Sugar and them, cause it's right bout this time they'll be ordering pizza or something to tide them over till Great Ma Drew can get the supper together" (*Gorilla, My Love,* 165).

The story develops by showing the narrator gaining not a respect for Ma Drew, but a sense of the intrinsic folk community of her own group. The message seems to be that because the problems, needs, and possibilities of black women remain the same, each generation will naturally move toward the traditional forms of expression. The forms most prevalent here are the folktale, black music, and the sermon with its call-and-response structure. The ritual quality of these forms is appropriate to the initiation of the narrator into the community of black women.

Nonetheless, the story focuses not on the narrator but on Inez, the narrator's older cousin, who has been deserted by her lover. Inez is simply a more mature version of her younger relative; they both prefer maintaining as much control as possible over their own lives to taking the advice of

111

others. What this identification means is that the narrator, seeing what happens to Inez, in effect watches and learns about herself. Given his stubborn individuality, this is the only way the initiation can occur.

The loss of Roy occasions a community ritual:

> And it always winds up to a moment like this when there's some big thing in Inez's life and all her friends gather, mostly the in-group. And everybody lays out their program, most times movin on incomplete information cause Inez don't give up much, so they make up whatever's missing and then exchange advice and yell at each other's stupidities and trade stories and finally lay the consensus thing to be done on Inez. Who turns right around and does exactly what she's going to do in the first damn place, cause that too is her way. (*Gorilla, My Love,* 170)

As Victor Turner has suggested in *The Ritual Process,* ritual functions to bring the person from one fixed state through a liminal process to a reintegration into the community.[3] In this case both Inez and the narrator must be moved away from a narrow self-reliance into a recognition of the value of shared experience. The communal, as opposed to individualist, perspective redefines identity and opens up possibilities for a richer, more complex sense of self. For the narrator and Inez, the black folk forms used in the ritual mean that the new self will be one that is integrated into the black community.

Sugar's secular sermon is the primary example of group sensibility:

> "I am in the prime of my life and I am ready to cop. And I mean to cop. And I want it all and all on one damn plate. Am I coming through?"
> "Loud and clear, Sugar," say Gail.
> "And if I can't have the blue-plate special I have been readying up for these thirty-some odd years, then I'll settle for the half loaf Nez say Roy is. Any day. Any time of any day at all. Big black dude with fat thighs pushing through his slacks. Deep brown voice sayin righteous reasonable lovin things. Beautiful hands and teeth. And when he moves and them corduroys go swish swish I just holler do it do it. Do you understand?"
> "You smokin," say Gail. (*Gorilla, My Love,* 172–73)

The questions and responses are as crucial to the performance as the statements themselves, for Sugar is not attempting to express a private, individual concern, but rather to articulate the values of the group. In the call-and-response tradition of the spirituals and the black sermon, validation comes in the form of the group's active participation in her performance.

Gail contributes another element to the ceremony in the form of a cautionary tale about the nature of men. After she tells about Rudi and the double standard that permits him to mistreat his wife, Inez demands to know the meaning: "Parables usually have a lesson" (*Gorilla, My Love,* 175). Her insistence on a fixed meaning suggests her position outside the community, since the black folktale, unlike the parables of other cultures, speaks indirectly within the experience rather than abstracting from it. The story, in other words, has no independent existence; it "means" within the context of the values of the group.

The larger narrative itself follows folk forms by being constituted of all the voices. In effect, it is a secularized version of a religious service, with the improvisational qualities of jazz. Each solo voice develops variations of the basic themes of the nature of men and the needs of women within the framework established by the group. The climax of the narrative comes when both the narrator and Inez add their voices to the emerging song. First, the narrator feels that she needs to hear what the others have to say: "And I'm waitin on Gail to speak. Not so much for Inez, cause Inez just don't care what's goin on in other people's heads, her program's internal. But speak for me, cause I'm keepin a notebook on all this, so I won't have all this torture and crap to go through when I jump into my woman stride and stalk out on the world" (*Gorilla, My Love,* 173–74). The very desire to learn reflects both the narrator's eagerness and her innocence. Her reference to keeping a notebook suggests her commitment to a written, Eurocentric culture rather than a black folk culture. Moreover, what she fails to grasp at this point is that the group wisdom and the forms that structure it point to the inescapability of "all this torture and crap." She would have the happiness without the suffering; to be truly initiated, she must understand the dialectical relationship of the two.

That knowledge comes in the conjunction of two incidents at the end of her narrative. First, she has an insight into the power of her own womanhood:

> "I'll send Thumb for cigarettes," I said, certain in a sudden way that I could send Thumb for anything anywhere at any time and to Turkey for smokes if necessary. And just like some telepathic happenin, here come Thumb taking six steps at a time and smilin his smile and his eyebrows up as if to say, Can I do somethin for you, baby. So I mime a puff and he split

through the door and I'm kinda diggin him as I turn back into the room.
(*Gorilla, My Love,* 177)

The discovery of her sexual power leads her not into narcissism but rather into an openness to and appreciation of another.

And this very fact creates in her the vulnerability that Sugar, Gail, and Marcy have been describing and that Inez is experiencing. "Digging" Thumb makes it possible for him to cause pain as well as happiness. The centrality to black womanhood of this double-edged situation is epito-mized by Inez's agreeing to share her experience with the group. Her rela-tionship with Roy supersedes her individualism. She sacrifices some of her identity and control to find comfort in the community of women. To the narrator, this sacrifice measures the depth of love and pain. "I look at Inez and she's sittin so forward I see the tremor caterpillar up her back. And I can't breathe. Somebody has opened a wet umbrella in my chest." And she also sees the implications for herself: "I shudder for me at the preview of things to come" (*Gorilla, My Love,* 177). She is blessedly condemned to the human condition: to love and suffer.

Significantly in terms of this realization, her narrative, told in the past tense, is spoken in the dialect of black urban speech. It is, as is Hazel's in "My Man Bovanne," a repudiation of the language of the dominant culture; the language in this sense is a metaphor of the knowledge arrived at through the folk ritual.

The stories of *Gorilla, My Love* are largely devoted to the lessons offered girls and young women within their local community or through represen-tatives of the larger black folk community. Whether the lessons are learned or not, the tendency is to assume that the older members of the group have insights to pass along. Even in "The Johnson Girls," where the women are all young, the forms they use to share their experiences are the traditional forms of black expression. What happens in *The Sea Birds Are Still Alive* (1977), a second collection of stories, is that Bambara expresses some doubt about the validity of folk experience in the process of trying to link folk wisdom to feminist, and to some degree nationalist, ideology. This doubt grows out of a more overt ideological perspective in these stories. The central, often narrating characters are pitted on the one side against very hopeful political activists and on the other against the harsh condi-

114

tions of the black community. Bambara moves the central figures from their doubt toward an acceptance of revolutionary action. But in the process her characters must raise important questions about ideology that cannot be easily answered. Ultimately, and despite the apparent intentions of the author, the acceptance of ambiguity, which is the condition of folk reality, seems a more powerful narrative force than the positive identity of ideological imposition. The results are uneasy narratives that sometimes must strain to make their points. In three stories from the collection that roughly parallel the three discussed above, both the changes in surface narrative and continuity of deep structure can be revealed.

"A Girl's Story," as is evident from its title, reverses the perspective of "My Man Bovanne." Its point of view is that of a girl entering womanhood and at odds with the older members of her family. Ideology is represented by Dada Bibi, who has set up a center where children acquire a knowledge of black history and a sense of black pride. Here, as in all the stories of *Sea Birds*, the activist is shown to be tolerant of those who disagree with her and understanding of the community's occasional hostility.

The story focuses on Rae Ann's first menstrual period and the reactions of various characters to that initiatory event. In her total innocence, the child is terrified by the bleeding, completely unaware of its source. Her thoughts move among three things: stopping the bleeding, hiding her condition from her grandmother and brother, and getting to Dada Bibi for aid and comfort. Fear of her grandmother and desire for the outsider suggest the values the narrator has given Rae Ann. Such values are reinforced when the grandmother returns and presumes that the condition is caused by either a sexual encounter or an abortion: " 'Watcha been doin?' she hissed through clenched teeth. Rae Ann backed up as a whole bunch of questions and accusations tumbled out of the woman's mouth ramming into her. 'You been to the barbershop, haven't you? Let that filthy man go up inside you with a clothes hanger. You going to be your mama all over again. Why didn't you come to me? Who's the boy? Tell me his name quick. And you better not lie.' "[4] Unlike Hazel of "My Man Bovanne," who recalls everything about the lives of her family, this woman's ignorance almost matches that of Rae Ann herself. Her refusal or inability to communicate means that she completely misreads the significance of the blood. But she also assumes that the child has gained knowledge from some source, perhaps simply as a function of being born female. Part of her own folk wisdom is obviously that such matters do not need to be communicated because they are intrinsic to the experiences of women. As a consequence, the grandmother gives Rae Ann the items she needs, but refuses to explain their significance.

Such failure, however, does not necessarily lead to the conclusion that the more communicative Dada Bibi provides greater comfort. Despite Rae Ann's affection and the woman's awareness, help is not provided even when it is offered. The day before the story's present time, Dada Bibi had spoken to Rae Ann: " 'My sister,' she said into her ear, gently releasing her with none of the embarrassed shove her relatives seemed to always punctuate their embraces with. 'You're becoming a woman and that's no private thing. It concerns us all who love you. Let's talk sometimes?' " (*Sea Birds*, 155–56). Rae Ann refuses this opportunity "cause, she figured she might have to hear one of them one-way talks like M'Dear [the grandmother] do about not letting boys feel on your tits" (*Sea Birds*, 155). Despite the obvious differences, the girl occasionally equates the two older women.

Such an equation is made only to the extent that Dada Bibi identifies herself with the Center, which is just as one-sided in its values as the grandmother. We learn early on that Rae Ann's brother no longer is welcome: "Besides, he didn't go round the Center anymore since they jumped on his case so bad about joining the Army. He didn't want to hear no more shit about the Vietnamese were his brothers and sisters, were fighting the same enemy as Black folks and was he crazy, stupid or what" (*Sea Birds*, 153). Moreover, Rae Ann has come to expect the Center to engage in intimidation: "Yesterday Dada Bibi had hugged her hello and didn't even fuss where you been little sister and why ain't you been coming round, don't you want to know about your heritage, ain't you got no pride?" (*Sea Birds*, 153–54).

In fact, Dada Bibi attracts Rae Ann to the extent that she slights ideology in favor of folk practices. She tells traditional African stories and contains call-and-response within the form, even when the responses run counter to the moral of the story: "Course Gretchen got to interrupt the story to say the sister chumping the dude, taking his money to have her some boss jewelry made and what a fool he was. But the girls tell her to hush so they can hear the rest. Dada Bibi maintaining it's important to deal with how Gretchen seeing things go down" (*Sea Birds*, 154–55). Rae Ann, who has so much difficulty communicating otherwise, "liked to retell the stories to the kids on the block. She always included Gretchen's remarks and everybody's response, since they seemed, in her mind, so much a part of the story" (*Sea Birds*, 155). She has an instinct for the liberating exercise of imagination and storytelling. Such a capacity can be used against ideology: when a speaker describes the glories of dying for the people, Rae Ann's ability to construct a mental movie of that idea leads her to contradict it.

She admires Dada Bibi to the extent that the woman passes on, not the political statements of the Center, but rather the folk wisdom that both the family and the activists seem to have lost. This position includes her own growing reputation as a "crazy" woman: "She even hugged the dirty kids from Mason Street. And drank behind them too without even rinsing the cup. Either Dada Bibi had a powerful health to combat germs, she thought, ripping open the packages, or the woman was crazy" (*Sea Birds*, 165). The "crazy" woman is the member of the community who does what every one else fears to do and manages to survive. She defies the conventional wisdom for reasons unclear to those who abide by that wisdom. Such a figure is common to the novels and stories of contemporary black women writers, but not to those of men.[5] Her role seems related to that of the bad man: she keeps alive a sense of alternatives to the existing order, while reminding the community of the danger of enacting such alternatives. For Rae Ann then, Dada Bibi is important as difference from both her family and the Center; she is the option of an imaginative, fluid identity to be pursued in the girl's emerging womanhood. It is the difficult possibility of living rather than dying for the people.

But Dada Bibi does not provide the immediate help that Rae Ann needs. At the end of the story, she knows no more about menstruation than she did at the beginning. It is in fact the grandmother who provides the materials to meet the girl's present physical necessities, but she too does not explain. Thus, while the story offers its message about self-creation through the joining of political and folk perspectives, it does not link these to the symbolism implicit in the beginning of Rae Ann's womanhood. The personal is not linked to the cultural as it was in the earlier stories.

"The Organizer's Wife," like the story of Mississippi Ham Rider, tells of a young woman brought to awareness by the folk. In this case, however, the whole community rather than an individual revives her. Virginia's initial situation is the traditional one of "troubles" for the rural southern black:

her husband is in jail, drought ruins the land, and the whites are seeking to displace the blacks for profit. Like others before her, she seeks a way to escape. The way she originally chose, marrying Graham, the man who comes to organize the blacks to fight white exploitation, only proves to be a trap when he decides to stay.

But this desire to escape, which isolates her from others, conflicts with her identification with her husband's values, insofar as she is disdainful of those who lack his courage. Her self-righteousness results from these two influences: she can afford to be haughty because she believes her residence to be only temporary, though it has lasted her entire life, and because the failure of the others is her proof to Graham that the situation is hopeless and thus that it is useless to remain.

She soon discovers the danger of language, for it ties her to the world she wants to escape. In the terms of the community she has never learned to "speak her speak," to give public expression to her sense of reality. She finds that doing so carries a price. To gain her freedom, she must get from the minister the word that he has betrayed the black community by selling out to white interests. But her own words and not his shock her:

> "Enough granite under this schoolhouse alone"—she stamped, frightening him—"to carry both the districts for years and years, if we developed it ourselves." She heard the "we ourselves" explode against her teeth and she fell back. . . . His legs buckled under and he slid down, his face frozen in disbelief. But nothing like the disbelief that swept through her the moment "we ourselves" pushed past clenched teeth and nailed her to the place, a woman unknown. (*Sea Birds,* 18)

Finding her voice situates her in history and makes clear to her the falseness of the desire to evade that history. She realizes that that evasion in fact reinforces white oppression.

But it does not guarantee an identity or make her task in life any less difficult. After considering how her confrontation with the minister would be reported in the community, she has only questions: "But would the women be able to probe and sift and explain it to her? Who could explain her to her?" (*Sea Birds,* 20). Later it becomes clear that the future does not hold any sentimental triumph of the folk; it will be a continuing struggle using the traditional combination of deception and attack: " 'Mother Lee who's secretarying for the board has held up the papers for the sale. We

118

came to tell you that.' He waited till she smiled to laugh. 'We're the delegation that's going to confront the board this evening. Us and Frankie Lee Taylor and—' " (*Sea Birds*, 19). This folk-based activism emerges from a seemingly permanent distrust of whites that shapes so much of its lore: "When we ever invited the beast to dinner he didn't come in and swipe the napkins and start taking notes on the tablecloth 'bout how to take over the whole house?" (*Sea Birds*, 22). Black history constantly negates systematic oppression, and the black voice finds its true expression not in a dominating monologue, but in a chorus of nay-saying. The young woman stays not because life necessarily will be any better but because she now understands that she is truly home.

A discordant note is struck in the language of political action. While Graham is said to be a native son of the folk community who enjoys telling the old stories, his political talk is abstract and Latinate: " 'What can defeat greed, technological superiority, and legal lawlessness,' Graham had finished up, 'is discipline, consciousness, and unity' " (*Sea Birds*, 13). Even in his stories, "the point always the same—the courage of the youth, the hope of the future" (*Sea Birds*, 5). This use of language to define reality in a one-dimensional way contrasts with the signifying and metaphoric statements, as well as the danger of "speaking her speak" that Virginia discovers. Bambara seeks to bring resolution in the story in the final sentences: "All she wished to tell him was the bail'd been paid, her strength was back, and she sure as hell was going to keep up the garden. How else to feed the people?" (*Sea Birds*, 23). The question implies a passive role for "the people"; much as whites expect blacks to accept exploitation, so the narrator assumes that the community must be taken care of rather than caring for itself. The main thrust of the story, which shows the folk taking care of themselves, is called into question by this conclusion. Bambara obviously desires to join folk wisdom and political action, but in "The Organizer's Wife" this conjunction threatens the coherence of the narrative.

"Witchbird" tells the story of another woman who seeks to escape the community (a community of women as in "The Johnson Girls") in which she finds herself. Appropriate to the collection's motif of voices, Honey is a blues singer and actress. The recurrent theme of the blues, the lover who is both a trouble and a delight, informs her narrative. The story oscillates between Heywood as the man of her dreams and Heywood as the one who has imprisoned her by leaving with her the women he accumulates in his exploits.

Repeatedly, Honey describes her life as a form of containment. She alternates between portraying herself as the thing contained and as the container filled to overflowing. Of Heywood, she says: "A good looker and all, but always makes me feel more mother or older sister, though he four months to the day older than me. Naaw, I conclude, Heywood just my buddy. But I'm thinking too that I need a new buddy, cause he's got me bagged somehow. Put me in a bag when I wasn't looking" (*Sea Birds*, 183).

Similarly, she feels that her acting can be a form of confinement: "Got to fight hard and all the time with the scripts and the people. Cause they'll trap you in a fiction. Breath drained, heart stopped, vibrancy fixed, under arrest. Whole being entrapped, all possibility impaled, locked in some stereotype. And how you look trying to call from the box and be heard much less be understood long enough to get out and mean something useful and for real?" (*Sea Birds*, 172).

This external entrapment is largely male-created. One of the sources of Honey's blues is the feeling of frustration and anger at being a manmade object and not an organic, natural being. Moreover, she believes that such objectification is the destiny of women. The women in the story seem incapable of escaping the men who treat them in such a manner.

However, the language of the second quotation suggests that Honey is, to some extent, self-imprisoned. She operates within the discourse system of the dominant culture, in contrast to the folk speech of the first quotation. Thus, when her argument moves into the political ("they'll trap you") as opposed to the personal ("he's got me bagged") realm, her language, like that of Graham, becomes abstract. Her political discourse is emptied out of concrete historical content; she is in this sense dependent for self-definition on the very culture that has boxed her in.

But she sees an alternative possibility in the inversion of the box image. One of the functions of the image is to absorb and contain as well as to be restricted. Though this generally means absorbing all the irresponsibilities of men, such as all of Heywood's castoff lovers, it makes possible a receptiveness to the experiences of those women. For Honey, this is part of the burden of her life: "Not that Heywood puts a gun to my head, but it's hard to say no to a sister with no place to go. So they wind up here, expecting me to absorb their blues and transform them maybe into songs. Been over a year since I've written any new songs. Absorbing, absorbing, bout to turn to mush rather than crystallize, sparkling" (*Sea Birds*, 170).

The very closeness to suffering makes difficult the traditional conversion of that experience into art. Dealing with the human reality robs Honey of the aesthetic distance and creative energy necessary to give that reality expression. That such expression is possible is evident from her cataloging of the women blues singers who have gone before her and also her contemplation of the dramatic potential in the history of black women, both famous and anonymous, in America:

> Mamy Pleasant, was it? Tubman, slave women bundlers, voodoo queens, maroon guerrillas, combatant ladies in the Seminole nation, calls from the swamps, the tunnels, the classrooms, the studios, the factories, the roofs, from the doorway hushed or brassy in a dress way too short but it don't mean nuthin heavy enough to have to explain, just like Bad Bitch in the Sanchez play was saying. But then the wagon comes and they all rounded up and caged in the Bitch-Whore-Mouth mannequin with the dead eyes and the mothball breath, never to be heard from again. But want to sing a Harriet song and play a Pleasant role and bring them all center stage. (*Sea Birds*, 173)

Implicit here is the desire not merely to recount the heroic actions of great women but also to expose the systematic dehumanizing of all black women, for the history she describes coincides with her own experience. To give voice to these women would be to liberate her own powers of articulation.

But her problem in some sense is having too many voices and too many roles. In addition to being Heywood's buddy, mammy for his many women and a stereotype on the stage, she had made herself the perpetuator of a blues tradition and spokeswoman for the suffering black females of the past and present. The truth about herself is found in a comment she makes about the witchbird at the beginning of the narrative: "I'm sucking my teeth but can't even hear myself good for the caterwauling that damn bird's already set up in the woods, tearing up the bushes, splitting twigs with the high notes. Bird make me think some singer locked up inside, hostage" (*Sea Birds*, 169). Honey spends so much time "splitting twigs with the high notes" of the songs of others that she cannot free the singer that is herself. This dual role of singer and spokeswoman is inherently problematic. On

121

the one hand, she seeks expression for its own sake, while on the other she wants her expression to serve an essentially political end. The blues performer creates a mood by rendering a personal experience in the appropriate form; the music's function is to entertain. The political speaker, in contrast, tries to persuade the audience to change the relationships of power in the world. To force these two forms together is to deform both. The result is the frustrated voice that is Honey's.

Her experience in the beauty shop, which is a natural space for a community of women, breaks down that barrier in a number of ways. First, the owner of the shop strips away the physical disguise: " 'Come on out from under that death, Honey,' Mary says soon's we get halfway in the door. 'Look like you sportin a whole new look in cosmetics. Clown white, ain't it? Or is it Griffin All White applied with a putty knife?' Mary leaves her customer in the chair to come rip the wig off my head. 'And got some dead white woman on your head too. Why you wanna do this to yourself, Honey? You auditioning for some zombie movie?' " (*Sea Birds,* 181). The narrator, who a few pages before had been talking about her pride in black history, is revealed as a product of the oppressive side of that history. Despite her knowledge of the victimizations of black women, Honey cannot avoid putting herself in the costume society demands. She has not previously revealed this aspect of her character, and it reinforces the implication of her use of the speech of the dominant culture that she helps perpetuate the very oppression she tries to resist.

Moreover, Mary reminds Honey of a recent encounter with Heywood. The telling of that incident deromanticizes the relationship by showing his open insensitivity and her submission to it. One of the other women drives home the point: " 'I'm getting tired of men like that,' grumbles Bertha after while. 'Either it's "Hey, Mama, hold my head," or "Hey, Sister," at three in the morning. When it get to be "Sugar Darlin"? I'm tired of it. And you, Honey, should be the tiredest of all' " (*Sea Birds,* 185). The constant role playing forced on black women not only denies them their own identity, but it also makes it possible for men to evade their responsibilities. Women who continue to accommodate that practice conspire in their own oppression. As long as they play the strong, ever-absorbent mother, their males do not have to become men.

The destructive impact of that is seen in the story a nameless voice tells of

Helen and Amos, also unknown to Honey. Amos has become addicted to drugs, and Helen does not know if she can deal with it. Paradoxically, because of her strength, Amos feels free to use drugs, knowing that she will take care of him; without that strength everything disintegrates. The ultimate blame falls on the dominant society: "No jobs, nary a fit house in sight, famine on the way, but the dope just keep comin and comin" (*Sea Birds*, 185). But it works so effectively because the victims cooperate in their own destruction.

The story has a dramatic impact on Honey: "I crumple up too hearing it" (*Sea Birds*, 185). "Crumpling" suggests the collapsing of the Chinese boxes she and others have built around herself. It also means the release of all she has absorbed: "No amount of towel's gonna stop the flow, I'm thinking. I don't even try to stop. Let it pour, let it get on out so I can travel light" (*Sea Birds*, 185). In this undamming of anguish, resentment, pain, and sacrifice, she frees the singer inside herself. That voice floats lightly, like that of the witchbird, which has associations with the devil and the night.[6] While she may sing the old blues numbers, she will do so in the knowledge that she calls hell by its true name. She begins not by singing someone else's words but by speaking her own. These "talking blues" constitute the narrative and give expression to Honey's loves and troubles for the first time.

The Salt Eaters (1980), like Bambara's previous works, concerns a woman on a quest for identity and freedom. The novel resembles Gaines's *In My Father's House* in its sense of the disintegration of black community values. Disintegration is the primary concern of Bambara's only novel, as the black community, the main character, and the book's structure are all decentered. The principle action takes place in a clinic room where Velma Henry, a political activist who has attempted suicide, is being treated by Minnie Ransom, a root worker. The cause of Velma's action seems to be her inability to deal with the conflicting demands of the black community. Groups committed to feminism, ecology, political activism, revolution, black capitalism, voodoo, astrology, and cynicism threaten her sense of self because she believes in achieving selfhood through work in the community and these groups all insist on her loyalty to the exclusion of the others. The impact of this atomization is reflected in the structure of the novel; many of the scenes are only marginally related to each other or to the central subject of Velma's treatment. This narrative form has the effect of showing the world as disordered as Velma believes it to be, though the point of view is not hers but that of an omniscient narrator. In this way a pattern becomes apparent in the disorder: each movement, which begins as a form of resistance to oppression, takes on an oppressive character as it seeks to compel agreement with its principles; it becomes itself a closed system. Similarly, Velma deals with the centrifugal forces of the community, which resist her unifying desires, by closing herself off from the unsafe realm of personal relationships: "She tried to withdraw as she'd been doing for weeks and weeks. Withdraw the self to a safe place where husband, lover, teacher, workers, no one could follow, probe. Withdraw herself and prop up a borderguard to negotiate with would-be intruders."[7]

She protects her self in this manner from dissolution, but at the same time she precludes the possibility of healing. Minnie doubts that Velma wants to recover: " 'Are you sure, sweetheart? I'm just asking is all,' Minnie Ransom was saying, playfully pulling at her lower lip till three different shades of purple showed. 'Take away the miseries and you take away some folks' reason for living. Their conversation piece anyway' " (The Salt Eaters, 15–16). Velma has constructed her innermost identity by steeling herself against vulnerability and suffering; her suicide attempt is her ultimate gesture at self-protection. But to keep that center, she needs to keep alive the pains and disorders that justify it. In other words, she finds her security in maintaining a constant state of antagonism, which she helps to generate, thus completing the cycle, by her withdrawals from love and happiness.

Minnie seeks to break this self-destructive, self-oppressive pattern through the use of all her folk arts. She expresses her view of Velma and the world at large through conversations with Old Wife, the ghost of a long-dead conjure woman:

> Dancing in mud with cowries. Mmm. Twisting and grunting for the reward-applause of a bloody head on a tray. Lord, have mercy. What is wrong with the women? If they ain't sticking their head in ovens and opening up their veins like this gal, or jumping off roofs, drinking charcoal lighter, pumping rat poisons in their arms, and ramming cars into walls, they looking for some man to tear his head off. What is wrong, Old Wife? What is happening to the daughters of the yam? Seem like they just don't know how to draw up the powers from the deep like before. Not full sunned and sweet any more. Tell me, how do I welcome this daughter home to the world? (The Salt Eaters, 43–44)

124

The daughters have ignored the ancient beliefs in loas and spiritual healing and pursue power through feminism, capitalism, ecology, or some other ideological system. The problem lies not in the values of such systems, but in their separation from the black folk roots of these ideas. In other words, the daughters seek ahistorical forms of power. For example, the activist women of the community feel that they have been exploited by the men of their organization. Although doing all the crucial organizational and administrative work that makes possible political change, they are excluded from policy making and from the rewards of political success. But their method of responding to this male domination is to use countervailing power: "We'll notify you about the meetings, and you are welcome to join us at my sister's studio, which will be the temporary headquarters of Women for Action until we get a more permanent place. . . . You all continue lollygagging at Del Giorgio's, renting limousines and pussyfooting around town profiling in your three-piece suits and imported pajamas while the people sweat it out through hard times" (*The Salt Eaters,* 37). In effect, their resistance consists of accepting the principle of domination and subordination and simply reversing the direction of oppression. In doing so, they perpetuate the very system that has so adversely affected them.

A very different approach is used by the Seven Sisters, a performing troupe of minority-group women. Their experience offers a model for Velma's recovery. In each case, the woman has found her creative potential by recovering the past of her people. Mai, for example, remembers the experience of Japanese Americans:

> Maybe . . . an old story passed down on Mai's maternal side huddled together in the internment camps of '42, keeping themselves alive with the stories. But keeping separate even then, even there, the threads of the Japanese, Chinese, Filipino elders. Stories keeping the people in the camps alive while the bill in Congress to sterilize the women of the camps got voted down by one vote, one vote. And then the silence. A whole generation silent about the camps. Then the hand reaching back, the pen dipped, the stories alive again to keep the people going. (*The Salt Eaters,* 222)

Mai's stories form part of the performance of the troupe, which, like the blues, retains both the sense of suffering and the means of coping with that suffering. The Seven Sisters exists specifically to remind women of their pains and their strengths. The performers do so by linking imagination, concrete folk history, and political awareness in a more effective pattern than others in the book have achieved. Theirs are stories about the stories created by the oppressed; since they come from different backgrounds, the experiences they articulate are simultaneously specific and universal. Moreover, they do not demand any particular political gesture; their end is remembrance of the true history of suffering, which is intrinsically opposed to the false history perpetrated by those in power.

Velma's healing follows the pattern of the troupe, but because that pattern demands concreteness, she must delve into her own personal and racial past, aided by Minnie Ransom, to find an identity deeper than any of those afforded to her by various ideologies:

> Day of Restoration, Velma muttered, feeling the warm breath of Minnie Ransom on her, lending her something to work the bellows of her lungs with. To keep on dancing like the sassy singer said. Dancing on toward the busy streets alive with winti, coyote and cunnie rabbit and turtle and caribou as if heading for the Ark in the new tidal wave, racing in the direction of resurrection as should be and she had a choice running running in the streets naming things—cunnie rabbit called impala called little deer called trickster called brother called change—naming things amidst the rush and dash of tires, feet, damp dresses swishing by, the Spirits of Blessing way outrunning disaster, outrunning jinns, shetnoi, soubaka, succubi, innocuii, incubi, nefarii, the demons midwifed, suckled and fathered by the one in ten Mama warned about who come to earth for the express purpose of making trouble for the other nine. (*The Salt Eaters*, 263–64)

Her role is not to order the chaos but to be the one who names in the act of running, which is also dancing. In this vision she is outside of ordinary time and space and in a sacred space, as Minnie realizes when she senses the presence of a pentagon, the emblem of a magical area for those who practice the black arts. In this space Velma can know the shifting shapes of the trickster and can recognize the different forms of the demons. She senses that true knowledge consists not in fixing identities and establishing closed structures but rather in tracing the patterns of change: "To have dominion was not to knock out, downpress, bruise, but to understand, to love, make at home. The keeping in the sights the animal, or child, man or woman, tracking it in order to learn their way of being in the world. To be at home in the knowing. The hunt for balance and kinship was the thing. A mutual courtesy. She would run to the park and hunt for self. Would be wild. Would look" (*The Salt Eaters*, 267).

But the process of being at home is not as sentimental and easy as it may sound, for it is based on a crucial paradox: the true home is found by being wild, untamed, undomesticated. To live in a free world means a constant running, shape shifting, and renaming. The world of mutual consent is also the world of demons and succubi, who seduce with their attractive but life-denying forms. Velma must give up the security of the various well-meaning ideologies to follow the path of the conjure woman, the "crazy" woman. At this moment of awareness, she also knows the price she must pay:

> Velma would remember it as the moment she started back toward life, the moment when the healer's hand had touched some vital spot and she was still trying to resist, still trying to think what good did wild do you, since there was always some low-life gruesome gang bang raping lawless careless pesty last straw nasty thing ready to pounce, put your total shit under arrest and crack your back—but couldn't. And years hence she would laugh remembering she'd thought *that* was an ordeal. She didn't know the half of it. Of what awaited her in years to come. (*The Salt Eaters*, 278)

The shift in verb tense at this point signifies the success of Velma's healing, but it also demonstrates that recuperation makes possible greater, not reduced, struggle. She can now reenter the world, but it is a world of apocalypse, not peace.

The black community, for which she is synecdoche, is undergoing the the same process of death and renewal. For Obie, her husband, the overpowering sense of disintegration of black unity and pride must be nullified. But the shift to a future perspective suggests that, as in Velma's case, healing can come only through a ritual of death. The ritual for society is the carnival, a ceremony that marks the end of winter and also, in traditional cultures, the death of the old symbol of power, the king. It is sometimes the occasion for the celebration of the death of Death. Simultaneously, it signifies the advent of summer and the new order, the resurrection of life. As a form, it is a unity comprised of diverse events and practices, an overflowing rather than a containment of experiences.[8] It is appropriate that Obie leads this ritual, since his name makes him the obeah man, the conjurer of African and Afro-American folk belief.[9] As such, it is his role to call forth the spirit of healing.

He enacts his role by finding a unifying theme in that same history that restored Velma to life; the project that will join the men and women, ecologists and astrologists, the revolutionaries and the reformers is a reenactment of a slave insurrection. Such a performance will remind the groups that their true history is in resistance and not in system building; furthermore, the rumors that Obie's Academy is a warehouse for a black arsenal suggest that the history continues into the present. The unverifiable nature of the rumor reasserts the part of that history that sees masking as a valuable strategy.

But as was the case with Ernest Gaines, Toni Bambara does not show the moment of achieved unity. The carnival itself is projected beyond the closing of the narrative. Despite a sense of apocalypse throughout the text—through character disintegration, ideological warfare, rumors of race war, and even the weather—the end of the old order is never actually shown. Comments about Velma's recovery hint at it, but even those are intentionally vague. The reason is clearly that the narrative itself is situated in history and could only project a new order by compelling an end to that history. In order to be true to that dialectic of resistance that gives it form, it cannot resolve its own tensions. It must end on the edge of time, and not at its conclusion. In the novel, Bambara brings together the various elements of her shorter fiction—folk speech, the search for voice, healing, and political activism—in a text that is itself unified less by the devices of plot resolution than by the theme of caring in the context of a diverse universe where possibility is more important than uniformity of belief. Her desire for political change is conditioned by an awareness that the universes of her fiction must remain open if real change, rather than a new form of oppression, is to come about. She grounds that hope in the stories of the rural and urban folk that populate her narratives.

Alice Walker, in both short stories and novels, makes much more explicit use of history than Bambara, but ironically, she has a greater tendency to construct political solutions that run counter to the thrust of that very folk history. This history takes public and private forms. Whether recreating the rural black South of the thirties or the civil rights movement of the sixties, Walker seeks to place her narrative within the framework of the social-political history of blacks in America. On the other hand, she gives her characters a very strong sense of their own pasts; in many cases, they are haunted by what has happened to them. Since she is, like Bambara, primarily concerned with black women, she writes stories that show these doubly oppressed figures searching for their own voices in the context of social and psychological conditioning that would deny them expression.

128

In her first novel, *The Third Life of Grange Copeland* (1970), Walker's overt concern does not immediately seem to be with female characters. After all, the title character and his son Brownfield occupy center stage. Their development and inevitable conflict form the focus of the novel. In this sense the story resembles those by Ernest Gaines, who even in *The Autobiography of Miss Jane Pittman* concentrates on males. Walker, however, insists on testing the meaning of male development by its impact on female characters. The achievement of self-consciousness or identity is thus doubly dialectical: it occurs in relation to both race and gender. In shaping the narrative, Walker uses folklore on both these subjects in showing the operation of the dialectical patterns.

The characterizations of both Grange and Brownfield draw on folk figures, principally the bad man and the moral hard man.[10] Brownfield lives out the selfish, violent, malevolent existence with which his father begins. In addition to being sexually promiscuous, he mistreats his wife and ultimately kills her, and he puts his newborn albino son outside on a winter night so that he will freeze to death. When his wife goes against his wishes in trying to create a more decent life for the family, he patiently and coldly calculates his revenge; he succeeds in returning the family to the barely human conditions from which they sought to rise. In all this, his attitudes resemble those of the bad man of black legend: the Great McDaddy, Billy Dupree, Stagolee.

But in the process of using this folk material to give her character vitality, Walker simultaneously demystifies the legend by showing its roots in self-hatred and its impact on female characters. By such a process, she calls into question the cultural functions of such folk images; like Gaines in "Three Men," she implies that the bad man figure can be a justification for inhumanity. Brownfield undergoes two experiences in his early life that give him a sense of his fate under the existing social order. In the first of these, he is shown another world, symbolized by the car his northern uncle drives:

> The automobile was a new 1920 Buick, long and high and shiny green with great popping headlights like the eyes of a frog. Inside the car it was all blue, with seats that were fuzzy and soft. Slender silver handles opened the doors and rolled the astonishingly clear windows up and down. As it bumped over the road its canvas top was scratched by low elm branches. Brownfield felt embarrassed about the bad road and the damage it did to his uncle's car.

129

> Uncle Silas loved his car and had spent all morning washing it, polishing the wheel spokes and dusting off the running board.[11]

Brownfield sees in his uncle's care for the car a pride of possession and thus a bourgeois sensibility that he himself under the conditions of his life could never attain. Nothing in his world is worth any pride. Moreover, his embarrassment implies that that sense of worthlessness extends to himself, since he assumes blame for the existence of the conditions. Thus, a desirable life is not possible, and he holds himself somehow responsible. Later, when he learns that Uncle Silas dies during a robbery designed to help support his drug habit, it serves to show him that middle-class dreams for blacks are only pretensions.

The second part of Brownfield's education comes in seeing his father's relationship to the white boss. His northern cousins had told him that the man "owned" Grange, but he only slowly comes to understand what that means:

> Brownfield's father had no smiles about him at all. He merely froze; his movements when he had to move to place sacks on the truck were rigid as a machine's. At first Brownfield thought his father was turned to stone by the truck itself. The truck was big and noisy and coldly, militarily gray. Its big wheels flattened the cotton stalks and made deep ruts in the soft dirt of the field. But after watching the loading of the truck for several weeks he realized it was the man who drove the truck who caused his father to don a mask that was more impenetrable than his usual silence. Brownfield looked closely at the man and made a startling discovery; the man was a man, but entirely different from his own father. When he noticed this difference, one of odor and sound and movement and laughter, as well as of color, he wondered how he had not seen it before. (*Grange Copeland*, 8)

But his response is not simply one of curiosity: he was "filled with terror of this man who could, by his presence alone, turn his father into something that might as well have been a pebble or a post or a piece of dirt, except for the sharp, bitter odor of something whose source was forcibly contained in flesh" (*Grange Copeland*, 9). Grange and the white man Shipley are different orders of being, with Shipley having the God-like capacity to change the black man into something nonhuman. The mask that Grange wears is not the strategically adopted one of the trickster but one assumed to hide the involuntary reactions of fear and hatred. The emotions suppressed here find expression in a variety of behaviors often associated with the bad man: promiscuity, insensitivity, and violence directed against other blacks, including his wife.

Seeing the futility of ambition and the power of whites, Brownfield quickly becomes fixed in his perceptions of the world. The narrative reinforces this by having him replicate the life of his father in an almost too perfect way. After Grange abandons his family and the boy's mother kills her child by Shipley and then commits suicide, Brownfield sets off in quest of his father, though he is not certain of the reason for this. He gets as far as the Dew Drop Inn, run by Josie, who, along with her daughter, provides for the young man, both nutritionally and sexually. Later, he learns that she was the mistress of his father for many years.

Brownfield falls in love with Mem, Josie's niece, and feels for her very much as Grange felt for his own wife, Margaret, early in their marriage. But this bliss is short-lived, as Mem's middle-class values come into conflict with her husband's experience of fear and impotence in the face of white power. In order to maintain some semblance of manhood, he beats her and their daughters and turns to Josie for sexual satisfaction. As one manifestation of his resentment of the dominant culture, he forces Mem to change her speech patterns. Her educated language represents access to that world he can never reach, so he berates and abuses her until she talks to his satisfaction: "He wanted her to talk, but to talk like what she was, a hopeless nigger woman who got her ass beat every Saturday night. He wanted her to sound like a woman who deserved him" (*Grange Copeland*, 56). The voice that is the product of her effort to change her life is denied her; it is replaced by a voice that confirms Brownfield's static vision of life.

The depth of his malevolence comes with Mem's efforts to improve the lives of her family. Brownfield moves them from one uninhabitable shack to another, following a pattern of accepting whatever the white man, in his omnipotence, chooses to give them. Though hard labor and sheer strength of character, Mem accumulates enough money to move them into a house in the town. She obtains a job for Brownfield in the factory, doing work much easier than the field tasks to which he has been accustomed. Gradually, they acquire the beginning of a middle-class existence. But he has not changed:

Brownfield lay in wait for the return of Mem's weakness. The cycles of her months and years brought it. The first early morning heavings were a good sign. Her body would do to her what he could not, without the support of his former bravado. The swelling of the womb, again and again pushing the backbone inward, the belly outward. He surveyed with sly interest the bleaching out of every crease on her wrinkled stomach. Waiting. She could not hold out against him with nausea, aching feet and teeth, swollen legs, bursting veins and head; or the grim and dizzying reality of her trapped self and her children's despair. He could bring her back to lowness she had not even guessed at before. (*Grange Copeland,* 101)

His success in doing this carries out the logic of the existence Grange ran away from. Brownfield's sense of identity and manhood, so circumscribed by the white economic and racial system, finds expression in domination of those weaker than himself. He will control his family even if it means depriving them of the benefits of a better life; in this, he becomes the omnipresent figure that his own father failed to be.

One reason that this drive for control overpowers all other concerns is that Brownfield sees in middle-class life a denial of his racial as well as personal identity. Living in town changes him: "Now he could shit, and rising, look at himself, at the way his eyes had cleared themselves of the hateful veins and yellow tigerish lines, without much odor or rain, and much like a gentleman; or, as he invariably thought of it, like a white man" (*Grange Copeland,* 102). His rejection of this image can be seen in two ways. On the one hand, his acquiescence to white power and his belief that whites are a different order of being suggest that he sees himself as unworthy of the status to which Mem aspires. The strength of his self-hatred leads him to deny to himself and his family a life of even minimal comfort. On the other hand, the rejection operates in the context of distrust of anything white that is a traditional part of black folk life. Mem's belief in economic progress is an act of self-deception; no matter how many things she acquires, she will never achieve respect and security in a racist society. To be more and more like a white man would be to Brownfield a measure not of success but of his loss of good sense. The return to the brutal cycles of the land marks a return for him to a true sense of time and place. In making this, his only true choice, Brownfield displays the bad man's disdain for social conventions, but he finds in his choice not liberation but imprisonment, both psychological and physical after he murders Mem. He cannot be freed by his rejection because he lacks the bad man's anarchistic courage. He believes in domination and systems of oppression. He lives in the folk world to the extent that he values its fatalistic and cyclical world view. His replication of the life of his father reinforces that; it demonstrates to him that he has no control over his life. The suffering he endures and that which he inflicts are matters of indifference to those who do have control, and thus it is better to be a stone like his father was. In effect, this self-reification ultimately serves the purposes of white supremacy as much as or more than Mem's middle-class values. Even the bad-man elements of his character are manipulated, since they are turned against other blacks and not against the oppressive system itself.

Brownfield carries to its logical extreme the first life of Grange Copeland. In terms of narrative structure, this frees Grange himself to develop in an alternative way. By having the father rather than the son go out into the larger world, Walker sets up not only a conflict of generations, but also conflicting senses of history. Brownfield, in living his life, relives his father's up to a certain point. As suggested above, this experience implies the changelessness of time. Grange, by going beyond that point, but within a folk context, offers an organic view of time much richer than his son's. The patterns of return are still present, but within them are growth and self-determination.

Just as Brownfield's character is shown through relationships with female characters, so with Grange two women are crucial to his experience. The first of these is an unnamed white woman he sees in New York's Central Park. Having escaped the brutality of the South, he has encountered the different brutality of the North, which treats him with indifference rather than hostility. He survives the winter by stealing whatever he can. Under these circumstances, he discovers the universality of human suffering as well as the depth of racial hatred. He watches from a hiding place as a pregnant woman meets the soldier who is the father of her unborn child. He gives her a ring and then tells her about his wife:

> Grange had watched the scene deteriorate from the peak of happiness to the bottom of despair. It was the first honestly human episode he had witnessed between white folks, when they were not putting on airs to misinform the help. His heart ached with pity for the young woman as well as for the

soldier, whose face, those last seconds, had not been without its own misery. And now the perhaps normally proud woman sat crying shamelessly—but only because she thought herself alone. There she sat, naked, her big belly her own tomb. Or at least it must have seemed so to her, for from cry to cry she pressed with both hands against her stomach as if she would push it away from her and into the pond. (*Grange Copeland,* 147)

This moment signifies not merely Grange's first experience of white humanity, but, in its language, his own first expression of self-transcending sympathy. Here he wears neither the mask of submission nor that of domineering masculinity, but a very human face.

The woman, in contrast, refuses to be vulnerable, and she quickly suppresses her emotion:

But abruptly, when she apparently considered she had cried enough, the young woman stopped, blew her nose and wiped her eyes. Quite containedly. He could almost see the features settle into a kind of haughty rigidity that belied the past half-hour. Her face became one that refused to mark itself with suffering. He knew, even before he saw them, that her eyes would be without vital expression, and that her lips and cheeks and old once-used laugh wrinkles would have to do all her smiling from then on. . . . At the same time her icy fortitude in the face of love's desertion struck him as peculiarly white American. No blues would ever come from such a saving of face. (*Grange Copeland,* 148)

The woman's face in this passage resembles Grange's own face when he must deal with white men. Moreover, the suppression of feeling is not that different from his own treatment of his wife and child. (In one passage Brownfield describes Grange's inability to touch him, even when he thought the boy was asleep.) What distinguishes the woman is her denial of the experience of suffering; she does not merely control it, but, more important, she refuses to recognize its existence. Grange sees this refusal as peculiarly white, since the blues are evidence that blacks do not engage in such willed erasure.

The full meaning of her denial comes when Grange seeks to comfort her. Her initial fear that he intends to rob her is quickly replaced by racism:

"Look at the big burly-head," she said, and laughed again. Grange swallowed. He hated her entire race while she stood before him, pregnant, having learned nothing from her own pain, helpless except before someone more weak than herself, enjoying a revenge that severed all possible bonds of sympathy between them. She stood there like a great blonde pregnant deified cow. She was not pretty, but only a copy of a standardly praised copy of prettiness. She was abandoned, but believed herself infinitely cared for and wanted. By somebody. She was without superiority, but believed herself far above him. (*Grange Copeland*, 151)

Her attitude duplicates that of Brownfield; victims of an oppressive system (the woman in her ersatz beauty as well as her betrayal), both deny their condition by practicing oppression themselves. The life-denying quality of this perspective is made clear when the woman falls through the ice into the pond. Grange, despite his anger, tries to help her because "he realized that to save and preserve life was an instinct, no matter whose life you were trying to save" (*Grange Copeland*, 152). But this instinct has been supplanted in the woman by another one: "She reached up and out with a small white hand that grabbed his hand but let go when she felt it was *his* hand" (*Grange Copeland*, 152). Life itself is less important to her than her feeling of superiority. And in killing her unborn child in the midst of her self-destruction, she duplicates Brownfield's killing of his own son. Not content with suicide, either physical or psychological, they feel compelled as well to murder the future.

But Grange resists the death wish that drives them. He takes responsibility for the woman's death by naming it murder. In that act he finds liberation and what he believes to be the dialectical heart of black reality:

He felt in some way repaid for his own unfortunate life. It was the taking of that white woman's life—and the denying of the life of her child—the taking of her life, not the taking of her money, that forced him to want to try to live again. He believed that, against his will, he had stumbled on the necessary act that black men must commit to regain, or to manufacture their manhood, their self-respect. They must kill their oppressors. He never ceased to believe this, adding only to this belief, in later years, that if one kills he must not shun death in his turn. And this, he had found, was the hardest part, since after freeing your suppressed manhood by killing whatever suppressed it you were then taken with the most passionate desire to live! (*Grange Copeland*, 153)

Killing is the necessary condition for life under a system of oppression. In accepting this idea, Grange becomes the true "bad nigger" that Brownfield only imitates. In acquiring a sense of justice, he moves beyond that role into that of the moral hard man, who acts not for himself but for some greater social good. Such a figure remains outside the sphere of social conventions and may even commit acts of violence, but he does so for righteous reasons.

He proves his change by moving back to the South, marrying Josie, and trying to force Brownfield to treat his family with decency. He takes responsibility for his past, including the death of Margaret. He buys land, hoping that he can withdraw as fully as possible from the world dominated by whites; in this way, he can maintain his dignity without being compelled to kill again. This second life, one of isolation, makes it possible to continue his hatred and still do good for those blacks closest to him.

The third life is Ruth, the granddaughter he takes in after Brownfield murders Mem and goes to prison. She represents for him the opportunity to perpetuate his values. He seeks to make her independent by passing on the folk wisdom he has accumulated, giving special emphasis to the trickster tales, which he hopes will instill in her a profound distrust of whites. His problem lies in passing on the complex tension between hatred and the affirmation of life that necessitates their isolation. Even after she realizes the racist nature of the formal schooling she receives, her feeling is one of wariness and resistance, not active personal hostility. In this, she comes closer than Grange himself to folk attitudes.

But his obsession with nurturing her, even to the neglect of his marriage to Josie, most influences her, for it teaches her that resistance and responsibility are larger than the individual. By taking care of her, he creates in her a sense of history more optimistic than her father's changelessness and more substantial than her mother's naïve meliorism. The act of nurturing, through education in folk wisdom and the example of dignity and independence, demonstrates the intimate relationship of past and future. It encourages hope while preserving an awareness of suffering.

The third life culminates in two episodes that take it into the larger world. The first of these is a visit to Grange's farm by a group of civil rights activists urging him to vote. He finds it remarkable that the white members of the group stay in the background, letting the young blacks do all the talking. Moreover, these whites have themselves endured suffering while aiding the movement. Even more surprising is the attitude of the blacks, who combine seriousness with joy and hope. He cannot reject them as simple-minded fools, since they have grown up in the country and understand the conditions. But his hatred will not allow him to believe what they believe: "He felt about them as he felt about Dr. King; that if they'd just stay with him on his farm he'd shoot the first cracker that tried to bother them. He wanted to protect them, from themselves and from their dreams, as much as from the crackers. He would not let anybody hurt them, but at the same time he didn't believe in what they were doing. Not because it wasn't worthy and noble and inspiring and good, but because it was impossible" (*Grange Copeland*, 241). His perspective is necessarily limited by that very system he has struggled so valiantly against. He sees resistance as inherently individual. He has been conditioned as much as Brownfield to view the wall of whiteness as impenetrable; his conscious education of Ruth has been aimed at teaching her how to act alone, although his methods—folk narratives and values—are inherently social.

The measure of his unintentional success with her becomes apparent in her very different response to the civil rights workers. Unlike him, she unselfconsciously welcomes the whites to the farm. She also has a reaction to the young black man that combines admiration and sexual attraction: "She was laughing a shy but bubbly delighted laugh; forgotten completely was the fact that nobody ever visited the farm without her grandfather's permission" (*Grange Copeland*, 237). Even after she realizes that he is married to the young woman, she sees him as a standard against which to judge other men. The extent of her difference from her grandfather is evident in their later conversation:

"I bet *all* the *good* ones have got taken!" she moaned, frowning at him.

"You really got a kick out of him, didn't you, girl?" asked Grange. "One day another one'll come and he won't have a wife and you can grab him before he starts looking for one."

"I don't expect a whole stream of 'em to come passing by *here*," she said with dismay. "I think I'm going to have to go out and *find* the one I want."

"What about this farm?" Grange asked.

"Oh, good grief!" she said, and stormed into her room, slamming the door and throwing herself across her bed. (*Grange Copeland*, 242)

She has no use for Grange's strong need for security and isolation. The very success of her training has expanded the boundaries of the world for her. She thinks it more important to seek out life than to hide from its difficulties. She takes for granted the future that Grange has struggled to create.

The act that enables her to enter that future comes in the last episode of the book. Here, the three lives of Grange Copeland are brought together in a final confrontation that reveals their interrelationship. Brownfield, freed from prison, seeks to regain custody of Ruth. His purpose seems again to be the stopping of history. He would suppress the ambitions of his daughter just as those of his mother and wife were suppressed. Ruth alone cannot stop him, not only because she is young but also because she has been conditioned to reject violence and to see all people as human beings rather than objects. Her encounters with her father are filled with ambiguity:

> "I'm not yours," Ruth said humbly, for she felt, momentarily, a great dam about to fly open inside her, and when and if it broke she wanted it to be soft and gentle and not hurtful to him, although whatever she said, since she could never forgive him, or even agree with him, would have to hurt some. But suddenly he reached out for the first time to touch her. And his touch was not, as some of his words had been, either pathetic or kind. He grasped the flesh of her upper arm between thumb and forefinger and began to twist it. Her defenses went up again, higher than before, and bitter tears came to her eyes. (*Grange Copeland*, 219–20)

She lacks the simple purity of hatred or obsession necessary to blot him out of her life; even he is human, and so her response must be a defensive rather than an offensive one.

But Grange, who comes between their worlds, can act in ways she cannot and in ways that make her world possible. Having retained his capacity for hatred and added to it a sense of justice and change, he can unhesitatingly kill Brownfield when an indifferent white judge grants custody of Ruth to her father. By this gesture he frees her from the old world, but he condemns himself to death as punishment for his crime. But this self-sacrifice itself affirms life, since it symbolizes the belief that the taking of a life is the ultimate immorality, even if the victim is someone as life-denying as Brownfield.

This existential ethic reflects Walker's early interest in Camus,[12] but it also can be found in the folk value of improvisation. Ruth's future is not guaranteed; Grange's act has robbed her of both father and guardian. She

138

stands at the beginning of Grange Copeland's third life, a life that of necessity must create its meaning at every moment, guided only by the wisdom of her heritage. She exists in difference from both Brownfield and Grange, as well as the dominant white culture, yet all of those condition the improvisational possibilities that will be her life. In this dialectic of history and self-creation, she repeats the theme and form of black life and black art.

The stories in *Of Love and Trouble* (1973) repeat the tension between folk wisdom and conventional systems of order. And again, as in all the writers previously discussed, black as well as white characters must be shown the limits and oppressiveness of those systems. "Strong Horse Tea," "The Revenge of Hannah Kemhuff," and "Everyday Use" provide the best examples of the working out of this theme. In each case a strong folk female figure must deal with the unbelief of a woman who has, either consciously or unconsciously, adopted an antifolk system of values. The validity of that system must be called into question and then the folk alternative given primacy.

"Strong Horse Tea" embodies this form in its conflict between a local healer and the mother of a sick child. Rannie Toomer believes that the cure for her child can only come from the white doctor, with his instruments and scientific knowledge. Her faith in the white order of things is so strong that she believes the mailman will carry her message. She fails to understand that her voice will not be heard in the white world. The mailman goes only as far as the home of Sarah the root worker to deliver his message. As far as he is concerned, no more is necessary: "He half believed with everybody else in the county that the old blue-eyed black woman possessed magic. Magic that if it didn't work on whites probably would in blacks."[13] Trudier Harris has traced the folk history of the blue-eyed black as a magical figure with great power in the black community.[14] Rannie's initial rejection of such power suggests how far she has removed herself from folk belief.

When Sarah arrives and explains the true situation of the doctor, Rannie mourns the wasted time: "Her feeling of guilt was a stone" (*In Love and Trouble*, 95). Though she still distinguishes between the old woman and the "real" doctor, she begs Sarah's help in saving the baby. In her desperation, she regains the faith. But Sarah knows that it is too late to heal the baby; she announces almost immediately that he is dying.

She undertakes instead the saving of the mother. She sends Rannie out into the rain and mud to collect "strong horse tea," urine from the farm's mare: "Rannie Toomer was close enough to catch the tea if she could keep up with the mare while she ran. So alternately holding her breath and gasping for air she started after her. Mud from her fall clung to her elbows and streaked her frizzy hair. Slipping and sliding in the mud she raced after the mare, holding out, as if for alms, her plastic shoe" (*In Love and Trouble*, 97). In this purgatory she does penance for her lack of faith. Sarah understands that the ritual, while meaningless for the child, which has died in the meantime, relieves Rannie of her guilt and restores her to the life of the community. She has done something for her child instead of waiting for some "superior" knowledge; by acting, even if ineffectively, she regains some control over her existence. To this extent, the horse tea does in fact have a healing effect. The story very carefully defers the question of the rootworker's capacity to effect physical cures, but it does clearly show the psychological value of folk belief.

In a similar manner, "The Revenge of Hannah Kemhuff" gives primacy to the mental rather than physical power of folk practices. In this story Walker makes explicit use of Zora Neale Hurston's *Mules and Men*, an early study of folklore practice among southern blacks.[15] Hannah, a sickly old black woman, appeals to a conjure woman for justice. She claims to be a good Christian but she feels that God "seemed to have other things on his mind" when she needed him in the past. In order to secure the justice she feels she deserves, she seeks out Tante Rosie to supplement the work of the Lord.

Her story is one of suffering and injustice. During the Depression, she dressed her children in the best clothes they had when she took them into town to receive government relief supplies. But this effort at dignity was used by Sarah Sadler Holley, the white distribution agent, to deny Hannah's request. As a result, her husband left her, and over the winter her children sickened and died. Hannah herself was forced into prostitution in order to survive; later she became an alcoholic. Meanwhile, Sarah was happily married, wealthy, and the mother of healthy children. Hannah seeks a redress of grievances through conjuration. She does not feel the necessity of witnessing justice; she only wants the assurance that it will come. When Tante Rosie assures her that Sarah will not outlive her by more than six months, "Mrs. Kemhuff turned and left, bearing herself grandly out of the room. It was as if she had regained her youth; her shawls were like a stately toga, her white hair seemed to sparkle" (*In Love and Trouble*, 70).

Hannah's renewed life comes not from anything done, but from the belief that something *can* be done to counteract the seemingly invincible power of whites. The curse prayer that she recites along with the narrator, an apprentice of the conjure woman, serves more to give voice to her anguish and anger than it does to evidence any real belief on her part. In fact, if the story can be taken in part as the education of the narrator in certain folk ways, then the lesson is about the power of language more than the power of demonic forces.

Tante Rosie never receives the things from Sarah necessary to enact the curse; it is not clear whether she ever intended to get them. Instead, she sends the apprentice to ask for the items—nail parings, hair, urine, feces, a bit of clothing—and to explain the reason for the request. Mrs. Holley, "the great white innovator and scientific scourge, forced to man the Christian fort against heathen nigger paganism" (*In Love And Trouble*, 76), denies both responsibility for Hannah's experience and belief in the power of conjuration.

Shortly after this encounter, Hannah dies, and a few months later, so does Sarah Holley. After the white woman's death, stories reach the narrator:

> A week after I'd talked to them [Sarah and her black maid] Mrs. Holley began having her meals in her bedroom upstairs. Then she started doing everything else there as well. She collected stray hairs from her head and comb with the greatest attention and consistency, not to say desperation. She ate her fingernails. But the most bizarre of all was her response to Mrs. Kemhuff's petition for a specimen of feces and water. Not trusting any longer the earthen secrecy of the water mains, she no longer flushed. Together with the nanny Mrs. Holley preferred to store those relics of what she ate (which became almost nothing and then nothing, the nanny had told Caroline) and they kept it all in barrels and plastic bags in the upstairs closets. (*In Love And Trouble*, 79–80)

Not the curse, but the effort to make the curse impossible, destroys Sarah Holley. Again she seeks to deny Hannah her needs, but the denial, in a perfect balancing of history, becomes the vehicle of satisfaction. And again, as in the case of Miss Jane Pittman's curse on Albert Cluveau, the word and not the act is effective. The ability to call up not spirits but the truth of history is the power of the powerless. And it works because the powerful, no matter how strong their ideology or how effective their oppression, cannot erase the reality of human experience, because, as Sarah Holley's obsession with her body demonstrates, they are themselves part of that reality. Despite their efforts, traces always remain of suffering and joy; giving voice to those traces delegitimizes whatever claims the system may have to truth. Those who remember and who find the strength to speak save themselves and damn the oppressors.

The pervasiveness of erasure and the persistence of traces are found in "Everyday Use." On the surface it seems, like Bambara's "My Man Bovanne," a rather simple story of the conflict of generations. A rural black mother tells of the return of her daughter from the city, where she has acquired a new, African name and a black nationalist ideology. In an argument over some family heirlooms, between this daughter and another, self-effacing one who has remained at home, the mother sides with the one who stays and the nationalist leaves in anger. But underlying this family spat is a deeper difference between the world views of the ideologues and the folk; fundamental to this difference are their opposed perspectives on history and art. Ultimately, the irony emerges that the ignorant rural folk are more true to the principles of nationalism than the far more educated nationalists themselves.

The narrator establishes very early on that she is a woman very much at home in her world, but also that she is marked by the larger world of the dominant society. She records a recurring dream in which she and her daughter Dee are reunited on a national television program, and she engages in witty repartee with Johnny Carson. This dream to her symbolizes success. But she always awakes to a less pleasant reality: "But that is a mistake. I know even before I wake up. Who ever knew a Johnson with a quick tongue? Who can even imagine me looking a strange white man in the eye? It seems to me I have talked to them always with one foot raised in flight, with my head turned in whichever way is farthest from them" (*In Love And Trouble*, 49). A woman who feels safe in her own home, she lacks the confidence to confront anything outside. She mixes a fear of the white world with an admiration of it as presented to her by mass culture.

This lack of confidence is only intensified in her younger daughter: "Maggie will be nervous until after her sister goes: she will stand hopelessly in corners, homely and ashamed of the burn scars down her arms and legs, eying her sister with a mixture of envy and awe" (*In Love And Trouble*, 47). Maggie cannot even feel secure in her own house or in the presence of her sister, much less in confrontation with a larger world. The burns came from a fire a dozen years earlier that destroyed their home and marred Maggie's life permanently. Such characterizations suggest that the folk do not contain some mysterious spirit that enables them to transcend the conditions of their lives. Within history, whatever strength they achieve must develop in that context.

In contrast to them is Dee, who "would always look anyone in the eye" (*In Love And Trouble*, 49). She seems to have stepped outside of the history that has so determined the lives of her relatives. This difference is the product of constitution more than education: her main response to the fire that scarred Maggie was joy that such an undesirable home was destroyed. Her appearance on this trip home only heightens the differences:

> A dress down to the ground, in this hot weather. A dress so loud it hurts my eyes. There are yellows and oranges enough to throw back the light of the sun. I feel my whole face warming from the heat waves it throws out. Earrings gold, too, and hanging down to her shoulders. Bracelets dangling and making noises when she moves her arm up to shake the folds of the dress out of her armpits. The dress is loose and flows, and as she walks closer, I like it. I hear Maggie go "Uhnnnh" again. It is her sister's hair. It stands straight up like the wool on a sheep. It is black as night and around the edges are two long pigtails that rope about like small lizards disappearing behind her ears. (*In Love And Trouble*, 52)

Even with a narrator struggling to be sympathetic, the portrayal reveals some distaste. The animal references (sheep, pigtails, lizards) suggest a different order of being, despite the accompanying sense of admiration.

Dee reinforces this alienation when she starts taking Polaroid snapshots of the house, its inhabitants, and the farm animals, as though she were a tourist or a social scientist preserving exotic phenomena. She then introduces herself as Wangero Leewanika Kemanjo, because, she explains, Dee is dead: "I couldn't bear it any longer, being named after the people who oppress me" (*In Love And Trouble*, 53). The mother then explains the long history of the name within the family, a bit of heritage which her daughter finds frustrating.

The narrator's ability to take this conversation seriously is open to question. For the next two pages, "Wangero" is the designation used to identify that speaker of dialogue. "Dee" completely disappears, and so does the use of the pronoun *she*. After this section, she consistently places one of the names in parentheses as an appositive to the other, thus: Dee (Wangero). Even in the most intense moments of conflict, she uses this designation. Similarly the young man accompanying Dee introduces himself as Hakim-a-barber, and the narrator thinks to herself, "I wanted to ask him was he a barber, but I didn't really think he was, so I didn't ask" (*In Love And Trouble*, 54). Despite dismissing this little joke, she later refers to him as "the barber." By foregrounding names in this manner, the narrator, as narrator but not as active character, undercuts the pretensions of her daughter. Thus, in typical trickster fashion, she can be two things at once.

A serious concern underlies this masking. In African and Afro-American lore, naming invokes the soul of the individual.[16] Dee's name embodies the spirits of her ancestors, and in denying it, she denies her heritage and the essence of her being, which are in fact the same thing. The self she chooses to create through the name Wangero is a false self because it is based on a false sense of her past. The narrator's implicit rejection of the new name in effect affirms the truth of history.

This rejection becomes explicit when Wangero indicates that she has come to collect artifacts rather than to see her family. She lays claim to a butter churn, thinking she can do something "artistic" with it, and, most important, to take a group of quilts made by her grandmother. When the narrator objects that the quilts have been promised to the younger sister, Wangero protests, " 'Maggie can't appreciate these quilts!' she said. 'She'd probably be backward enough to put them to everyday use' " (*In Love and Trouble*, 57). The richness of irony lies in the word "backward," for precisely such "backward" people as her ancestors created such works of art in the first place. Moreover, such objects gain much of their significance precisely because they were intended for "everyday use." In this sense,

144

they exist in an African artistic tradition that does not distinguish aesthetic and utilitarian functions;[17] it is Wangero's desire to put them on display—she intends to hang the quilts on a wall—that is part of an "alien," Eurocentric conception of art.

For the mother, the using of the quilt in her family is most important; if it is "used up" in the process, that is simply a condition of history not to be especially regretted. Maggie's real inheritance is not the object but the skill: " 'She can always make some more,' I said. 'Maggie knows how to quilt' " (*In Love And Trouble*, 58). While Dee has gone out into the world and now returned to repossess her history, Maggie, in her own "backward" way, has been living and perpetuating it. Thus, aesthetically, the artistic work gains its value and meaning in its social and historical context. To remove it from that context, even in the names of History and Art, reduces it to a mere object.

Linked to this aesthetic point is a psychological one. Maggie, seeing herself as one of life's victims, offers to surrender the quilts to her more forceful sister: "When I looked at her like that something hit me in the top of my head and ran down to the soles of my feet. Just like when I'm in church and the spirit of God touches me and I get happy and shout. I did something I had never done before: hugged Maggie to me, then dragged her on into the room, snatched the quilts out of Miss Wangero's hands and dumped them into Maggie's lap. Maggie just sat there on my bed with her mouth open" (*In Love And Trouble*, 58). The passive resistance to Wangero that has been going on throughout the story finally emerges not merely as rebellion but as affirmation of something else. For the first time, the narrator sees Maggie not as an object to be pitied but as a subject with intrinsic worth. It is not Dee-Wangero, with her education, ideology, and African name, but Maggie, with her scars, her humility, and her talent, who is the truest descendant of the family. In this sense, the quilts rightly belong to Maggie not because of the mother's whim, or even because of her promise, but because Maggie herself is the context in which they have their fullest value; she carries within her the family history that gives them meaning. And her everyday use of them will be their fulfillment as works of art.

Ironically, the narrative, as a written text, both affirms and denies its aesthetic theme. It is not merely an artistic object but is useful both for the author and the reader as a way of communicating certain aesthetic, politi-

145

cal, and moral principles. It achieves the same combination of functions as the quilts it describes. It also carries within it a sense of its historical context; the references to Johnny Carson, to the Black Muslims, and to black nationalism place it in time. Yet its usefulness and its context do not lead to its being used up; as long as any copies of it exist, it has permanence. Moreover, no matter how many students read it or how many scholars interpret it, the text remains untouched. In this sense, it has no history; it cannot be a folk form like quilt making or oral narrative. Thus, for the black literary artist, there is a perpetual enactment of a contradiction: the very forms that give value to the experience the artist renders cannot be the form by which the rendering is done.

Meridian (1976) is Walker's most impressive effort to incorporate history, folk forms, and the conditions of women into fiction. While the time frame in which it operates is not extended, taking in only the period just before and during the civil rights movement, the use of legends and folk tales adds historical depth in matters of race and gender. In addition, the technique of repetition moves it into the realm of cyclical time. As in *The Third Life of Grange Copeland,* the tension is between those who see that time as changelessness, which reduces people to ciphers, and those who see it as the pattern of growth and individuation. In *Meridian,* as in *Invisible Man,* the powerful have a reductive, mechanistic vision, which is opposed by those who have or seek some connection with the folk in order to achieve an individual voice. The conflict in Walker's novel operates on three levels: gender, sexual politics, and race. These are not mutually exclusive categories, but rather dynamically related aspects of the basic quest for expression and, through it, power.

Gender in this book has to do with the imposition of certain definitions on the lives of women. The opening chapter establishes the basic pattern with the story of Marilene O'Shay, whose body, "Preserved in Life-Like Condition," is carried around in a trailer by her husband and put on display for the paying public. A flier explains her history:

> According to the writer, Marilene's husband, Henry, Marilene had been an ideal woman, a "goddess," who had been given "everything she *thought* she wanted." She had owned a washing machine, furs, her own car and a full-time housekeeper-cook. All she had to do, wrote Henry, was "lay back and be pleasured." But she, "corrupted by the honeyed tongues of evildoers that

146

dwell in high places far away," had gone outside the home to seek her "pleasuring," while still expecting him to foot the bills. [18]

When Henry finds her with another man, he kills them both and throws their bodies in the Great Salt Lake. As a consequence, one observer notes, he "explained everything to the 'thorities up there and they forgive him, preacher forgive him, everybody forgive him. Even her ma. 'Cause this bitch was doing him wrong, and that ain't right!" Later, her body washes up on shore, and Henry recovers it. "Thought since she was so generous herself she wouldn't mind the notion of him sharing her with American public. He saw it as a way to make a little spare change in his ol' age" (*Meridian*, 8–9). His concern for her well-being during her life is directly related to his ability to turn her into an object for his own purposes. When she asserts her own preference, she must be destroyed. Dead, she becomes a nonthreatening object he can again manipulate.

But his own grotesque behavior is aided and abetted by that of society. At all levels, it reinforces his belief that she is merely a piece of property to be handled in whatever way pleases him. In sanctioning his definition of marriage and womanhood, in forgiving his crime, and in paying to see the freak show, the social order reifies Marilene. The exhibition itself functions in the same way as a cautionary tale: for both men and women, it demonstrates the permissible limits of female behavior.

Variations on this theme appear in a number of stories told early in the novel. The Wild Child, an abandoned girl who lives on the garbage of the community, is refused a home by the "decent" people of the college Meridian attends. When she dies, the president will not permit her funeral to be held in the campus chapel. The commemoration of Fast Mary of the Tower is a secret ceremony disguised as a May Day celebration. It recalls a girl who, fearful of discovery, killed and chopped to pieces her illegitimate baby as soon as it was born. Found out, she was flogged in front of her parents and teachers, then locked in her family's attic, where she shortly after committed suicide.

The most folk-oriented of the stories is the legend of Louvinie, a very dark slave woman who told terrifying tales. Part of the legend was that her parents in Africa functioned as detectives. When a crime had been committed, the mother would visit the village to learn as many details as possible.

Then she and her husband would weave them into a narrative told to the entire village. In a manner not explained, they were thus able to get the criminal to reveal himself. Louvinie's tales, on the contrary, seem to serve only as entertainment for children. On one occasion, a child of the master is so frightened that his weakened heart fails and he dies. The truth of his condition, unknown to Louvinie, is brought into the open by her narrative just as the murderers were revealed by her parents. For this "crime" of too-effective storytelling, she is punished by having her tongue cut out. She buries it under a scraggly magnolia tree, which slowly develops into the largest tree on the plantation. Named the Sojourner, the tree is said to have magical qualities: a slave hidden in it would be invisible to whites. Much later, it becomes Fast Mary's one friend on campus; it served as a trysting place for lovers (none of whom are ever caught); and it is the site of the Wild Child's funeral. After the funeral the students, in a frenzy of anger over the administration's behavior, riot, but the only damage is the cutting down of the Sojourner.

In every case, the female character or image is mutilated and destroyed for expressing the truth of her own being. Failure to become simply an object leads inevitably to destruction. For Meridian, who must deal with all of these tales in trying to form her own identity, there is clearly a warning of the difficulties she must face. But the problem is complicated for her by the story of her mother, who, unlike the others, does conform. She gave up the life of the single schoolteacher, because she thought that there was something in wifehood and motherhood she was missing: "There grew in her a feeling that the mothers of her pupils, no matter that they envied her her clothes, her speech, her small black car, pitied her. And in their harried or passive but always overweight and hideously dressed figures she began to suspect a mysterious inner life, secret from her, that made them willing, even happy, to endure" (*Meridian*, 40).

She soon discovers that the only secret is a horrible one: "The mysterious inner life that she had imagined gave them a secret joy was simply a full knowledge of the fact that they were dead, living just enough for their children" (*Meridian*, 40–41). She has fulfilled the socially imposed role of woman, only to find it a living death. "Creativity was in her, but it was refused expression" (*Meridian*, 41). In her only real contact with her daughter, she inflicts on her a sense of guilt; whenever Meridian seeks to

148

express her feeling to her mother, she is answered with, "Have you stolen anything?"

Thus, the conditions for Meridian's life as a woman are established: acquiescence to the social role means frustration and guilt, while efforts at self-realization will be met with ridicule, criticism, and even violence. When she cannot take seriously her responsibilities as housewife and sexual partner, her husband feels justified in being unfaithful and is supported in this by the community. When she tries to take care of her child, she cannot prevent the upwelling of a desire to murder him, but when she gives him up in order to attend college, her mother and other women accuse her of irresponsibility. She is burdened with a triple load of guilt: for her mother's unhappiness, for her own ambitions, for her son's loss of a mother. One of the motivations for her behavior throughout the book is her desire to understand and perhaps alleviate this burden. She refuses to surrender her quest for identity, but she also refuses any simplistic escape from the guilt. The narratives of other women help her to see the larger pattern of oppression, but they do not offer hope for change. That must come within the context of her own concrete experience.

The opportunity for her comes in the form of oppression of a different kind: racism. The book concerns itself not so much with acts of oppression by white supremacists, though those occasionally are presented, as with the impacts of such acts on the victims. Again, as in the case of the stories of women, a basic story is repeated. The initial tale concerns Meridian's father, a history teacher who discovers that his land is an ancient burial ground for Indians. He becomes obsessed with their traditions and sufferings and cannot escape a sense of responsibility. When his wife disclaims any black involvement in the treatment of native Americans and points out that Indians held slaves and fought for the Confederacy, her husband can only respond, "I never said either side was innocent or guilty, just ignorant. They've been a part of it, we've been a part of it, everybody's been a part of it for a long time" (Meridian, 47). He attempts to redress some of the historical wrong by deeding his property to a wandering Indian, but, in a manner consistent with his own traditions, the man stays on the land for a few months and then returns the deed. He lacks the Western sense of private ownership of land that conditions the father's gesture.

But this conditioning does not exclude him from the sacred experience

149

of the land. Like his grandmother before him and Meridian after him, he knows ecstasy at certain moments in the center of the serpent mound. Feather Mae's experience is typical:

> When she stood in the center of the pit, with the sun blazing down directly over her, something extraordinary happened to her. She felt as if she had stepped into another world, into a different kind of air. The green walls began to spin, and her feeling rose to such a high pitch the next thing she knew she was getting up off the ground. She knew she had fainted but she felt neither weakened nor ill. She felt renewed, as from some strange spiritual intoxication. Her blood made warm explosions through her body, and her eyelids stung and tingled. (*Meridian*, 49–50)

The ecstasy seems directly connected to locating oneself in the center of the mound; Meridian and her father debate whether the "craziness" they share with her great-grandmother is an experience of death or life. They do know that the past contains much more than facts and bones.

The negation of their understanding comes when the state discovers the historical value of the land and takes it over with minimal compensation to Mr. Hill. They then set up a state park, and refuse to allow blacks into it. Thus, the true history of the sacred serpent becomes the cycle of dispossession. The spiritual significance of this is made clear when Meridian returns after the park has been integrated and tries to find ecstasy. "But there were people shouting and laughing as they slid down the sides of the great Serpent's coil. Others stood glumly by, attempting to study the meaning of what had already and forever been lost" (*Meridian*, 52). The state, by considering history primarily as entertainment, has succeeded in suppressing the meaning of history.

Similarly, Meridian finds both outside and within the civil rights movement an effort to suppress concrete experiences of both ecstasy and suffering. One evidence of this is a partial listing of those assassinated during the 1960s; included in the list are both those who represented hope, such as John Kennedy and Martin Luther King, and those who represented anger, such as Malcolm X and Patrice Lumumba. These well-known acts of violence are repeated in Meridian's story of the cheerful nameless young girl she encourages to join a march, only to see her arrested and beaten by the police. Also, Tommy Odds, one of the young activists who has succeeded in getting a group of street-corner men to participate in the voter registration drive, is shot coming out of a church. His arm is amputated, and the only way he knows to express his rage is by raping the white wife of his friend Truman. In all of these cases, the attempt to articulate historical wrongs and to demand change is met with violence. Just as women seeking expression were killed, so those desiring an end to racism were silenced.

The movement itself engages in suppression, for it, like racism, has an ideology and a history. Walker traces the changes from a somewhat awkwardly integrated organization to one that is almost exclusively black, and from a nonviolent one to one that argues for self-defense and even armed revolution. Meridian goes through these changes but, unlike others, her sense of suffering and responsibility makes the transition a difficult one. In a confrontation with the members of her group, she is asked the crucial question: "Would you kill for the revolution?" She explains that she is perfectly willing to die, but that killing is another matter, since the snuffing out of life, even that of one's enemies, cannot be taken lightly:

> Meridian alone was holding on to something the others had let go. If not completely, then partially—by their words today, their deeds tomorrow. But what none of them seemed to understand was that she felt herself to be, not holding on to something from the past, but *held* by something in the past: by the memory of old black men in the South who, caught by surprise in the eye of a camera, never shifted their position but looked directly back; by the sight of young girls singing in a country choir, their hair shining with brushings and grease, their voices the voices of angels. When she was transformed in church it was always by the purity of the singer's souls, which she could actually *hear,* the purity that lifted their songs like a flight of doves above her music-drunken head. If they committed murder—and to her even revolutionary murder was murder—*what would the music be like?* (*Meridian,* 14–15)

The revolution, because it would deny the songs, is ultimately no different from the oppressive system it seeks to destroy. Both would efface the concrete history of suffering and joy and replace it with a mechanized order intolerant of variety and thus of human life itself. Meridian's choice, incomprehensible to the revolutionaries, is to return to the people and to preserve the songs.

This new life for her is one of struggle rather than pleasure. The return to the folk seems to intensify rather than relieve the burden of her personal history. Haunted by the images of her mother and son, she questions the value of her actions. To Truman Held, who is haunted by *her*, her behavior seems absurd. In the opening scene, she leads a protest by children who want to see the corpse of Marilene O'Shay. Mostly but not exclusively black, these are the children of workers in the town's guano factory. They are restricted to one day's attendance at the freak show because the other residents believe that they, like their parents, smell of dung. Meridian and the children confront the town authorities, who have even threatened to use a tank against them, and achieve a victory. The point, Meridian later explains to Truman, is not that some great moral principle has been defended but rather that the children have seen for themselves, without having to spend their money, that the display is fake. Implicitly, she has taught them the value of resistance to the false images of the dominant society, both the image of Marilene O'Shay and the image of themselves as lesser beings. Both Truman and Anne-Marion, a revolutionist friend also obsessed with Meridian, fail to see the value of actions that do not contribute to the grand sweep of History. Meeting the concrete needs of small groups of individuals seems to them an ineffective (or undignified) way to bring about social change.

Moreover, she pays a high price for such small gains. She has given up almost all possessions and depends on the people she helps for food, clothing, and shelter. She is physically deteriorating: her skin is sallow and her hair has fallen out. Most important, she seems to suffer from the inversion of her youthful ecstasy. Each time she leads a public demonstration, she lapses into a catatonic state shortly after its conclusion; she requires several hours of rest in order to recover. Her behavior is that of someone seeking not merely salvation, but sainthood. She punishes her flesh in an attempt to purge all guilt and achieve spiritual perfection; she serves others because "they *appreciate* it when someone volunteers to suffer" (*Meridian*, 12). But her quest is ultimately a secular one, for she seeks not religious but political conversion. The spirit for her is human, and the goal is the revolution of the social order. All her acts resist the present structure and instill in the powerless a sense of their own potency. She seeks the renewing of her own and the people's spirits because that will preserve the songs while bringing about the revolution.

The plot device which unifies the themes of sexism, racism, and spiritual quest is the romantic triangle. The complex relationships of Meridian,

Truman, and Lynne are the working through of these themes. Lynne, a white woman who comes from the North to participate in the Movement in its early days, has complicated motives for coming and staying:

> To Lynne, the black people of the South were Art. This she begged for-giveness for and tried to hide, but it was no use. To her eyes, used to Northern suburbs where every house looked sterile and identical even before it was completely built, where even the flowers were uniform and their nicknames were already in dictionaries, the shrubs incapable of strong odor or surprise of shape, and the people usually stamped with the seals of their professions; to her, nestled in a big chair made of white oak strips, under a quilt called The Turkey Walk, from Attapulsa, Georgia, in a little wooden Mississippi sharecropper bungalow that had never known paint, the South— and the black people living there—was Art. The songs, the dances, the food, the speech. . . . If Mississippi is the worst place in America for black people, it stood to reason she thought, that the Art that was their lives would flourish best there. (*Meridian*, 128)

To see people as Art is the reverse side of seeing them as interchangeable cogs in the social machine. It makes them more than human for enduring their suffering and making a worthwhile life despite it. But like the mechanistic vision, the artistic one rejects the painful reality of that suffering. By seeing it as good and meaningful, it does not take seriously the importance of alleviating it. Lynne's recognition of the error of her thought does not prevent her from using blacks as a way of dealing with her private difficulties. She marries Truman in part because he is a highly desirable expression of that Art. Moreover, to marry him is to escape from the constraints of her Jewish parents. When these acts backfire as Truman leaves her and her parents treat her as dead, she turns to Meridian as the all-enduring black woman who will relieve her anguish.

Truman, on the other hand, defines both his manhood and his identity through women. Like Lynne, he has a degree of courage in his politics, but his identity must come through others. Meridian is at first overwhelmed by his sophistication: he is an artist, he speaks French, he knows the larger world. He finds her attractive because she is beautiful, black, and unafraid of the violence activists face in the streets and jails. But this interest is short-lived: he is soon drawn to the white college women who participate in the summer marches. To him, they represent the world he wishes to be a part of. As he tells Meridian at one point, "They read *The New York Times*" (*Meridian*, 141). This quest for identification with the white world, both as a positive ambition and as a desire to escape his blackness, leads him to abandon Meridian and eventually to abandon the movement in order to live in New York. Later, when black rather than white is in vogue, he seeks to return to Meridian. When she refuses him, he goes back north, leaves Lynne, takes a studio apartment where he does massive paintings and sculptures of maternal black figures, and simultaneously cohabitates with a beautiful blonde from Alabama. In the present time of the novel, he has returned to Meridian because, like Lynne, he needs her to soothe his troubled mind.

But Meridian, as noted above, herself needs healing. Her service to others does not seem, in and of itself, to provide sustenance; in fact, it robs her of her strength. She gives others their voices, but she cannot seem to find her own. She begins to recover it in a church service. What she notes first are the changes: the songs are more militant, the minister talks about political change rather than heaven, and the stained glass window pictures not a passive Jesus, but a vibrant B. B. King, guitar in one hand and sword in the other. This image of the joining of the sacred and the secular realms appropriately has music as its motif; the linking of the spirituals and the blues makes possible an integrated folk expression that is one way of keeping alive the songs. Thus, she discovers that even within the traditions, there is change and a refusal merely to endure the suffering.

The focal point of the service is a ritual of remembrance. At the altar sits the picture of a young civil rights activist slain a few years earlier. The father of the young man stands before the congregation. He had gone temporarily insane at the time of the boy's death and had destroyed his own home out of grief and lost love: "He had thought that somehow, the power of his love alone (and how rare even he knew it was!) would save his son. But his love—selfless, open, a kissing, touching love—had only made his son strong enough to resist everything that was not love" (*Meridian*, 201).

Now he stands in front of the church to say the three words he always says, "My son died" (*Meridian*, 202). After a few moments he sits down and the service winds down to its conclusion. The function of the ceremony is to make forgetting impossible for the congregation:

154

"Look," they were saying, "we are slow to awaken to the notion that we are only as other men and women, and even slower to move in anger, but we are gathering ourselves to fight for and protect what your son fought for on behalf of us. If you will let us weave your story and your son's life and death into what we already know—into the songs, the sermons, the 'brother and sister'—we will soon be so angry we cannot help but move." (*Meridian*, 204)

The forms created are not arbitrary or abstract; they emerge as the natural expression of the people for embodying their own sense of their experience. The change that they facilitate will be organic because it will grow out of their concrete needs. In this sense, the ceremony exists for "everyday use," to change history by recalling the fullness of the suffering.

For Meridian, the ritual serves as liberation more than remembrance:

In comprehending this, there was in Meridian's chest a breaking as if a tight string binding her lungs had given way, allowing her to breathe freely. For she understood, finally, that the respect she owed her life was to continue, against whatever obstacles, to live it, and not to give up any particle of it without a fight to the death, preferably *not* her own. And that this existence extended beyond herself to those around her because, in fact, the years in America had created them One Life. (*Meridian*, 204)

This ritual, which emerges out of the concrete history of the folk, teaches her the difference between suffering and victimization. The pain occurs, but the service is a reminder to her that suffering is not a natural and necessary state of existence, that accepting it as such is an act of cooperation with those who inflict it. The guilt that she had felt for her son, her mother, and her own efforts is cleansed in her refusal to be a victim any longer. By choosing life—personal, sexual, racial—she cures her diseased soul. By taking responsibility, she rejects the guilt that has been imposed on her. She will be the singer of the old songs that make possible the new world. And this world is the world of the black community, which shares her vision and understanding.

But before she enters this new life, she must bring the old one full circle. She does this by producing a symbolic new son, Truman. In the last few chapters, she teaches him all she knows about caring for the people; he must be brought fully into the folk world and made to see it as a real and human world if he is to find his truest self, free of the stipulations of the

155

white world and his dependence on women for his identity. In the end, he inherits her role: "Truman turned, tears burning his face, and began, almost blindly, to read the poems she had left on the walls. He could not bring himself to read the letters yet. It was his house now, after all. His cell. Tomorrow the people would come and bring him food. Someone would come and milk his cow. They would wait patiently for him to perform, to take them along the next guideless step. Perhaps he would" (*Meridian*, 228). Meridian has left him to find his own song through the burden of responsibility. Having found her own voice, she leaves him to find his. In this painful quest, he is not even permitted her guidance, for the past is his and so the song must be as well. Thus, the text implies a cyclical pattern in history; the return is always necessary for true change. Paradoxically, one makes progress only by going back to the beginning, which is to be found among the people. Meridian has gone through her initiation and can move on; Truman begins his, and Anne Marion, we are led to believe, must follow him. The ritual allows one to cease attempting to become a self in terms of the values of the dominant culture or the revolutionaries that are its mirror image; and instead to be the healed, growing self that the folk world makes possible.

The oppression of women has become so important a theme to Walker that it has come to dominate her most recent works. The stories in *You Can't Keep a Good Woman Down* (1981) have a polemical thrust that leads many of them to resemble the propagandistic black art of the 1960s. What distinguishes such pieces from the political implications of *Meridian* is the lack of a dialectical sense of character and theme. Certain figures resist sexism, but they are not conditioned by the history that it is a part of. The impulse, in other words, is to create ciphers on both sides of the polemical fence. Significantly, folk material is seldom used in these pieces. The two best stories do use such material.

"A Sudden Trip Home in the Spring" literally returns its main character to the folk world. Sarah Davis, a young southern black, attends Cresselton, a prestigious northern women's college. She sees her life here as an escape from her past: "Talfinger [Hall] was her home now; it suited her better than any home she'd ever known."[19] But this sense does not blind her to her position in this world: she is very much aware that the other women see her as something rare: "Her friends often teased Sarah about her beauty; they loved dragging her out of her room so that their boyfriends, naïve and worldly young men from Princeton and Yale, could see her. They never guessed she found this distasteful" (*Good Woman*, 125). Like Lynne in *Meridian*, they tend to see "their" black as a work of Art.

What makes Cresselton valuable to Sarah, despite her friends' unconscious condescension, is that it gives her access to the achievements of Western culture. Chagalls hang in the lobby, and she studies and talks about Cummings, Camus, and Giacometto. For her, these are the models for art and thought; the extent of her escape from the South is measured by her accumulation of the physical and intellectual artifacts of the dominant culture. But this does not mean that she simplistically denies her race. She uses the skills taught in art classes to paint images of black women that she hangs on her walls. But these are tied to white culture: "Sarah Davis's room was next door to the gallery, but her walls were covered with inexpensive Gauguin reproductions, a Rubens ("The Head of a Negro"), a Modigliani and a Picasso. There was a wall full of her own drawings, all of black women. She found black men impossible to draw or to paint; she could not bear to trace defeat onto blank pages. Her women figures were matronly, massive of arm, with a weary victory showing in their eyes" (*Good Woman*, 126).

The source of her art is less her experience of her heritage than her experience of other art. Her black women fit the stereotype of the marnmy, just as Truman Held's did. The fact that they are all the same suggests that she is working out of a white image much like the one-dimensional image her friends assume she is. Moreover, her inability to draw black men at all means that in fact she has erased the concrete history of her family that has enabled her to attend the school in the first place; the daughter and granddaughter of "defeated" men would have neither the energy or ambition to acquire such an education.

Having set up this state of certainty, Walker then puts Sarah through a ritual process that forces her to reevaluate both her past and her art. The death of her father means a return to the South and to all the emotional connections she has there. At first, the experience seems to validate her assumptions. Her father had been a sharecropper, a role she uses to compare him to Richard Wright's failed father. The mother was the strong one: "Her mother had stood stout against the years, clean gray braids shining across the top of her head, her eyes snapping, protective. Talking to her father. 'He called you out your name, we'll leave this place today. Not tomorrow. That be too late. Today!' Her mother was magnificent in her quick decisions" (*Good Woman*, 131). Sarah holds her father to blame for indecisiveness, a temperament she believes ultimately killed her mother. But her memory will not erase something more complex in her father's response to the mother's righteous anger: "But what about your garden, the children, the change of schools?" (*Good Woman*, 131). In other words, he desires stability and nurture for his family. What Sarah has always taken as weakness reveals itself to be a willingness to sacrifice his pride in order to obtain the greater good. Thus a complex pattern emerges wherein the parents together in a dialectical way attempt in the face of racism to have dignity and still provide for the future. The father gives up an appearance of manhood by giving in to his wife, but his way of doing so signifies his true understanding of fatherhood. As Sarah remembers, *"The moving killed her,* her father had said, *but the moving was also love"* (*Good Woman*, 132).

Her confrontation with her dead father aids in coming to terms with the family, but it is through her still-living grandfather that she begins to understand her heritage and possibilities. Unlike the father, he lacks even the appearance of defeat:

> He did not seem to bend under the grief of burying a son. His back was straight, his eyes dry and clear. He was simply and solemnly heroic; a man who kept with pride his family's trust and his own grief. *It is strange,* Sarah thought, *that I never thought to paint him like this, simply as he stands; without anonymous meaningless people hovering beyond his profile; his face turned proud and brownly against the light.* The defeat that had frightened her in the faces of black men was the defeat of black forever defined by white. But that defeat was nowhere on her grandfather's face. He stood like a rock, outwardly calm, the comfort and support of the Davis family. The family alone defined him, and he was not about to let them down. (*Good Woman*, 134–35)

The only way she has previously conceived of him has been as an abstraction, a symbol of eternal blackness rather than as a specific black man who has suffered and endured. Of course, if she had been able to consider him concretely, she would have come up against the extent to which the white world had defined her own sense of black men, including her father.

158

In this moment, she recognizes some difference from her fixed ideas, but there is a hint of sentimentality in her description of the grandfather. She wishes to turn him into art, to paint him. But he insists on something else: "If you want to make me, make me up in stone" (*Good Woman*, 135). To work in stone is to work in three dimensions and to work in the materials of the earth. Moreover, sculpting is associated with African art much more than painting. To carve his head in rock is to pay tribute to him as an ancestor who is full-bodied, not one that is an abstraction. His particular phrasing of the request has related connotations. In African cultures, the spirits of the ancestors inhabit the images of themselves; thus the figure Sarah crafts will, in a spiritual sense, *be* her grandfather.

In her enthusiasm for her rediscovery of her black past and its artistic possibilities, she sentimentally decides not to go back to Cresselton. But her brother, a "radical preacher," to whom she says, "You deliver your messages in person with your own body," has a more complex understanding of reality. Sentiment is not the same thing as craft: " 'You learn how to draw the face,' he said, 'then you learn how to paint me and how to make Grandpa up in stone. Then you can come home or go live in Paris, France. It'll be the same thing' " (*Good Woman*, 136). His wisdom is that repeated in folktales and slave narratives: take what you can get and make it your own. Learning to sculpt and paint no more commits one to surrender to the dominant culture than learning to read committed Frederick Douglass to believing in slavery. Only when one believes that "masters" define the possibilities of the craft is one imprisoned. Sarah must acquire the skills, not to imitate Giacometti or Rubens, but rather to give shape to her sense of the world and give expression to the values of her parents and grandparents. Once this knowledge is acquired, then she no longer needs to be in that place because she will carry that place in her through memory and imagination. Black art, then, is not so much a particular technique, use of language, or political position, as it is an attitude toward the experiences—aesthetic, personal, and cultural—that have made one an artist.

"1955" develops another aspect of the relationship of art and culture. Here we have the parallel developments of a legendary blues singer and a successful white singer who tries to understand the meaning of her music. The moral of the story is rather obvious: the white man, patterned after Elvis Presley, gains great success by singing her songs, but he fails to find either meaning or happiness in life. She, on the other hand, has much less but lives a fully human life and is around at the end to comment on his death and the superficiality of society.

What makes the story more than a simplistic allegory is the quest for the meaning of the song. From beginning to end, Traynor is obsessed with finding out what Gracie Mae Still's song means. Even though he sings it well enough to launch a meteoric career, he believes that it contains a secret only she can reveal. The form of the story is a series of repetitions of this quest. The dating of the various sections shows how Traynor changes externally but never with regard to the song. In each, he pays his respects to Gracie Mae, offers her some grand gift, and then renews his questioning. The first meeting after his initial celebrity establishes the pattern.

> I done sung that song seem like a million times this year, he said. I sung it on the Grand Ole Opry, I sung it on the Ed Sullivan show, I sung it on Mike Douglas, I sung it at the Cotton Bowl. . . . I don't have the faintest notion what that song means. Watchumean, what do it mean? It mean what is says. All I could think was: These suckers is making forty thousand a *day* offa my song and now they gonna come back and try to swindle me out of the original thousand. It's just a song, I said. Cagey. When you fool around with a lot of no count mens you sing a bunch of 'em. I shrugged. (*Good Woman,* 8)

He then gives her a new white Cadillac as a Christmas gift.

What Traynor never understands, because he cannot, is that the song grows out of the concrete history of this particular black woman and her community. It thus expresses a reality that cannot be purchased or investigated by himself or even articulated by Gracie Mae herself except by singing. The central problem is history:

> Now if I was to sing that song today I'd tear it up. 'Cause I done lived long enough to know it's *true*. Them words could hold me up.
> I ain't lived that long, he said. (*Good Woman,* 14)

Because he has not lived the life, he cannot truly sing the song. And this absence robs him of the enjoyment of his success. The relationship between the two is dialectical: the success came initially because he could effectively bring to the popular culture an inherently dishonest version of the song because he performed it with its history erased. But that very success, with its forms empty of content, became his history and thus made it even more difficult to comprehend the meaning.

Thus, the story becomes a comment on the relative natures and values of popular and folk art forms. The popular ones empty out the content that is the history: even Gracie Mae's children and grandchildren talk of the song as though it were Traynor's. In this manner the forms become meaningless but infinitely communicable. Thus, Gracie Mae's name appears on millions of copies of the record, but the meaning of her act is lost. On the other hand, the folk art maintains an organic connection between form and content, but for this reason, the art cannot be mass produced. It functions within history, and its meaning is subject to that history. Gracie Mae cannot tell Traynor what the song absolutely means because that meaning changes with each experience of her life, including her dealings with him. His death suggests the death-wish inherent in the drive for control and empty forms, while her continued life and energy constitute an appreciation of the vitality of the "dying" folk arts.

The Color Purple (1982), Walker's award-winning and much-praised novel, has achieved immense popularity. In part, this success can be explained because the book is, in essence, a "womanist"[20] fairy tale. Like Snow White, Celie is poisoned (psychologically in the novel) by an evil step-parent; like Cinderella, she is the ugly, abused daughter who ultimately becomes the princess; like Sleeping Beauty, she is awakened from her death-in-life by the kiss of a beloved; and like them all, she and her companions, after great travails, live happily ever after. Moreover, the fairy-tale quality is more than metaphoric, since major plot elements are worked out with fairy-tale devices. The story is generated out of what Vladimir Propp calls interdiction and violation of interdiction.[21] Celie is told by her evil stepfather, after he rapes her, that she must tell no one but God what he has done; she chooses to write her story, which, as shall be seen below, makes it a public text. Transformation from a life of shame to one of self-esteem occurs when Celie receives the physical embrace of the regal Shug Avery. Finally, the plot is resolved and the characters reunited through the exposure of villainy and the death of the primary villain, an event which reverses the dispossession of Celie and her sister Nettie.

Since the fairy tale itself is a folk form, albeit a European one, there is no obvious contradiction between it and the Afro-American and African materials that enrich the narrative. In fact, such materials enhance the sense of a faerie world where curses, coincidences, and transformations are possible. The power for healing and change latent in folk arts and practices important to black women—quilting, mothering, blues singing, "craziness," and conjure—fit the pattern of the female character in the fairy tale who is victimized but then saved through love and magic. One of the things that mark Walker's text as womanist is her insistence that these female capacities are a superior way of bringing about change. One trait that distinguishes *The Color Purple* from her earlier work is her setting up of an opposition between male and female folk wisdom; the former wisdom, passed from father to son, claims, in Walker's view, the natural inferiority of women and the need to keep them under control, through violence if necessary. What was implicit in *Grange Copeland* becomes explicit here as part of the oral tradition.

The dominating male voice is present as the first words of the narrative: "You better not never tell nobody but God. It'd kill your mammy."[22] These statements simultaneously demand female silence and place the responsibility for illicit behavior on the woman. They are spoken by the man Celie believes to be her father after he has raped her. In effect, he makes her voice rather than his action the fatal force in the family. By his definition, it is not his violation of taboo but Celie's violation of his command that will kill the mother. He presumes that his rules of order transcend those of the social order. But silence does not protect the women; the mother dies anyway, and Celie continues to be sexually assaulted. In fact, the father uses the silence as evidence of acquiescence to his desires. Neither Celie nor her mother exists for him except as ciphers to which he can arbitrarily assign meanings.

Appropriately, in this context, Celie chooses to write rather than speak to God. At one point, Nettie recalls a comment by her sister: "I remember one time you said your life made you feel so ashamed you couldn't even talk about it to God, you had to write it, bad as you thought your writing was" (*The Color Purple*, 110). On the one hand, the statement suggests the effectiveness of the father's threat; one so degraded as Celie denies herself even the most private speech act. Nonetheless, she can write. In this sense, the process of writing is itself associated with shame; it is the expression of

162

those beyond salvation, those who have been dehumanized. Writing, then, takes on those characteristics of the disreputable that, as indicated earlier, are linked with the folk culture. In entering the culture, it becomes dialectical. For example, the act of writing, though apparently motivated by Celie's desire to obey the original interdiction against speech, is clearly a violation of the command. Spoken words are transient; writing lasts as long as ink and paper. By putting down her thoughts, Celie makes possible discovery of her pain and victimization. The fundamental violation here is that she writes herself into humanity and thereby contradicts the stipulation that she be a mere cipher. She gives herself an inner life and a concrete history and thus an otherness that the patriarchal order denies her. In the folk tradition, then, her letters subvert oppression in the process of affirming it.

Celie's story concentrates first on the tyrannies exemplified by the initial interdiction. The first letter makes clear the source of her troubles: "He never had a kine word to say to me. Just say You gonna do what your mammy wouldn't. First he put his thing up gainst my hip and sort of wiggle it around. Then he grab hold my titties. Then he push his thing inside my pussy. When that hurt, I cry. He start to choke me, saying You better shut up and git used to it" (*The Color Purple,* 3). When she becomes pregnant, her dying mother blames her for bringing shame to the family. The father steals the baby and apparently kills it. Celie fears for the life of the second one. Then he marries again, casting her aside as waste material, but this does not end the threat to the family: "I see him looking at my little sister. She scared" (*The Color Purple,* 5). When Nettie attracts the interest of a widower, Celie advises her to take advantage of the opportunity: "I say Marry him, Nettie, an try to have one good year out your life. After that, I know she be big" (*The Color Purple,* 7). But the father has other ideas; he offers the older sister to Mr. _____ instead, arguing that she will make a better wife because she is ugly and not "fresh." The discussions between the two men take the form of negotiations over livestock; the deal is closed when a cow is included with the woman. Celie literally has become a commodity, one with a low exchange value.

Life with Mr. _____ (the designation Celie uses through most of the book) is no better. He continually beats and berates her, and he allows his children to treat her like a servant. He goes into periods of melancholy

163

during which he leaves the arduous tasks of the farm to Celie and his son Harpo. Moreover, he does not consider marriage a deterrent to his desires. He pursues Nettie when she comes to live with them, eventually forcing her to run away to avoid rape. His true love has always been Shug Avery, a blues singer with whom he lived years earlier. His affection for her produces the central irony of the book: though it initially damages Celie's self-esteem and their marriage, it eventually is the means of revitalization and rehumanization for both of them.

But the role of the blues singer, to be discussed in more detail below, is only one of the folk images in the book. Quilting, for example, functions as a way of creating female community in a world that represses female expression. Early in the story, Celie, who has largely accepted the male definition of woman's place, advises Harpo to beat his new wife into submission. She does this in part because she has trouble with the concept of an independent woman, since such a figure implicitly calls into question her own submissiveness. When Sofie confronts her with the consequences of her advice, she cannot adequately explain her action, but faces for the first time her hatred of her own womanhood. This awareness enables the two of them to establish rapport through the folk arts of the dozens and quilt-making. The exchange of insults allows them to vent any remaining hostility:

> I'm *so* shame of myself, I say. And the Lord he done whip me little bit too.
> The Lord don't like ugly, she say.
> And he ain't stuck on pretty.
> This open the way for our talk to turn another way. (*The Color Purple,* 38)

This ritual, usually associated with males, creates an equality and intimacy between them that guilt and anger had previously made impossible. It leads to the quilting, which has a healing influence: "Let's make quilt pieces out of these messed up curtains, she say. And I run git my pattern book. I sleeps like a baby now" (*The Color Purple,* 39). Later on, sewing on the quilt occasions opportunities to discuss various problems; moreover, the process itself is a way of literally keeping one's history. The yellow stars Celie makes out of Shug's dress recall the designs she used to make for her daughter Olivia's diapers. And in Africa, Nettie uses a quilt to force that

164

daughter's adoptive mother to remember Celie, a recollection that absolves Nettie of accusations against her and that allows Corrine to die in peace.

The African traditions, made available through the device of Nettie's letters, suggest the universality of oppression. The African male order, just like its American counterpart, denies the validity of female expression; girl children are not permitted to participate in the education provided by the missionaries, and they are considered the property of first their fathers and then their husbands. As a sign of their entry into womanhood, they undergo a ritual of scarification which literally marks their role in society. Interestingly, while Walker indicates here the African women's suffering, the only form of resistance she provides them is the Western education they surreptiously get from Nettie and Olivia. When whites appropriate the land, the very traditions of generosity and trust which the Olinka display lead to the destruction of the land and the tribe. The only option for the group is the *mbele*, a hidden area from which occasional acts of resistance can be carried out. But such a space is essentially an escape from rather than an engagement with the oppressive world. Significantly in this context, the missionaries return to America rather than stay to share the Africans' fate.

Afro-American women, in contrast, develop with models for resistance as well as healing. The first of these is the "crazy" woman, mentioned in the discussion of Bambara. The story of Sofie is explicitly the story of a woman who will not accept the rules of an oppressive order. She refuses to allow Harpo to beat her and in fact always wins their physical battles; some of the most humorous moments in the book are his attempts to explain away his inability to control her: "He say, Oh, me and that mule. She fractious, you know. She went crazy in the field the other day. By time I got her to head for home I was all banged up. Then when I got home, I walked smack dab into the crib door. Hit my eye and scratch my chin. Then when that storm come up last night I shet the window down on my hand" (*The Color Purple*, 35). Her more serious struggles are against white authority figures who presume to dictate her role. She talks back to the mayor's wife and then strikes the mayor when he attempts physically to put her "in her place." She is then beaten by the police and thrown in jail for assault. In prison, she constantly dreams of murder.

She is saved from further violence when Harpo, Celie, and Mr. _____ devise a Brer Rabbit scheme to ameliorate her situation. They send Harpo's new girlfriend, Squeaks, who is an unacknowledged relative of the warden, to tell him that Sofie would rather rot in prison than work as a maid for the mayor's wife. He, of course, immediately assigns her that task. Because this woman has already seen what she considers the black woman's crazy behavior, she is intimidated and Sofie suffers much less than she would have otherwise. "Craziness," then, is a form of resistance that allows for the expression of the frustrated humanity and creativity of black women.

Celie herself functions at one point as a conjure woman. When she decides to travel to Memphis with Shug, she delivers herself of a curse on Mr. _____: "Until you do right by me, I say, everything you even dream about will fail. I give it to him straight, just like it come to me. And it seem to come to me from the trees" (*The Color Purple*, 176). Walker uses here Zora Neale Hurston's notion[23] that the voice speaking is in fact that of a god using a human instrument: "A dust devil flew up on the porch between us, fill my mouth with dirt. The dirt say, Anything you do to me, already done to you" (*The Color Purple*, 176). The voice, whatever its source, speaks the truth of Celie's pent-up anger and sense of injustice. Speaking forth carries with it its own authority; the voice exposes the suffering that has been her life and gives her an interiority and humanity that others have denied her. Her conjuring, in other words, has creative moral force. Its effect is shown in Mr. _____'s decline, both physical and mental, during her absence; only when he takes steps to right the wrongs he has done her does his strength return. Significantly, his major wrong has been the withholding of correspondence between Celie and Nettie. When he accepts their right to expression, the curse is lifted.

The most important of the folk figures is the female blues singer Shug Avery. Like her music, she embodies both love and trouble. For Mr. _____, who has always loved her, she is the source of his dissatisfaction over everything, including Celie, that is not her. Moreover, she has had a negative impact on his reputation in the community; Celie's father uses their affair as an excuse not to allow him to marry Nettie. But that same love is his one saving virtue. When Shug becomes ill, he brings her to the house and nurses her back to health. Similarly, her encouragement allows Squeaks

(Mary Agnes) to find her own voice as a blues singer and to demand that she not be "called out of her name" by Harpo, who has previously treated her as insignificant.

Her most complex effect is on Celie. From the very beginning she makes a powerful impression: "Shug Avery was a woman. The most beautiful woman I ever saw. She more pretty than my mama. She bout ten thousand times more prettier then me. I see her there in furs. Her face rouge. Her hair like somethin tail. She grinning with her foot up on somebody motocar. Her eyes serious tho. Sad some" (*The Color Purple,* 8). Shug exists as something other than the reality in which Celie lives, and yet she is connected with that reality through Mr. _____. Thus she is not pure fantasy, a being representing escape from the harsh world of the present. The seriousness and sadness in her face suggest that she too has had unpleasant experiences and has lived through them. In addition, she opens for Celie the realm of the unconscious, giving this cipher another dimension of being.

The emergence of this dimension (which makes possible the conjuration described above) receives expression in the connection between Shug and Celie's gradual awareness of her own body. Walker emphasizes a relationship between the development of selfhood and the acceptance of female biology. Repeatedly, Celie talks of making herself wood, of not responding to either abuse or sexual intercourse. She protects herself, much as Velma did in *The Salt Eaters,* by denying the reality of her own flesh and emotion. Her rehumanization begins with her involuntary response to Shug's body: "First time I got the full sight of Shug Avery long black body with it black plum nipples, look like her mouth, I thought I had turned into a man" (*The Color Purple,* 45). Since Celie herself has never experienced sexual arousal, she assumes that stimulation is a male attribute. She feels urges that frighten her: "I feel like something pushing me forward. If I don't watch out I'll have hold of her hand, tasting her fingers in my mouth" (*The Color Purple,* 46). Part of what elicits this response is Shug's beauty, which sets a standard that Celie, who believes in conventional notions of female attractiveness, cannot hope to meet. Only when she learns the beauty of her own femaleness can she begin to accept her body and the self of which it is a part: "Stick the looking glass tween my legs. Ugh. All that hair. Then my pussy lips be black. Then inside look like a wet rose. It a lot prettier than you thought, ain't it? she say from the door" (*The Color*

Purple, 69). The discovery, not of an abstract, spiritual beauty, but of a physical one inherent in womanhood begins the psychological change in Celie. She now becomes someone worthy of the love of Shug, and someone who did *not* deserve the treatment she received from her stepfather and Mr. _____.

For both Celie and Mr. _____, Shug's beauty is linked to her singing. She can give voice to the pains they each endure silently. For Celie, she implies the possibility of creativity in a context other than the endless cycle of reproduction:

> What that song? I ast. Sound low down dirty to me. Like what the preacher tell you its sin to hear. Not to mention sing.
>
> She hum a little more. Something come to me, she say. Something I made up. Something you help scratch out my head. (*The Color Purple*, 48)

Though Shug sings the "devil's music," Celie must balance this "sin" against her affection for the singer/sinner. A tension is created between the rules of the church and the attractiveness of the violation. Again Celie is implicated in a crime of verbal expression, just as she was at the beginning of her story.

But if Shug brings love and creativity, she also brings and experiences troubles. She holds herself responsible for the death of Mr. _____'s first wife, who took a violent lover when she could not counteract her husband's infatuation with the singer. Moreover, her story of her inability to stay with one man is a tale of loneliness; she loved Mr. _____ (whom she calls Albert), but she wanted her freedom more than love. Thus, her history is the classic blues dilemma she describes in her songs. She creates the same tension for Celie, whose very love for Shug makes her vulnerable to despair when her beloved finds another man; the opening of her life involves pains which she did not experience before she felt worthy of love. Thus, Shug as a folk figure opens possibilities rather than constructs completed orders of reality.

However, another of her contributions to creativity leads to a resolution of the text's conflicts that is more appropriate to the fairy tale than to Afro-American folklore. At her suggestion, Celie begins making pants, especially purple ones (a color associated with Shug's regal bearing), for herself and others. At first, this traditional art works in a folk manner; though she desires to kill Albert for suppressing the letters, she puts her energy into sewing instead: "A needle and not a razor in my hand, I think" (*The Color Purple*, 125). But, when the immediate motive passes, pants making becomes a business and Celie a petty capitalist who turns her farm into a home factory. When it is revealed that Albert has always enjoyed sewing, any lingering hostility vanishes, and they sit on the porch stitching "folksy" pants and shirts.

This resolution is part of a larger pattern of closure in the narrative. Harpo turns his house into a blues club where Shug and Mary Agnes sing, while he works at his favorite activity, cooking. When the stepfather dies, a long-hidden will appears which shows that the land, house, and store he had possessed for years in fact were left to Celie and Nettie. And, finally, the long-lost sister escapes from Africa and turns up at the farm with Celie's children, Olivia and Adam, who has scarified his own face to identify himself with the suffering womanhood of his African bride. Thus, all the characters are reunited in a feminized space with female traits and free of the hostility, oppression, guilt and cruelty of the male and white worlds.

But this very liberation contradicts the nature of the folk sensibility on which it is based. History, with the suffering and joy it brings, cannot, in the folk worldview, be transcended; it must be lived through. Walker seeks to resolve the dialectic by making all males female (or at least androgynous), all destroyers creators, and all difference sameness. In this process, she must move outside the very conflicts that generated the sewing, the blues singing, and the voice of Celie herself. Such an effort makes sense for one who wishes to articulate a political position; resolution creates a sacred, utopian space which justifies the ideology on which it is based. But this creation is in fact another system that requires the same denial of history and difference as the order it has supplanted. To live "happily ever after," as the folk characters do in *The Color Purple*, is, ironically, to live outside the folk world.

Alice Walker's feminist and antiracist perspective has given her access to new literary material by allowing her to see the value of the folklore of black women and the history which has shaped that lore. In *The Third Life of Grange Copeland*, *In Love and Trouble*, and *Meridian*, she has emphasized suffering and the struggle to resist it through folk values. In much of *You Can't Keep a Good Woman Down*, she moves away from storytelling into polemic, even within narratives. Questions of race and sexual identity become more absolute, and much of the complexity of historical sensibility that feeds folk material is lost. In *The Color Purple,* she has in effect moved to allegorical form in order to transcend history and envision the triumph of those principles she espouses. But in doing so, she has neutralized the historical conditions of the very folk life she values.

Four

Beyond Realism: The Fictions of Gayl Jones and Toni Morrison

GAYL JONES AND TONI MORRISON create bizarre, oppressive worlds that are naturalized by the folk wisdom of the black communities that constitute their narrative settings. Within these worlds are found aliens, characters who seem abnormal because they fail to adjust to the conventions of the social order. They are seen as insane, grotesque, or perhaps merely a bit "crazy," in the sense meant by Alice Walker.[1] In the interaction between alien and world, it becomes clear that the world itself, in its pursuit of sexual, racial, or economic domination, is most thoroughly insane. Thus the works of Jones and Morrison reinforce Flannery O'Connor's point about grotesque characters: "They seem to carry an invisible burden; their fanaticism is a reproach, not merely an eccentricity."[2] The characters in the books under discussion become grotesque either by being victims who personify and exaggerate their society's obsessions or by resisting its conventions, sometimes by carrying them to their logical and violent extreme. The resisters demonstrate the denaturalizing potential of folk material, in the case of Jones, by turning narrative into blues performance, and, in the case of Morrison, by turning the resister into an embodiment of folk sensibility. Thus, in their work, folk material is double-edged; it can either reinforce the cultural hegemony[3] of the dominant society or it can provide an alternative to that domination. For Morrison and Jones, then, the primary conflict occurs within the black community itself.

Gayl Jones, of all the writers discussed thus far, creates the most radical worlds. Not only are the societies depicted the most thoroughly and directly oppressive, but she also denies readers a "sane" narrative center

171

through which to judge world and narrator. Most frequently, her narrators have already been judged insane by the society; and this assessment, given the teller's actions and obsessions, seems reasonable. But we cannot therefore assume that we have entered a Poesque world of confessors of personal guilt or madness, for it is equally apparent that society has its own obsessions and that its labeling of the narrators as mad facilitates evasion of the implications of those obsessions.

Given the irrationality of both narrator and world, the reader must rely on the text itself to provide whatever sense is to be made of the story. Jones's stories and novels work because they effectively give voice to those who have suffered. By structuring the experiences, the texts become blues performances, rendering as they do stories of the convolutions and complications of desire. Patterns of repetition, identification of sufferer and solo performer, and use of the audience as confidant—all characteristics of the blues—suggest that the worlds of White Rat, Ursa Corregidora, and Eva Canada, no matter how disordered, are worlds of human experience.

While most of Jones's stories deal with sexual obsession, "White Rat," the title story of her short story collection (1977), focuses on racial identity; nonetheless, it is representative of the collection in its emphasis on self-destructive obsession. The narrator has the name White Rat because he is so light-skinned that he could easily pass for white. This condition of pigmentation is the source of his difficulties because he has been raised to identify with blacks, but he can only do so by insisting on his race in a society that attaches a stigma to blackness. In order to marry, to associate with black friends, to perform all the normal social functions in the Kentucky town where he lives, he must repeatedly name himself a "nigger." That he uses such a pejorative indicates the degree of self-hatred implicit in his behavior. He has been taught by his father to hate all "hoogies" (whites), yet he himself can only be distinguished from them by deliberately identifying with those that whites despise and debase. Despite the fact that in his case the semiotics of race seem especially arbitrary, family and society conspire to keep him from developing an effective self-image.

To prevent the psychological suicide encouraged by his experience, he turns his frustration and anger outward. He creates a persona of the "hard man" who does not recognize any faults in himself and does not tolerate them in others. Though his wife Maggie is "high yaller" in color, he is

172

constantly berating her for having "chicken-scratch" (nappy) hair. Thus the only trait that physically marks either of them as black becomes a source of derision.

The birth defect of their son serves a similar psychological function. He tries to blame Maggie:

> I said there weren't never nothing like that in my family ever since we been living on this earth. And they must have come from her side. And then I said cause she had more of whatever it was in her than I had in me. And then she said that brought it all out. All that stuff I been hiding up inside me cause she said I didn't hated them hoogies like my daddy did and I just been feeling I had to live up to something he set and the onliest reason I married her was because she was the lightest and brightest nigger woman I could get and still be nigger.[4]

Later, in a drunken state, he confesses to a bartender that the responsibility is in fact his. He does this by telling the story of a black priest who renounces his vows in order to marry. The child of this marriage has a club foot:

> The nigger blamed hisself cause he said the God put a curse on him for goin' agin his vows. He said the God put a curse on him cause he took his vows of cel'bacy, which mean no fuckin', cept everybody know what *they* do, and went agin his vows of cel'bacy and married a nigger woman so he could do what every ord'narry onery person was doing and the Lord didn't just put a curse on him. He said he could a stood that. But the Lord carried the curse clear over to the next gen'ration and put a curse on his little baby boy who didn do nothing in his whole life . . . cept come. (*White Rat,* 12)

While the confession serves as a corrective to the tendency to blame blackness for the difficulties of his life, the narrator makes this adjustment by claiming sacred status for the hatred of whites his father had advocated. He sees himself, his wife, and his child as actors in a religious allegory that inverts conventional thinking by making black good and white evil. He acts out penance for his sin by desisting from drunkenness and by allowing his wife to run off with a much darker man, only to return supposedly pregnant. By assuming responsibility for this future child, White Rat believes himself to have made right the sin he committed.

But such a view corrects the previous one only by going to the opposite extreme. To hate white and love black fails to recognize the ambiguity of

173

the narrator and his family. White Rat is a white black man and his wife and son are of similar mixed ancestry. To hate white is to hate a part of himself and them. Thus, the resolution he seems to claim at the conclusion of the story in fact only points to the limitations of his perception; he cannot yet live in the state of tension between blackness and whiteness that is his total self. His narrative, however, by showing the human suffering involved in a dualistic sensibility, does point to such a dialectical truth.

"The Women" is a female initiation story with the twist that the young girl comes to sexual awareness through antagonism to her mother's lesbianism. The narrative develops by paralleling Winnie's growing understanding of the nature of her mother's relationships with her own emerging sexuality. Contributing to her sensibility is her increasing knowledge about the larger society's attitude toward her mother's behavior. These three elements join in the opening scene where Winnie's cousin Freddy explains the significance of the visits of Miss Maybell in terms that both explain and deride the women's relationship:

> "It mean she a pussy willow."
> "What that mean?"
> "It mean what I hear my momma say. It mean she a woman that want to be a man." . . .
> "You got a fake fucka daddy." . . .
> "Moustache Woman still be in there then. Ain't got no cock to crow."
> (*White Rat*, 26–27)

While the labels do not clarify the relationship for the five-year-old Winnie, Freddy's accepted offer to do to her what Miss Maybell does to her mother does inspire in the child a dislike for sex:

> He raise my dress up and take my panties down and then he was doing something to me but I didn't know what he was doing. I wont to get away but was scared to scream cause my mama'd come down here and then Miss Maybell'd come down here and see we doing what they been doing, and then he did it. And then he put his hands down there and wipe it on my dress, but I just sit there. He say, "Cover up your ass 'fore you get a cold pussy." (*White Rat*, 28)

The sense of fear, secrecy, and derision that accompanies the act make this first lesson both painful and unpleasant. Shortly after, the mother fights with her lover and tells Winnie that Miss Maybell is a "bitch's whore." Thus, the bitterness of the adult world reinforces the child's own experience.

All the mother's relationships go through cycles of devotion and hostility. This pattern is in contrast to the linear development of Winnie's life. The middle stages of her initiation involve other girls, who first can share her innocent fascination with the female body and later can talk with her about heterosexual relations.

But the full emergence into sexuality must be understood in the context of the mother's actions. Winnie's attitude toward young men is one of indifference and distrust, the product of the lessons taught by Freddy and her mother. This attitude is apparently reinforced when she accidentally sees her mother passionately kissing another woman. As the most explicit act she has witnessed, it forces on her a full awareness of her mother's behavior which, combined with the derogatory comments about lesbians she has heard from her girlfriends and their parents, leads her to a renunciation of such a life for herself: "I get under the covers and say, 'I ain' goin' be like my mama when I grow up. I ain' goin' be a bitch's whore' " (White Rat, 43).

Her initial reaction to the experience is to avoid sexuality altogether. She adopts a hard exterior that discourages all advances. Only when one boy is persistent in seeking to break through her defenses does she discover desire in herself. When Garland comes to her house, she finds little reason to resist his efforts. However, the geography of her submission suggests something deeper than adolescent hormones at work: "We got up and I started in my room, but changed my mind, and take him into my mama's bedroom. Then I lay down on my mama's bedspread, and let him get on top of me" (White Rat, 52). Heterosexual copulation in the space her mother has made homosexual defines Winnie's own womanhood in direct opposition to that of the mother. It is less a statement of what the girl is and will become than it is an assertion of what she refuses to be. In acting out this rebellion, Winnie in effect uses Garland in much the same way that Freddy used her and her mother uses women to fulfill her own needs. Given that the mother defames her lovers once they leave, the implications for Winnie's experiences are clear.

The characterization of sexuality as manipulative, often dehumanizing, and a source of obsession is common throughout Jones's work. Lesbian relationships are seen as narcissistic, while heterosexual ones are egocentric, in the sense that (usually) men are depicted as viewing women as nothing more than man-pleasing genitalia. Women either accept the resultant dehumanization to the point of being victimized, or they resist it in violent ways. In either case, neither men nor women can escape obsession with sexuality.

"Asylum" is an extreme case of Jones's attitude. The narrator, a young woman committed to an asylum because of her irrational behavior, refuses to allow the doctor to examine her genital area, yet she was admitted after deliberately urinating in the living room when her nephew's teacher visited their home. She explains to the reader (though not to the psychiatrist) her motive for the latter action: "She [the teacher] just sit on her ass and fuck all day and it ain't with herself" (*White Rat*, 79).

Obsessed with acts of violation, whether sexual, intellectual, or psychological, she reveals her madness in rendering this sense of violation in graphic terms. Thus, her feeling that the teacher functions as an exploiter of children and thus provides a humanly worthless education is effectively expressed by presenting and using the family slop jar. Significantly, when the psychiatrist explains the means by which she is to be made "normal," she sees those means as schoolwork (*White Rat*, 80).

She considers the whole process of physical and mental examination to be rape. Whenever she has been examined, she sees a "big black rubbery thing look like a snake"[5] emerging from either her vagina or her anus. Those examining her define her resistance and sensibility as narcissistic sexual obsession, needing correction by experts. What Jones accomplishes through selection of narrator is a rebuttal of such a reductive notion. Even if the narrator is insane, our access to her thoughts informs us that the probing and objectification of her by the doctors is woefully inadequate. The pain and disorder she experiences are unrelieved and even aggravated by such clinical cliches as: "libido concentrated on herself" (*White Rat*, 81).

Moreover, she associates this reification and violence with whites. In a dream, the narrator sees the black nurse becoming "chalk white" when she assists in the examinations. More important, the narrator dreams that she herself takes on white characteristics and is thereafter unable to prevent the vaginal exploration.

The final conversation of the story suggests the dilemma facing the narrator:

"What does this word make you feel?"

"Nothing."

"You should tell me what you are thinking?"

"Is that the only way I can be freed?" (*White Rat*, 82)

The asylum is a microcosm of the totalitarian state. Those in authority determine what constitututes sane behavior and thought. Not to speak is to condemn oneself to imprisonment as a mental incorrigible. But the act of speaking is collaboration in one's dehumanization since it leads to categorization and "treatment," which in effect is imposition of values and modes of behavior designed to make one a functioning cog in the social machine. In other words, there is no freedom, no escape from this "refuge."

The only possibility is the narrative told to an audience willing to hear her story *as* a story rather than as confession or self-analysis. At the end of the narrative we are no closer to a rational explanation of her strange behavior than we were at the beginning. What we do have is an understanding of the human context of that behavior and a sense of the price of insisting on rational explanation. Thus, the story liberates because it preserves the humanity that would be destroyed by either rebellious silence or collaborative speech.

Jones's two novels, *Corregidora* (1975) and *Eva's Man* (1976), extend and enrich the themes of her stories. The earlier novel makes the association between race and sexual domination that "Asylum" makes, while *Eva's Man* expands upon that story's interest in madness. As in "The Women," lesbianism is introduced into both books as a questionable alternative to the exploitative nature of heterosexual relationships. Finally, both Ursa and Eva must confront the problem of White Rat: how to achieve a strong sense of identity in a society that devalues individual worth on the basis of race or sex. *Corregidora* ultimately insists on love and history as creators and preservers of identity, while *Eva's Man*, more in line with the pessimistic tone of "Asylum," sees the expression of the self's experiences as the only hope.

In *Corregidora*, sexual domination coincides with racial domination in the family history narrated by Ursa Corregidora. According to the legend preserved by the women of the family, Corregidora was a Brazilian slave owner and procurer who fathered both Ursa's great-grandmother and her grandmother. Keeping alive the truth of this humiliating experience of incest and possession becomes the life-purpose of these women and their descendants. Each generation produces the next primarily to protect against the destruction of the truth by those in power. Part of the story is the claim that written records can and are destroyed so that only procreation and narration will save the truth of history.

The problem for Ursa, who is, appropriately, a blues singer, is that she is barren as a result of mistreatment by her lover, Mutt. Suspicious of the men who come to watch her perform, he pushes her down a flight of stairs, causing her to lose both the child she is carrying and the possibility of producing any more. Like her mothers, she experiences possession and violence by a man obsessed with her; unlike them, however, she experiences guilt at being unable to pass on the family story to a daughter. Mutt seems to have succeeded where the slave owners failed: they could only destroy the record while Mutt can destroy the truth itself by effacing the future. At this level, the tale rather straightforwardly attacks male domination, which repeatedly assaults female identity and integrity. Ursa's experiences with other men and the story of her mother's love affair reinforce this theme.

But another theme, dialectically related to the first, slowly emerges. Out of her own hatred and guilt, Ursa begins to consider the usefulness of hatred to the victim of such assaults as those that form her personal and familial history. Through the ferreting out of the story of her father and the thinking through of her relationship with Mutt, she comes to see that it is not only men who are obsessed. The hatred of domination and possession itself becomes obsessive. Keeping alive the story of Corregidora and blaming Mutt for her troubles reveal more than a desire for justice; they also reveal evasion of one's own responsibility. The drive for power is not gender-specific; it only manifests itself in different ways. Thus, keeping alive the story of Corregidora's evil serves as a way of defining and thereby controlling him. Moreover, the teller, by making the story her own, can suppress whatever ambiguities of responsibility and power might detract from her allegory of evil against innocence.

The necessary element for Ursa's discovery of this truth about herself and her family is her blues singing. Significantly, her mother opposes this career from the beginning. Given the ambivalent nature of the music,[6] her opposition is not surprising. The blues makes a personal statement of trouble and love's vagaries, but the performer is not only the victim but also, by virtue of the performance itself, the ultimate power. In women's blues, especially the "classic" form recorded by Bessie Smith, Ma Rainey, and others, the lyrics are rich with a mixture of joy and sorrow. Men are both good lovers and dirty dogs. The voice rendering the lyrics is always sensual, authoritative, and in control of the emotion described.[7]

Ursa's insight comes with her awareness that her injury has the effect of deepening and improving her musical performance: "Your voice sounds a little strained, that's all. But if I hadn't heard you before, I wouldn't notice anything. I'd still be moved. Maybe even moved more, because it sounds like you been through something. Before it was beautiful too, but you sound like you been through more now."[8] At one level, this enhancement merely reiterates the cliché that beauty is deepened by suffering. But more important, her singing has acquired a power that it previously lacked: " 'You got a hard kind of voice,' he said now. 'You know, like callused hands. Strong and hard but gentle underneath. Strong but gentle too. The kind of voice that can hurt you. I can't explain it. Hurt you and make you still want to listen' " (*Corregidora*, 96).

This quality in Ursa's voice is precisely the power that women have over men. This paradox of desire pervades Jones's work: men are obsessed by women, even though they know that their obsession makes them vulnerable. Moreover, women are most often the victims of their own power, since men evade their own weakness by demonstrations of domination and possession. Because of this sex-role conditioning, women cannot openly exercise power, for to do so is to invite the violence of insecure men. Alternatives to this situation explored in *Corregidora* include lesbianism, mystification of male obsession, and the wisdom of the blues, which acknowledges and then conceals female power.

Lesbianism becomes here, as in "The Women," a form of narcissistic evasion. In the case of Cat Lawson, Ursa's friend, it serves as a way of not having to "feel like a fool in my own bed" (*Corregidora*, 64). Because another woman knows this feeling, the bed can become a place of refuge. But in this sense the relationship is marked by absence and negation rather than by creative assertion. It is a space of not-men rather than of women. This point is reinforced in the character of Jeffry, Cat's obsessive and domineering lover, or in other words, an ersatz man.

179

The second option, mystification, is the one chosen by Ursa's mothers. Corregidora becomes for them an embodiment of absolute evil. He is incestuous, cruel, promiscuous, racist, and tyrannical. He defiles everything he touches, including the innocent young slave women. Such a characterization makes it possible to make the innocence as absolute as the evil. The women, who keep the name Corregidora no matter whom they marry, achieve through their myth making a dualistic universe in which all women are victims regardless of their behavior. The self-destructive sexual obsessiveness of men is the never-sufficient price that they must pay for being born male. The only good men serve is in engendering daughters to be taught the evil nature of their fathers, husbands, and sons. Ursa uses this message to justify her hatred of Mutt.

But her music tells a different story. It tells her that men are both weak and strong, good and evil, and that women have the same mixed character. The story of her mother, which is very much a blues tale, concerns a relationship that failed in part because of the hatred of men perpetuated by the family history. The mother's inability to love and make love, more than the father's evil, caused the breakup of the relationship. Only when Ursa goes back home in pain and guilt to discover history rather than myth does she find out the truth about her parents. The mother hates the blues in part because they speak all too clearly of the pain in her own dilemma.

Out of the sense of ambiguous personal history and her strengthened artistic expression, Ursa begins the reassessment of her relationship with Mutt. She begins to see that the Corregidora women have done as much to deny her an awareness of Mutt's humanity as social conditioning has trapped him into thinking of her as a piece of sexual property. What results is not sentimental resolution but epiphany, in which she is suddenly conscious of both her power and her love. In this moment, she also realizes the male-female attraction-repulsion that is the dynamic of her family history:

> We got out of our clothes. I got between his knees. . . . It had to be sexual, I was thinking, it had to be something sexual that Great Gram did to Corregidora. I knew it had to be sexual: "What is it a woman can do to a man that make him hate her so bad he wont to kill her one minute and keep thinking about her and can't get her out of his mind the next?" In a split second I knew what it was, in a split second of love and hate I knew what it

180

was, and I think he might have known too. A moment of pleasure and excruciating pain at the same time, a moment of broken skin but not sexlessness, a moment just before sexlessness, a moment that stops just before sexlessness, a moment that stops before it breaks the skin: "I could kill you." (*Corregidora*, 184)

This moment of choice between life and death, between manhood and unmanning is the moment of female power. But this power, which manifests itself when the woman seems most clearly in a posture of submission, expresses itself most effectively by not being exercised. Its latency becomes its greatest proof, and also its greatest excitement. To not kill keeps the power in reserve as a constant reminder to the oppressor of his vulnerability.

Corregidora ends with the embrace of Ursa and Mutt. But that embrace is less a resolution of the issues raised than an acceptance of the need to live in a state of tension. Love, according to Jones, can exist only in a dialectic with hate. Only when the power of the dominator can be countered with that of the dominated can something resembling human caring be established. Thus love is not a presence but a process of affirmation and negation.

In *Eva's Man*, the woman does what Ursa refused to do, and this difference marks the boundary between sanity and madness. Eva refuses to live in the state of tension that Ursa ultimately accepts. Because Eva is the narrator, we see very clearly those forces she perceives to be acting against her. Through the use of this mad narrator, Jones denaturalizes and defamiliarizes the system of male sexual domination. Eva, in her blues performance, articulates in extreme form the experience of women and rebels against it. Since Eva is obsessive, she exaggerates the oppression, and thereby forces the reader to reconsider this aspect of the social order. The effect is a novel of the gothic and grotesque.

The book opens with Eva in a prison for the criminally insane; she is kept here because she has poisoned the man with whom she was living and then bitten off his penis. Though she retains a near-total silence when addressed by various authority figures and other men, she seems to tell the reader everything about her past and her relationships. Everything, that is, except what is most needed: the motive for murder and dismemberment.

Structurally, the narrative operates as a whirlpool in its downward, ever-tightening, ever-faster, spiraling movement. J. Douglas Perry has described this pattern in another literary context:

> The three structural principles are simply ways in which a whirlpool is shifted from a visual representation to the printed page. The process down the sides of the whirlpool becomes the sequential experiencing of levels, funneling into the final one. The sequence is predetermined because the whirlpool cancels free will and random motion. To move through the whirlpool is to find oneself moving in smaller and faster circles; a novel conveys this sensation by repeating its initial event or situation in more and more strident ways, creating for us a sense of concentricity. Finally, there is the matter of character repetition, the recurrence of archetypal figures, or clusters of them, throughout the various subplots of the novel, in an obsessive and stereotypical fashion.[9]

Eva's Man follows this pattern rather closely in the first-person narrative of Eva Medina Canada. She describes for us her movement through ever more intense experiences that the reader can see are more and more destructive of her sanity. Repeated images, scenes, and words reflect the increasing restriction of her range of response. At the climax, obsessed with an object she believes to hold the secret of power and truth, she takes violent possession through sexual dismemberment. In the end, she is locked in a literal prison where she derives sexual pleasure from a mirror-image female character whose attentions are nearly as manipulative as those of the men Eva has repeatedly encountered.

The folk elements seem on the surface to reinforce this pattern. Miss Billie, the voice of the community, repeatedly suggests that sexual domination is the natural obsession of men and submission the natural role of women. The story of Eva's cousin Alphonse and his convoluted relationship with his wife, Jean, is the acting out of a blues destiny. He cannot live without her, yet he becomes so enraged at times that he publicly assaults her. Nonetheless, Jean endures and, according to her brother Otis, seems to instigate and thrive on this ritual of violence: "*She* starts it, Marie. Not him. She starts it and then he finishes it. She's the one wonts it, though, Marie. . . . Like they were working all that blues out of them, or something."[10] The story as told by Eva, with her self-dividing feelings of attraction and repulsion for sexuality and men, is itself a kind of blues performance, with its repetitions and reversals and themes of love and violence. Eva's stories of various women who have trouble with men who prove unreliable and violent but still somehow desirable, draw on a pattern in women's blues that strengthens the sense of irreversible female destiny.

The most compelling of these narratives, that of the Queen Bee, is also the one which through its folk connections provides a negation of that destiny. The Queen Bee has the misfortune of falling in love with men who die shortly thereafter. The community comes to believe that her love is somehow a fatal sting. Finally, the Queen Bee commits suicide when she falls in love one last time. Because she believes the lore about herself, she sacrifices that self rather than unavoidably threaten the life of her lover. She is thus an emblem of the condition of all women in the book. In all the male-female relationships, the women cannot resist their sexuality but they are nonetheless blamed and punished for it. The repetition of this pattern reinforces the structure of the novel by showing such characters as victims swept downward by their passion and self-deprecation.

But the tale of the Queen Bee has at its heart an inversion of this passivity. The very name suggests power, fertility, and creativity.[11] If women are, like queen bees, destined to a sexual function, men, like drones, are obsessed with satisfying that need. The woman, in her apparent helplessness, has the power to affirm or deny manhood. Given the intensity of this male obsession, the affirmation or denial literally becomes a matter of male life and death. As in *Corregidora,* so in *Eva's Man,* victimization creates in women significant power.

Eva, unlike the other women and as a sign perhaps of her madness, chooses to literalize the metaphor of the queen bee's power to destroy the drones. Davis imprisons her in an apartment where he does not permit her any amenities, not even a comb to control her ever-wilder hair; thus she serves as a Medusa whose function is to keep him perpetually in a state of sexual hardness. The epitome of sexual domination is reached; the actions and attitudes of her father, her husband, her cousin, and all other men she and other women encounter culminate in Davis's reification of her. But like the queen bee, Eva finds in her cell the source of her power. The phallus, both literal and figurative emblem of male control, is also the point of greatest weakness. Eva demonstrates the illusiveness of masculine power by biting off Davis's penis, wrapping it in a silk handkerchief, and then placing it back inside his pants. She carries to its logical end the insight of Ursa Corregidora.

But Eva goes beyond even this point by accepting responsibility for her action. She reports the crime herself and then returns to the scene to be captured. In this way she reenters the world of male domination, represented by the police and the psychiatrist. But she enters now not as a victim but as an alternative power, a queen bee. Consistent with this role, she refuses to explain, to defend herself, in fact even to speak at all. This silence is her refusal to rationalize her behavior in terms of the system she has so pointedly assaulted.

For her action and her silence she is criminally insane. But as Michel Foucault has indicated, a judgment of madness is an act of domination.[12] Eva must be declared insane so that the meaning of her act can be evaded and suppressed. Through the symbolic significance of her violence, she threatens to expose male domination for the dehumanizing and exploitative system that it is. She has challenged in a primal way the right of that system to be considered natural and rational. Both her crime and her silence call into question this particular universe of discourse.

But of course Eva does speak; as narrator, she provides the reader with the entire story. And the patterns of narration are those of madness. Time and space displacement, obsessive emphasis on sexuality and violence, and increasingly confusing and obscure references clearly indicate an insane speaker. But this very insanity makes possible a different discourse; we enter a recognizably different realm, yet one that has grotesque resemblances to those we are both familiar with and accept as natural. And like the police and psychiatrists, we quest for rational explanation. Unfortunately for us, Eva explains and justifies nothing about her crime. Instead, she expresses her sense of the world, just as the blues is expressive rather than explanatory. She tells her story to an audience that she forces to listen rather than to ask questions. And that very compulsion turns the focus back on those who dominate and dehumanize, not as an act of political and social reform but rather as an act of memory.

In contrast to the anguished narrative consciousnesses of Gayl Jones's fiction, Toni Morrison creates conventionally stable central characters. Moreover, she adds even greater reliability by using primarily omniscient narrations; even when there is a first-person narrator, as in *The Bluest Eye*, that voice is complemented by an omniscient perspective. Thus, it would seem that Morrison's fiction is much closer to that of the traditionalists discussed earlier. But in fact, she uses the narrative to present disordered, violent, perverse worlds less overt but no less troubling than those of Jones. These novels present us with murder, incest, necrophilia, child abuse, insanity, terrifying family secrets, and a general sense of life teetering on the edge of dissolution. Such material presented through reliable narration creates a tension that intensifies the emotional impact of the fiction.

The rational telling of extreme events forces a radical reconsideration of commonly held assumptions about black life and black-white relationships. Through its extremism, it defamiliarizes the reader by pointing to the violent effects of such ordinary phenomena as popular culture, bourgeois ideas about property, love, sexual initiation and sex roles, family, and the past. Perhaps more than any other writer under consideration in this study, Morrison shows the exploitative nature of logocentric orders.[13] She dramatizes the destructive power implicit in the control of various symbolic systems. In her fiction that power creates grotesque victims, often including those who seem to be in positions of domination. Her novels are quest tales in which key characters search for the hidden sign capable of giving them strength and/or identity. In a significant twist, those who find what they seek become the most thoroughly victimized, while those who are turned in their searches toward some other goal (which is usually an absence rather than the originally desired presence) are most often triumphant. The changed pursuit is in the direction of some black folk value, such as true community, true family name, or authentic black history. The revision of goals makes possible a loosening of the control of logocentrism so as to achieve a black selfhood that negates that control.

In *The Bluest Eye* (1970) the destructiveness of control rather than the creativity of negation predominates. Pecola Breedlove, a black girl thought by everyone to be ugly, finds herself enthralled by the blue eyes of Shirley Temple. Everywhere in her world, white skin and blue eyes are taken as signs of beauty. The image manifests itself in movies, billboards, children's drinking cups, Mary Jane candies, other characters, and in the excerpts from a primary-school reader that constitute both epigraph and chapter titles in the novel. Conversely, the lack of such traits in Pecola leads her and virtually everyone else in the book to consider her worthless. Black children deflect their self-hatred by verbally assaulting her; lighter-skinned blacks, children and adults, proclaim their superiority by alternately patronizing and attacking her; and her own mother makes clear her preferences when she slaps Pecola aside in order to comfort a white child.[14]

In response to this psychological violence, Pecola takes up a quest for blue eyes. Initially, she limits herself to drinking white milk from a cup with a Shirley Temple decal and to buying and eating Mary Jane candies. Through this popular-culture Eucharist, she hopes to be transubstantiated from common black clay into spiritual whiteness. At this stage, she achieves only the momentary happiness of seeing the white faces and wishing to have one. Later on, after the trauma of being raped by her father, she loses all sense of reality, visits a self-styled conjure man, and believes that she has actually undergone the change in eye color that she so strongly and pathetically desired. Claudia, part-time narrator and childhood companion, points out the moral of Pecola's story:

> All of us—all who knew her—felt so wholesome after we cleaned ourselves on her. We were so beautiful when we stood astride her ugliness. Her simplicity decorated us, her guilt sanctified us, her pain made us glow with health, her awkwardness made us think we had a sense of humor. Her inarticulateness made us believe we were eloquent. Her poverty kept us generous. Even her waking dreams we used—to silence our own nightmares. And she let us, and thereby deserved our contempt. We honed our egos on her, padded our characters with her frailty; and yawned in the fantasy of our strength.[15]

Perhaps more significant than the catalogue of forms of victimization in the above quotation is the "we" that makes Pecola the victim. More than the melancholy story of a little girl driven mad by the world's hostility, *The Bluest Eye* tells the story of the community and society that persecutes her. Pecola may be the central character, but she is far from the only victim of the blue eyes. "We" individually and collectively are both victimizer and victim; and, while the roles vary with each character, it is also the case that the role of victimizer results from that character's own victimization by a larger society. Each person fantasizes that he has real self-determining power. But Claudia, at the end, knows better: "We substituted good grammar for intellect; we switched habits to simulate maturity; we rearranged lies and called it truth, seeing in the new pattern of an old idea the Revelation and the Word" (*The Bluest Eye*, 159).

This pursuit of the Word entraps the characters. Pauline Breedlove differs from her daughter Pecola only in the sense that the image she believes in comes from the movie screen rather than the milk cup. Whiteness is goodness, and she feels more at home in the white kitchen where she works than in the rundown house she shares with her family. In the chapter giving her history, we learn that she has compensated for her lameness and putative ugliness by creating order wherever possible. In most cases the order is a trivial arrangement of objects, but she learns from the movies that a white home is the paragon of order. Her work in such homes makes possible a control in her life that is impossible in her own existence as a poor black woman with a family suffering under the manipulations of that very white world she loves.

She only overcomes the self-hatred implied by such values through the self-righteousness of her religion. To reinforce this goodness she needs the evil of her husband Cholly: "She was an active church woman, did not drink, smoke, or carouse, defended herself mightily against Cholly, rose above him in every way, and felt she was fulfilling a mother's role conscientiously when she pointed out their father's faults to keep them away from having them, or punished them when they showed any slovenliness, no matter how slight, when she worked twelve to sixteen hours a day to support them. And the world agreed with her" (*The Bluest Eye*, 102).

Cholly inverts Pauline's values. He deals with self-hatred and oppression by becoming as evil as possible, even to the point of raping his daughter and burning his own house. Behind this "bad-nigger" persona lies a history of distortions of the principal relationships and rituals of life. He is abandoned in a junkyard by his mother, who was never certain of the identity of the father. His first sexual encounter is interrupted by white men whose derisive comments render him impotent. His search for the man he believes to be his father ends at a dark alley dice game when the man chases him away, believing he has come only for money. Such events make him both anti- and asocial. He hates the girl of his sexual humiliation rather than the white men because she was a witness to his powerlessness; he has

no sense of socially acceptable behavior because he has been denied primary socialization; and he is incapable of appropriate fatherly behavior because he has had no parents.

The most perverse act of his life, the rape of Pecola, is a product of his
confusion of violence and love.

> She was washing dishes. Her small back hunched over the sink. Cholly
> saw her dimly and could not tell what he saw or what he felt. Then he
> became aware that he was uncomfortable; next he felt the discomfort
> dissolve into pleasure. The sequence of his emotions was revulsion, guilt,
> pity, then love. His revulsion was a reaction to her young, helpless, hope-
> less presence. Her back hunched that way; her head to one side as though
> crouching from a permanent and unrelieved blow. Why did she have to
> look so whipped? She was a child—unburdened—why wasn't she happy?
> The clear statement of her misery was an accusation. He wanted to break
> her neck—but tenderly. Guilt and impotence rose in a bilious duet. What
> could he do for her—ever? What give her? What say to her? What could a
> burned-out black man say to the hunched back of his eleven-year-old
> daughter? If he looked into her face, he would see those haunted, loving
> eyes. The hauntedness would irritate him—the love would move him to
> fury. How dare she love him? Hadn't she any sense at all? What was he
> supposed to do about that? Return it? How? What could his calloused
> hands produce to make her smile? What of his knowledge of the world
> and of life could be useful to her? What could his heavy arms and
> befuddled brain accomplish that would earn him his own respect, that
> would in turn allow him to accept her love? His hatred of her slimed in his
> stomach and threatened to become vomit. But just before the puke moved
> from anticipation to sensation, she shifted her weight and stood on one
> foot scratching the back of her calf with her toe. . . . The timid, tucked-in
> look of the scratching toe—that was what Pauline was doing the first time
> he saw her in Kentucky. Leaning over a fence staring at nothing in
> particular. The creamy toe of her bare foot scratching a velvet leg. It was
> such a small and simple gesture, but it filled him then with a wondering
> softness. Not the usual lust to part tight legs with his own, but a tender-
> ness, a protectiveness. A desire to cover her foot with his hand and gently
> nibble away the itch from the calf with his teeth. He did it then. . . . He did
> it now. . . . The confused mixture of his memories of Pauline and the doing
> of a wild and forbidden thing excited him. . . . Surrounding all of this lust
> was a border of politeness. He wanted to fuck her—tenderly. But the
> tenderness would not hold. (*The Bluest Eye*, 127–28)

The various ways in which society has conditioned Cholly so as to control him have had the effect of denying him a socially acceptable means of expressing an authentic human emotion. Having learned that he is nothing but an object of disgust, he, like Pauline, can do nothing other than objectify Pecola. Each of them exploits her because his own exploitation makes it impossible to do otherwise.

In the larger community, objectification is also common. White storekeepers, light-skinned children, and black middle-class adults all see this black child as a piece of filth repugnant yet necessary to their own senses of cleanliness.

Alternatives to this pattern of victimization can be found in two sets of characters, the whores and the McTeer family. Though diametrically opposed in both values and ambitions, both groups offer ways of coping with the pain of experience. The whores accomplish this by being what they are:

> Three merry gargoyles. Three merry harridans. Amused by a long-ago time of ignorance. They did not belong to those generations of prostitutes created in novels, with great and generous hearts, dedicated, because of the horror of circumstance, to ameliorating the luckless, barren life of men, taking money incidentally and humbly for their "understanding." Nor were they from that sensitive breed of young girl, gone wrong at the hands of fate, forced to cultivate an outward brittleness in order to protect her springtime from further shock, but knowing full well she was cut out for better things, and could make the right man happy. Neither were they the sloppy, inadequate whores who, unable to make a living at it alone, turn to drug consumption and traffic or pimps to help complete their scheme of self-destruction, avoiding suicide only to punish the memory of some absent father or to sustain the misery of some silent mother. (*The Bluest Eye*, 47)

They are women who do their work without illusion, self-hatred, or guilt. They have no use for their customers or for those dishonest women who pretend virtue but are in fact unfaithful. They respect only the innocents, like Pecola, and truly religious women who they see as having the same honesty and integrity as themselves.

They are also the primary folk figures in the novel. Even their names—Poland, China, Maginot Line—suggest larger-than-life characters. Maginot Line entertains Pecola with outlandish stories of past loves and adventures.

She keeps alive the idea of love in her recollections of Dewey Prince, the only man she did not sell herself to. China is adept at verbal dueling, constantly drawing Maginot Line back from the edge of sentimentality with sarcasm. Poland is "forever ironing, forever singing" (*The Bluest Eye,* 44). Her songs are blues, which serve less to express personal problems than to entertain through reminders of the nature of the world in which they live. These folk arts enable them to transcend the private obsessions of other characters. The world may well be a place of misery and doom, but folk wisdom dictates that one adapts to circumstances rather than resignedly move toward evasion or self-destruction. Blues and folk tales imply that trouble is *both* personal and communal and that life is a matter of adaptation and survival rather than resignation and death. The whores treat themselves and Pecola with consideration because they neither despair nor hope.

Ironically, the McTeer family, although hostile to the behavior and attitude of the whores, make a decent life for themselves by working from the same principles. One of the functions of the family in the novel is to serve as a counterpoint for the Breedloves. Pauline slaps Pecola and protects a little white girl, whereas Mrs. McTeer takes in the black girl, even though it is a strain on her family's resources. Cholly rapes his own daughter, whereas Mr. McTeer nearly kills a boarder who fondles his daughter. The Breedloves are so absorbed in variations of self-hatred that they see each other only as objects, whereas the McTeers make themselves into a family despite all the economic, psychological, and social forces opposing them.

This is not to suggest that the McTeers are sentimentalized into the Dick-and-Jane family of the school reader. Morrison insists that it is in fact those who refuse such sentimentality who are the most heroic. The McTeers live without illusion as much as possible. The parents whip their children, complain about the burdens of life, and struggle only semisuccessfully to acquire the necessities for survival. The children must face embarrassment because of their cheap clothing and lack of money and must deal with the same assaults on their race as Pecola. But unlike the Breedloves and the light-skinned Geraldine and Maureen, they do not measure their human worth by the symbols of the dominant white culture. Although the Shirley Temple cup belongs to the McTeers and although Frieda, Claudia's sister, loves the child actress's movies, no one in the family defines himself or herself by a lack of whiteness. They accept their difference from whites as a given of their existence, not as a deprivation to be evaded or mourned.

Claudia, the narrator, is the most emphatic in asserting this difference. She serves for a while as a rebel figure, similar to the young Jane Pittman in Ernest Gaines's novel. She plots insults and attacks on Maureen Peel, who glories in her lack of melanin. More important, she almost ritualistically destroys the white doll she receives for Christmas:

> The other dolls, which were supposed to bring me great pleasure, succeeded in doing quite the opposite. When I took it to bed, its hard unyielding limbs resisted my flesh—the tapered fingertips on those dimpled hands scratched. If, in sleep, I turned, the bone-cold head collided with my own. It was a most uncomfortable, patently aggressive sleeping companion. To hold it was no more rewarding. The starched gauze or lace on the cotton dress irritated any embrace. I had only one desire: to dismember it. To see of what it was made, to discover the dearness, to find the beauty, the desirability that had escaped me, but apparently only me. Adults, older girls, shops, magazines, newspapers, window signs—all the world had agreed that a blue-eyed yellow-haired, pink-skinned doll was what every girl child treasured. . . . I could not love it. But I could examine it to see what it was that all the world said was lovable. Break off the tiny fingers, bend the flat feet, loosen the hair, twist the head around, and the thing made one sound—a sound they said was the sweet and plaintive cry "Mama," but which sounded to me like the bleat of a dying lamb, or, more precisely, our icebox door opening on rusty hinges in July. Remove the cold and stupid eyeball, it would bleat still, "Ahhhhh," take off the head, shake out the sawdust, crack the back against the brass bed rail, it would bleat still. The gauze back would split, and I could see the disk with six holes, the secret of the sound. A mere metal roundness. (*The Bluest Eye*, 20–21)

The doll is an emblem of a manipulative, inverted order. Adults and children are encouraged to believe that this combination of wood, cloth, and metal is an idealization of girlhood and that the noise it makes is a human cry. Claudia herself confuses illusion and reality when she does violence to real white girls who seem to her imitations of the doll. Claudia's instinct to penetrate to the secret of the doll's voice and demystify it is appropriate, but her identification of objects and human beings is a measure of her acceptance of the culture's dehumanization. Even if the white girls take their identity from the doll, as its deliberate design and mechanism implies that they should, even if, in other words, they take the object as more real than themselves, their voices nonetheless remain human voices and their pain human pain. Claudia ultimately fails, not because of her confusion, which she overcomes, but because she refuses to live in her demystified knowledge:

> When I learned how repulsive this disinterested violence [against white girls] was, that it was repulsive because it was disinterested, my shame floundered about for refuge. The best hiding place was love. Thus the conversion from pristine sadism to fabricated hatred, to fraudulent love. It was a small step to Shirley Temple. I learned much later to worship her, just as I learned to delight in cleanliness, knowing, even as I learned, that the change was adjustment without improvement. (*The Bluest Eye*, 22)

The state of rebellion cannot be sustained because it requires a perpetual opposition and negation without hope of victory. *The Bluest Eye*, then, is about the difficulty of achieving individuality and full humanity in an objectifying and manipulative society. To refuse that state of tension and negation is to accept self-hatred, illusion, and even madness. In this novel, the best that can be accomplished is an intimation of what a fully human condition might be.

Sula (1974) probes even more deeply for the origins of oppression, victimization, and social order. In the process, it also explores the possibilities for negating such control. Consistent with the dialectics of language, Morrison finds both control and its negation in naming. When a place, person, thing, or event is labeled, the namer assumes it to be fixed, present, and under his or her dominion. By such a practice, experience can be organized and even reified. But in *Sula* the process of designation creates possibilities not intended by the namer, possibilities that can be realized in human history, though frequently only with great suffering. The effort to escape this dialectic, as Sula does, is doomed, as she is. She cannot avoid being part of the social order, since even rebellion is named and used in the community.

The uses of naming are developed in the book long before the title character appears. The novel opens with a "nigger joke" associated with the origin of the black community. According to the legend, a white man promised freedom and land to his slave if a particularly difficult task were performed. When the work was done, the freedom was given without a second thought, but the land was a different matter. The white man convinced the black one that the rocky hill country was bottom land, since it was the "bottom of heaven." Thus, the black community of Bottom was created above the white town of Medallion. Here, as elsewhere, Morrison suggests the economic underpinnings of racism, as well as the function of language in establishing and maintaining social control. The white man manipulates the ambiguity of language to his advantage and thus determines the economic condition of blacks for generations.

But this control is not necessarily absolute: "Still, it was lovely up in the Bottom. After the town grew and the farm land turned into a village and the village into a town and the streets of Medallion were hot and dusty with progress, those heavy trees that sheltered the shacks up in the Bottom were wonderful to see. And the hunters who went there sometimes wondered in private if maybe the white farmer was right after all. Maybe it was the bottom of Heaven."[16] Thus the attempt to control through language is always subject to negation by the very nature of language itself. Compulsion can cause suffering and sorrow, as it does in the exploitation that creates and maintains the Bottom, but it cannot be totalitarian. Traces of meaning exist that make for other possibilities. Black refusal to be dehumanized by the "nigger joke" creates the ironic realization of the joke's language.

The second instance of control through naming comes in the form of National Suicide Day, created by Shadrack, a psychologically damaged veteran who walked through the fires of World War I. He suffered shell shock when, during battle, "he turned his head a little to the right and saw the face of a soldier near him fly off. Before he could register shock, the rest of the soldier's head disappeared under the inverted soup bowl of his helmet. But stubbornly, taking no direction from the brain, the body of the headless soldier ran on, with energy and grace, ignoring altogether the drip and slide of brain tissue down its back" (*Sula*, 8). The surprise and the messiness together render Shadrack nearly insane.

The bullet dissolves not merely the soldier's head but also Shad's sense of reality and identity. The world ceases to have any inherent order, and he has no name. After he leaves the hospital, "a haven of more than a year, only eight days of which he fully recollected," he is on his own, "with no past, no language, no tribe, no source, no address book, no comb, no pencil, no clock, no pocket handkerchief, no rug, no bed, no can opener, no faded postcard, no soap, no key, no tobacco pouch, no soiled underwear and nothing nothing nothing to do" (*Sula,* 12). He is deprived of all the markers of an identity, which are also the markers of a social existence. Without such possessions and the social and economic orders implied by them, he cannot be a human being.

Only when he finds by accident someone who knows him, a town to live in, a job to do, and a language (that of obscenity) to speak can he begin to function. But this order cannot counteract the primal chaos of death. To live with this obsession, he must create an order for it, which he does in National Suicide Day: "In sorting it all out, he hit on the notion that if one day a year were devoted to it [death], everybody could get it out of the way and the rest of the year would be safe and free" (*Sula,* 14).

Significantly, this private neurosis becomes part of the social order: "As time went along, the people took less notice of these January thirds, rather they thought they did, thought they had no attitudes or feelings one way or another about Shadrack's annual solitary parade. In fact they had simply stopped remarking on the holiday because they had absorbed it into their thoughts, into their language, into their lives" (*Sula,* 15). Though the designation lacks for the community the traumatic significance that it holds for Shad, nonetheless its incorporation into the group's language holds *in potentia* meaning that will later be catastrophically realized. The mad rituals of a madman seem to be naturalized and thus neutralized by the community, but that very folk process makes the actualization of the name, through repetition, in fact feasible.

An entirely different kind of order, one that appears to be no order at all, is created by Eva, Sula's grandmother. Eva begins as the victim of a white- and male-dominated society. When she and her children are abandoned by her husband, she is left with little food and no money in the middle of the winter. She saves the life of her baby by using the last of her lard to remove fecal stones from his bowels. Realizing the hopelessness of the situation, she leaves her children with a neighbor and disappears for eighteen months. When she returns, she is missing a leg but has a substantial income. The mystery of her quest becomes the material of folk legend, and she becomes a symbol of the will to survive. With the money she builds a ramshackle house and takes in boarders and various kinds of stray beings. She establishes herself as a queen, sitting on an ersatz throne constructed from a rocking chair and a children's wagon. From this position, she entertains the men of the community.

A key element in the order Eva maintains is this relationship with men. While Morrison suggests that both Eva and her daughter Hannah are enthralled by "manlove," the men themselves seem very much mere playthings. While Hannah expresses the idea by having intercourse with any willing man, Eva is more derogatory. Her former husband is nicknamed Boyboy, while her son is called Plum, and an apparently white tenant Tarbaby. In the most bizarre naming, three boys she adopts are designated "the deweys," though they have neither appearance nor background in common. As a manifestation of Eva's power of naming, the boys become identical in mentality and sensibility; in fact, they become virtually a separate species.

In some sense, Eva sees herself as a god figure. She held the power of life and death over her children, she created the race of deweys, she names and manipulates men as she sees fit. When Plum returns from the war addicted to heroin, she chooses to destroy the remnants of his being by setting fire to him. Later on, she is punished for this hubris by having to watch helplessly as Hannah becomes accidentally engulfed in flame and then seared when neighbors throw water on her to put out the fire. Moreover, it is Eva's lack of the leg she apparently chose to sacrifice for money that makes it impossible to reach and save her daughter. Thus, the very sign of Eva's power comes to be the negation of that power.

The underlying order of which Shadrack and Eva are extreme metaphors is that of the community. It establishes the forms of male-female, parent-child, individual-society, and good-evil relationships. It creates rituals recognizing the mysteries of birth, sex, and death; it codifies acceptable attitudes toward power, whether personal, sexual, or racial. In other words, it makes the conventions that define life in the Bottom.

Morrison is at her best perhaps when showing how such rites and conventions operate in ordinary experience. At the funeral of a child, the women participate in a mourning ceremony:

> As Reverend Deal moved into his sermon, the hands of the woman unfolded like pairs of raven's wings and flew high above their hats in the air. They did not hear all of what he said; they heard the one word, or phrase, or inflection that was for them the connection between the event and themselves.

195

> For some time it was the term "Sweet Jesus." And they saw the Lamb's eye
> and the truly innocent victims: themselves. . . . Then they left their pews.
> For with some emotions one has to stand. They spoke, for they were full and
> needed to say. They swayed, for the rivulets of grief or of ecstasy must be
> rocked. And when they thought of all that life and death locked into that
> little closed coffin they danced and screamed, not to protest God's will, but to
> acknowledge it and confirm once more their conviction that the only way to
> avoid the Hand of God is to get in it. (*Sula*, 65–66)

The need here is to express, not to explain. The funeral is not the cause but
the occasion to reaffirm a position as both victim and elect. The ritual trans-
forms an absence into a presence, makes a private, physical loss into a
communal, spiritual gain. The language of the passage, which modulates
into a litany, reinforces the pattern by suggesting the recurrence and thus
permanence of structures.

But the treatment and attitude toward Sula most overtly reveal the patterns of the community. National Suicide Day could be naturalized by the
people, as could Eva's arrogance. Each in some way recapitulates the need
for an order, a name. But Sula refuses ordering and naming, so for the
community she becomes the embodiment of evil. By ignoring or deliberately violating the conventions, she threatens the assumptions by which
life in the Bottom is organized and made meaningful. By naming her evil,
they seek to bring her within the framework of their worldview, but, as we
shall see, this effort is itself inherently ambiguous.

Morrison establishes early on the events that make Sula's identity an
essentially negative one. Sula overhears a conversation between her mother and other woman during which Hannah remarks: "You love her, like I
love Sula. I just don't like her" (*Sula*, 57). Later the same day, a little boy
drowns when he slips from her hands while they are playing. "The first
experience taught her there was no other that you could count on; the
second that there was no self to count on either. She had no center, no
speck around which to grow" (*Sula*, 118–19). For a time she has an epi-
center of sorts in Nel, her girlhood friend. Some of the best passages are
devoted to the rites of passage they go through together. Their experiences
of emerging womanhood, of personal bonds, of death and guilt are very
effectively rendered.

Ultimately, however, a break must come, for Nel eventually defines herself by community conventions, while Sula exists outside such structures. Nel's wedding, which marks the end of part 1, is the occasion of the break. It marks the moment at which Nel actualizes her underlying desire for order by making an identity through a man rather than through herself: "The two of them together would make one Jude" (*Sula,* 83). From this point on, Nel becomes one of the voices of the community; the last half of the novel is built around her position as one who has some understanding of Sula, yet who cannot see the world in the same way. She serves, then, as a character in the middle, between the polarities of Sula and the community.

Nel's ambivalent position becomes clear early in part 2, when Sula returns after a ten-year absence. The marriage to Jude has been frustrating in large part because of his inability to find rewarding work in a white-dominated economic system. These frustrations become self-pity which Nel is expected to nurse, in both senses of healing and feeding. Sula, however, cannot take such an attitude seriously: "I mean, I don't know what the fuss is about. I mean, everything in the world loves you. White men love you. They spend so much time worrying about your penis they forget their own. The only thing they want to do is cut off a nigger's privates. And if that ain't love and respect I don't know what is" (*Sula,* 103). She goes on to talk in the same vein about white women, black women, children of both races, and other black men. She does not permit an identity created by oppression or self-hatred. By this method she restores laughter and perspective to both Nel and Jude.

The same disregard for social convention leads to the dissolution of both the marriage and the friendship. Because she finds Jude interesting, Sula entices him into sexual play that is discovered by Nel. Having no sense of possessiveness or conventionalized identity, Sula feels no responsibility either to her friend's marriage or to Jude's need for love. Truly amoral, she can understand neither Nel's humiliation and outrage nor the husband's desire to leave.

For this crucial part of the story, Morrison shifts to Nel's perspective. This point of view makes it possible to see another character's experience of absence as an experience much different from that of Sula:

> Now her thighs were really empty. And it was then that what those women
> said about never looking at another man made some sense to her, for the

real point, the heart of what they said, was the word *looked*. Not to promise
never to make love to another man, not to refuse to marry another man, but
to promise and know that she could never afford to look again, . . . never to
look, for now she could not risk looking—and anyway, so what? For now
her thighs were truly empty and dead too, and it was Sula who had taken
the life from them and Jude who smashed her heart and the both of them
who left her with no thighs and no heart just her brain raveling away. (*Sula*,
110)

The loss of Jude is the loss of identity and the loss of life. More specifically, it is the loss of what filled her thighs that has deprived her of identity.
Jude's penis was her life, both personally and socially. Whatever the conditions of the marriage, having his name and his body gave her an acceptable
place in the community. The absence of the phallus means a loss of status
in the social order. She now becomes a "woman without a man" and
unable to raise her eyes. For this change she blames Sula who, without a
sense of ownership, cannot conceive of Jude as an object to be taken.

Nel's private experience is a metaphor for the community's treatment of
alien behavior. Sula's refusal of positive identity cannot be tolerated, so she
is explained as a demon. A folklore is created that includes both tales of her
evil actions and interpretations of "signs" associated with her. Like her
mother, she has sexual intercourse indiscriminately with the men of the
Bottom. But unlike Hannah, her behavior is seen as arrogant rather than
complimentary. Without evidence, she is accused of having had liaisons
with white men, which is considered the essence of degradation. Her decision to put Eva into a nursing home is attacked, with everyone ignoring the
old woman's previous behavior.

The "signs" are the means of objectifying the general feeling of distaste.
They become the evidence necessary to fit Sula negatively into the social
order. The "plague" of robins that accompanies her return is taken as an
omen. Accidents are said to be caused by certain dark practices in which
she engages. The most important of the signs is the birthmark over her eye.
Each observer reads it in such a way as to validate his or her own interpretation of Sula's identity. When she is a child, it is seen as a rose bud.
Jude, believing her both threatening and enticing, sees it as a snake.
Shadrack, who fishes for a living and who thinks of her as a kindred alien
spirit, sees it as a tadpole. The community reads it as ashes, symbolizing

both her presumed indifference to her mother's fiery death and her associa-tion with hellish forces. The assignment of meaning to an accident of pig-mentation makes it possible to bring Sula within a structure set up by the interpreter. Bringing her in, even as evil, brings her under control: "There was no creature so ungodly as to make them destroy it. They could kill easily if provoked to anger, but not by design, which explained why they could not 'mob kill' anyone. To do so was not only unnatural, it was un-dignified. The presence of evil was something to be first recognized, then dealt with, survived, outwitted, triumphed over" (*Sula,* 118).

To make her *their* evil was to limit and explain the damage she could do. To recognize her as truly different and alien would be to accept discon-tinuity, disorder, and absence. She must be named so as to render her power manageable. She came to serve an important function in the com-munity as a scapegoat. She took on for them the evil they had previously done to each other. They became righteous as a way of defining themselves as different from her. Mothers previously indifferent to their children be-came fearful and then protective as stories of Sula's evil power spread. Wives threatened by her promiscuity became more attentive to their hus-bands. The group banded together for good now that it had identified evil. A fantasy of power is thus created that enables them to evade conscious-ness of the true oppressors: death and white society.

Nel, though conventional enough to blame Sula for robbing her of her marriage and thereby both her happiness and her identity, does not engage so directly in the social fantasy. Instead, she creates a new identity that equates her suffering with goodness. Thus, when she learns that Sula is dying, she goes to her out of Christian charity, but not out of friendship. What she learns at the bedside again disturbs the center around which she has organized her life. Sula shows not gratitude or remorse, but a candor that is disorienting. When Nel demands an explanation for the affair with Jude, she is told that it was merely a passing fancy. And when she attempts a moral definition of friendship, the response is even more troubling:

> "What did you take him for it you didn't love him and why didn't you think about me?" And then, "I was good to you Sula, why don't that matter?"
>
> Sula turned her head away from the boarded window. Her voice was quiet and the stemmed rose over her eye was very dark. "It matters, Nel, but only

to you. Not to anybody else. Being good to somebody is just like being mean to somebody. Risky. You don't get nothing for it." (*Sula*, 144–45)

Finally, Sula even asserts that perhaps she, not Nel, was the one who was good (*Sula*, 146).

For years, Nel manages to evade the implications of this confrontation. She escapes her own responsibility for self-creation and action by believing that she has been a mere victim. Like the community, she achieves a false innocence by constructing a moral hierarchy with herself at the top and Sula at the bottom. To use the language of *The Bluest Eye*, both she and the Bottom clean themselves on Sula. But such a stance cannot be maintained in the realities of the concrete historical world. The death of Sula, taken to be a sign of better times, brings trouble for the community. Unable to use the strength of the evil one, the people fall back into their selfish, antagonistic ways. The condition is exacerbated when jobs promised by the whites in power do not materialize. On Suicide Day, frustrated citizens join Shad's parade, which ends at the construction site. Here their anger is vented in destruction of the tunnel, with the attendant deaths of dozens of people.

For Nel, the impact is delayed and results in insight rather than cataclysm. As an expression of her goodness, she visits the women in the nursing homes. Twenty-five years after Sula's death and the mass death at the tunnel, she goes to see Eva. Though the old woman is senile, she still makes disturbing observations, such as identifying Nel with Sula, and accusing her of participation in Chicken Little's drowning. Though Nel denies complicity, the accusation has an effect because she was there and did nothing to prevent the death. Thus, Eva, like her namesake, forces on another the knowledge of good and evil and thereby brings Nel out of her self-created innocence into the world of history, experience, and responsibility. The mark of this fortunate fall is her embrace of the spirit of Sula:

> "All that time, all that time, I thought I was missing Jude." And the loss pressed down on her chest and came up into her throat. "We was girls together," she said as though explaining something. "O Lord, Sula," she cried, "girl, girl, girlgirlgirl."
> It was a fine cry—loud and long—but it had no bottom and it had no top, just circles and circles of sorrow. (*Sula*, 174)

200

The cry is "fine" because it is not self-protective or dehumanizing. It expresses sorrow for what had not merely been lost but thrust away through a desire to control and order one's experience. Its lack of conventional structure—no bottom and no top—makes possible the natural and human order of circles, which accepts absence as absence, irreducible yet infinitely meaningful. Nel achieves her true humanity by giving her emptiness its rightful name. This right name makes possible insight but not manipulation; as nearly pure blues expression, it offers not domination but a working through to the truth of experience.

In *Song of Solomon* (1977) the quest is explicitly rather than implicitly for a name. Milkman Dead, a central character with very conventional values, comes to a point at which he feels the need to find out his family's true name. The discovery of this name carries with it a sense of his own humanity and also certain magical qualities connected with black folklore. Naming here has associations with African cultures in which the name is the expression of the soul; because of this, the choosing and keeping of the name is a major ritual.[17] To lose the name or, in Afro-American terms, to be "called out of one's name" is an offense against the spirit.

Consistent with these folk beliefs, the Dead family, whose name was given to them accidentally after the Civil War by a drunken white soldier, act out the designation. The father, Macon Dead, has perverted his own father's efforts to acquire and work the land by becoming an exploitative landlord and real estate speculator. He defines himself and others by accumulation of alienated property. Milkman's mother, Ruth, rejects the present by literally embracing only the past and the future. Macon tells the story of seeing her lying naked on the bed with her father's corpse. And Milkman acquired his nickname by being discovered still nursing at his mother's breast when he was four years old. Ruth, as the daughter of the town's first black doctor, displays the values of the old black bourgeoisie by assuming an attitude of hauteur toward her nouveau riche husband. Their daughters, Magdalene and First Corinthians (whose names were selected by the family tradition of choosing names at random from the Bible), despite their names, are adult virgins who have never been permitted to experience love, either because all men in the community were socially beneath them or because these men lacked sufficient property. Milkman's friend Guitar becomes associated with the Seven Days, a secret society of black men dedicated to exacting retribution for the deaths of blacks killed by whites. The murder of a black child must be avenged by the similar death of a white one on the same day of the week.

Milkman, then, is born and reared in a family that is life-denying. As a sign of this, his birth is simultaneous with the suicide of a man who leaps from the roof of the hospital. As he grows up, he acquires the attitudes of his family and friends. He becomes narcissistic and selfish and treats the members of his family with disdain.

The dialectical movement necessary to move him away from this death-house begins with his discovery of the home of his Aunt Pilate, a woman his father hates for some yet-to-be-determined reason. Pilate has a history and a true name, which she literally carries with her in a small brass box fashioned into an earring. Inside is the piece of paper on which her illiterate father painstakingly copied the word Pilate, the name he insisted she have despite the objections of relatives. Her mother died while giving her birth, and she and her brother later saw their father killed by whites who wanted his land. Having given birth to herself, Pilate creates a family of women much like that of Eva Peace. She herself makes money by selling illegal liquor, and the attendant disrepute is accompanied by a certain folk status since she has no navel and thus is thought to be a child of the devil. Her daughter Reba (whose proper name is the biblical Rebekkah) is marked by her luck; she wins every contest she enters and even those she accidentally happens into. Hagar is the spoiled child of her mother and grandmother, who spend their money to satisfy all of her whims.

Milkman is initially fascinated with this matriarchal household because of its difference from his patriarchal one. Here stories are told, food is tasty and plentiful, and none of the rigidity of his own home is present. Moreover, here he has his sexual initiation with Hagar.

But fascination breeds not understanding but exploitation, which takes two forms. The first is the treatment of Hagar, whom he considers a sexual object to be used at his convenience, but never to be part of his life with his family's and his own respectable friends. Finally, he decides at Christmas to break off the affair, but he chooses to do so in a letter that is the emotional equivalent of his father's eviction notices: "He went back to his father's office, got some cash out of the safe, and wrote Hagar a nice letter which ended: 'Also, I want to thank you. Thank you for all you have meant to me. For making me happy all these years. I am signing this letter with love, of course, but more than that, with gratitude.' "[18]

This male domination through words has the effect of driving Hagar crazy. She sets out to kill him but repeatedly cannot do so. While this insane quest goes on, Morrison introduces other stories of the suppressed humanity and creativity of women. The effect is to provide a sense of a folkloric and historical tradition of oppression. In the barber shop a recent killing is said to be the work of Winnie Ruth Judd, a white woman who kills and dismembers her victims and periodically escapes from the state hospital. For these black men, she serves as a sign of the lunacy of whites who can kill for no good reason; her private torment and motivation is irrelevant to her symbolic usefulness. More pertinent to Milkman is his dream about his mother, which he is not at all certain is in fact a dream. In it, Ruth plants tulip bulbs which immediately emerge as plants and flowers; Milkman expects her to be frightened, but her response is very different: "She leaned back from them, even hit out at them, but playfully, mischieviously. The flowers grew and grew, until he could see only her shoulders above them and her flailing arms high above those bobbing, snapping heads. They were smothering her, taking away her breath with their jagged lips. And she merely smiled and fought them off as though they were harmless butterflies" (*Song of Solomon*, 105). The chaos of creation, which the male fears, is embraced by the female. His mother, who is passive and serious, has a secret garden where she generates and plays with life.

It is in this context that Milkman receives a revisionist version of family history, one that reveals the importance of female creativity to his own life. He follows his mother one night on a long journey to the cemetery where her father was buried. Upon her exit, he confronts her with her monumentalizing tendency, including the incident of necrophilia told him by his father. She responds by expressing the feeling that the doctor was the only one who ever loved her and that she had reacted to his death by kneeling to kiss his hand, not by any perverse sexual gesture. More important, she explains to her son that she was the one who saved his own life. Her husband desired no more children, and insisted that she abort him. She appealed to Pilate, who helped her to defeat Macon's attempts. Thus, Milkman owes his existence to the life-affirming efforts of the two women.

He responds to her story by seeking a way to escape the entire family. In this second act of exploitation, he conspires with his father to steal a green sack from Pilate, a sack which they believe contains gold. Macon tells his son about hiding out with his sister after their father's murder, in a cave where they find buried treasure. They are discovered by a white man whom Macon kills. They flee, but the brother believes that Pilate later returned and took the gold, which is now in the green sack. Milkman and Guitar, who needs money to carry out an assassination, steal the sack, only to discover that it contains human bones.

Still obsessed with the idea of getting money and thereby power, Milkman sets out to find the cave near the old family property. He is at this point also evading both the knowledge that the women have offered and the responsibility that accompanies that knowledge. Just as his father distorted the values of the first Macon Dead by emphasizing possession over creation, so Milkman distorts his father's values by taking on his greed without any sense of responsibility and seriousness. And when he arrives in the family hometown, the folk recollections reinforce this idea. His grandfather and father are remembered, but he hears in the memories a respect for material possession and manipulative energy that validates his self-image.

Only when he encounters the incredibly old woman Circe does he begin to question the object of his quest. Circe was the servant of a white family, the head of which was responsible for the murder of Milkman's grandfather. She recalls the relationship of his ancestors and the real name of his grandfather. She is also the voice of a larger history, for she tells him of the injustices committed by whites throughout the past and implicitly questions his identification with white middle-class values. She also shows him one way to act: she lives in the house of the white family with an ever-increasing pack of dogs, which she intentionally keeps inside so that they will destroy all of the objects that were purchased through the exploitation of black labor. She has willfully outlasted the whites so as to destroy everything they found precious. But she knows the price of revenge; she fully expects the dogs to eat her when she is no longer strong enough to feed them. She has reached the time envisioned by the Invisible Man's grandfather in his admonition to "agree 'em to death and destruction,"[19] but she also accepts full responsibility for her action. Her vengeance contrasts with that of Guitar in that hers is embedded in a concrete history and not an abstract, dehumanizing concept of justice.

Milkman leaves in search of the original home of his grandfather, but his quest is now ambivalent. On the one hand he wants the gold, which he still believes Pilate has hidden; on the other, he wants to know the story of his family. He has worked through concentric relational circles from himself to his parents to his grandparents. At each level the more he has probed the more he has found difference rather than the expected identity. In Shalimar he will move through one more circle, but in the process he will find a new definition of himself.

In the village he for the first time is the alien, for here his city clothes, city talk, and city values are not privileged. He is taken not as one returning to his roots, but as a threatening "white-hearted" presence. To succeed in his quest, he must undergo rituals that will strip him of his false culture and prepare him for authentic knowledge. He hears the children reciting ancient rhymes that are vaguely meaningful to him. But in order to decode them, he must become a member of the community. This happens first with a fight that demonstrates his alien status but also tests his courage, then through the opportunity to participate in a hunt. This serves as the male initiation rite that Milkman has never had and thus his possibility of moving out of his perversely extended, narcissistic childhood. He is stripped of all the symbols of the dominant culture, much as Ike McCaslin is in Faulkner's "The Bear." Though inept, he survives the test, including an unexpected murder attempt by Guitar, who feels he has been betrayed in the pursuit of the gold. Milkman discovers that he wants to live and thus is not truly Dead. He endures and thereby receives the symbols of his success: the throbbing heart of the bobcat killed in the hunt and a woman he can truly enjoy without dominating.

Most important, he begins to decipher the children's song and finds in it the narrative of his family. It is the folktale of the flying African, Solomon, who one day discovers his magical power and uses it to fly from slavery back to his African home. He left behind a wife Ryna and twenty-one children, including Jake, Milkman's grandfather. Ryna, like Hagar, goes crazy over the loss of her man, and her children are cared for by Heddy, an

Indian. The random elements of the past become a coherent family story. The men (Solomon, Jake, Macon, Milkman) seek power, either magical or material; the women (Ryna, Sing, Ruth, Hagar) must suffer for this pursuit; the children are abandoned because of it, but they are saved by a surrogate mother (Heddy, Circe, Pilate) who keeps alive the history for whoever might later need it. It is also preserved as a functional part of the community, in children's songs. Thus the narrative of power and suffering and love dialectically becomes play.

He also learns the relation of the story to identity:

> Under the recorded names were other names, just as "Macon Dead,"
> recorded for all time in some dusty file, hid from view the real names of
> people, places, and things. Names that had meaning. No wonder Pilate put
> hers in her ear. When you know your name, you should hang on to it, for
> unless it is noted down, it will die when you do. . . . He closed his eyes
> and thought of the black men in Shalimar, Roanoke, Petersburg, Newport
> News, Danville, in the Blood Bank, on Darling Street, in the pool halls, the
> barbershops. Their names. Names they got from yearnings, gestures, flaws,
> events, mistakes, weaknesses. (*Song of Solomon*, 329)

Names have a concrete history; they keep alive the complex, painful, disorderly, creative reality of human experience that dominant, logocentric structures seek to suppress. They register the hidden expressions of life in defiance of the controlling Word. They are also liberating and magical. They free Milkman from his death-wish and thus make it possible for him to die if necessary. And he frees Pilate, knowing as he now does that the sack of bones belongs not to the white man Macon murdered but to her own father. Aunt and nephew return them to the cave for proper burial. As part of the ritual of purification, Pilate rips off the earring containing her name; it is unnecessary in the presence of the body of the man who gave it to her and who now himself has his right name. At this moment, she is killed by Guitar, who, like the white man who murdered her father, values possession over human life.

With the elimination of these two generations, Milkman can achieve identity with Solomon/Shalimar the flying African:

> He could just make out Guitar's head and shoulders in the dark. "You want
> my life?" Milkman was not shouting now. "You need it? Here." Without
> wiping away the tears, taking a deep breath, or even bending his knees—

206

> he leaped. As fleet and bright as a lodestar he wheeled toward Guitar and it did not matter which one of them would give up his ghost in the killing arms of his brother. For now he knew what Shalimar knew: If you surrendered to the air, you could *ride* it. (*Song of Solomon*, 337)

This act of identification is simultaneously an act of differentiation, for unlike Solomon, Milkman flies into history and responsibility rather than out of it. And in the process he creates the meaning for his own name. From being the one who sucks nourishment and life from others, he becomes the provider, giving Jake his name and home, Pilate freedom from guilt, and Guitar the life he needs to take. His riding the air implies both play and control, or perhaps control through play, and is thus life-affirming even in the moment of death. The magic word, the true name, conquers for a moment of history, the Word.

While *The Bluest Eye* shows us the victimization that comes in a black community without a sustaining folklore and *Sula* shows us the oppressive nature of a community that uses its folk material as a means of control and evasion, *Song of Solomon* reveals the power that can be achieved through the embrace of a folk history. Claudia tells us of her own failure to overcome oppressive forces in the process of telling of Pecola's madness; Nel achieves an insight that makes true sorrow possible; and Milkman acquired the magical power that can hold joy and sorrow together. In *Tar Baby* (1981), Morrison makes use of the same dialectic of dominant culture and folk experience, but does so in a more complex fashion. Unlike her other works, this novel personifies the dominant culture in the two characters of Valerian and Margaret Street. One purpose seems to be to dramatize the sexually differential effects of the culture on those who wield its power. Another difference is the division of the middle character into two parts: Son and Jadine. In this way it is possible to have both success and failure in achieving insight. Finally, the setting is not the American Midwest and South, but an isolated Caribbean island, Isle des Chevaliers. Though all the major characters are American, the setting is useful in clarifying the effects of the dominant order on personality. Separated from the context of American society, the Americanness of the characters, especially in regard to race, can be more directly observed. The inclusion of native black characters serves not merely as counterpoint but also to suggest a broader sense of Afro-American folk experience.

Isle des Chevaliers is a perverse Eden. Valerian Street, a wealthy American candy manufacturer, purchased it years earlier and gradually built it into a clean, sterile paradise for himself and the few white families to whom he sold some of the land. He has created a carefully controlled environment, but primeval nature constantly threatens to reassert its authority, as is suggested by repeated personifications of butterflies, trees, flowers, and the land itself. Valerian, who has retired from his inherited business, has brought with him to the island his wife, a former beauty queen; two black servants, Sydney and Ondine; and Jadine, the niece of the blacks. Also present are two native workers, known as Yardman and Mary because no one has bothered to learn their real names.

Two elements trouble this paradise. One, an absence, is Michael, the son that Margaret perpetually believes will return but who never in fact makes an appearance. Valerian, who considers her an obsessively protective mother, can rather easily handle the absence until he learns the horrifying history of the mother-child relationship.

The other disruption is an intrusive presence in the form of Son, a black seaman who has jumped ship. Though Valerian tries to naturalize this alien influence by in effect making Son a surrogate for Michael, he is ultimately devastatingly unsuccessful. Son is a traditional figure in black history and lore, the fugitive from an unfair system; but he has reversed the journey of runaway slaves by escaping south to the plantation and its white patriarchy, loyal blacks, and tragic mulatto. He has many identities, but he very quickly learns the true names and relationships of everyone else, including the natives.

The responses to his intrusion reveal the natures and insecurities of the residents. Margaret, in whose closet he is found, has the southern white woman's rape fantasy (even though she is from Maine); she believes that a strange black man would be in a white woman's room only because he intends to sexually assault her. Sydney and Ondine, being proper "Philadelphia Negroes," see in Son a threat to the racial respectability they have achieved. Though they are servants, they have taken on middle-class values, and being black, they feel contaminated by anyone of their race who does not uphold the image they have created. Valerian, considering himself in total control, experiences no fear; he invites Son into the group, confident that his patronizing liberalism will neutralize any threat.

The response of Jadine is the most complex, for she blends together elements of the others. A sensual woman, she is both terrified and fascinated with the sexual energy of Son: she both fears and invites rape. Having an even more refined aura of respectability than her relatives, she is repulsed by his unkempt appearance, uncouth behavior, and lack of education. And yet, like her benefactor, she wants to be in control of situations and people; Son provides an opportunity to test her manipulative skills.

These conditions and personalities set up the double quest that structures the book. Jadine's is epitomized by an African woman she has seen in Paris:

> Under her long canary yellow dress Jadine knew there was too much hip, too much bust. The agency would laugh her out of the lobby, so why was she and everyone else in the store transfixed? The height? The skin like tar against the canary yellow dress? The woman walked down the aisle as though her many-colored sandals were pressing gold tracks on the floor. Two upside-down V's were scored into each of her cheeks, her hair was wrapped in a gelee as yellow as her dress. The people in the aisles watched her without embarrassment, with full glances instead of sly ones.[20]

Later, when the woman leaves the grocery, she pauses outside the door and spits on the sidewalk. In this image is all that Jadine wants: racial pride, arrogance, power in the white world yet disdain for it. In her present world, power and race are divided into the characters of Valerian and Son, and she seeks what each has. But the quests are as separate as the men, and her struggle is to unite them.

On the other hand, Son wants beauty and blackness, which are characterized for him by Jadine and the native woman Therese. In Jade he sees pulchritude, intelligence, and sophistication, all things not previously available to him. In Therese, he discovers the powerful though subterranean forces of his race.

Jade and Son serve as tarbabies for each other. Their contact with each other and the attachment of each to what the other represents denies them the freedom to pursue the goal which is truest for each of them. Ultimately, Morrison establishes a hierarchy of values that sees Son's freedom as success and Jadine's as failure. The hierarchy is based on what is earned by each character, in the sense that the struggle with the tarbaby either does or does not force the character to confront and work through the truth of the self and history. The hierarchy, which is an inversion of surface realities, can be seen in the personifications of the opposed goals Jade and Son free themselves for.

Valerian, the model of Jadine's pursuit of power, was named for an emperor and had a candy bar named after him. The bar, a pink and white confection, was successful only in black neighborhoods, while white boys thought its name and color vaguely homosexual. The family provided Valerian with everything, including a good wife when the time came. Deciding that he would not have the same obsession with the company that his relatives had, he used some of his income to purchase Isle des Chevaliers as a place of retirement and escape. When his first marriage did not work out, he discovered Margaret, Miss Maine, whom he loved in large part because her complexion reminded him of his candy bar. When Jadine was orphaned, Valerian financed her education and early modelling career as a favor to Sydney and Ondine. He created, in effect, a perfect patriarchal system, with everyone created in his own image. Despite flaws in the order, such as Michael's absence and Margaret's mental aberrations, Valerian considered himself a successful deity.

But like his candy bar, his world was an insubstantial confection. One of his eccentric schemes, to have the servants join the family for Christmas dinner, backfires when Ondine, in a moment of stress, reveals Margaret's compulsion as a young mother to abuse Michael with sharp pins and lighted cigarettes. This history destroys Valerian, not because of its horror, but because it exposes his arrogant innocence and impotence. Because he refused to see Margaret and Michael as other than his creations, he could not see the depth of human frustration and suffering implied by such behavior. What he has always taken as his wife's stupidity was in fact the expression of her guilt, a guilt that makes her totally other and thus beyond his control. His power has been an unearned one, and is therefore destroyed by concrete reality. At the end of the novel, he sits in a chair mumbling, while Sydney feeds him and Margaret runs the house.

In Therese we find a very different blindness, one that is both literal and magical. Repeatedly, she and other characters refer to her failing eyesight, but this is compensated for by her ability to see what others cannot. For example, she knows of Son's presence days before Margaret finds him. She names him the chocolate-eater and thus predicts his ultimate commitment

210

to his color rather than Valerian's. She sees the past as well as the present and future: she is said to be one of the blind race, for whom the Isle des Chevaliers is named:

> Son asked who were the blind race so Gideon told him a story about a race of blind people descended from some slaves who went blind the minute they saw Dominique. . . . Their ship foundered and sank with Frenchmen, horses and slaves aboard. The blinded slaves could not see how or where to swim so they were at the mercy of the current and the tide. They floated and trod water and ended up on that island along with the horses that had swum ashore. Some of them were only partially blinded and were rescued later by the French, and returned to Queen of France and indenture. The others, totally blind, hid. The ones who came back had children who, as they got on into middle age, went blind too. What they saw, they saw with the eye of the mind, and that, of course, was not to be trusted. Therese, he said, was one such. . . . "They ride those horses all over the hills. They learned to ride through the rainforest avoiding all sorts of trees and things. They race each other, and for sport they sleep with the swamp women in Sein de Veilles." (*Tar Baby*, 152–53)

Therese believes Son to be one of the race; what she does not see is that he must be enslaved before he can become one of the blind and free.

Valerian and Therese are the polarities between which Jade and Son will move. And they are interacting polarities even though they have no contact with each other. Therese defines herself in part over against the white world, both that of the Valerian Streets who dominate Caribbean life and the white slave masters who originally brought her race to the islands. And Valerian carves his empire out of and against the world of the black natives; he judges his power in part by his ability to keep natural growth out of his palace and his intellectual superiority by his ability to dismiss such folk history as the blind horsemen.

Morrison does not arrange parallel movements between these poles for Son and Jadine. Rather, she has each move between a pole and that in the other which resembles the opposite pole. Thus Son literally and figuratively alternates between Therese and those sophisticated qualities in Jade that she shares with Valerian.

Jadine stands at a crossroads: she has received her advanced degree in art history and has achieved substantial success as a model in Europe. As a consequence of the latter, a wealthy European has asked to marry her. She comes to the island to make a choice without interference. Her choices, however, are all within the realm of white society, consistent with the values taught her by Ondine and Sydney and the opportunities provided her by Valerian.

The costs of such values are indicated in her childhood memory of Baltimore after her first encounter with Son. She remembers female dogs being in heat and willing to be mounted by males in the middle of the street. A neighbor tries to get rid of them:

> Every goddam dog in town'll be over here and he went back inside to get a mop handle to run the males off and crack the bitch over the back and send her home, she who had done nothing but be "in heat" which she couldn't help but which was her fault just the same so it was she who was beaten and cracked over the head and spine with the mop handle and made to run away and I felt sorry for her and went looking for her to see if she was hurt and when I found her she was behind the gas station standing very quietly while another dog sniffed her ass embarrassing me in the sunlight.
>
> All around her it was like that: a fast crack on the head if you let the hunger show so she decided then and there at the age of twelve in Baltimore never to be broken in the hands of any man. . . . When her mother died and she went to Philadelphia and then away to school, she was quick to learn, but no touchee, teacher, and no, I do not smile, because Never. It smoothed out a little as she grew older. The pugnacious lips because a seductive pout— eyes more heated than scary. But beneath the easy manners was a claw always ready to rein in the dogs, because Never. (*Tar Baby*, 124)

She has ordered and defined her life by a firm control of sexual desire. She has equated sexuality with animality and desire with exploitation and has chosen to make herself into a gemstone rather than a woman. But Son disturbs her order: "He did not know that all the time he tinkled the [piano] keys she was holding tight to the reins of dark dogs with silver feet" (*Tar Baby*, 158). Eventually, his sheer physical beauty, obvious desire for her, and "savannahs in his eyes," which suggest an African nobility, compel her to loosen the reins.

After the Christmas revelations make the Street house unbearable, the two of them go to New York, which in its modernity and sophistication is her natural territory. Here the influence of Valerian becomes clear as she seeks to remake Son into her image of the African prince, which is ultimately the only way she can accept him. Mutual affection for a time disguises this manipulative impulse, and because he loves her, he does not resist the education, the parties, and the pretensions. Finally, after a visit to his home, a Florida village she finds unbearably provincial, she realizes that he will always be a native Son, never an African prince, and she leaves him to return to her European suitor.

She rejects not merely him but her own Afro-American heritage and her blackness, the first represented by Florida and the latter by the Caribbean islands. She chooses the fixed life of white values, which are repeatedly associated with death, to the uncertainties of her race, which Morrison consistently associates with life and nature. Moreover, she chooses in effect to be a creation rather than a creator, an art historian rather than artist, a model rather than designer, a wife rather than woman. Thus, the very choice to have a clearly defined identity denies her access to origins and thus negates the very thing she seeks.

For Son, the struggle is much harder because he works from absence toward and then finally away from presence. His values are not dominant, his identity is not fixed, his origin is ambiguous. He lacks conventional identity:

> He was dwelling on his solitude, rocking in the wind, adrift. A man without human rites: unbaptized, uncircumcised, minus puberty rites or the formal rites of manhood. Unmarried and undivorced. He had attended no funeral, married in no church, raised no child. Propertyless, homeless, sought for but not after. . . . In those eight homeless years he had joined that great underclass of undocumented men. And although there were more of his kind in the world than students or soldiers, unlike students and soldiers they were not counted. They were an international legion of day laborers and musclemen, gamblers, sidewalk merchants, migrants, unlicensed crewmen on ships with volatile cargo, part-time mercenaries, full-time gigolos, or curbside musicians. What distinguished them from other men (aside from their terror of Social Security cards and *cedula de identidad*) was their refusal to equate work with life and an inability to stay anywhere for long. (*Tar Baby*, 165–66)

What marks Son and others like them is their refusal to participate in those social orders which categorize and systematize; they create identities by deliberately evading the conventional markers of identity—family, job, education, religion, politics—and they equate this evasion with life. In Son's case, the absence of positive identity literally keeps him from imprisonment since he was responsible for the death of his wife.

Jade tempts him from this world of uncertainty and anonymity by offering visible signs of success: education, money, herself as physical presence and as the actual picture of elegance: in their first encounter, Son is enthralled by photographs of her printed in a Paris fashion magazine. Just as she sees in him a primitive energy to be channeled into civilization, so he sees in her sophisticated beauty in need of passion. In New York he realizes his ambition as long as she is willing to center her existence on him. But once she moves out into her world and tries to take him with her, he begins again to feel the impingement of the documented world.

He tries to overcome this by taking her to Florida, back to his origins, where the name Son has meaning because his father is called Old Man. But the language of this world is one she refuses to understand, seeing it as an alien culture unworthy of her interest. Blackness, so appealing when mediated by Son's beauty, is unattractive in its ordinary folk form of uneducated people, sexual circumspection, and the clothes of working people rather than fashion models. Most disturbing is Son's at-homeness in this world and his ability to love it and her simultaneously. This capacity for inclusion is one she lacks precisely because she, like Sydney and Ondine and Valerian before her, has created her visible and positive identity by excluding such blackness, by making this reality an invisibility and negation. But that very act renders it an ever-present, intolerable part of her existence. Son, who loves both beauty and blackness, and in fact sees them as a totality, cannot understand her need to escape this black village.

Back in New York, the conflict reaches a climax, as each of them assumes the role of savior:

> She thought she was rescuing him from the night women who wanted him for themselves, wanted him feeling superior in a cradle, deferring to him; wanted her to settle for wifely competence when she could be almighty, to settle for fertility rather than originality, nurturing instead of building. He thought he was rescuing her from Valerian, meaning *them,* the aliens, the people who in a mere three hundred years had killed a world millions of years old. . . . Each was pulling the other away from the maw of hell—its very ridge top. Each knew the world as it was meant or ought to be. One

214

had a past, the other a future and each one bore the culture to save the race in his hands. (*Tar Baby,* 269)

The inability to achieve resolution is fundamentally an insistence by both on an origin that can be made present. Each in effect denies history: Son by believing in the possibility of returning to a prewhite black purity and Jadine by assuming that blackness was merely an aberration from the truth of Eurocentric Progress.

But Morrison makes it clear that Jadine's is the greater flaw. She must turn Son into an abstraction; her love is totalitarian and cannot incorporate the differences that are part of his concrete being. When he will not submit, she goes to the island, then to Paris to her wealthy European. He comes, on the other hand, to realize that his love must assume difference; because of this, he leaves, returns, and then pursues her back to the Caribbean.

This very gesture makes possible his rite of passage, for it brings his experience into the realm of folk experience in the sense that he cannot have that which he most needs to live, yet must go on living nonetheless. He goes to Therese, thinking she will help get back Jadine, but she knows better the meaning of his return. She deceives him by letting him believe he is going to Valerian's house, but in fact lets him off on the part of the island inhabited by the blind horsemen: " 'The men. The men are waiting for you.' She was pulling the oars now, moving out. 'You can choose now. You can get free of her. They are waiting in the hills for you' " (*Tar Baby,* 306). Fearful and unable to see, he stumbles over the rocks at first. "By and by he walked steadier, now steadier. The mist lifted and the trees stepped back a bit as if to make the way easier for a certain kind of man. Then he ran. Lickety-split. Lickety-split. Looking neither to the left nor to the right. Lickety-split. Lickety-split. Lickety-lickety-lickety-split" (*Tar Baby,* 306).

Tar Baby marks the final step of immersion into the black folk world. Son achieves his truest nature by becoming one, not with the tellers of tales, as in Ellison, Gaines, and Walker, but with the tales themselves. Like the horsemen, he has been blinded by the prospect of enslavement, but also like them, this very handicap gives him freedom and power. He does not go back to the womb, as Jadine thought, but into the domain of the true black man.

Significantly, such a conclusion is only possible in a magical fictional

215

world, one which in some ways mirrors the submerged Afro-American world of voodoo, conjure, and tricksters. Morrison takes as ordinary experience what more realistic black writers assume to be fantastic. She differs from Jones in taking for granted that what is considered irrational is in fact only a perversion of the natural order by a mechanistic, oppressive social system, whereas Jones is concerned to show that that system generates madness. Thus, for the author of *Tar Baby,* the sight of the blind, the magical power of the impotent, and the spiritual vitality of nonhuman nature makes greater sense than the insanities, grotesqueries, and ironies of the realm of "normality" and order. The particular dialectical structure of her work serves to develop the interrelated irrationalities of white and black culture.

Five

Voodoo Aesthetics: History and Parody in the Novels of Ishmael Reed

ZORA NEALE HURSTON, in *Tell My Horse*, a study of Jamaican and Haitian folk beliefs, describes the practices of the loa (spirit) Guede, said to be the god of the common people:

> He delights in an old coat and pants and a torn old hat. So dressed and fed, he bites with sarcasm and slashes with ridicule the class that despises him. But for all his simple requirements, Guede is a powerful loa. He has charge of everyone within the regions of the dead, and he presides over all that is done there. He is a grave-digger and opens the tombs and when he wishes to do so he takes out the souls and uses them in his service. Guede is never visible. He manifests himself by "mounting" a subject as a rider mounts a horse, then he speaks and acts through his mount. The person mounted does nothing of his own accord. . . . Sometimes Guede dictates the most caustic and belittling statements concerning some pompous person who is present. A prominent official is made ridiculous before a crowd of peasants. It is useless to try to answer Guede because the spirit merely becomes angry and may reprove the important person by speaking of some compromising event in the past in the coarsest language or predicting something of the sort in the near future.[1]

Ishmael Reed, who specializes in verbal attack in both his fiction and his essays and reviews, embodies the spirit of Guede. The connection is in part deliberate: Reed practices what he calls Neo-HooDoo art, which has as one of its functions the challenging of authority.[2] But the parallel runs even deeper, for the method by which Reed makes his challenge is the calling forth of the dead of Western history. He conjures up presidents (Abraham Lincoln, Warren G. Harding, Dwight Eisenhower), religious figures (Moses,

Pope Innocent), and cultural figures (Harriet Beecher Stowe, Marie Le Veau, Sigmund Freud), as well as myths and legends (Osiris, Antigone, Santa Claus). In each case he manipulates the dead to his satiric purposes. Structurally, he takes over the forms of popular literature—the Horatio Alger story, the western, the detective story, *Uncle Tom's Cabin*, Dickens's "A Christmas Carol"—and speaks through them in his own voice.

In a fundamental way it is pointless to evaluate Reed by conventional literary standards, since the cultural assumptions on which these standards are based are themselves his primary target. The pertinent question is whether he in fact creates and practices a new aesthetic or whether, like the black nationalist writers and critics he so often attacks, he turns literature into polemic. Like his opponents, he castigates, satirizes, and vilifies white cultural values; like them he views the dominant society as excremental, repressive, and death-driven. Both implicitly and explicitly, he sees blacks as allies of the life force and whites as death seekers. Unlike the nationalists, however, who emphasize present oppression, Reed seeks nothing less than the demystification and deconstruction of cultural history. He works backward to Egyptian myth to locate the source of the black-white conflict, which he sees as coinciding with the Osiris-Set conflict. From this primal struggle, apparently won by the forces of death, has come the underlying pattern of human experience, which is the effort of life, fertility, and creativity to assert themselves against the control of death, sterility, and repression. Through systemization and violence, the dominant culture has not only maintained its power, but has made itself appear as the true, beautiful, and natural. It presumes to be the only valid voice, the only Word. But because creativity is anarchic, individualistic, and irrepressible, it continually intrudes itself upon the controlling patterns. It is this intrusion, this breaking of the pattern, that Reed designates Neo-Hoo-Doo. His fiction consistently operates dialectically: it exposes and denigrates the oppressive nature of Western culture so as to free the non-Western voices which express life and creativity. And this very act of exposure is the saying of the words which in voodoo practice give one access to the spirits. Thus, Reed serves the function not only of Guede, but also of the houngan (priest) whose litany opens the way to an alternative world.

His six novels—*The Free-Lance Pallbearers* (1967), *Yellow Back Radio Broke-Down* (1969), *Mumbo Jumbo* (1972), *The Last Days of Louisiana Red*

(1974), *Flight to Canada* (1976), and *The Terrible Twos* (1982)—are variations on this theme of cultural conflict. Each presents some aspect of human history and makes clear the continuous character of the struggle by collapsing conventional literary time structures. In such simultaneity, as in the use of the forms of popular literature such as the western and the detective novel, Reed calls into question the dominant society's control of both history and language. His play with time and genre is a way of denaturalizing assumptions about these aspects of culture and revealing the underlying manipulative functions of both. In this, he resembles postmodernist white writers like John Barth and Donald Barthelme. However, his fictions differ from theirs in that his undercutting of literary and cultural values is premised on an alternative value system, Neo-HooDoo. The similarity to metafictional practice is clearest in the early nihilistic works, but, beginning with *Mumbo Jumbo,* he lays claim to a different mythology and aesthetic.

The Free-Lance Pallbearers is Reed's parody of the success-story genre. The "hero," Bukka Doopeyduk, pursues a dream of finding a place as one of the intimates of Harry Sam, the ruler of the land named after himself. Bukka seeks the truth as a Nazarene apprentice, one who studies the texts produced by Sam. Through a series of sacrifices and humiliations, the hero reaches the center of power, only to find the leader to be engaged in disgusting behavior, including cannibalism. Bukka exposes this corruption in an attempt to overthrow Sam, but he himself is sacrificed at the moment of his success. What distinguishes Reed's version of this Horatio Alger story is his excremental vision. Sam's throne is a toilet on which he sits for weeks at a time; the waters around his island are filled with waste materials; his sexual practices are anally oriented. Bukka himself sacrifices his education so as to work in a hospital cleaning bedpans, while U2 Polyglot, the hero's intellectual mentor, pushes a huge ball of dung with his nose to test a theory he has about Kafka's "Metamorphosis." Money, power, sexuality, and language are all metaphorically associated with feces.[3]

The languages of advertising, of politics, of scholarship, of bureaucracy, of medicine, and of religion are specifically shown to be forms of human waste. More important perhaps, the speeches of black community leaders, nationalists, and academics are placed in the same category. In addition, literary references to T. S. Eliot, Ralph Ellison, and Kafka are used reductively in the text, as though they were cultural detritus. Finally, the genre Reed chooses to work in is itself a form of "pulp" fiction which has not been taken seriously (if it ever was) since Nathanael West's *A Cool Million*.

The targets of this parodic quest, the cultural, political, and economic underpinnings of the American Dream, are quite obvious. Less clear are the functions of two motifs—the text and hoodoo—that become increasingly important in Reed's fiction. The text in *The Free-Lance Pallbearers* is the book of Nazarene writings, which is taken to be the key to understanding Harry Sam. The credo shows the proper relationship between Sam and his subjects: "Harry Sam does not love us. If he did, he would come out of the John and hold us in his lap. We must walk down the street with them signs in our hands. We must throw back our heads and loosen our collars. We must bawl until he comes out of dere and holds us like it was before the boogeyman came on the scene and everybody went to church and we gave each other pickle jars each day and nobody had acne or bad breath and cancer was just the name of a sign."[4]

The statement of belief connects Reed's attack on the political system with the anti-Christian tone of the book. The believers, not the God-leader, are held responsible for the failure of communication and love. Thus, the Word coerces even greater efforts on the part of the powerless. For their suffering there may be the reward of the return to a Golden Age, though even in the framework of the novel this Age is absurd. Labor and sacrifice might make possible a time of trivial blessings. But even this hope is undercut when Bukka (Booker/Book) learns at the end of the novel that Sam has never heard of the Nazarene creed: "There was somethin' else puzzlin' me and it confused SAM too but he didn't say anything to you about it because he thought it was some special custom your people had, and didn't want to seem ignorant about it. What was that Nazareeny thing you kept yapping about?" (*Pallbearers*, 154). The lack of relationship between text and reality here suggests a self-imprisoning practice, in this case one engaged in by blacks ("your people") which is superadded to the various oppressive structures imposed by the powerful.

The potentially liberating element, hoodoo, receives relatively little attention in this novel. At one point when Bukka has developed some skepticism about his life and belief, he is said to be under a hoodoo influence which needs to be counteracted. It is the counteraction, in the form of

"Mojo Retraining" that achieves some prominence. "Mojo Retraining" serves as a means of neutralizing the subversive possibilities of hoodoo. Repeatedly in Reed's fiction, the creative potential is challenged by another spiritual force that is manipulated by those in power. Thus, hoodoo must combat not only a mechanistic system but also an antihoodoo which uses magical means to achieve its ends.

The Free-Lance Pallbearers itself can be seen as the hoodoo alternative not present in the story. From behind the mask of the success story, Reed voices the unpleasant, vulgar truth of America as he sees it. Like Guede, he reveals the embarrassing, compromising realities that the powerful, both black and white, want to keep hidden. In this sense, he is not interested in extensive characterization; he has argued elsewhere that his figures are types on the model of African art.[5] Such types quite clearly serve the purposes of his satire, which is directed more toward exposure than reformation. Thus, he works largely by negation; except in his generalized preference of life over death, Reed does not seek to impose an alternative system to replace the existing one. His art depends in fact on the continued existence of oppressors. Like Guede, he needs the powerful in order to have his own voice. The test of the power of his art is his ability to expose and negate, not to assert and control.

Yellow Back Radio Broke-Down (1969) differs from *Free-Lance Pallbearers* in that its hero, while seeming to fail in his objective, comes to understand that life-affirming love is more important than the power he sought. The genre used here is the western, and the Loop Garoo Kid is the black cowboy hero. Loop, whose name is derived from the Haitian Congo spirit Bacca Loupgerow, an especially powerful loa,[6] is characterized as a demonic figure who resists the forces of order and oppression. As in *Free-Lance Pallbearers*, Reed provides an inverted version of popular myth: the forces of law and order become the evil to be done away with by the lone figure whose love of freedom is here seen as the primal satanic threat. The corrupt rancher, Drag Gibson, is the defender of traditional cultural and religious values. Thus, Reed both enacts and reverses the belief system espoused by the genre: good does triumph over evil, but the good is the satanic Loop Garoo.

The title of the book, as explicated by Reed elsewhere, suggests the interrelationships of power, hoodoo, and literary form:

The title *Yellow Back Radio Broke-Down* was based upon a poem by Lorenzo
Thomas called *Modern Plumbing Illustrated.* . . . I based the book on old radio
scripts in which the listener constructed the sets from his imagination—that's
why radio, also because it's an oral book, a talking book; people say they
read it aloud, that is, it speaks through them, which makes a loa. . . .
"Yellow Back" because that's what they used to call old West books about
cowboy heroes—they were "yellow covered books and were usually lurid
and sensational," and so the lurid scenes are in the book because that is
what the form calls for. They're not in there to shock. "Broke-Down" is a
takeoff on Lorenzo Thomas's *Illustrated.* When people say "Break it down"
they mean to strip something down to its basic components. So *Yellow Back
Radio Broke-Down* is the dismantling of a genre done in an oral way like
radio.[7]

Assuming that this analysis represents accurately the design of the novel,
then the concerns of the book reflect the basic theme of Reed's entire canon: the relationship of art and ideology. The western genre, with its lone
hero defending freedom, justice, and goodness against the forces of corruption and evil, becomes a vehicle for examining the society's commitment to
principle. But in the process of breaking the form down to its components,
the author exposes an underlying aesthetic and cultural totalitarianism and
thereby breaks up the form altogether. In a system where law and order are
equated with repression and corruption, the "good" cowboy must be presented as anarchic and demonic. Thus, the dualistic formula of the western, with its clearly defined categories of good and evil, breaks down into
something more closely resembling a dialectic in which good and evil are
defined historically and functionally rather than absolutely. Moreover, the
chronological, cause-and-effect design of the genre cannot be applied,
since the dismantling makes clear the arbitrary nature of the form. Without
fixed relations of story elements based on fixed ideological assumptions,
anything becomes possible.

That "anything" for Reed is the reconstruction of the formula, through
the narrative of its deconstruction, into a new kind of fiction, the hoodoo
western. Essential to this reformulation is its oral character; thus the emphasis on radio. But of course the novel is written; to become a loa requires
that the reader turn it into a litany. Reed seeks a nonlogocentric text, a text
whose power is not in itself but in its ability to call forth that which is not
present. As Loop Garoo says: "What if I write circuses? No one says a novel

has to be one thing. It can be anything it wants to be, a vaudeville show, the six o'clock news, the mumblings of wild men saddled by demons."[8] This freedom and versatility are both the form and content of *Yellow Back Radio Broke-Down*. Loop Garoo's resistance to the forces of control reflects Reed's refusal to follow the formula of the yellow backs or the conventional assumptions about representations of time in the novel.

Loop's methods of resistance are the power of voodoo and the exposure of a related repressed history of culture and religion. Early in the novel, after Drag Gibson's men have attacked the circus with which the black cowboy travels, a dying conjure woman tells him where his power lies: "Flee boy, save yourself, I'm done for, the woman murmured pressing something into his hand. It's a mad dog's tooth it'll bring you connaissance and don't forget the gris gris, the mojo, the wangols old Zozo taught you and when you need more power play poker with the dead" (*Yellow Back Radio*, 26). Loop uses this power to get revenge on Drag Gibson and on the town of Yellow Back Radio for killing his friends. He causes Drag's cattle to die and his crops to wilt and creates a conjure in the traditional manner that makes the rancher go into a physical decline. Every attempt to resist the voodoo power is ineffectual: for example, John Wesley Hardin, the legendary outlaw, is brought in to destroy the Kid, but he goes insane when attacked by Loop's snake.

But Reed has not simply reversed the pattern of good and evil, black and white, in this novel. Loop Garoo fits the model of the Afro-American folk badman: he was a pimp before joining the circus, he literally brands one of the women, and he enjoys humiliating and murdering his opponents. He represents all that is destructive of the existing moral, political, religious, and social order. Moreover, he exposes the manipulative and exploitative motives of those who challenge the dominant ideology with a system of their own; his statement defining art as circus comes in response to the arguments of Bo Shmo and "the neo-social realist gang," who wish to limit literature to a political gesture. The chief evidence of Loop's nihilism is the loa to whom he prays: Judas Iscariot.

This latter point suggests the larger target of Reed's satire: the whole Judeo-Christian tradition of Europe and America, which throughout history has justified the suppression of cultural, religious, and racial differences. For Loop, the real enemy is not Drag Gibson, but God the Father and God the Son. Pope Innocent, called in to neutralize the power of the Kid, explains to Gibson that the church has always been engaged in the destruction of African-based religious practices, which have consistently challenged both ecclesiastical and political power: "It's important that we wipe it out because it can always become a revolutionary force" (*Yellow Back Radio*, 154). In a later scene that is a parody of Dostoyevsky's "Grand Inquisitor," we learn that Loop himself is a Son of God, the satanic one cast out of heaven. As he explains it, he left not out of a desire to supplant patriarchal power, but out of disgust with the smugness and lack of taste and imagination on the part of both Father and Son: "And the Hoo-Doo cult of North America. A much richer art form than preaching to fishermen and riding into town on the back of an ass. And that apotheosis. How disgusting. He had such an ego. . . . Publicity hound, he had to prolong it for three hours, just because the press turned out to witness. And his method had no style at all" (*Yellow Black Radio*, 163).

Here Reed inverts the whole Western aesthetic tradition. Art and imagination are not the expression of order and standards but the subversion of them. They are not the sublimation of a desire for power and authority, but the refusal of these. In fact, authoritarian power is the inadequate substitute used by those suffering from stylistic impotence. Unable to understand this, the pope misreads Loop's motive for allowing himself to be captured and martyred:

> Loop reflected. Remember when he came home that day Innocent? The old man made love to him as if they were man and wife. He licked his punctures and fed him from the breast.
>
> So you think by allowing yourself to be humiliated by mortals he'll respect you too, huh?
>
> No, I just wanted to show the world what they were really up to. . . .
>
> Seems to me that people are getting sick of daddies. (*Yellow Back Radio*, 165)

Loop rejects the notion that he wishes simply to be reinstated in the patriarchy. But his alternative explanation implies a dependence on the father for a sense of his role and identity; his willingness to die rebelliously is still an acknowledgment of the death impulse and not a repudiation of it. His decision to go back with the pope when his execution does not occur seems a resignation and return to patriarchal authority.

But a motif running through the narrative offers another possible read-

224

ing, one consistent with the theme of black expression. Repeatedly Loop and others talk about the woman Diane who "went uptown" on him. She is connected at various times with Mary Magdalene and the Virgin Mary. Her abandonment left him distraught and desperate to get her back, though his pride keeps him from going after her. Thus, we have a typical blues situation: "I almost went out of my mind to suicide, but she went on" (*Yellow Back Radio*, 166). Innocent brings him word that she regrets her action: "Ever since her ascension she's been with the blues" (*Yellow Back Radio*, 161). In fact, God desires Loop's return primarily because she is out of control and threatening the heavenly order: "He wants you to come home too—she's driving them batty. O Loop she's so bitchy, you know how she is. He even put a curse on her but she found a way to absorb that. Matter of fact she's getting a following up there. Both of them are afraid she might start something that'll make your uprising look quite small" (*Yellow Back Radio*, 165). In a final inversion of the western format, Loop Garoo can be seen as riding into the sunset, not away from love and in affirmation of patriarchal order, but toward the beloved and the creative anarchy of the blues relationship. While the satanic, erotic, expressive force leaves the world of history, it does so to become an eternal principle.

In *Mumbo Jumbo* (1972), the hoodoo aesthetic is again the subject and again it fails to be realized. The succeeding work, *The Last Days of Louisiana Red* (1974), may be seen as a companion piece in that both use a detective format with Papa LaBas, a New Orleans houngan, as the investigator. In both novels, the conflict of forces is clear-cut, with a conspiracy by whites designed to destroy the power of hoodoo belief. *Mumbo Jumbo*, with its devices of anachronism, uncovers the mythological and historical sources of conflict and oppression, while *Louisiana Red* exposes a local manifestation of the universal crime. From Reed's perspective, the detective genre fits perfectly his purpose, since "being a Negro in this society means reading motives in a complicated way."[9] LaBas fits into this pattern since his name is the American version of the Haitian Legba, the god of crossroads and beginnings. Since the mysteries to be solved in these two novels are more spiritual than material, it is necessary to have a detective who can interpret the spiritual evidence properly. In this sense, LaBas serves as a guide for the reading of the fictions in which he appears; to read the novels with conventional assumptions about time, plot development, characterization, and verisimilitude is to miss the point. A literal reading renders a nonsensical text, a "mumbo jumbo" narrative; only openness to a symbolic level makes possible an adequate understanding. At this level, the two novels portray battles for voice and power; they depict struggles between the forces of life and those of death.

In *Mumbo Jumbo,* this conflict occurs in its broadest possible historical, cultural, and mythological context. The story, set in the 1920s, concerns the emergence of an "epidemic" called Jes Grew, which manifests itself as anarchic, hedonistic behavior. The "disorder" is explicitly linked to black culture: "He said he felt like the gut heart and lungs of Africa's interior. He said he felt like the Kongo: 'Land of the Panther.' He said he felt like 'deserting his master,' as the Kongo is 'prone to do.' He said he felt he could dance on a dime."[10] Political and economic leaders, fearful of the threat such an outbreak of unstructured pleasure and vitality poses to their control, seek some antidote to the "disease." Hinckle Von Vampton, who understands the spiritual basis of the disorder, is brought in to determine the origin and direction of Jes Grew. Both he and Papa LaBas, who runs the Mumbo Jumbo Kathedral, a center of hoodoo practices, know that Jes Grew is a spiritual energy seeking embodiment in its Text. The main plot line involves the efforts of these two men to locate the Text, Von Vampton to destroy it, and LaBas to preserve it. The methods of Von Vampton—manipulation, exploitation, and violence—are those Reed consistently shows to be associated with the dominant culture. On the other hand, LaBas concentrates on feeding his loas and on uncovering the truth of black history. Eventually LaBas gets his antagonist carried off to Haiti, only to discover that the Text has been burned by Abdul Hamid, a black nationalist who found the work immoral and contrary to his own designs for black life. At the end, Jes Grew dies out, and LaBas returns to obscurity with the hope of the "epidemic's" rebirth. He is last seen speaking to a black studies class in the 1960s and being considered a relic of the Jazz Age.

Consistent with the detective formula is LaBas's discovery of a hidden past relevant to his quest for the Text. Moreover, in a scene common to such fiction, this "cosmic detective" reveals this history, with its complex of motives, means, and opportunities. Unlike the narratives of Dashiel Hammett and others, however, this revelatory scene moves beyond personal history into human prehistory and even mythology. To explain Jes Grew and Von Vampton, LaBas must go back to ancient (and black) Egypt, with its legends of Osiris and Set, who represent respectively the erotic-vitalist impulse and the mechanistic-thanatogomonic impulse. Osiris (the "Black Bull"), through dance, sexuality, and magic, makes the land and people productive and happy. Set, jealous of his brother's popularity, kills him and imposes an order based on exploitation and guilt. Nonetheless, the Osirian beliefs are kept alive, in part through the Book of Thoth, an anthology of the magic and dance designed to give some form to creativity without imposing an absolute structure. LaBas then traces the attempts of the Atonists (named after Akhnaton, who introduced monotheism and thus uniform belief to Egypt) to control the lives of the masses by denying them pleasure and creativity through such ideological devices as Christianity, Islam, the Protestant ethic, and rationalism. Underground are the various manifestations of Osirian values, especially in LaBas's view voodoo, which emphasizes fertility, multiple spirits, and variety of expression.

Human history, in LaBas's version, becomes a conflict for power between Eros and Thanatos. Moving from ancient Egypt to the Crusades to twentieth-century America, Reed shows a consistent pattern of suppression and reemergence of creative, anarchic impulses. This pattern explains history: conquest, religion, economic domination, social control, racism, sexual suppression, and even modernist art can be explained as the efforts of those who have or seek power to eliminate the complexities and thus possibilities of humankind. Eros, taking creation as an end in itself, cannot sufficiently structure itself so as to give its strength direction; thus, it always appears to be dominated. Thanatos, which has order and stasis as its objective, can only continue by bringing more of life under its control; but doing so means that it must constantly change. The Book of Thoth is Reed's metaphor for the artist's ability to make a structure for the articulation of Eros. *Mumbo Jumbo* seeks to be the Text by breaking an established form to allow the intrusion of vital spiritual truth. Appropriately, its disruption of chronological time through the use of anachronism, historicized myth, photographs, drawings, simultaneous narrations, and mixture of historical and fictional events and characters creates a kind of eroticized narrative in which all time exists in a single intense moment. In hoodoo fashion, Reed seeks to take the materials present to him and fashion them into a fetish which provides access to the loas. The narrator goes beyond LaBas, whose mistake was to think that the Text was a fixed word that would bring power when filled with the spirit of Jes Grew. From the perspective of the narrator of *Mumbo Jumbo*, the text is a process, a continuing movement between form and energy that changes with each reader.

In *The Last Days of Louisiana Red*, Reed brings his mythology and aesthetic to bear on a specific community—Berkeley, California—and on relationships within black political and cultural areas. This time, LaBas's investigation focuses not on the universal conflict, but on the particular ways various black groups manifest aspects of that conflict. The Louisiana Red Corporation, a permutation of the Atonist Order, is seen largely through its black agents and fellow travelers. Its antagonist is the Solid Gumbo Works, the organization of hoodoo workers that sets up factories to provide the materials believers need to gain access to the loas. LaBas is sent by the Board of Directors to investigate the death of Ed Yellings, the manager of a Works factory in Berkeley. In working out the details of the crime, the detective uncovers connections with the Corporation and with the Moochers, Reed's parody of black nationalists.

Despite the local setting and limited time frame, the author does move freely in history to show the universality of the issues raised. Minnie, the leader of the Moochers, is implicitly connected with Antigone and Marie LeVeau, the nineteenth-century New Orleans conjure woman. A central point in the book is the destructive, essentially Atonist attitude and behavior of women, especially black women. Reed rewrites the Antigone story as a parable of a female embrace of death rather than an act of rebellion and liberation. Marie LeVeau, the Voodoo Queen, is interpreted as an entertainer who compromises the Work and uses devious means to destroy the reputation of Doctor John, her chief competitor and a true Worker. More immediate to the plot, Nanny, Ed Yellings' maid, works as an agent of Louisiana Red in conjunction with a white man sent to carry out the assassination.

But the real targets here are those labelled as Moochers. Their view of their role is articulated by Minnie:

> "Nothing can stop my Moochers. Next time the sacrifices will be more terrible, bloodier."
> "Why is there always the need for blood, Minnie? Why do you always see 'many casualties' as being victorious?"

"We Moochers understand nothing but blood. Blood is truth. Blood is life. Drink blood, drink it. Blood. Blood."[11]

The vampirish quality of the statement has a double significance. On the one hand, the Moochers teach and practice violence; they thrive on death. Minnie is, in this context, associated with an Antigone who becomes a heroine by embracing her brother in death rather than saving him in life. Minnie repeats this behavior by turning her brother Street, who is a common criminal made political hero, against their brother Wolf, who is the heir to his father's Works. Thus, one measure of the flaw of Moocherism and hence nationalism in this form is its antagonism to the real source of black life in folk values.

On the other hand, the Moochers embody their name by using their militancy as an excuse to siphon off the meager economic gains of the black community. Kingfish and Andy Brown, characters brought in from the "Amos and Andy" radio and television programs, are Moochers who attempt to burglarize the home of their friend Amos, who has achieved some success through hard work rather than mooching. A direct correlation is made between the Business of Ed Yellings that the Moochers want to suck dry for their ideological purposes and the businesses that black men try to create. LaBas makes the point: "You couldn't stand for your Dad and your brothers to run a Business as they sought. You and your roustabouts and vagrants just couldn't stand negro men attempting to build something; if we were on the corner sipping Ripple, than you could love us, would want to smother us with kindliness" (*Louisiana Red*, 125). The statement is a slight variation of one Reed makes elsewhere about a man who owned a bar: "I used to kid him about being a 'capitalist,' and he used to kid back. That was before I found out that an independent black businessman or worker threatens the status quo more than those who spend a lot of time saying that they do." A page later, he remarks, "The Pee Wees of this world, the spine of black manhood."[12]

These observations draw together the thematic and structural threads of *Lousiana Red*. Misogyny, antimilitancy, black entrepreneurship, and hoodoo Business are part of Reed's argument, in allegorical form, that black manhood is the manifestation of the life-force; the qualities of that manhood are diligence, creativity, responsibility, and quiet self-confidence. The black women and ideologues who in any way neutralize these qualities, even in the name of black pride, are in effect coconspirators with whites, who have a long tradition of dehumanizing and castrating black men.

The conflict between Marie LeVeau and Doctor John is presented in precisely these terms:

> "Doc John, as he called himself, didn't need the Madison Avenue-styled show-biz tricks to get his gumbo across because he had gone even beyond Marie, whom Business people all over the world acknowledged as a distiller, successfully fusing the Business with Catholicism. . . .
>
> "Wasn't long after that Doctor John showed up dead. They say he got her daughter pregnant and that infuriated Marie. He was too dark-skinned for her daughter." (*Louisiana Red*, 138, 141)

Doctor John must be killed both because he is too successful and authentic about the "Business" and because his blackness is an affront to the world Marie LeVeau seeks to control. He is an inconvenient reminder, both as a practitioner of voodoo and as a black man, of the "disreputable" source of her power.

Thus, the misogyny of the text serves not only as an attack on women but also as a metaphor for the destructive potential within the black community; it is premised on the belief that the real vitality of black culture is male and that black women who challenge that tradition invite the destruction of their own culture. Reed implicitly makes use of the strongly masculine strain in black folklore. His male characters are versions of John Henry and occasionally Brer Rabbit as well as the male voodoo gods. Similarly, the antimilitancy of the narrative is not a denial of political reality but an assertion of the oppressive nature of any ideology. LaBas makes the point clear: "They are the moochers who cooperate with their 'oppression,' for they have the mentality of the prey who thinks his destruction at the fangs of the killer is the natural order of things and colludes with his own death. The Workers exist to tell the 'prey' that they were meant to bring down killers three times their size, using the old morality as their guide: Voodoo, Confucianism, the ancient Egyptian inner duties, using the technique of camouflage, independent camouflages like the leopard shark, ruler of the seas for five million years" (*Louisiana Red*, 172).

As in *Mumbo Jumbo*, LaBas's function is to stand between the two worlds, to identify the real truth behind the appearances, to explain the true nature of power and voice. He is not an actor but a guide, just as Legba is the loa one goes through to get to the active spirits. As the figure in the middle, he is taken by other characters as ineffectual and irrelevant; but this is precisely his usefulness to the reader. He stands as the interpreter of the apparent noise of the text; by absorbing it all he can shape it into a coherent pattern. Freed from conventional assumptions about time, space, and causality, he has a certain omniscience that both defamiliarizes and brings order. As "cosmic detective," he forces the reader out of ordinary patterns of response so as to make possible the understanding of larger, more significant patterns. In essence, LaBas in *Mumbo Jumbo* and *The Last Days of Louisiana Red* forces the reader to become a "cosmic detective."

The ideas of camouflage and working so important in *Louisiana Red* are carried over to *Flight to Canada* (1976). In this fifth novel, Reed becomes more metafictional than ever. References to texts, discussions of writing, and a range of forms of expression are present throughout the narrative. The genre most obviously being used is the slave narrative, but it emerges not so much in parody forms as in dialectical opposition to Harriet Beecher Stowe's *Uncle Tom's Cabin*, which is itself seen as a distortion and plagiarism of the narrative of the former slave Josiah Henson. In this sense, authentic black forms of expression are set over against false, sentimental, exploitative forms, whether black or white. The title *Flight to Canada* is specifically a reference to a poem by Raven Quickskill, the central character; but the poem, designed to assert its author's independence, is itself a fiction, since Quickskill only goes to Canada long after it is written. In fact, the poem both makes it possible for him to get there and compels him to go, since its publication puts slave-catchers on his trail. Moreover, the narrative that is actually being undertaken at the conclusion of the novel is not that of the poet, but rather that of Uncle Robin, who has achieved his freedom by never leaving Virginia. Rather, he has reached his goal by rewriting the will of his master. We have, then, a version of literary tricksterism consistent with the folk forms of such behavior. Thus, in *Flight to Canada*, the relationship of freedom and literacy, which Robert Stepto has identified as the central motif of black literature,[13] is a highly ambiguous one. Crucial to freedom and identity are the abilities to sort among the false meanings of

231

the Word in order to find the true one, and also to create one's own true text, even if it must appear false. Raven Quickskill, who has no Papa LaBas to guide him, must undertake the quest himself.

Unknown to Quickskill, a conspiracy goes on behind the scenes, as in all of Reed's fiction. The creator of this political-economic order is Arthur Swille, the poet's owner. Swille, who is indirectly identified with the Rockefellers, runs the country through his manipulations of the economic system; he even has Abraham Lincoln under his control. The weakness in his pattern is that he believes the images he has helped to manufacture. He thinks that Lincoln fits the stereotype of the country rube and therefore is incapable of such an act of liberating authorship as the Emancipation Proclamation. He is so taken with the versions of life created by Edgar Allan Poe and Sir Walter Scott that he engages in necrophiliac incest with the body of his sister while literally forcing his wife into the shape of the southern belle. Later, the woman and the ghost kill him. Most important, he believes that the Uncle Tom image of black slaves makes it impossible for them to be anything other than loyal and submissive. He even encourages literacy as a tool for work, not realizing the subversive potential of writing. When slaves like Quickskill run away, he explains it "scientifically" as drapeto-mania, a disease that causes blacks to run away. Seeing and shaping the world in terms of superficial literary figures rather than immediate reality leads directly to Swille's death and the acquisition of his empire by his own Uncle Tom, the manservant Robin. This occurs because Robin, like Frederick Douglass, learned that literacy can be the vehicle of freedom and rewrote Swille's will to make himself the heir of a fortune built on black sweat and blood.

Quickskill's problem is also one of the relation of language and reality. He takes literature much more seriously than Swille; he says of the theft by Stowe of Henson's narrative: "A man's story is his gris-gris, you know. Taking his story is like taking his gris-gris. The thing that is himself. It's like robbing a man of his Etheric Double. People pine away. It baffles the doctors the way some people pine away for no reason. For no reason? Somebody has made off with their Etheric Double, has crept into the hideout of themselves and taken all they found there. Human hosts walk the streets of the cities, their eyes hollow, the spirit gone out of them. Somebody has taken their story."[14]

The narrative is the self, the ordering of identity that gives body and voice through language. Quickskill's problem is determining both the nature and control of the narrative. He must contend not only with other voices, such as Swille's, that claim control over his story, but also with the power of the story to act independently of him. He repeatedly attempts to find out when, if, and where his poem has been published, who has read it, and how they have interpreted it. The poem gains him a reputation, including an invitation to the White House, but it also makes him visible as a fugitive. Thus, the writing always exceeds its author's designs. It is more than his life; it has a life of its own.

One of the narrative purposes of Quickskill's travels seems to be to give him opportunities to debate the nature and function of art. One of his fellow fugitives, 40s, contends that art is a luxury that blacks can ill afford:

> "You got to be kiddin. Words. What good is words?"
> "Words built the world and words can destroy the world, 40s."
> "Well, you take the words; give me the rifle. That's the only word I need. R-i-f-l-e. Click." (*Flight*, 81)

Another member of the group has chosen to use his talents as a producer and actor in pornographic films. Leechfield argues that Quickskill's principles and poetry have had no practical effects: " 'We did it' wasn't paying my rent" (*Flight*, 74). Pornography does, and since Leechfield believes that money is what the nation understands and respects, he does what he has to to get some.

On another level, the poet argues with Princess Quaw Quaw, an Indian dancer, about the validity of ethnic art. She contends that the only true art is that which develops universal themes, a position he contends is only another form of slavery: "They're going to get your Indian and my Slave on microfilm and in sociology books; then they're going to put them in a space ship and send them to the moon. And then they're going to put you on the nickel and put me on a stamp, and that'll be the end of it. They're as Feudalist and Arthurian as [Jefferson] Davis, but whereas he sees it as a political movement, they see it as a poetry movement" (*Flight*, 96). He sees art as an act of subversion that those who control the culture try to neutralize by trivializing it or turning it into nonart, just as slaveholders turn blacks into nonhumans. "Flight to Canada" serves his purposes by being an overt rejection of both the image of black illiteracy and the "proper" poetic forms.

But in order to go beyond rebellion, Quickskill must come to terms with the idea of Canada. He persists in believing that the physical Canada matches the image in his mind. Like Swille, he assumes no difference between signifier and signified. And like his master, his misreading brings him to the brink of disaster. Canada was the site of Josiah Henson's failed utopian dream, and it is the home of whites who hate blacks as much as southerners do. Learning this harsh truth makes it possible for Quickskill to grasp the meaning of his own gris-gris: "Canada, like freedom, is a state of mind" (*Flight,* 178). His flight to Canada can only be fulfilled by a return to Virginia. As the Raven, an outlaw scavenging bird, he finds both his subject and his vocation in the story of Robin, the seemingly domesticated slave who has built his nest by camouflaging his true colors. Quickskill's literary talents are realized in beginning the narrative of deception, which is also the narrative of truth. In the tradition of black folk expression and slave narratives,[15] the two can never be separated. Through the use of such black materials, Reed brings us around to the paradox of art: only in artifice is reality to be known. There is no origin, no fixed ascertainable reality prior to images of that reality. The games played with time, character, and form serve to point out the deceptiveness of conventional perception by foregrounding its arbitrary nature. Canada is real, but only as a state of mind. The moral significance of this point, and that which takes Reed beyond metafiction, is his contention that in imposing one image of reality for the purpose of controlling real human beings, those who dominate the culture create slavery and bring about suffering and death. The freedom of artistic expression, then, has political and social consequences. Like the slave narrative, the very existence of imaginative art contends against uniformity and oppression. For Reed, such art works most effectively when it operates in the black folk tradition.

The Terrible Twos (1982) attempts to bring this claim of freedom into the very heart of white society. For the most part, Reed's earlier works have equated black with life and freedom and white with death and oppression. Failed black characters were those who in one way or another did the bidding of white masters. In *Twos,* however, he looks to one of the central legends of the dominant American culture, Santa Claus, for evidence of

234

imaginative and moral freedom. Such a choice makes sense in Reed's aesthetic, for as one character says of the Christian figure, "Nicholas was a
model capable of producing endless variations."[16] Reed makes use of the
European legends of Saint Nicholas, in some of which he is a vaguely disreputable figure accompanied by a small black man named Black Peter.
According to the narrator, stories differ as to whether Nicholas or Peter
was the servant. The plot follows a typical Reed pattern: a conspiracy
exists to make the image of Santa Claus the private property of the North
Pole Development Corporation, which plans to build a massive shopping
complex at the North Pole and to lease the rights to Santa Claus to various
stores. Opposed to this monopoly are the Nicholasites, led by the Boy
Bishop and Black Peter, a former street ventriloquist. Within the cult, a
debate goes on over the proper image of the Saint, with Peter arguing that
Haile Selassie ought to have equal standing as a figure of generosity; he
contends that Santa Claus is the white American offshoot of the legend (an
offshoot that excludes the Black Peter stories) and blacks ought to be allowed their own version. Meanwhile, a political plot is developing that will
make possible the destruction of Third World populations as well as American minorities, with whites, American and Soviet, then in firm control of
the earth.

The narrative structure is loosely based on Charles Dickens's "A Christmas Carol," complete with Christmases past and future, a Tiny Tim figure,
and a variety of Scrooges. The two plot lines come together through this
structure as the President, a male model being manipulated by his aides, is
taken to hell by Santa, who introduces him to the "duppies" (ghosts) of
Dwight Eisenhower and Harry Truman, who are suffering because of their
crimes against Africans (specifically Patrice Lumumba) and the Japanese
(specifically Hiroshima and Nagasaki). Made to see his responsibility, President Clift first brings gifts to the crippled grandson of his black servant and
then makes a television speech exposing the threat to the Third World.
Simultaneously, Black Peter has kidnapped the Corporation's Santa Claus
and substituted a figure through whom he tells the people of their right to a
Christmas free of coercion and uniformity. The result is a violent confrontation with the Corporation's henchmen. Santa and Peter are last seen flying
off into the night.

Clearly, Reed's targets are his usual ones: those, primarily white, who seek cultural, political, and economic control over what he sees as a diverse, creative, and potentially great society. The key to resisting this homogenizing oppression is again folkloric material, which in this case must be stripped of its commercial trappings and revealed in all its anarchic, rebellious ambiguity. America's arrogant assumptions about itself are shown to be the selfish attitudes of a terrible two-year-old that has not yet learned the ancient, beneficent character of its ethnically-diverse civilization. Its monopolizing impulses are deadly versions of the narcissism of an infant that sees the world only as an extension of itself. The legends and folklore challenge this national egocentrism by showing the central image of consumerism, Santa Claus, to be a figure who cannot be reduced to a symbol of accumulation. Significantly, his black companion voices through him this refusal of a materialist orientation.

Black Peter is a trickster who kidnaps, throws his voice, and uses the dead to his own benevolent purposes. A black man with red hair (like Reed), he is also an artist figure and "whatever his art lacked in technical craftsmanship, it made up for in originality" (*Twos*, 83). His role as artist is to bring variety by recovering subjects and approaches that have been lost. Thus he paints Haile Selassie as Saint Nicholas; he makes himself into that saint's ancient companion; and he gives Santa Claus true words to say about the significance of the saint. He is not entirely successful in his efforts; the North Pole Corporation continues to exist, just as those conspiring against the Third World remain in power after committing the President to a sanitarium. But as with traditional black tricksters, small gains, not revolution are the object. The Corporation's Santa announces that he is starting a mission to aid the needy, and the son of a powerful white lawyer goes to a secret New Year's party where the walls are covered with posters of Selassie-Nicholas. Thus, even though Black Peter is not a voodoo figure, like Loop Garoo or Papa LaBas, he serves the same function as the vehicle through which Reed attacks the structures and images of white American society. The achievement here is in finding in one of that society's own myths a contradiction of its values.

Ishmael Reed, as fictionist, seeks to enact the functions of the various loas of voodoo. As Guede, he attacks, often viciously, those he opposes, including white cultural, political, and business figures; black ideologues and critics; women who cooperate with white oppressors by undercutting black manhood; and religious teachers of both races. Like his model, he frequently sharpens his satire by references to private sexual behavior. As LaBas (Legba), he connects the material world with the spiritual world, both thematically by showing the delusion of material prosperity and power and structurally by using his material allegorically. He decodes the signs so as to reveal the message of the ongoing conflict between the affirmers of life and the merchants of death. Generally speaking, he inverts conventional sign systems by associating black with life and white with death. Finally, as a loup garou, he invades various genres and reshapes them to his own purposes. Thus, the detective story, usually a vehicle for affirming the validity of rationality, becomes a means of exposing order as oppressive and proclaiming the priority of disordered life. As an artist, Reed has no problem in using contemporary, often metafictional techniques to make social and cultural criticism. He uses anomalous materials, anachronism, cartoonlike characters, radical time shifts quite self-consciously and often self-reflexively to undermine what he considers to be indefensible values. In this he shares the aesthetic principles of Barth, Barthelme, and Pynchon. But unlike them (except, perhaps, Pynchon), his undermining is premised on an alternative value system, one that includes diversity, creativity, artistic freedom, and cultural democracy and that he insists has its true basis in the black folk system. This combination of method and value can be called his voodoo aesthetic.

Six

Orphans and Circuses: The Literary Experiments of Leon Forrest and Clarence Major

LEON FORREST AND CLARENCE MAJOR, though experimentalists like Ishmael Reed, differ from him, just as they differ from each other. Whereas Reed relies on parody and social criticism, the work of the others is much more self-contained. Forrest writes surreal, stream-of-consciousness stories that owe some debt to Faulkner, Joyce, Proust, and, in their intensity of language, Dylan Thomas.[1] Major, on the other hand, is postmodernist in his attitudes toward fiction. His work reveals a background of Henry Miller, William Burroughs, and Jorge Luis Borges. Forrest and Major, of course, are not mere imitators; like all good writers and like generations of blacks, they use what they find to their own advantage. Along with Reed and others, such as Charles Wright and the early Imamu Baraka, they have redefined what is possible in black fiction. Following the lead of Ellison, they tend to emphasize the telling more than the tale and have thereby added a new dimension to black writing.

The fictions of Leon Forrest are surrealistic in their effects. They figure forth nightmares and apocalyptic visions; they collapse and confuse the sense of time; they portray intense, often destructive, emotional states; they present personal and family histories filled with coincidence, violence, and madness; and they do all this in a language that moves rapidly across biblical, street-slang, mythic, folkloric, and literary systems of discourse. He presses both language and the fictive realities it conjures up to the point of incomprehensibility. At the same time, he establishes clear boundaries: *There Is a Tree More Ancient than Eden* (1973) concerns a day in the life of Nathaniel Turner Witherspoon, an adolescent coming to terms with the

238

death of his mother. *The Bloodworth Orphans* (1977) again uses Nathaniel as a center but focuses on the black community of which he is a part. In both cases the stories move across time and space with these fixed reference points.

The surrealism is in part a function of the sense of displacement and disorientation that many black writers (as well as the artists of other oppressed groups) have articulated as inherent in a racist world. Frederick Douglass, W. E. B. Du Bois, Richard Wright, Ralph Ellison, and Toni Morrison, as a small sampling, have recorded the nightmarish, irrational quality of lives in a world where the arbitrary quality of skin color has labeled characters grotesque and inhuman. The extent to which whites in these fictional worlds (and in the real world they represent) take racial distinctions as the natural and normative state of reality only heightens the surrealism. In some cases the writers choose to let the irrationality stand as an indictment of American society.

In the case of Forrest, however, and those with whom he chooses to identify himself (such as Ellison and Morrison[2]), the desire is to go beyond condemnation in order to register an affirmation of the resources that blacks bring to bear on their condition. "Black writers have the special duty to reveal how our people have been dominant carriers and reshapers in a very fundamental way in the cultural life of America."[3] The very richness of cultural material carried by blacks itself becomes part of the surreal quality of Forrest's fiction. Blues, spirituals, biblical stories, folk narratives, folk speech, folk and popular heroes, Greek and Egyptian myths, strong mother figures and heroic father figures, religious faith and folk "superstition," mother-wit, and world, national, racial, familial, and personal history are readily and simultaneously available to the characters in these novels. By using a style that is breakneck and that does not distinguish among these resources in creating stream-of-consciousness passages, Forrest reinforces the irrational aura of his fictions while displaying the spiritual and cultural wealth of a group denied political power, social recognition, and material prosperity. The dialectic at work here, perhaps as clearly as in *Invisible Man*, is between this folk wealth and political and social deprivation; the deprivation actually seems to enhance the wealth, while the folk materials make possible the endurance and occasional overcoming of the oppression.

Forrest's image for this condition is the orphan who experiences abandonment, anger, guilt, namelessness, and alienation, yet for this very reason must call on very deep human resources to find the strength to endure
and create a self. Orphanhood reflects not only the political reality of blacks
but also their history. Kidnapped from African societies where extended
families were the primary social units, victims were additionally separated
during various stages of slave trading from other members of their cultural
group. Once on the plantation, blacks were not permitted legal recognition
of whatever marital arrangements they made; moreover, they had no re-
course or appeal if white masters chose or were financially forced to break
up families. Added to this was the fairly common practice of miscegenation, which produced black children who were not recognized by their
white fathers and who could not claim either their fathers' heritage or their
fathers' name. Thus, from Forrest's perspective, we have created in America a group of millions of people dispossessed and orphaned.

There is a Tree More Ancient than Eden, unlike *The Bloodworth Orphans,*
deals with the personal and private rather than social condition of orphanhood. Nathaniel Turner Witherspoon, during the progress of the
novel, has to come to terms with the death of his mother (and the unex-
plained absence of his father through much of the text). He must deal not
only with the loss itself but also with what that loss means for his developing sense of self. His problem on this second point is less one of deprivation
than of excess. His family is Catholic, but the strong "aunt" figure in his life
is devoutly Protestant; within his light-skinned family are those who hate
and those who embrace darker blacks; he knows religious songs and stories as well as blues and "bad nigger" tales; there is a tradition of strong,
rebellious male figures in his family; he has friends who are both creative
and disreputable. Without parents to direct him, he is in danger of diffusing
his self. These problems of loss and excess are presented through the mind
of Nathaniel in sections entitled "The Nightmare," "The Dream," "The Vision," and "Wakefulness." After an initial part called "The Lives," which
serves to provide names and relevant background information, the book
moves through these sometimes orderly, sometimes apparently chaotic,
vaguely associational sections. Presenting the narrative through such
stages of consciousness makes it possible for Forrest to give a full inventory
of the cultural resources of even a young, innocent black man. Even the

240

"Wakefulness" section shows little constraint on the pouring forth of images and experiences. When all the stages have been endured, Nathaniel can give expression to his grief and can begin the process of self-definition.

Though the images and allusions vary widely, they tend to fall into two categories: vertical and horizontal. Analogously, the text alternates between metaphoric and metonymic patterns. The vertical images and references are trees, birds, ladders, spirituals, and angels while the horizontal ones are trains, wagons, rivers, blues, and riders. The metaphoric patterns are those that add levels of meaning to a particular image. For example, the train variously refers to the gospel train of the spirituals, the underground railroad Jericho Witherspoon used to escape slavery, the death train that returned the body of Abraham Lincoln home to be buried, and the hearse that carried Nathaniel's mother. A metonymic pattern, one that develops an image, character, or situation through narrative or argument, is apparent in the short biography of Jamestown Fishbond included in "The Lives" section. These patterns are not exclusive: metaphoric elements are often elaborated in a linear fashion while metonymic elements, consistent with the surreal character of the text, often proceed through shifts in the shape or meaning of images. Each section involves rapid changes in kinds of images and allusions and in structural patterns.

Such form shifting is evident even in the opening section, where relevant figures for Nathaniel's consciousness are described. The catalogue includes not only his relatives and friends but also historical figures somehow important to him: Louis Armstrong, Frederick Douglass, Harriet Tubman, Abraham Lincoln. Persons so clearly identified with the slavery-freedom dynamic of black life suggest the constant presence of a dialectical history in black life. Even Armstrong fits this pattern: "Press-music-money magnates always kept out of the news the very substantial contributions Armstrong made to the freedom movement, as they enjoyed dividing Dipper from the young and his own people on the shaky grounds that he was a Tom when in the end it was from the people themselves that Armstrong's towering and revolutionary power issued."[4] The tension inherent in black experience is clear even in its popular music. The real source of artistic power must be suppressed because all black expression by its very nature has political implications. Designating Armstrong a "Tom" is a form of "calling him out of his name," denying his true identity and his true origins so as to control the effect of his art. Thus Nathaniel, in describing Armstrong in such terms, makes him another of the orphans.

In describing his own life, Nathaniel focuses on male figures like Armstrong. He talks of the influence of his father, who refused to share the status of his mulatto family, which had made its fortune with bleaching creams and slaveholding; he is an idealist with an edge of bitterness: "And him, Father, rather than 'becoming anything' became nothing if he couldn't be everything—but became everything to me, even as he trained and demanded that I try to catch the stars in orbit, without expostulation; yes, and how to appreciate a flower and to listen to a poem, and how to switch-hit and how to love and yes, something of hate as well" (*Tree*, 4). But the "everything" here is an evasion which cannot be continued, just as is the refusal in this section to address the event which triggers the narrative, the death of his mother. The potential conflict emerges: "But also contemplating that, in a very real fashion, I had depended so much upon the people closest to me to give definitions to my life and to the events, courses, orbits, and directions, yet juxtaposed to this dependence was that something else lurking and brooding underneath: eruptive violence and a fierce desire to mold and sculpt out of my dreams, a world in flight" (*Tree*, 5).

The opposition of dependency and the "something else" suggests a struggle against the father as part of the process of creating a world. The violence necessary for self-creation is in large part precisely the effort to supplant the father as maker and namer. Most of the narrative concentrates on that "something else" characterized by both chaos and form. The dreams themselves manifest certain possible shapes in the lives, songs, folk narratives, and bits of history and myths kaleidoscopically joined in the last four sections of the novel. Nathaniel seeks the Word that will be the beginning of his world. But this word must carry him beyond his dependency if he hopes to gain self-determination; the end is not an absolute freedom but rather a tension between the fixity of a formed world and the motion of flight.

In searching for a shape, Nathaniel undergoes a "Nightmare" dominated by figures of father-defiance. He sees himself as a fallen angel, his "wings, lamblike on the outside but yellowed like an ancient scroll, greasy, black and purplish blue, like bruised blood, tough and wolfish underneath"

242

(*Tree*, 42). He has become Lucifer, cast out of heaven for presuming to be God's equal. Forrest indicates in *The Bloodworth Orphans* that Lucifer was rejected because he was so beautiful that he became prideful and God became jealous.[5] Set over against this image is one of heaven and Jacob's ladder, but with the distinction that this ladder segregates the angels into black and white: "And atop each star, milk-white angels dance—yet some are kneeling and praying with tears in their dreaming eyes like waves gushing through lily-white sands. And behind them those other angels—black skeletons tossed and driven, clacking together, as if they had been hatcheted down from the uppermost tops of the most massive trees in Eden, then caught and divided into black dancing limbs and branches" (*Tree*, 42). This image condenses the levels of meaning of the tree of the title. It functions simultaneously as a cross, as a lynching tree, as the Edenic Tree of Knowledge, and as the mythic Tree of Life. Blacks are thus presented as Christ-scapegoat figures, an idea more fully developed in "The Vision," but also linked, because of their race, both with the knowledge of good and evil and with a life principle. Their persistent presence reminds whites of the "blood on the leaves and blood at the root," a Billie Holliday blues line Forrest uses as epigraph and as refrain throughout the novel. They are the certain signs of the nation's guilt, and its refusal to do penance for that guilt. Like Nathaniel's wings, their apparent quietude conceals the harsh realities of physical and spiritual struggle. But the persistence also symbolizes a belief in life. The skeletons are not dead: "The black angels shift inside of the balloon-jawed [like Louis Armstrong] rhythms as if a streak of lightning had shot up and through them and made their heads, shoulders, hips, fingers, and feet move with a supple, switchblade swiftness" (*Tree*, 42). Like Lucifer refusing to submit to God's authority, these angels refuse the death of their lynching-crucifixion-dismemberment.

Other chapters in the "Nightmare" section develop these linked ideas of defiance and vitality in more human contexts. Chapter 3 tells some of the story of Jamestown Fishbond, who Nathaniel recalls primarily riding with his stepfather in a wagon filled with fresh fruit and vegetables. Juxtaposed to this is the memory of his own extended mulatto family and its disdain of darker members of their race. These two recollections collide when Jamestown, insulted by being refused admission to the Witherspoon house by black-hating Uncle DuPont, retaliates by nearly decapitating the man with a cantaloupe thrown off the wagon. The mulatto arrogance grows out of a sense of physically identifiable closeness to the white father and thus the source of all they consider strong and good. Jamestown fires his cantaloupe at exactly this presumption.

Jamestown's defiance and creativity go further than his street life, however. A talented painter, he must deal with the ideological demands of the educational system. He wins an art contest by submitting, at the insistence of his teacher, a painting of Lincoln comforting a slave. But he is then expelled, in part because he secretly enters a second painting, entitled "Fear No More the Stench of the Dying Sun, for Heaven Is a Reefer and Salvation a Lost Bottle of Wine, Worth a WEE Bit More than Thirty Pieces off the Eagle's Ass," rumored (since neither Nathaniel nor any of the other students are permitted to see it) to include "a huge black man, a broken crucifix, a wine bottle. . . . and there was a flag with thirteen holes in it, a Bible going up in flames, two crazy clowns, a great bird that looked, so we heard, like an eagle, a golden cord running all through the picture and a crazy-looking black man" (*Tree*, 55–56). In talking to Nathaniel, Jamestown makes a clear distinction between this work—"the one I washed out of myself for love"—and the other, "out of my Uncle Tom side" (*Tree*, 57). Thus, a key theme of the novel emerges: expression of the truth of the self, and of experience, no matter how violent, fierce, angry, disreputable, or even obscene, will be necessarily an expression of love. "Uncle Tomming" may be necessary to survival but it can never have the same status as true art; it serves only as a mask to hide the real identity of the actor.

For Nathaniel, a more direct metaphor of the sensibility he is trying to shape into a self is the story of his great-grandfather, Jericho Witherspoon, a slave who refused to tolerate his incarceration and who hated those who presumed to enslave him. Like Jamestown, he combines the roles of badman, trickster, and freedom-lover:

> Known to be a potential leader and *always* a dangerous nigger who apparently thinks of himself as a white man. . . . Armed constantly and must be taken, if he is to be taken by any white men, by at least a platoon of Our best, or Your best up there, where no doubt he is. . . . Very, very foul of mouth and evidently despises the ground upon which the master race walks; yet dangerous too because he knows the way of the house so well that he

can pose and even out-pose a true-born, true-blue son of the legitimate. (*Tree*, 33–34)

His distinguishing mark is the brand "J.W." burned into his shoulder by his master in a vain attempt to control him, "scalded into place to know his place, his right from his left, his wrong from his right" (*Tree*, 67). But the marking and labeling succeed in an unintended way, for they inspire Jericho to fill his name with his own meanings, to preserve the brand as a record of his ability to endure the pain, defy the master, and live to tell his story to his great-grandson.

Two other images, drawn from black culture, reinforce the notion of resistance in this section. The first is Charley "Yardbird" Parker, jazz saxophonist who helped to revolutionize music by undermining, through bebop, the sterile, white-dominated music that jazz had become. But his flights of artistic freedom were bought at the price of derision and harassment, and also of the self-destructiveness of heroin addiction. But another bird, the gray goose of black ballads, provides another option. Like Parker, Jericho, and Jamestown, the goose is attacked and mistreated; specifically it is "shot, plucked, boiled, parboiled, thrown to the hogs, run through the buzz saw." But it is too tough to be defeated: "in the end [it] would be seen flying off with his progeny, quink-quanking derisively at his tormentors."[6] The song suggests that refusal to succumb results not only in freedom but also in the expression of the voice. All of these males provide Nathaniel with alternative Father-God figures, who seek not domination but the creative possibilities of the voice gained through suffering.

"The Dream" responds to the call of "The Nightmare" by emphasizing faith and community in counterpoint to the freedom of the individual. Hattie Breedlove, Nathaniel's "aunt" figure, has the key voice in this section. She speaks more of the necessity of belief and the social conditions of black experience than of private struggles to overcome oppression. The God of Breedlove may be questioned, but he is not arrogantly defied. Moreover, in contrast to the God-Father-Master, the deity shares the condition of orphanhood, since he himself has no father. Such a humanized God also is fallible; Nathaniel begins the dream by suggesting that God is the "nightrider" who has taken away his mother, apparently as an act of divine self-preservation: "Yet to save yourself, *You* had to gather at her glorious

245

hem, and that lilac lovely, blazingly beautiful dress before *you* fell—or was it jumped?—off that high Sinai cliff into the valley of DEATH, as you looked into the faces of horror and which mirrored *you* and your face and what you had created in the furnace You, fatherless" (*Tree*, 80).

With the father lacking the divine power to control the chaos, the mother must be turned to as the source of nurture. Hattie, as the principal maternal figure, herself relies on religious faith, not because it has changed the world, but because it represents the only hope for change. But her faith and hope are not sentimental, but rather ways of being tough like the gray goose:

> He is the only light you can ever really trust and test against the rocks and read the dawn by: yes and son see by as well, to understand what's happening to you or the crushing world flooding in on you, as them baby-blinding cataracts are shed off your eyes by tragedy and the wisdom of your hands carving your way down this unfriendly, steel-cold world of constant binds and the long, shifting journey road . . . the only blazing justice, thundering and rocking with light and giving you seeing eyes and a speaking tongue, so as you can see deeper down into the stark cup of life's river-wide, soul-sucking, muddy waters—uplifting you to see the length of the journey and the weightiness of your burdensome cross; so as you can strip down your body—like a runner, yes and toughen up your woolly spirit for the breadth and depth of your tragic flight down that mouth-opening freedom journey. (*Tree*, 87–88)

Belief does not save one from the world or give him control over it; rather it makes it possible to endure the suffering and realize the freedom. Hattie argues, in effect, that faith is, for her at least, the means by which the ends sought by Jamestown and Jericho can be achieved.

"The Vision" attempts to penetrate, through apocalyptic allegory, to the heart of the black experience in America. Several of the images from previous sections are repeated and intensified in order to show the function and nature of black suffering and the meaning of enduring that suffering and thereby turning it into an affirmation of life. At the center of the vision is a crucifixion-lynching-dismemberment of a black man. This is carried out as a ritual of two contending groups who seek apparently to unify themselves through his sacrifice. Significantly, the narrative lacks any suggestion that he is in any way being punished for any real or imagined wrongdoing. Repeated mention is made of his "majesty." Thus he seems to combine the elements of the virgin and the fisher-king, two mythic sacrificial figures who die to bring fertility to the land.[7] The ritual begins as a crucifixion, but the crowds seem to need even greater sacrifice. Upon the discovery of his race ("HE IS A NIGGER!"), the killing turns into a lynching, which makes more intense attacks upon his body possible. He is hung in a tree next to the river, called variously Styx and Jordan, and is castrated when the crowds demand more violence. But the scapegoating does not bring peace; instead nature erupts with storms and floods and the people attack each other. The river meanwhile fills with objects:

> I rush my hand into its steaming depths and touch ashes, feces, fishes, eyes, cancer-slabs of skin, blood, chains, hooks, scales, irons, calves, leg chains, duck butter, sperm, wings, wedding gowns, dice, nine-pound hammers, WANTED signs, ropes, rosaries, empty wine cups, free papers, bibles, diamond-eyed necklace crucifixes, whale eyes, flags, skeleton bones, luck-dream books, washboards, spittoons, washtubs, jugs, congo drums, tin whistles, flour barrels, sticks, glistening trumpets, kazoos, knocking bones. (*Tree,* 129)

This list resembles the Invisible Man's recording of the artifacts accumulated by the evicted old people,[8] and its purpose seems much the same. It catalogues in objects the human reality of black life. Represented are occupations, arts, diseases, beliefs, imprisonment, families, body functions—all the things that constitute human life. But as in the case of *Invisible Man,* the objects are meaningless trash outside that human reality. Their very lack of order in the list (which continues for several lines beyond those quoted) is an appeal for their historical connections.

The same order-disorder occurs in the dismembering of the black man's body. His arms, legs, and other parts, removed in response to the crowd's frenzy, are cast away into the river with the other detritus. As a final gesture of sacrifice, they order his head severed from his trunk and placed on a pole in the middle of the river. When this is done, an eagle lands on it and plucks out the eyes. These fall to the ground, but efforts to smash them only cause more of them to develop. Meanwhile angels gather up the body parts and the rock on which the eyes were smashed. These reunite themselves, and the re-membered man, with the scars of his ordeal, flies off like the indestructible gray goose.

At one level, the allegory is clear: competing sides (North and South)

247

contend over the black man, not for his good but for their own. But the very effort to save their souls, or their land, or their wealth by sacrificing him only serves to worsen their condition. The nation (the eagle) seeks to deprive him of his awareness (his eyes), but the attempt produces its opposite by giving him even greater sight than before. And finally, his long suffering is rewarded when he is made whole again and soars above his tormentors.

On another level, however, one directly related to Nathaniel's story, the meaning is more complex. The shifting of rituals from crucifixion to black lynching to Osiris-dismemberment implies a deep human need for scapegoats and sacrifice. The killing of a significant figure as a communal gesture reflects the tradition of destroying the fisher-king in order to renew and revitalize the society itself. The black man crucified, lynched, and dismembered is thereby associated with powerful figures sacrificed in order to bring prosperity, fertility, and salvation. The murder in "The Vision" seems designed to bring the divided people back to a state of unity and purity. But the return to origins must fail because the victim is not a god but a human being, and thus the society's guilt is increased, not assuaged, by his death. His refusal to die marks not the community's renewal, but his own spiritual toughness.

The need and resources for such toughness constitute Nathaniel's final awareness in "Wakefulness." The struggle between faith and freedom, brought about by the irreversible, inexplicable death of his mother, continues: "Knowing and not knowing that by changing my name i could not change the track, or the switch of the train, or the splattered rainbow" (*Tree*, 154). But knowing this, according to Breedlove, should not cause despair: "Upon this earth young man you will learn to understand that there are some places where there are no seats to sit down in, and places to choose, but that's not a judgment upon you, or against you, rather it's a challenge to your vision, and you've got to make them/us honor until the dying lamb, the letter and spirit of the word" (*Tree*, 155).

Nathaniel seeks the freedom and the faith without the struggle, to be the gray goose without being boiled, to be God's son without suffering the crucifixion that is black history. But none of the images and voices will allow it; so he must shape a self that has no fixed center: "Upon this earth young man you will learn the advantages of changing your name and your ways when attempting to ford dangerous, marshy country" (*Tree*, 155). Fearful of such a world, he hides naked under his mother's bed. But he emerges to confront his manhood:

> And the fist of my bloody right hand coming down hard and well-deep into the pit of my stomach and howling as if death's mothering-birthing switch-blading force had sliced across my face, as i did come from up underneath the bed and stood in all of my nakedness before my mother's body-length mirror, locked away in the enframing reflection as my bloody hands clasped away at my loins and i crumbled upon the floor rising and falling rising and falling and rising and falling. (*Tree*, 163)

Nathaniel is reborn into black manhood, an orphan facing the absence of his origins and the necessity of making his own name. But his situation is not an existentialist one, for he has the resources of a culture and a history upon which to draw. The last image suggests this by combining in the rising and falling not only grief but also masturbation, the "threshing floor" of religious experience, and the struggle of the gray goose to fly. Death, sexuality, faith, and endurance-freedom are the necessary elements present to make possible his black identity.

The Bloodworth Orphans (1977) seek to do on the social level what *There Is a Tree More Ancient than Eden* did on the individual level. Rather than focus on the isolation of Nathaniel Witherspoon, Forrest here creates a variety of figures characterized by orphanhood. Nathaniel serves as the collector of their stories, all of which deal with the destructive effects of fatherlessness and the desperate need for a paternal image. But the record also indicates that the quest for the image is self-destructive; those who must search for their origins are destroyed in finding them. The only hope lies in accepting one's condition and drawing from the motherlike culture the strength necessary for survival.

Dominating the book are the Bloodworths, a white slaveholding family who over several generations and through several name changes produce black offspring scattered throughout the country. The narrative follows this bloodline through its meanderings and its frequently grotesque turns, leading eventually to incest and apocalyptic floods. The story then shifts to three orphan lives only tangentially connected to the Bloodworths; these tales involve Nathaniel directly and bring him to an awareness of the brotherhood of man created by the common condition of being "lost-found," to use a recurring expression of the book. The section ends with an apocalypse of riot and fire. In this sense, the novel may be said to have a biblical structure, divided between a testament on the power of the Father and the wandering of the children and a testament on salvation through love. This structure is more thematic than chronological, since *Bloodworth Orphans*, like *There is a Tree*, often shifts radically in time, space, and language. Linking the theme of orphanhood and the biblical structure is a line from a spiritual, which also serves as an epigraph: "Jesus told me the world would hate me if he changed my name . . . changed my name." Variations are played on this refrain throughout the book; it reinforces the identity quests and victimization of the orphans, as well as the costs and benefits of faith.

The Bloodworths themselves, like YHWH of the Old Testament and the early Greek gods, lack individualizing qualities. They are powerful, lustful, and arbitrary, but distinguishable only by the number that follows the name Arlington Bloodworth. Only Pourty has a story, and he is in fact not a Bloodworth, but an orphan raised by the family. Like all the lost-found, he carries a curse; in his case, the elder Bloodworth, on casting him out of the family for having raped a black Bloodworth half-sister, predicts that he will be killed by his own child. Later a fortune teller adds the condition that the mother of the murdering child will be Pourty's own sister. This curse, described very late in the book, is fulfilled in distorted ways throughout the narrative. The only Bloodworth who did not participate in the rape of the half-sister is murdered by her son; the elder Bloodworth is unknowingly killed by Pourty, who himself is killed by his black mistress; and his black son commits both fratricide and incest with his sister. Thus, the language of the curse, like the bloodline, takes its own directions, testifying to the unpredictability of both words and human history. Those who seek, like Bloodworth, to dictate human experience, may find it boomeranging on them, just as it did in *Invisible Man*. And Pourty, who sought to supplant the father, is similarly doomed.

But history is not the working out of some divine plan of punishment for evil, for the innocent suffer as well. The novel even suggests, ironically, that the suffering of the innocent may well be even more exaggerated than that of evildoers, precisely because their goodness is intolerable in a flawed world. The interrelated stories of Rachel Flowers, Regal Pettibone, and

LaDonna Scales point to the necessity of the community to "scandalize" the names of these strong, virtuous figures. Rachel herself is both a motherless child and, like her biblical namesake, a mother who has lost her children. The story of her early life, as rendered by Reverend Packwood, who is responsible for her conversion, reveals that she was the product of brother-sister incest, was sent off by her grandfather, and produced two sons by Arlington Bloodworth III by the age of fifteen. She goes temporarily insane when she discovers that Bloodworth also had intercourse with sheep. Having been deprived of a family and having had her name scandalized in what personal history she does know, she comes to salvation in search of origins: "This merchandized and scandalized daughter is gonna learn of the origins of her banished royal father and she's gonna learn of the radiance of my Kingly Father" (*Bloodworth Orphans*, 39). Symbolically, Packwood's sermon, which leads her to a state of grace, has both religious and cultural roots. Packwood himself worked as a blues musician before becoming a preacher, and his style reflects both the call-response form and blues language used for religious purposes: "Spit him out, Dear Sister, LOOOOOOSE HER, LUCIFER, LET MY DAUGHTER GO; take your lying, filthy, polluting and scandalizing hands from her throat, her temple, her insides, her outsides, her backbone. . . . OPERATE, PACKWOOD, OPERATE! CLEAN HER UP AND OLD LUCIFER OUT" (*Bloodworth Orphans*, 36).

Rachel sees her religion as compensation for her suffering, but like Breedlove in *There Is a Tree*, she is not blind to the world's realities. She makes use of her position as the church's Mother-Witness to denounce social activism and to attack implicitly those, who through jealousy, try to scandalize her name. She views suffering and sacrifice as necessary conditions of the Christian life; in fact, she keeps the unbelieving, profligate Bee-More Flowers as a husband in part as a test of her virtue. Moreover, she imposes on the church an annual Easter performance by herself and Regal, an orphan she has raised who is widely known in the community as a pimp and numbers racketeer. Since she is old, frail, and blind, only the power of her voice filled with religious authority makes her so effective.

Regal Pettibone, who also has a powerful voice, adds to that the power of his male potency. For this reason, he combines for the women of the church qualities of Lucifer and Christ: "But nearly all were united in their passion to take some of the spiritual garment, for he was in the throes of a miracle, and 'touched by the Hand of God,' to take part in his gloryhood. (He was brilliant and radiant to look upon, yes, like Lucifer, a few observed, and filled with the new black oils and the old colored scents and perfumes.)" (*Bloodworth Orphans*, 214). These women simultaneously desire his destruction and his embrace, for he reminds them of both human possibility and human desire. Such an ambivalent feeling cannot be comfortably maintained, and so this church, like God the Father, takes its opportunity to cast out this beautiful demon. Moreover, they make him the literal sacrifice for all their spiritual failings.

Regal himself, however, perceives his condition differently. He sees himself as an orphan clinging to the only mother he has known but dreaming of other relationships; he writes love songs and poetry, takes special care of his prostitutes, has a passionate need for origins, and suffers nightmares of dispossession: "This nightmare was a feverish companion to Regal's days and nights. He was constantly trying to find the power centers of his origins and of his life, and to manipulate them, use them, employ them. A sorrowful pilgrim, without brothers and sisters, torn, driven and tossed in many directions" (*Bloodworth Orphans*, 9). His elaborate lifestyle and concern for Rachel in large measure reflect his means of compensating for this sense of absence at the heart of his being. Only exaggerated possessions and emotions can come close to satisfying his need.

Similarly, La Donna Scales, who becomes his lover, lives a disproportionate life as a way of dealing with her loss. She becomes a Catholic and then a nurse so as to find a father figure and to care for the suffering of others. But merely being helpful does not suffice; she castigates the priests and nuns whom she considers lackadaisical in their attention to patients. She cannot comprehend why they do anything less than surrender their entire being to their work. In addition, she has an extended dream in which she finds herself the daughter of the bishop, a powerful man married to his sister. These conditions of paternity and incest are not morally offensive to her, but merely reinforcements of her need for love. In the dream she gradually becomes jealous of the mother-aunt for having intimate access to the father-priest in a way she cannot. The dream turns to nightmare as she acquires from a hag the means of making herself more desirable and her mother less so. But the potions have the reverse effect and, like Regal, she dreams herself from love to dispossession.

In each case, including that of Pourty, the character conceives of him or herself as an emptiness that can only be filled by discovering origins—a father or some father-substitute, such as God, or the church, or the father's property. Haunted by the absence, each fears, in dreams or curses, that the substitute will never be sufficient. To evade this fear, ever more elaborate substitutions must be made. But since the primal Father-Presence can never be made manifest, satisfaction can never be achieved.

The threat of such a condition is made clear in two episodes, the doomed Regal–La Donna romance and the religious troubles of Maxwell Saltport. Regal and La Donna come together as a result of their concern for others: each is devoted to comforting Rachel during her terminal illness. Out of this shared experience comes their passion for each other, which they consummate the night of the old woman's death. They find in one another a filling of the emptiness unlike any of their previous experiences. But they are star-crossed lovers; at Rachel's funeral a recently discovered brother of La Donna reveals that Regal is a child of the same parents. In a fight shortly thereafter between Amos-Otis and Regal, La Donna is shot and Amos-Otis is also killed. While carrying his sister-lover to Rachel's grave, Regal is attacked and his body partially dismembered by a gang of church members who hold him responsible for bringing disgrace and trouble to them. The children of Pourty Bloodworth are thus brought to their deaths by knowledge of his paternity.

Contrasting motifs of the Tree of Life and the Tree of Knowledge from *There Is a Tree* are important here as well. Like their mythic models Isis and Osiris, La Donna and Regal rejuvenate the world with their love; theirs is a potent, fertile union, both for themselves and others.[9] Amos-Otis, the Set figure, insists upon introducing factual knowledge which in a modern civilization damns that love. Thus, a life-affirming relationship that negates the internal necessity of such knowledge is destroyed by it.

A slightly different distinction operates in the story of Saltport, where knowledge is separated into categories of ideological realities and mother-wit. Saltport becomes a convert to the Black Muslim faith, and, because of his talents, rises quickly in the organization. He is so successful at reforming black criminals and exconvicts that the president of the United States offers him a medal of honor, which he believes he accepts with the approval of the head of the church. Shortly thereafter, he receives notice that he is to be stripped of his authority. He turns in confusion to Gladstone, the man responsible for his conversion. The older man then explains political realities to him, much as President Bledsoe did for the narrator in *Invisible Man*. And like Bledsoe, Gladstone condemns the initiate for mistaking appearances for realities. Saltport learns of intrigue and obscure alliances in the organization and of the jealousy of some superiors over his success. His flaw is in believing that he has arrived at the very origins of Truth and therefore no longer needs the "street smarts" that had previously enabled him to survive.

These lessons are not lost on Nathaniel, who, after having been an observer-learner, becomes a participant in the story he tells. Imprisoned by unknown forces in the Refuge Hospital, he is locked up with Noah Grandberry, who turns out to be another child of Pourty Bloodworth. Also kept in the hospital is Ironwood Rumble, a blind blues pianist whose music brings home to Nathaniel both the terror and the joy of black experience:

> Then he commenced to transport his homeless patrons on out of that cellar
> kitchen. Ironwood "Landlord" Rumble, navigating blue-melted steel
> through a forest on fire, through Job's-tear grass; wisteria; cotton fields and
> patches of maize; through the tumbledown razor-strapped gospels and epis-
> tles of tracks to glory of chained stars; lost tar-babies gathering in the black-
> berries, canceled notes, wigs, strait jackets, as abandoned rib cages, upon a
> ferris wheel, whirring, choking, raging; pinch-nerved abandoned children,
> foundlings, chalking the grotto blackboard, tiptoeing up charred ladder
> rungs, arising from the blood of Niobe's children. (*Bloodworth Orphans*, 295)

Like the music in the prologue of *Invisible Man*, the blues here not only affects the listener emotionally, but actually embodies the history and experience of his race.

Similarly, Grandberry's story of his own past clarifies both the condition and the possibilities of life. First, he tells of his experiences with Ford, a character who has appeared in various guises throughout the novel. An orphan, Ford uses his lack of a past to become a master trickster and shape changer. Like Rinehart of *Invisible Man*, he is all things to all people: con man, fortune teller, salesman, preacher, father, brother, ancestor, male, female. He is pure possibility, pure form, pure expression, and as Grandberry's great-grandfather (or so the story goes) he passes his freedom to new generations. Without history, he is poles apart from Rachel Flowers, who turns painful experience into a religion. Neither provides a basis for a nurturing community.

Nathaniel and Grandberry create that basis by using their wit to escape the hospital, which brings them back into a world of chaos and the violence that makes more orphans. While running they find an abandoned baby, which they take with them to a place of momentary safety. By nurturing it, they discover the new possibility, a community of orphans, who make a history by telling the stories of orphanhood.

The larger meaning of Forrest's work, then, is clear: blacks have been made fatherless, motherless, and pastless by a racist society that scandalizes their being and makes them scapegoats. But this last ritual in itself implies a certain power in black life that even its enemies recognize. This orphanhood and violence, though devastating, also make of all blacks a community, defined by outsiders in scandalizing terms, but from within by a determination to survive through the wisdom of a folk culture, by a belief in the power of their voices, and by an awareness brought by those voices of a life-affirming history of suffering and joy.

William Gass says in *Fiction and the Figures of Life* that in metaphors, both elements of the comparison are often changed for the reader by the creation of the figure. In his example of a character described as a mouse, both our understanding of the character and our sense of mice are affected by the image.[10] In the fiction of Clarence Major, it can be argued that his use of metafictional techniques sets up writing as a metaphor for the black experience; in the process he forces his readers to reconsider both things. A common image in his novels is imprisonment, which works for both the characters he describes and for the exigencies of writing itself, upon which he frequently comments within the narratives. Characterization, plot development chronology, causation, and stylistic consistency constitute arbitrary impositions on the novelist, and Major deliberately violates them. But he also, having proven this point, chooses to create central black characters who go through significant experiences in their efforts to achieve freedom and identity within the imprisoning worlds of the fictions. In the metaphor, then, we are compelled to see writing as a constant struggle against aesthetic oppression, while also seeing the black experience as an effort to find expression. His fictions are dramas of craftsmanship, in which the narrator seeks to shape his story against opposing forces of experience and conven-

255

tion, both historical and literary, just as blacks seek to shape identities within and against social, political, and historical conditions.

Major's fiction, though experimental from the beginning, has become more and more insistent on its own arbitrariness. *All-Night Visitors* (1969) reduces its central character to a single aspect, his sexuality, but it develops his story largely in sequential fashion. *No* (1973) continues to question characterization, but it also breaks up the chronology. *Reflex and Bone Structure* (1975) confuses characterization further by making the implied author a participant who is sometimes identified with a totally different character and who frequently comments on his inability to create full characters. Finally, *Emergency Exit* (1979) dissolves plot and causation, and has characters remark on their sense of being imprisoned within the narrative.

One point of reference for Major's work, as he has suggested, is African aesthetics.[11] Crucial to this view of art is the concept of "nommo," the word that gives meaning to the object created. Thus, a mask of a dead person need have no resemblance to that person because the artist will give it its proper name and thereby its meaning. Likewise a group of identical artifacts can be individually distinguished by the designations given them by their creator. The objects mean nothing in themselves; they are granted significance by the artist.[12] In terms of story, this means that the narrator does not discover a message in his tale but imposes one on it. In the case of Major's novels, the narrators struggle to discover this power in themselves. They feel imprisoned by the conditions of private, familial, social, or literary experience; they are victims of their own stories. They gradually come to understand their power as narrative voices to give shape to their experiences. This realization frees them from false quests for meaning and identity; they become like the singers of blues who rearrange the verses or invent new ones in order to create a certain mood or the singers of spirituals who put new words to old tunes or old words to new tunes. The object, whether a song, a mask, or a story, is merely a product to be put to use in whatever way the artist sees fit. Thus, characterization, plot, chronology, and causation are created effects, only valuable to the extent the narrator finds them functional. Major demonstrates repeatedly the artificiality of such constructs, as well as the arbitrariness of such concepts as freedom and identity in a literary fabulation. They are made things serving the story, not preexis-

256

tent realities governing the narrators. The novels address this very issue by making narrators and implied authors central characters trying to make sense of their material. Ultimately, they discover their potential, and their stories end, which means they begin, since the successful struggle with the material makes the story possible. Major's ultimate concern, then, like that of McPherson, Morrison, Reed, and others, is the right of expression, which for blacks cannot be taken for granted.

All-Night Visitors alternates between paeans to the phallic powers of Eli Bolton, the narrator-central character, and dramatizations of the psychological price of living in a world that defines his identity in terms of this one characteristic. The identification is made at the very beginning: "My dick is my life, it has to be. Cathy certainly won't ever come back. I've stopped thinking about the possibility. Eunice has of course gone away to Harvard, and I'm taking it in my stride. My black ramrod *is* me, any man's rod is himself."[13] The egocentrism and attendant irresponsibility implicit in this self-definition emerge in a variety of ways. Eli thinks of women principally as objects of desire: "I want to fuck her, like she's a *thing*. I don't want to see her eyes when I screw her, because sometimes they are *too* sad. The overpowering rapture of just grinding gently with her, without compassion, because I know there is no future for us, no real reason why we should protect each other's feelings" (*All Night Visitors*, 5). Even more indicative of his sense of himself is a passage of a dozen pages which goes into minute detail about a single act of fellatio. With his cornucopia of names for his sexual organ, Eli even outdoes Henry Miller, who seems to be the influence here.

The restriction of the self to sexuality is partially involuntary, as indicated by the imperative clause in "My dick is my life, it has to be." We learn, as the narrative progresses, that Eli is an orphan, which deprives his life of a familial history through which he could organize certain experiences. He served as infantryman in Vietnam, where he repeatedly saw white soldiers rape and then murder Vietnamese children. The two jobs he holds during the narrative, drugstore soda jerk and night clerk in a rundown hotel, bring him into contact with life's losers: drunks, worn-out prostitutes, petty bureaucrats, non-English-speaking poor families. All these experiences point to the loss of meaning in any realm beyond the private one. Human beings have become objects, a condition Eli does not want to fall victim to, even as a character in a novel:

> This thing that I am, this body—it is me. *I* am it. I am not a concept in your mind, whoever you are! I am *here,* right here, myself, MYSELF, fucking or being driven to the ends of my ability to contain myself in the ecstasy her little red mouth inspires as it works at the knobby head of my weapon, or if I am eating this goat's cheese, the pumpernickel, drinking the beer I have just bought, or whatever I happen to be doing, I am not *your idea* of anything. (*All-Night Visitors,* 4–5)

Whether Eli functions here as a narrator addressing his listener or as character addressing the author and/or *his* reader, a double irony manifests itself. On the one hand, Eli, as a character in fiction, *is* simply an idea, a pattern of words created by the writer and interpreted by readers. Even his proclamation of his reality comes to us in the code operative in this particular novel. Major has said elsewhere that "always writing correlated as one of the main tools for enslaving people," and Eli seems very much a fictional case in point.[14] On the other hand, the self he insists on is in fact very much the stereotype of the sexually prodigious black man, whose oversized penis corresponds to his insatiable sexual appetite. Thus, even the one normal human expression available to Eli, the one where his verbal and physical creativity make possible a self, has already been defined and controlled by the outside world.

The narrator responds to this outside control in the traditional manner of the black trickster: his appearance of submission to them itself becomes a means of subversion. He succeeds by showing the control he does have and by humanizing the abstractions of himself. The sexual acts themselves reveal his control. In his declaration of reality cited above, he speaks of "being driven to the ends of my ability to contain myself," and in the fellatio scene, much of his pleasure is derived first by getting Anita to participate in the act without being asked and then by delaying his orgasm and slowing his ejaculation once it begins. He repeatedly and successfully tests his will against those of his sexual partners and against his own body. In doing so, he demonstrates that his true power is not physical but psychological; he thereby calls into question the image of the mindless black stud.

Parallel to this is his control over the depictions of the sexual scenes. By rendering them in loving and extended detail, he eroticizes the text, which serves to resist any moralistic presuppositions the reader might hold. Major goes so far as to say that the book is not Christian because of its sexual explicitness; in addition, it confronts the notion that black literature specifically somehow ought to treat sexuality in a different way.[15] Because the sexual material goes beyond what is necessary for the development of the narrative, it becomes almost an end in itself and in the process subverts the idea that the parts of the fiction are merely functions of the text.

Eli humanizes his story by pointing toward a private suffering related to his eroticism. The identity imperative cited above applies not only to the world's treatment of him and others, but also to certain of his relationships with women. The flexibility of time in the narrative makes the significant women in his life seem omnipresent. Thus, Cathy, the dominant figure, coexists with Eunice and Anita, though she left Eli several months before the present time of the story. In each case some problem exists that one or the other in the relationship refuses to face. Eunice is beautiful, unpretentious, and talented, but she remains rather childish and spoiled. Anita, though strikingly attractive and sexually very adept, disturbs Eli because she lacks a sense of her black identity: "She believed religiously in the values of the White Knight Ajax cleaner Kraft Foods Wildcat and Impala cars, the existential reality of Aerowax and the divinity of jet-age plastic Sperry Rand Frank Sinatra George Burns Maxwell House coffee Jack Benny and Texaco gasoline; she thought the Hully Gully was a game invented by Jewish kids in Israel, that who Stagger Lee shot was his mama, that a Blood was an Indian and that C.C. Rider was a civil service technician" (*All-Night Visitors*, 175). Though Anita provides the pleasure of the fellatio described earlier, her cultural inadequacies exceed her sexual aptitudes. Even when she later attacks Eli for caring more for the white Cathy than for herself, her insufficient blackness undercuts her argument.

Cathy is the heart of the narrative. While other episodes are brief and developed in a linear fashion, this relationship is a recurrent topic and is told from end to beginning, as though Eli were working psychoanalytically back to its origins. What gets told at the end of the book involves the narrator only marginally, but the necessity of telling it reveals some clues to the relationship's problems. Significantly, the narrator in fact provides *only* clues; he does not presume to claim absolute truth for his version of events: "It is very simple: the universe is not *ordered*, therefore I am simply pricking the shape of a particular contruct, a form, in it" (*All-Night Visitors,* 21).

Early in their time together, Cathy tells Eli of the abuse that she suffered as a child from both her mother and her stepfather. This mistreatment made her sexually frigid, a condition which Eli helps her overcome through his own sexual skills. But in improving her situation, he assumes the right to control her life just as her parents had. The situation becomes apparent in a scene where she has violated his control: "We even walked the dangerously expensive and sometimes repugnant streets of our Lower East Side, that night, just to think clearly, and I was still in shock at how she had told me to shut up—I had seen how her own voice had frightened her. She had covered her mouth at that moment. Suddenly I felt she had to pay her dues" (*All-Night Visitors,* 18). The full meaning of that last statement emerges when she uses her voice once again somewhat later to tell him that she is leaving. He then fantasizes killing and cannibalizing her to keep her with him. When she in fact goes out to the street, he follows her and rapes her in public view. Thus he seeks to return her to the status of thing, using the same sexual brutality her stepfather had.

From this point we move first into the present, where Eli lives a life of despair and sex without pleasure, and then back to the early stages of the relationship, when an authentic romance was developing. In very little of this is there evidence that Eli ever understands the extent of his responsibility. At two points near the end, however, he suggests some awareness. In the penultimate chapter, he describes his first meeting with Cathy. In the process of telling, he uses a score or more of diminutives and elaborations on her name: Kathea, Cathela, Katherina, Cathquel, Cat, and so forth. The manifold naming parallels the earlier cataloguing of synonyms and nicknames for his penis. The two acts of naming have a dialectical relationship: one is presence, the present, and physical, while the other is absence, the past, and psychological. Each is integrally related to the other: Cathy is the object of his desire and thus the stimulator of his manhood, while the equation of his manhood with domination caused the loss of Cathy. Furthermore, the overflowing of nomination in each case suggests that Eli's creative power lies in accepting and living within this tension of presence and absence.

The possibility for such a state is demonstrated in the final chapter, when a Puerto Rican mother and her children come to his apartment door, seeking refuge from a drunken husband and father. Eli, who to this point has done nothing for others that he was not forced to do, suddenly experiences compassion:

> I had stood there only a psychic inch into a moment of apprehension, the kind New Yorkers have about getting into other folks' business; the kind that lets people, bereaved, die on the windy, storm-swept sidewalks, being stepped over, like litter, when I realized that I could not rationalize my way out of my human responsibility to those ageless sounds of pain that were expropriating this mother from a kind of blemished but necessary social security, the tangible reality of herself simply in the world. (*All-Night Visitors*, 200)

Eli may not have come to an understanding of his own loss and guilt, but the nature of suffering has been communicated to him as a universal experience. And understanding and responsibility provide the deeper manhood he needs to survive: "I stood inside a doorway down the street, vibrantly alive, watching the rivers of water wash along the street, the giant dynamite-streaks of lightening [*sic*] pulverize the sky, felt it open the private crevices of this moment, in me; I had become firmly a man" (*All-Night Visitors*, 202–3). The double meaning of "firmly" effectively links the physical and psychological aspects of manhood. But the "private crevices" go even further by suggesting a female element in Eli's character which makes it possible for him to be nurturing and creative as well as strong; the joining of male and female enables him to engender a self that could not previously have come into being. Dialectically, this inner self comes into being not through introspection or self-indulgence, but through the fathering and mothering that protect and nurture other suffering human beings.

No makes overt use of the imprisonment metaphor implicit in *All-Night Visitors*. The narrator retells the story of his childhood and, more briefly, the influence of that experience on his adult life. In the process, he shows in each of the three parts instances of abuse of women, unmanning of males, attacks on children, and racial intimidation. Each case demonstrates the dehumanization implicit in being locked into a role. But, consistent with the Freudian element Major himself has commented on,[16] the crucial aspect of the book is the narrator's self-imprisonment that results from psychologically evading the violence and guilt that constitutes his past. The

261

novel moves from the social to the familial to the personal. Dreams, encounters with father and mother images, sexual experiences, and castrations both literal and figurative appear at each of the stages. These elements serve primarily to reinforce the sense of incarceration; offering counterpoints in each part are characters with some folk connection and social rituals with liberating influences—circuses, parties, and bullfights. As in *All-Night Visitors,* the narrator's achievement of a more complete manhood corresponds to an ever-greater acceptance of these characters and an ever-greater involvement in the rituals.

The first part of the narrative might be said to be a dialectic of circuses. A Barnum and Bailey circus has been promised by posters and by word of mouth, and seeing it is the great hope and desire of the Boy (the name given the narrator in this section to distinguish him from his father, Moses Westby). The Boy, living a restricted life, worries about the moral implications of the show: "Like laughter, I figured a circus had to be sinful. Shit, how could a circus *not* be sinful: it was happy! The soft curse of the invisible devil hid in the joy."[17] Enjoyment is evil, and as though to secure the point, the Boy immediately thinks of the legendary and criminal adventures of his father: "Like he was on the trail with that badass Ben Hodges, a notorious cattle thief and gyp artist. The man who once guarded us learned a lot by knocking around with that old badman. They rustled cattle all through the Southwest and westward, to the North, through Nebraska, where he wanted to rewrite all the road signs. . . . That's why I say Moses could've told me anything I wanted to know about the denomination of that particular circus" (*No,* 73).

The circus, with its variety, its color, its amoral emphasis on pleasure liberates the imagination and thereby calls into question the existing order of religious constraint and racial repression. But its influence can be even more subversive: "If I could put a name to each and everything in the circus I might then control it all. Manipulative magic" (*No,* 71). The show makes it possible for the powerless to conceive of the prospect of having the naming and controlling power. The quest of the narrator in *No* is to name not merely the circuses but also the terrors in his story; when he has completed this process by the end of the book, he gains his own identity.

The Boy's everyday life differs from the circus, not in being dull and

262

colorless, but in being horrific rather than pleasurable. The horrors are as varied and vivid as the pleasures, but they serve to suppress imagination and power rather than enhance them. Young Moses has a homosexual encounter that he does not quite understand. Then, while staying with his grandmother, he witnesses the sexual battles of his uncle and aunt, which culminate when Uncle John and one of Lucy's lovers capture her and paint her pubic area red. As part of this same sequence, John gelds one of Boy's cousins for being disobedient. Boy himself is viciously assaulted by a white man for refusing to call him "Sir." At the same time the victims themselves victimize: the boys drown a cat, have intercourse with a mule, and torment their paralyzed white grandfather. Thus, Boy finds himself locked into a world that is the distorted reflection of the circus; the only freedom is exercised in punishing the weak, while imagination is used only in devising new punishments.

The second section, "Witch Burning," focuses on the family and its associated rituals—sexuality, marriage, and funerals. Of these, only death offers some insight into the nature of reality. "Witch Burning" opens with the story of an Indian graveyard and the canyon from which Grandmother Thursday's Indian ancestors made suicidal leaps. She recalls the stories of the suffering and dying of earlier generations: "When she thought about the Indian side of her family, her ancestors, she would whine, sometimes out loud, the word, *genocide*. She could say it distinctly, slow: gen-o-cide" (*No*, 81).

The second death reveals more about the character of Moses Westby the father than it does about the victim. At a stock-car race to which Moses has taken his children, a white driver dies in an accident in front of them. While everyone else panics, Boy watches his father's coolness: "Moses Westby didn't move, so I didn't move. I looked up at his face, and he was busy lighting a fresh cigarette. Calmly, his good eyes squinted behind his dark sunglasses" (*No*, 83). Moses the badman has no time to concern himself with the death of a white man. Along with the legends, this experience shapes an image of black manhood that Boy takes as a model: "I really envied him as much as I loved him. If only I could be so smooth! So masculine, a *first* person! Moses had an acute accent, but I couldn't quite place it, yet I always tried to imitate it" (*No*, 85). Yet Moses also possesses a folk

263

intelligence, called by the narrator "penal wisdom." He knows how to avoid trouble in racially mixed situations without in any way sacrificing his pride.

But part of the knowledge of manhood transmitted by Moses is the impossibility of expressed emotional commitments by men. Strong fathers can only serve as models of strength if they teach their sons not to be dependent on anyone else, including perhaps even the father. Strength lies in silence and in repression. For Boy, this means that he can never hold his father's hand and that anger, frustration, and even love must take either parodic or violent forms. Boy is forced to go through a mock wedding ceremony with Oni (his love much later) in which he is deliberately made fun of. When he develops an innocent infatuation with a schoolmate, she takes him into an old refrigerator, shuts the door, and lifts her dress.

All of these events enhance the sense of imprisonment. Even Moses as badman is an image that locks Boy into a fixed definition of manhood. The death of the grandfather, however, provides, as did the circus, a kind of liberation. First, the dying old white man, in his senility, denounces his wife Thursday, essentially for not being white. His explosion opens up all the unexpressed hostility of a long marriage. It exposes a distorted masculinity through his claims to have taken her off the streets, to have suffered mightily for marrying her, and to have endured all of her infidelities; unable to express either his fear of dying or his need for Thursday's love, he reverts to the language and values of one who builds a self on domination.

In addition, his death sets loose a body of folk beliefs about death and ghosts. Miss Liza Jane, for example, was said to have danced on her husband's grave before her death and to have continued to do so on certain occasions afterward. The preservation of such tales disrupts the presumed order of things, as the narrator realizes: "I know I manage to convey a belief in weird things and at the same time a kind of scientific knowledge that would preclude such mental activity. It is true—I see only the clumsiest "order" anywhere; believe in nothing really, which is solid reason why I can afford a belief in all manner of "folly." If I say one thing and feel another, it's not uncommon. If I believe something and tell you I don't or vice versa what you do with the paradox is part of the bargain" (*No*, 125–26). Furthermore, "Grady's death gave me a vision of my own liberation. . . . I got a glimpse into the possibility of how death of entities with sensibilities can also serve the discontinuous nature of all life" (*No*, 126). Different things can be believed simultaneously; there is no life-rule that requires uniformity or consistency. Moreover, mortality makes possible such multiplicity by reminding us that the fathers do die, leaving us free to believe what we choose, even if it conflicts with the system they created.

Embodying this knowledge in a self becomes the narrator's task in the last part of his narrative. Necessary to this task is the destruction of those from the past. This happens in violent fashion when Moses, in an effort to save his family from suffering, tries to kill them all, including himself. He succeeds in every case except that of his son, who is only wounded. After this the narrator moves away, changes his name to Moses Eastby, and seeks primarily to suppress his experience. But the past cannot be escaped; in New York, he meets someone from back home who tells him the fates of those he left.

More importantly, he encounters Oni, his child-bride, now an actress. Much of this section is devoted to experiences of unsuccessful sexuality, with Moses apologizing and Oni trying to understand the source of his problem. He reflects on the past, but his absorption does not bring understanding, even when he says, "And if I am anybody I am Moses" (*No*, 159). His problem is that he is not his father but his father's son, lacking the intensity of experience and passion perhaps, but with a greater possibility of comprehending the meaning of the experience. Once he can transcend the necessity for identification with the father, he can create himself.

He does both these things through acts of sympathy, which culminate in one that threatens his life in the moment of affirming it. The first of these occurs when he picks up a young Puerto Rican whore but then decides to give her money without demanding sex in return. Instead he listens to her talk about her love of freedom and dancing: "Suddenly, I burst out laughing. I am happy, unexpectedly so" (*No*, 164). Rather than impose on Josefina either his own suffering or his socially determined definition of manhood, he simply accepts her otherness and therein finds pleasure.

His relationship with Oni also takes a sympathetic turn. At first he is defensive about his sexual performance and passion when she criticizes him and tries to tell him about her past, which includes a successful sexual encounter with his father. But even this can be put to use, because his very failure changes his status in an imprisoning world; he becomes an escapee:

"Part of the definition of an escapee is that he attains the curious status of adulthood. It may not really mean anything in terms of true liberation but the escapee is nevertheless stuck with not just the condition but also the stigma. An escapee does not come to know anymore about the Beginning than those strictly confined in one of the more terrible penal areas. An escapee who does not know his real name neither necessarily learns it nor makes peace with the one that has stuck to him" (*No*, 170).

Moses escapes with Oni to Latin America, hoping that life outside the country that drove his father to the point of murder and suicide will enable him to live the life of a free man. But his heritage of what W. E. B. Du Bois called "double consciousness" is unavoidable. Despite his blackness, the natives steal from him because they consider all Americans to be wealthy; meanwhile all white Americans he meets remind him, directly or indirectly, that he is black regardless of his location. Moreover, he discovers that Oni carries with her news clippings of his family tragedy.

He responds to all this by adopting a fatherly role: he tries to protect Oni from the locals, and he follows her when she goes out alone. He comes to accept her need for sexual satisfaction from other men. While this diminishes their sexual intimacy, he opens the gates of Oni's own history of suffering. Moses learns that she was sexually abused by a white janitor in her school when she was very young; he also learns of her petty crimes and her insecurities. "After Oni opened up she went on for days" (*No*, 198). He functions as a father-confessor, enabling her to purge herself of all the hidden anxieties of her life.

But Moses too must find freedom, which he does through an act which he may have dreamed, as Major has suggested.[18] At a bullfight, he suddenly jumps into the ring and confronts the animal. But rather than kill it in some Hemingwayesque test of manhood, he seeks only to touch it: "I felt that, if I could touch the bull's head, and survive such a feat, life, from this perhaps unworthy moment, would be invested with essence. In other words I had to give meaning to it and it had to contain courage. . . . He was bleeding and sweating and half dead *but* I touched his head and in a strange and beautiful way that single act became for me a living symbol of my own human freedom" (*No*, 204). The bull in Egyptian mythology is the symbol taken of masculinity, power, and fertility. Ismael Reed in *Mumbo Jumbo* links it to the Osiris legend and resurrection.[19] Moses' choice to face

266

death in order to create a meaning for his life identifies him with this tradition. He no longer will accept the name of either a prisoner or an escapee: "I do know this, though, I felt, there, for the first time, in that ring, for those few moments, that I was no longer a victim" (*No*, 203).

And the possibility that the experience is a dream strengthens rather than weakens the effect because, as he notes upon leaving South America, the ancient Indians used trances to detect thieves. His dream-reality exposed not only the fear that robbed him of his identity, but also the courage that will make recovery of that identity possible. And his identity, like his freedom, is not a fixed single thing, but the entirety of his experiences, both painful and joyous; it is all the names he has had. His freedom consists not in running but in creating the means of survival.

The text itself is an aspect of that creation, for its end was in the beginning, where the narrator outlined the major events of his story and proposed their meaning: "I didn't realize that I was really trying to crash out of a sort of penal system in which I was born and grew up" (*No*, 3). His success is not in escape; rather it comes in the recording of his history, which registers in full detail the imprisonment. Like the slave narratives, the words of *No* register the acquisition of a language and a voice in spite of the silencing efforts of wardens and masters.

In his next two novels Major takes another step by suggesting that the text itself can be a prison, with the author as the warden-master. In *Reflex and Bone Structure*, the implied author becomes a character who both enjoys and questions his freedom to do as he chooses with the characters and events of his story, while *Emergency Exit* is dedicated "to the people whose stories do not hold together," a condition which the narrative proceeds to reflect in part by having characters comment on being fixed images in a fictional narrative.

Reflex and Bone Structure presents itself at one level as a mystery: Cora Hull, the central female character, dies at some point in the story. But this mystery is simply a metaphor for another: "I came to see that what I had been trying to do in making a novel was the same thing I meant to do in producing a poem: to invest the work with a *secret nature* so powerful that, while it should fascinate, it should always elude the reader—just as the nature of life does."[20] Major's comment about his intentions is reflected in this novel; mysteries exist at every level.

The first of these is the nature of the narrator. On the one hand he claims to be the author, and he acts as one. He demonstrates his freedom by giving us different versions of Cora's death: he provides a variety of murder scenes, complete with detectives, weapons, and motives, as well as several plane crashes in different places under differing circumstances. Moreover, he mentions at several points characters from Major's earlier books, a device which points out the arbitrariness of the text, since these characters have no function in this narrative. They remind us that characters exist merely as words on a page, to be used at the author's discretion.

But just as identity in *No* was ultimately shown to be multiple, so here the "author" can be a character. Despite his power and freedom, he lacks full control. For example, he cannot clearly define the role or history of Dale, an apparently minor figure. At times he finds it necessary to ask the characters about their motives: "When she was like this, it often caused me to forget incidents or things I felt I should remember. Why, I don't know. But the inability to recall something would nag me until I'd have to ask Cora to help me."[21] In addition, he occasionally identifies (or confuses) himself with Canada Jackson, the central male character.

At yet another level, the narrator sometimes enters the story as though he were simply another character as limited as the rest. He has coffee with Canada, talks to the police officers, and, in an act of metafictional incest, has intercourse with Cora. In this role he is as susceptible to depression, mistakes, and criticism as any of his creations: "I find everything I touch falling to pieces, and the pieces themselves continue to break into smaller and smaller segments. Cora, who enjoys unusual conditions, considers this one. When I mention my misfortune to her the crisp edge in her voice always drops. She knows how to be very cynical" (*Reflex and Bone Structure*, 50).

The novel in one sense is clearly about the problems of writing a novel. How is character created? What should be the narrative voice and the point of view? What possibilities are there in certain plot lines and how is the choice to be made? It is also about reading a novel. How are we to take the narrator? Seriously? Ironically? With which character do we identity? Which one does the author sympathize with? What do we mean by "identify" and "sympathize," since we are dealing with words on a page? One point of the narrative is clearly to suggest the significance and inevitability of such questions in all fiction, not merely that which overtly calls them forth.

But with all these metafictional concerns, and perhaps through them, Major addresses his recurrent themes: freedom and identity. As in *No*, so in *Reflex and Bone Structure* these are not fixed qualities. The "author's" freedom to make characters creates prisons for himself, depending on the kind of story he wishes to tell. And his defiance of conventional narrative costs him his control over characters and situations. Moreover, his creation of characters makes him responsible for their lives and deaths. His repeated resurrection of Cora implies his desire to evade responsibility. He cannot avoid fate in this fashion, however, for as Canada tells him: "Once you stop there isn't likely to be any thing left" (*Reflex and Bone Structure,* 145). What the narrator struggles with is his own unfreedom, his own multiple identities, and even his own death when he stops writing. But paradoxically, to stop writing is to have a narrative, one which eternally resurrects Cora, Canada, Dale, and himself. And, because it does so through the ambiguous vehicle of language, it perpetuates the elusiveness of the secret nature of the fiction.

Emergency Exit, like *Reflex and Bone Structure,* has a narrator who struggles to tell his story. But in this case, the issue is less his doubts about his work than it is the constraints of form and language. He finds himself struggling to communicate through a system that does not allow for the kinds of messages he needs to deliver. Unlike the "author" of the previous book, this one seeks to work with his characters to free them from such oppression. His acts of defiance are directed against accepted styles and narrative expectations. Unlike Eli, Moses, and the "author," he is certain of his rebellion. A significant effect of his violation of convention is the resemblance his fiction comes to have to life itself: "Everything comes together in a novel—life is another matter."[22] In making a fiction that flouts plot resolution and character consistency, he renders experience much more like "the real world" than the most realistic novel. Of course, he is acutely aware that his world can be reexperienced any number of times, whereas reality is unrepeatable. Moreover, his world is truly a verbal one: any blood spilled or joy experienced occurs only in words. He works constantly against his condition; something like life must be rendered, but it must be done honestly, without the pretense that words are blood or joy.

To try to suggest this edge in his work, the implied author (who, like the speaker in *Reflex and Bone Structure*, is sometimes outside and sometimes a part of the story) creates a central motif of the threshold. He brings together various folk beliefs on thresholds and doorways and invents a Threshold Law as part of the world of Inlet, Connecticut. According to this law, men must carry females over the age of eighteen through any entranceway. The rule is said to have some connection with an ancient Jewish belief that blood is sacred and can be used for protection by being smeared over doorways. Because women menstruate, they inherently violate the sacredness of the fluid and for this sin they must never touch any part of a doorway. The novel, then, deals with entries, beginnings, changes, crossroads, and with the rules and violations associated with these. The metaphor also implies that these questions have an inherent sexual aspect, since the female body, though sinful, is also the threshold of birth. In addition, the threshold is intrinsically dialectical: "Hence the function of the threshold is clearly to symbolize both the reconciliation and separation of the two worlds of the profane and the sacred" (*Emergency Exit*, 74). Within the novel are found two principal threshold patterns: the black world separated from and joined to the white world, and the fictive world and that of the implied author.

The Ingram family constitutes the center of the narrative. Black, they share the American dream of prosperity and status. Jim, a successful businessman, takes his family on cruises and guided tours of Africa, from which they return with little more than tourist pictures. Deborah, his wife, tries to raise their children in typical middle-class fashion and with an apparently blind acceptance of conventional morality. The children attend private school and go off to college. But the family suffers the same problems as their white counterparts. Jim and Deborah have an unsuccessful marriage, in part the product of his ten-year affair with his white secretary. The children have trouble with their parents' expectations and moral values.

Despite their acculturation and very light skin color, the Ingrams know they are black. Occasionally, this awareness takes superficial forms: "Julie's hair and shoulders are true. Al sees them. Hi there shoulders! Then her legs and feet. But her hair, what lovely hair! Silky long brown hair soft and straight. She tried a bush and she tried an afro but the texture was too soft.

It wouldn't keep. Wants to prove she's Black" (*Emergency Exit*, 106). The threshold nature of their lives takes concrete narrative form in a parallel construction where Jim and a white man think about each other:

Jim meets a stranger in a bar his name is Barry Sands this guy seems young idealist Barry says no one hates the middle class more than the middle class and Jim thinks oh no another one who needs to listen to this young white Jewish dude still wet behind the ears but Barry goes on saying things like who hasn't gone back into the dirty clothes for a pair of clean socks

Barry Sands meets this older white-looking colored guy who has a nice smile Barry likes him but doesn't trust him in fact Barry doesn't trust people in bars period but he thinks this middle class colored man must have kissed a lot of ass to be where he's at and it's just so fucking disgusting to see this type of person who should be de-nouncing the system
(*Emergency Exit*, 56)

The space between the recorded thoughts is the doorway which separates rather than joins these men who otherwise could get along.

This sense of a double awareness is most apparent in Jim's recurrent dream:

> He was back in Africa in his office there. Ten years of respect, sane and clean. People appreciated his power. He appreciated his own power. Power is as hard as rock. He could smell his own rot, too. Even before he was thirty. In the dream his age doesn't matter. He was busy designing the Black American Dream. Three hundred and twenty-seven versions of it lined up in his sleep every night. The shadow of Martin Luther King loomed over them and over Jim. In the back seat of each dream Deborah was always making love to a snapshot of Booker T. Washington. Even in his dream Jim was an expert at collecting information for the United States. (*Emergency Exit*, 92)

The two historical figures in the dream represent two versions of the Black American Dream. Booker T. Washington, with his policy of accommodation and acceptance of white power, believes in the separating aspect of the racial threshold. Blacks should respect existing social conventions and strive to please whites and gain prosperity for themselves. Martin Luther King's program of integration suggests the threshold as a joining mechanism. For Jim, ideals lie with King but practice with Washington, as in his collecting of information for the government. The dream about Dreams thus manifests the two-sided status of being black and American. To be American alone involves some betrayal of his ethnic history (for example, spying on Africans) and a general sense of dissatisfaction with merely material success; but to be black alone is to be bitter and parochial, as is the case with the Black Professor:

> He was consumed by his racial identity. The Black Professor. He was Black. The only aspect of Inlet's history he cared about was that of its Black people. . . . He wouldn't eat in Inlet's finest restaurants because he was convinced that nobody could cook collard greens and corn bread and black eyed peas and ham hocks the way he could. So he cooked for himself and ate at home. . . . His courses were, Introduction to The Black Experience and a five-hundred level course called, The Sense of the Black Experience. . . . He had a secret ambition. One day he would go beyond these works in the field of the Black Experience. He would write and publish the definitive work on the Black Experience, especially in Inlet, Connecticut. . . . Meanwhile, he spoke only to Black people and for sure did not hang out with white faculty. (*Emergency Exit*, 198)

Such a life of deliberate and arbitrary narrowness not only unnecessarily restricts experience but also serves as a way of evading the central problematic, ambiguous condition of being both black *and* American.

The alternative offered by Jim and the implied author is to accept the tension as the nature of being and to live through it. Jim, despite his compromises and his infidelities, both personal and cultural, is the only character whose voice has equal status with that of the author-narrator. This occurs in a parallel construction similar to the earlier one; significantly, its subject is folklore:

everybody in town will have something to say about this situation discontinuous as it is and dangerous even gutbucket low full of tricksters and hot names and cool cats and squares and dittybops they'll speak out on the mythopoeic reality of true fiction watch and we'll get 'em all together in the Beulah Railway Station's waiting room and let 'em have their say just before we put 'em on the train for good they'll explain it all all the connections or hand it back to us saying so what and I can just see Mr. Coonshine and

hi reader Jim here again our narrator is showing how silly he can be he's never heard Inlet's Jubilee Beaters imitating the Cotton Blossom Singers and the Hampton Colored Students and he certainly never sang from my grandma's *Negro Singers' Own Book* of 1846 so when he says somebody with a gutbucket view of life can explain or eat narrative energy put on a page by say Patchen he's clearly out of touch with say Leadbelly's Becky Dean or the Little Albert Black Magic Book or the Prince Ali Lucky Star Dream Book which in-

Mr. Kneebone with a mouth full of   terprets dreams in three numbers
Beckett and Borges talking it out and   (*Emergency Exit*, 113)
spitting grape seeds in the grass

Granting Jim the power not only to comment on but to criticize his point of view places the narrator in a different relationship with his story. It violates the threshold law separating teller from tale. At another point, Jim comments on his sense of restriction as a character. In both cases, the narrative voice has conceded the right of being to the voice of the character.

Such literary democracy also includes the use of drawings and photographs, including one of Clarence Major in a field of cows across the page from: "I (your narrator) parked my car on the road went down to say hello to thirty cows eating grass they all came to the fence to greet me" (*Emergency Exit*, 10). The "author" also comments on his use of realistic detail, of naturalistic and surrealistic styles, and of flashbacks: "We haven't had any flashbacks have we how can we have a decent American novel without at least one good flashback?" (*Emergency Exit*, 184). This motley of devices and comments asserts the right of the author to make his novel a circus if he so chooses. He can do whatever he wants, even share the center ring with other voices and forms.

In the process he engages in a defamiliarization which demystifies narrative expectations. He frees his tale of conventional restrictions on what a narrator can do and say in telling his story. He garbles and sometimes deletes dialogue in what would normally be considered crucial scenes; he talks directly to the reader about the nature of fiction and criticism; he questions the effectiveness of his own plot. And at the end of the novel, in the ultimate crossing of boundaries, he marries his central female character, although he has previously been a voice and not an actor in the story.

He becomes a metafictional Rinehart or Ford, shifting the shapes of his art forms to fit his desires; in doing so, he defies all restraints on the expression of the imagination. His "nommo" makes a reality by deforming the given assumptions about the nature of narrative. He even recreates folk material by writing modernist parodies of it:

Al had warts. He killed a cat and put it into a supermarket shopping bag along with a transistor radio turned full blast he then went out to the edge of town and buried an afro-comb in black dirt stole a chicken from a chicken shack rung its neck cleaned it and buried it the burial took place at a busy

> intersection then he went out and found a pig pen he got in it and did it to one of the pigs and being the sort of person he was left a quarter in the pig's rear end. Tied a knot in his own shirt sleeves left his shirt in the graveyard. Invaded a group of boys shooting marbles counted out as many as there were warts on his body tied the marbles in a snotrag threw it in the river waited ten days and was cured. (*Emergency Exit*, 122)

While the content of the tale parodies folk belief, the use of the form recovers it for postmodernist writing. It becomes another resource for the extravagantly creative imagination. It is thus renewed and regained as a means of expression.

Clarence Major, then, has taken the concerns of this study in a metafictional direction. He resists the suppression of the voice by deforming the forms which conventional expression takes. He challenges fixed notions of identity by not pretending that his characters are real people and by making fluid the concepts of narrator and author. He affirms life, not by assuming that his fictions reflect it but by making the fictions themselves the products of a skilled and imaginative craftsman.

Conclusion

Just like a Tree: Implications of Folklore for Black Fiction

IN TWO KEY EXCHANGES of views over twenty years ago, Ralph Ellison set out what have been some of the guiding principles of the present study. In a discussion with Stanley Edgar Hyman, he described the value of black folklore as a literary discovery: "Taken as a whole, its spirituals along with its blues, jazz and folk tales, it has, as Hyman suggests, much to tell us of the faith, humor and adaptability to reality necessary to live in a world which has taken on much of the insecurity and blues-like absurdity known to those who brought it into being."[1] For Ellison, and for the others discussed, black culture, both as historical reality and literary material, exists in relationship to the whole of American culture. I have assumed in arguing my position that the long-running debate about whether black American literature is primarily black or primarily American is ultimately pointless; those who write out of an experience of being black *in* America have an inescapably dialectical heritage, both as human beings and as writers. Acknowledgement of such a situation is not, however, a resolution of the issue; rather, it is an opening to the complexities of living and writing within these polarities. In his 1963–64 *New Leader* debates with Irving Howe, Ellison again clarifies the issue: "More important, perhaps, being a Negro American involves a *willed* . . . affirmation of self as against all outside pressures—an identification with the group as extended through the individual self which rejects all possibilities of escape that do not involve a basic resuscitation of the original American ideals of social and political justice" (*Shadow and Act,* 132).

275

The refusal-as-affirmation that is the black experience in America is the content of contemporary black literature (and, for that matter, for most of black writing). For the fictionist, at least three problematic areas develop out of this context: morality, identity, and the nature of one's literary parentage. If questions of ideals and justice are intrinsic to black life, then the man or woman representing that life cannot avoid moral issues. What impact does oppression have on the character? What is the appropriate moral action in a society where conventional moral behavior so often reinforces injustice and violence? Similarly, what kind of identity can be created in a world where survival itself may depend on masking and deceit? And finally, to whom does the Afro-American writer turn as models of literary creation? If Richard Wright is inadequate for a modernist sensibility, is one denying the truth of racial experience by looking to Joyce, Faulkner, and Hemingway?

The responses implicit in the fiction suggest a worldview that these writers share with the folk culture. The use of folk material, not only as imagery and motif but as a basic element of the inner form of recent narratives, implies a fundamentally conservative, organic vision on the part of the writers. "Conservative" here connotes not any particular social or political belief, but rather a desire on the part of these fictionists to preserve the values, forms, and perspectives of the past as vital to their own sensibilities. This desire comes less from a nostalgia for a simpler era than from a recognition that such a vision of wholeness, creativity, endurance, and concreteness has relevance to a world increasingly atomistic, sterile, transient, and abstract. It implies a three-dimensional reality, full of contradiction, paradox, and masking, that contrasts with a society requiring one-dimensional humanity.

The organic nature of the folk culture has particular significance for questions of morality and identity in the fiction. By "organic" is meant a whole made up of interrelated parts and a slow, "natural" process of change over time. In this context, the folk culture generally rejects any fixed, absolute morality, especially one that functions by means of exclusion. Even the black church, a bastion of structured morality, began as illicit meetings of slaves and became a center for civil disobedience during the 1950s and 60s. Moreover, its claims of purity are qualified by a body of preacher tales that point out the hypocrisy of the religious leader. But re-

276

fusal of moral absolutes does not lead to moral anarchy. Rather, the good is linked to that which contributes to the vitality of the whole; evil is that which denies life. In the fiction, this means that the good is frequently associated with victims and with those who endure and survive suffering. Jane Pittman, Celie, Pilate Dead, and Papa LaBas are such figures. In contrast, Brownfield Copeland, the Moochers, Macon Dead, and the Bloodworths embody evil; they demand the sacrifice of others in order to achieve their ends, and therefore, regardless of how worthy those ends might be, the characters and the systems they represent are immoral. Actions that conventionally would be considered unacceptable, such as deception, infidelity (in Celie's case), theft, and even incest (in *Bloodworth Orphans*) can become moral if they enhance the possibilities of life. Morality, then, is a function of the processes inherent in the folk material.

Similarly, individual identity in these narratives does not exist separate from the community of which the individual is a part. Contemporary black literature in this sense is different from works of modern literature which emphasize either isolation or the drowning of identity in a mass, conformist society. In contrast, the threat in black fiction comes from a loss of connection to history and community. In *Invisible Man, The Salt Eaters, Mumbo Jumbo,* and other works, characters retain a sense of self only by recalling or returning to their folk roots. Even characters antagonistic to the community, such as Sula, Eli, and Marcus, can only be understood in relationship to that which they oppose; they are part of the folk whole. The self, in other words, is inclusive and processive. It is made in the concrete history of the individual and the folk, not given or fixed at some point. This is one reason the narratives tend to be open; the key characters, instead of achieving a definite, permanent identity, are still engaged at the end in becoming a self. Masking, roleplaying, and trickster behavior do not contradict this development, as the Invisible Man thought, since these are creative expressions of the emerging self and not falsifications of it; furthermore, they constitute part of the history of the character and thus have their own authenticity. Falsification comes in the belief that one facet of the self is its entirety. Repeatedly in the works discussed, characters have found in themselves possibilities for deceit, confrontation, or love that they did not expect; these do not supplant but rather complement earlier versions of their self-image. The writers do not present these complexities as evidence

277

of confusion or madness; instead, they are markers of health, creativity, and wholeness. The texts of madness, *Eva's Man* and *The Bluest Eye*, show characters and worlds that cannot acknowledge multiplicity and tension, but insist on categorization and permanence.

Another aspect of the themes of tradition and community is literary history. As mentioned earlier, a number of the writers, especially males, have pointedly emphasized the nonblack influences on their work. Given the clear thematic and formal connections between contemporary artists and earlier black writers, something like a racial anxiety of influence seems to be at work. But, unsurprisingly, such an anxiety needs to be considered dialectically. Ellison has revealed the complexity of the question in his responses to Howe, who argued that Ellison and James Baldwin should accept Richard Wright as their literary father and create the same kind of fiction. Ellison counters this by insisting that he, Baldwin, and Wright are all individuals who experienced their racial identities in different ways. To contend that they must speak with identical voices is to require a single black identity and experience, which is essentially a racist position. By claiming Hemingway, Faulkner, Joyce, and others as literary ancestors, Ellison is declaring his freedom to use all the materials available to him as a writer; he defends, in effect, artistic multiplicity. Just as blacks traditionally have laid claim to all of their cultural heritage, regardless of its source, in the process of building an Afro-American culture, so Ellison demands access to the full range of the materials and techniques of his art. Similarly, Forrest, Gaines, and Major have talked about the nonblack influences in their work without, either implicitly or explicitly, denying the importance of their racial identities.[2] As the author of *Invisible Man* explains, the two things are connected: "I use folklore in my work not because I am a Negro, but because writers like Eliot and Joyce made me conscious of the literary value of my folk inheritance" (*Shadow and Act,* 58). He chooses them over Wright not because they are white but because their techniques and insights are more useful to his particular literary needs. The tendency to deny black literary fathers, then, can be seen, in part at least, as a way of avoiding what Ishmael Reed has called ghettoization, the tendency to lump black writers together because they share a skin color and not because they share certain aesthetic concerns.

This study has undertaken, in a modest way, to participate in the ongoing process of defining black literature not as a racial category but as a matrix of literary characteristics. Political, social, and moral questions have been addressed not because the literature is primarily social document but because such issues are inherent in the materials black writers have chosen to use. Further, these elements have been analyzed here on the assumption that such usage has literary rather than political significance. Thus Alice Walker's feminism is viewed as having certain effects on her narrative structures; as an ideological stance, its validity or lack thereof has no relevance to this discussion. I have attempted to study the literature as literature because I believe that it is only through such attempts that it can receive the attention and appreciation it so richly deserves. Even if, as Baldwin says, "there is only one tale to tell," there are nonetheless many tellers and many ways of telling. If this study has accomplished its purpose, it has shown that the commonality of the story and the variety of the tellings have both contributed to the creation of a significant body of literature.

Notes

Introduction: Making a Way of No Way

1. See especially LeRoi Jones, "The Myth of a Negro Literature," in *Home*, 105–15; various essays in *The Black Aesthetic*, ed. Addison Gayle, Jr.; and Gayle's *The Way of the New World*.

2. Interviews with Ellison, Gaines, Morrison, Jones, Forrest, and Major consistently show their conscious use of a modernist tradition. See the bibliography for these interviews.

3. See Robert Stepto, *From Behind the Veil*, ix–xi.

4. "It is a peculiar sensation, this double-consciousness, this sense of always looking at one's self through the eyes of others, of measuring one's soul by the tape of a world that looks on in amused contempt and pity. One ever feels his twoness,—an American, a Negro; two souls, two thoughts, two unreconciled strivings; two warring ideals in one dark body, whose dogged strength alone keeps it from being torn asunder." W. E. B. Du Bois, *The Souls of Black Folk*, 3.

5. Recent social and cultural histories of blacks in America have given a great deal of attention to the dialectical character of the black experience. See Eugene Genovese, *Roll, Jordan, Roll*; Herbert G. Gutman, *The Black Family in Slavery and Freedom, 1750–1925*; Lawrence Levine, *Black Culture and Black Consciousness*; and Albert Murray, *The Omni-Americans*.

6. Many of these folk forms are discussed in various essays in Alan Dundes, ed., *Mother Wit from the Laughing Barrel*. Collections of Afro-American folk material include Roger Abrahams, *Deep Down in the Jungle* and *Positively Black*; B. A. Botkin, ed., *Lay My Burden Down*; J. Mason Brewer, *American Negro Folklore*; Harold Courlander, *Treasury of Afro-American Folklore*; Hughes and Bontemps, eds., *Negro Folklore*; Zora Neale Hurston, *Mules and Men*; and Newbill N. Puckett, *Folk Beliefs of the Southern Negro*.

7. See Janheinz Jahn, *Muntu*, 220–23; and Levine, *Black Culture*, 187, 209, 221.

8. Hennig Cohen, "American Literature and American Folklore."

9. Folk materials in black writing have received increasing attention in recent years. However, these discussions have focused primarily on the cataloging of such material and on its presence in earlier or nonnarrative writers. See Bernard W. Bell, *The Folk Roots of Contemporary Afro-American Poetry;* Susan L. Blake, "Ritual and Rationalization;" Stephen Henderson, *Understanding the New Black Poetry;* Robert G. O'Meally, *The Craft of Ralph Ellison;* Robert B. Stepto and Dexter Fisher, eds., *Afro-American Literature;* and Sherley Anne Williams, *Give Birth to Brightness.*

10. See Joachim Israel, *The Language of Dialectics and the Dialectics of Language,* 55–151.

11. Jacques Derrida, *Of Grammatology,* 23–24.

12. Jahn, *Muntu,* 220.

13. See H. C. Brearly, "Ba-ad Nigger."

14. See "Residual African Elements," 97–98.

15. *Negative Dialectics,* 146–51.

16. See Herbert Marcuse, *One-Dimensional Man,* 84–120.

17. "Negative dialectics" is a key concept for the critical theorists of the Frankfurt school, including Adorno, Marcuse, and Walter Benjamin. In part, it is analysis based on the assumption that every ideological system contains its own contradiction and thereby the seeds of its own destruction. It differs from more traditional Marxist dialectics in its rejection of an end to this dialectical process within history. See Susan Buck-Morss, *The Origin of Negative Dialectics.*

18. The self-reflexive fictions of John Barth, Donald Barthelme, and Thomas Pynchon, among others, as well as the critical work of William Gass (in *Fiction and the Figures of Life*) and Robert Scholes (*The Fabulators*), indicate that fictional creation has become a central, overt concern of contemporary fiction.

19. See Jahn, *Muntu,* 132–40.

20. See Levine, *Black Culture,* 106–21.

21. For a discussion of authorial control in black narrative, see Stepto, *From Behind the Veil,* 45–46.

22. John Dollard, "The Dozens," 284.

23. Logocentrism is the commitment to rational fixed definitions of reality. In the present context it refers to those who categorize black experience according to white supremacist, capitalist, black nationalist, or other ideological constructs. See Derrida, *Of Grammatology,* 10–18.

24. On domination through discourse, see Michel Foucault, *Language, Counter-Memory, Practice,* 51.

25. James A. Snead, "On Repetition in Black Culture," 150.

26. Jahn, "Residual African Elements," 100.

27. On the importance of style in black cultural experience, see Murray, *The Omni-Americans,* 84–100.

Chapter One: History Against History

1. Some critics have suggested that this is exactly what he has done. See, for example, Addison Gayle, Jr., *Way of the New World;* Blake, "Ritual and Rationalization;" and Ernest Kaiser, "A Critical Look at Ellison's Fiction and at Social and Literary Criticism About the Author."
2. See Buck-Morss, *Origin of Negative Dialectics,* 49–57.
3. See Blake, "Ritual and Rationalization"; Richard Kostelantez, "Politics of Ellison's Booker"; and O'Meally, *The Craft of Ralph Ellison.*
4. *Selections from Ralph Waldo Emerson,* 340.
5. Ralph Ellison, *Invisible Man,* 31. All further references to this work will be cited in the text.
6. Emerson, *Selections,* 340.
7. Ibid., 333.
8. Ibid., 339.
9. Jonathan Baumbach, *The Landscape of Nightmare,* 68–86; Selma Fraiberg, "Two Modern Incest Heroes"; Peter Hays, "The Incest Theme in *Invisible Man*"; and Marcus Klein, *After Alienation,* 118.
10. On the function of rhetorical devices in the novel, see Robert L. Bataille, "Ellison's *Invisible Man:* The Old Rhetoric and the New."
11. Ralph Ellison, "That Same Pain, That Same Pleasure: An Interview," in *Shadow and Act,* 18.
12. See Booker T. Washington, *Up from Slavery,* 153–58.
13. Frederick Douglass, *The Narrative of the Life of Frederick Douglass, an American Slave,* 137–39.
14. Ellison, *Shadow and Act,* 78.
15. James Baldwin, *Going to Meet the Man,* 121.

Chapter Two: Negotiations

1. See "An Interview: Ernest Gaines," 335; and Edith Blicksilver, "The Image of Women in Selected Short Stories by James Alan McPherson," 390.
2. James Alan McPherson, *Hue and Cry,* 5. All further references to this work will be cited in the text.
3. See Elliot Liebow, *Talley's Corner;* and Abrahams, *Deep Down in the Jungle.*
4. Ellison, *Shadow and Act,* 94.
5. James Alan McPherson, *Elbow Room,* 24. All further references to this work will be cited in the text.
6. Levine, *Black Culture,* 407–8.
7. For a discussion of signifying, the black verbal art of attacking another without necessarily appearing to do so, see Mitchell-Kernan, "Signifying," 321–326.
8. Ernest Gaines, *Catherine Carmier,* 174–75. All further references to this work will be cited in the text.
9. See Brearly, "Ba-ad Nigger," 578–85.

10. Ernest Gaines, *Of Love and Dust*, 258. All further references to this work will be cited in the text.

11. On the concept of defamiliarization, see Tomashevsky, "Thematics," 85–87.

12. Ernest Gaines, *Bloodline*, 71. All further references to this work will be cited in the text.

13. On the moral hard man in black folk culture, see Levine, *Black Culture*, 420–40.

14. "Concrete particulars" are the discrete, unrepeatable phenomena of history whose reality calls into question the homogenizing impulses of ideological systems. See Theodor Adorno, *Negative Dialectics*, 134–206.

15. Ernest Gaines, *The Autobiography of Miss Jane Pittman*, 89. All further references to this work will be cited in the text.

16. Ernest Gaines, *In My Father's House*, 3–4. All further references to this work will be cited in the text.

17. Ernest Gaines, *A Gathering of Old Men*, 80. All further references to this work will be cited in the text.

Chapter Three: Women's Blues

1. "Commitment: Toni Cade Bambara Speaks," 244.

2. Toni Cade Bambara, *Gorilla, My Love*, 6–7. All further references to this work will be cited in the text.

3. Victor Turner, *The Ritual Process*, 94–95.

4. Toni Cade Bambara, *The Sea Birds Are Still Alive*, 160. All further references to this work will be cited in the text.

5. The works of Alice Walker, Toni Morrison, Gayl Jones, and Paule Marshall contain such figures. See also Walker's "In Search of Our Mother's Gardens," 64.

6. See Puckett, *Folk Beliefs*, 149–50.

7. Toni Cade Bambara, *The Salt Eaters*, 5. All further references to this work will be cited in the text.

8. See Mircea Eliade, *Patterns in Comparative Religion*, 311–22; and James Fraser, *The New Golden Bough*, 144–47.

9. See H. Delos Dias, "Obeah," 452–54.

10. See Levine, *Black Culture*, 420–40.

11. Alice Walker, *The Third Life of Grange Copeland*, 3–4. All further references to this work will be cited in the text.

12. John O'Brien, *Interviews with Black Writers*, 187.

13. Alice Walker, *In Love and Trouble*, 92. All further references to this work will be cited in the text.

14. Trudier Harris, "Folklore in the Fiction of Alice Walker," 3–8.

15. For example, characters quote passages from this work in conjuration ritual.

16. See Puckett, *Folk Beliefs*, 335.

17. See Jahn, "Residual African Elements," 100.

18. Alice Walker, *Meridian*, 6. All further references to this work will be cited in the text.
19. Alice Walker, *You Can't Keep a Good Woman Down*, 126. All further references to this work will be cited in the text.
20. Walker uses this term to distinguish her position from mainstream feminism, which she considers to be dominated by the limited perspective of white, middle-class women. Though womanism implies similar things, she considers it more appropriate because it comes from the folk expression "womanish." See David Bradley, "Novelist Alice Walker," 35.
21. Vladimir Propp, *Morphology of the Folktale*, 26–27.
22. Alice Walker, *The Color Purple*, 3. All further references to this work will be cited in the text.
23. Zora Neale Hurston, *Tell My Horse*, 232–50.

Chapter Four: Beyond Realism

1. Walker, "Our Mothers' Gardens," 64.
2. Flannery O'Connor, *Mystery and Manners*, 44.
3. Antonio Gramsci has defined cultural hegemony as the complex of values, beliefs, and attitudes of a society which strengthen and justify the power of the dominating class. See Carl Boggs, *Gramsci's Marxism*, 39.
4. Gayl Jones, *White Rat*, 11. All further references to this work will be cited in the text.
5. "Black Snake Moan" is the name of a blues song with strong sexual connotations. See Samuel Charters, *The Poetry of the Blues*, 125.
6. See Ellison, *Shadow and Act*, 256–57; and Murray, *The Omni-Americans*, 86–90.
7. For discussions of the forms and themes of blues by women, see Charles Keil, *Urban Blues*, 55–56; and Giles Oakley, *The Devil's Music*, 99–121.
8. Gayl Jones, *Corregidora*, 44. All further references to this work will be cited in the text.
9. J. Douglas Perry, "Gothic as Vortex," 153–54.
10. Gayl Jones, *Eva's Man*, 92–93. All further references to this work will be cited in the text.
11. The voodoo loa Erzulie, like the queen bee, demands the absolute attention of males. Those who serve her must sacrifice their human sexual activities as well as marriages. To refuse obedience is to court death. See Hurston, *Tell My Horse*, 143–51.
12. See Michel Foucault, *Madness and Civilization*.
13. Here *logocentric* is used to suggest the assumption of a fixed relationship between signifier and sig-

nified that does not allow for the ambiguity of language. See Derrida, *Of Grammatology*, 3–5; and Christopher Norris, *Deconstruction*, 29–31.

14. As her own marker of such characters, Morrison consistently gives them names with the diminutive suffix *-ene:* Maureen, Geraldine, Pauline (*The Bluest Eye*); Helene (*Sula*); Magdalena (*Song of Solomon*); and Ondine and Jadine (*Tar Baby*).

15. Toni Morrison, *The Bluest Eye*, 159.

All further references to this work will be cited in the text.

16. Toni Morrison, *Sula*, 5–6. All further references to this work will be cited in the text.

17. See Jahn, *Muntu*, 125.

18. Toni Morrison, *Song of Solomon*, 99. All further references to this work will be cited in the text.

19. Ellison, *Invisible Man*, 13.

20. Toni Morrison, *Tar Baby*, 45. All further references to this work will be cited in the text.

Chapter Five: Voodoo Aesthetics

1. Hurston, *Tell My Horse*, 233–34.

2. See Ishmael Reed, "Neo-HooDoo Manifesto," in *Conjure*, 20–25.

3. See Michel Fabre, "Ishmael Reed's *Free-Lance Pallbearers*," 5–19.

4. Ishmael Reed, *The Free-Lance Pallbearers*, 26. All further references to this work will be cited in the text.

5. O'Brien, *Interviews with Black Writers*, 177.

6. See Hurston, *Tell My Horse*, 180.

7. Ishmael Reed, *Shrovetide in Old New Orleans*, 160.

8. Ishmael Reed, *Yellow Back Radio Broke-Down*, 36. All further refer-

ences to this work will be cited in the text.

9. Reed, *Shrovetide*, 15–16.

10. Ishmael Reed, *Mumbo Jumbo*, 5.

11. Ishmael Reed, *The Last Days of Louisiana Red*, 57. All further references to this work will be cited in the text.

12. Reed, *Shrovetide*, 334–35.

13. Stepto, *From Behind the Veil*, ix.

14. Ishmael Reed, *Flight to Canada*, 8. All further references to this work will be cited in the text.

15. Ishmael Reed, *The Terrible Twos*, 84. All further references to this work will be cited in the text.

Chapter Six: Orphans and Circuses

1. Forrest himself has suggested the influence of Thomas. See "If I Changed My Name: An Interview with Leon Forrest," 146.

2. Ibid., 156.

3. Ibid., 153.

4. Leon Forrest, *There Is a Tree More Ancient than Eden*, 34–35. All fur-

ther references to this work will be cited in the text.

5. See Leon Forrest, *The Bloodworth Orphans*, 1. All further references to this work will be cited in the text.

6. John Greenway, "The Flight of the Gray Goose," 171.

7. See Fraser, *New Golden Bough*, 53–54, 194.

8. See Ellison, *Invisible Man*, 265–66.

9. Fraser, *New Golden Bough*, 183–99.

10. Gass, *Fiction and the Figures of Life*, 67–68.

11. Clarence Major, *The Dark and Feeling*, 128.

12. See Jahn, *Muntu*, 121–40.

13. Clarence Major, *All Night Visitors*,

4. All further references to this work will be cited in the text.

14. Major, *Dark and Feeling*, 13.

15. Ibid., 118.

16. Ibid., 137.

17. Clarence Major, *No*, 72. All further references to this work will be cited in the text.

18. Major, *Dark and Feeling*, 142.

19. Reed, *Mumbo Jumbo*, 188–97.

20. Major, *Dark and Feeling*, 16.

21. Clarence Major, *Reflex and Bone Structure*, 29. All further references to this work will be cited in the text.

22. Clarence Major, *Emergency Exit*, 26. All further references to this work will be cited in the text.

Conclusion: Just like a Tree

1. Ellison, *Shadow and Act*, 58–59. All further references to this work will be cited in the text.

2. Black women writers seem much less concerned with the whole question of influence. They either willingly acknowledge a variety of literary ancestors or dismiss the matter as extraneous to their work.

Bibliography

Abrahams, Roger. *Deep Down in the Jungle: Negro Narrative Folklore from the Streets of Philadelphia*. Rev. ed. Chicago: Aldine, 1970.

———. *Positively Black*. Englewood Cliffs, N.J.: Prentice-Hall, 1970.

Adorno, Theodor W. *Negative Dialectics*. Translated by E. B. Ashton. New York: Atheneum, 1973.

Ambler, Madge. "Ishmael Reed: Whose Radio Broke Down?" *Negro American Literature Forum* 6 (1972): 125–31.

Andrews, William L. " 'We Ain't Going Back There': The Idea of Progress in *The Autobiography of Miss Jane Pittman*." *Black American Literature Forum* 11 (1977): 146–49.

Atlas, Marilyn Judith. "A Woman Both Shiny and Brown: Feminine Strength in Toni Morrison's *Song of Solomon*." *Society for the Study of Midwestern Literature Newsletter* 9, no. 3 (1979): 8–12.

———. "The Darker Side of Toni Morrison's *Song of Solomon*." *Society for the Study of Midwestern Literature Newsletter* 10, no. 2 (1980): 1–13.

Aubert, Alvin. "Ernest J. Gaines's Truly Tragic Mulatto." *Callaloo* 1, no. 3 (1978): 68–75.

Baker, Houston A., Jr. *The Journey Back: Issues in Black Literature and Criticism*. Chicago: University of Chicago Press, 1980.

———. *Long Black Song: Essays in Black American Literature and Culture*. Charlottesville: University Press of Virginia, 1972.

———. *Singers of Daybreak: Studies in Black American Literature*. Washington: Howard University Press, 1974.

———. "To Move Without Moving: An Analysis of Creativity and Commerce in Ralph Ellison's Trueblood Episode." *PMLA* 98 (1983): 828–45.

Bakerman, Jane S. "Failures of Love: Female Initiation in the Novels of Toni Morrison." *American Literature* 52 (1981): 541–63.

———. "The Seams Can't Show: An Interview with Toni Morrison." *Black American Literature Forum* 12 (1978): 56–60.

Baldwin, James. *Going to Meet the Man*. New York: Dial Press, 1965.

Bambara, Toni Cade. *Gorilla, My Love*. New York: Vintage, 1972.

———. *The Salt Eaters*. New York: Vintage, 1980.

289

_____. *The Sea Birds Are Still Alive.* New York: Vintage, 1977.

Bataille, Robert. "Ellison's *Invisible Man:* The Old Rhetoric and the New." *Black American Literature Forum* 12 (1978): 43–45.

Baumbach, Jonathan. *The Landscape of Nightmare: Studies in the Contemporary American Novel.* New York: New York University Press, 1965.

Beckham, Barry. "Jane Pittman and Oral Tradition." *Callaloo* 1, no. 3 (1978): 102–9.

Bell, Bernard W. *The Folk Roots of Contemporary Afro-American Poetry.* Detroit: Broadside Press, 1974.

Bell, Roseann Pope. "Gayl Jones: A Voice in the Whirlwind." *Studia Africana* 1 (1977): 99–107.

Bellamy, Joe David. *The New Fiction: Interviews with Innovative American Writers.* Urbana: University of Illinois Press, 1974.

_____. Review of *Flight to Canada,* by Ishmael Reed. *Saturday Review,* 2 October 1976, 35.

Benston, Kimberly W. "Ellison, Baraka, and the Faces of Tradition." *Boundary 2* 6 (1978): 333–54.

Bigsby, C. W. E. *The Second Black Renaissance: Essays in Black Literature.* Westport, Conn.: Greenwood Press, 1980.

_____, ed. *The Black American Writer.* 2 vols. Deland, Fla.: Everett/Edwards, 1969.

Bischoff, Joan. "The Novels of.Toni Morrison: Studies in Thwarted Sensibility." *Studies in Black Literature* 6, no. 3 (1975): 21–23.

Blake, Susan L. "Folklore and Community in *Song of Solomon.*" *MELUS* 7, no. 3: 77–82.

_____. "Modern Black Writers and the Folk Tradition." Ph.D. dissertation, University of Connecticut, 1976.

_____. "Ritual and Rationalization: Black Folklore in the Works of Ralph Ellison." *PMLA* 94 (1979): 121–36.

Blicksilver, Edith. "The Image of Women in Selected Short Stories by James Alan McPherson." *CLA Journal* 22 (1978): 390–401.

Bluestein, Gene "The Blues as a Literary Theme." *Massachusetts Review* 8 (1967): 593–617.

_____. *The Voice of the Folk: Folklore and American Literary Theory.* Amherst: University of Massachusetts Press, 1972.

Boggs, Carl. *Gramsci's Marxism.* London: Pluto Press, 1976.

Bolling, Doug. "A Reading of Clarence Major's Short Fiction." *Black American Literature Forum* 13 (1979): 51–56.

Bone, Robert. *Down Home: A History of Afro-American Short Fiction from Its Beginnings to the End of the Harlem Renaissance.* New York: G. P. Putnam's Sons, 1975.

_____. *The Negro Novel in America.* Rev. ed. New Haven, Conn.: Yale University Press, 1965.

Botkin, B. A., ed. *Lay My Burden Down: A Folk History of Slavery.* Chicago: University of Chicago Press, 1945.

Bradley, David. "Novelist Alice Walker: Telling the Black Woman's Story." *New York Times Magazine,* 8 January 1984, 35.

Brearly, H. C. "Ba-ad Nigger." In *Mother Wit from the Laughing Barrel: Readings in the Interpretation of Afro-American Folklore,* edited by Alan Dundes. Englewood Cliffs, N.J.: Prentice-Hall, 1973.

Brewer, J. Mason, comp. *American Negro Folklore.* Chicago: University of Chicago Press, 1968.

Broyard, Anatole. Review of *The Bloodworth Orphans,* by Leon Forrest. *New York Times Book Review,* 1 May 1977, 12.

––––––. Review of *There Is a Tree More Ancient than Eden,* by Leon Forrest. *New York Times,* 8 June 1973, 37.

Bruck, Peter, ed. *The Black American Short Story in the Twentieth Century: A Collection of Critical Essays.* Amsterdam: B. R. Gruner, 1977.

––––––, and Wolfgang Karrer, eds. *The Afro-American Novel Since 1960.* Amsterdam: B. R. Gruner, 1982.

Bryant, Jerry H. "Ernest J. Gaines: Change, Growth, History." *Southern Review* 10 (1974): 851–64.

––––––. "From Death to Life: The Fiction of Ernest J. Gaines." *Iowa Review* 3 (1972): 106–20.

Buck-Morss, Susan. *The Origin of Negative Dialectics: Theodor W. Adorno, Walter Benjamin, and the Frankfurt Institute.* New York: Free Press, 1977.

Burke, William. "*Bloodline:* A Black Man's South." *CLA Journal* 19 (1975): 545–58.

Burt, Della. "The Legacy of the Bad Nigger." *Journal of Afro-American Issues* 5 (1977): 111–24.

Burwell, Sherri Lynn. "The Soul of Black Women: The Hermeneutical Method of Analysis as Applied to the Novel *Corregidora.*" Ph.D. dissertation, University of California, Berkeley, 1979.

Butler, Thorpe. "What Is to Be Done? Illusion, Identity, and Action in Ralph Ellison's *Invisible Man.*" *CLA Journal* 27 (1984): 315–31.

Byerman, Keith E. "Black Vortex: The Gothic Structure of Eva's Man." *MELUS* 7 (1980): 93–100.

––––––. "Intense Behaviors: The Use of the Grotesque in *Eva's Man* and *The Bluest Eye.*" *CLA Journal* 25 (1982): 447–57.

Charters, Samuel. *The Poetry of the Blues.* 1963. Reprint. New York: Avon, 1970.

Christian, Barbara. *Black Women Novelists: The Development of a Tradition, 1892–1976.* Westport, Conn.: Greenwood Press, 1980.

––––––. "Community and Nature: The Novels of Toni Morrison." *Journal of Ethnic Studies* 7, no. 4 (1980): 65–78.

Clipper, Lawrence J. "Folkloric and Mythic Elements in *Invisible Man.*" *CLA Journal* 13 (1970): 229–41.

Coffin, Tristram, ed. *Our Living Traditions: An Introduction to Folklore.* New York: Basic Books, 1968.

Cohen, Hennig. "American Literature and American Folklore." In *Our Living Traditions: An Introduction to Folklore,* edited by Tristan Coffin. New York: Basic Books, 1968.

"Commitment: Toni Cade Bambara Speaks." In *Sturdy Black Bridges: Visions of Black Women in Literature,* edited by Roseanne Bell et al. Garden City, N.Y.: Doubleday, 1979.

Courlander, Harold. *A Treasury of Afro-American Folklore.* New York: Crown Press, 1976.

Covo, Jacqueline. *The Blinking Eye.* New York: Scarecrow Press, 1974. (Ralph Ellison bibliography.)

Culler, Jonathan. *Structuralist Poetics: Structuralism, Linguistics, and the Study of Literature.* Ithaca, N.Y.: Cornell University Press, 1975.

Davis, Arthur P. *From the Dark Tower: Afro-American Writers, 1900–1960.* Washington: Howard University Press, 1974.

Davis, Charles T. *Black Is the Color of the Cosmos: Essays on Afro-American Literature and Culture, 1942–1981.* Edited by Henry Louis Gates, Jr. New York: Garland, 1982.

Davis, Cynthia A. "Self, Society, and Myth in Toni Morrison's Fiction." *Contemporary Literature* 23 (1982): 323–42.

Davis, L. J. Review of *There Is a Tree More Ancient than Eden,* by Leon Forrest. *New York Times Book Review,* 21 October 1973, 48.

Derrida, Jacques. *Of Grammatology.* Translated by Gayatri Spivak. Baltimore: Johns Hopkins University Press, 1976.

Dias, H. DeLos. "Obeah." In *Negro Anthology,* edited by Nancy Cunard. London: Wishart, 1934.

Dollard, John. "The Dozens: The Dialectic of Insult." In *Mother Wit from the Laughing Barrel: Readings in the Interpretation of Afro-American Folklore,* edited by Alan Dundes. Englewood Cliffs, N.J.: Prentice-Hall, 1973.

Douglass, Frederick. *The Narrative of the Life of Frederick Douglass, An American Slave.* 1845. Reprint. New York: Penguin, 1982.

DuBois, W. E. B. *The Souls of Black Folk: Essays and Sketches.* 1903. Reprint. Millwood, N.Y.: Kraus-Thomson, 1973.

Dundes, Alan, ed. *Mother Wit from the Laughing Barrel: Readings in the Interpretation of Afro-American Folklore.* Englewood Cliffs, N.J.: Prentice-Hall, 1973.

Eagleton, Terry. *Marxism and Literary Criticism.* Berkeley and Los Angeles: University of California Press, 1976.

Eliade, Mircea. *Patterns in Comparative Religion.* Translated by Rosemary Sheed. Cleveland: World, 1963.

Ellison, Ralph. *Invisible Man.* New York: Random House, 1952.

———. *Shadow and Act.* New York: Random House, 1964.

Emerson, Ralph Waldo. *Selections from Ralph Waldo Emerson.* Edited by Stephen E. Whicher. Boston: Houghton Mifflin, 1957.

Erickson, Peter. "'Cast Out Alone / to Heal and Recreate / Ourselves': Family-Based Identity in the Work of Alice Walker." *CLA Journal* 23 (1979): 71–94.

Fabre, Michel. "Bayonne or the Yoknapatawpha of Ernest Gaines." Translated by Melvin Dixon and Didier Malaquin. *Callaloo* 1, no. 3 (1978): 110–24.

———. "Ishmael Reed's *Free-Lance Pallbearers:* On the Dialectics of Shit." *Obsidian* 3, no. 3 (1977): 5–19.

Fenderson, Lewis H. "The New Breed of Black Writers and Their Jaundiced View of Tradition." *CLA Journal* 15 (1971): 18–24.

Fikes, Robert Jr. "Echoes from Small Town Ohio: A Toni Morrison Bibliography." *Obsidian* 5, nos. 1–2 (1979): 142–48.

———. "The Works of an 'American' Writer: A James Alan McPherson Bibliography." *CLA Journal* 22 (1979): 415–23.

Fisher, Jerilyn. "From Under the Yoke of Race and Sex: Black and Chicano Women's Fiction of the Seventies." *Minority Voices* 2, no. 2 (1979): 1–12.

Fontenot, Chester J., Jr. "Black Fiction: Apollo or Dionysius?" *Twentieth Century Literature* 25 (1979): 73–84.

———. "Ishmael Reed and the Politics of Aesthetics, or Shake Hands and Come Out Conjuring." *Black American Literature Forum* 12 (1978): 20–23.

Forrest, Leon. *The Bloodworth Orphans.* New York: Random House, 1977.

———. *There Is a Tree More Ancient than Eden.* New York: Random House, 1973.

Foucault, Michel. *Language, Counter-Memory, Practice: Selected Essays and Interviews.* Edited by Donald F. Bouchard. Translated by Donald F. Bouchard and Sherry Simon. Ithaca, N.Y.: Cornell University Press, 1977.

———. *Madness and Civilization: A History of Insanity in the Age of Reason.* Translated by Richard Howard. New York: Pantheon, 1965.

Fraiberg, Selma. "Two Modern Incest Heroes." *Partisan Review* 28 (1961): 646–61.

Fraser, James. *The New Golden Bough.* Edited by Theodor H. Gaster. Garden City, N.Y.: Doubleday, 1961.

Gaines, Ernest. *The Autobiography of Miss Jane Pittman.* New York: Dial Press, 1971.

———. *Bloodline.* New York: Dial Press, 1968.

———. *Catherine Carmier.* 1964. Reprint. Chatham, N.J.: Chatham, 1972.

———. *A Gathering of Old Men.* New York: Knopf, 1983.

———. *In My Father's House.* New York: Knopf, 1978.

———. *Of Love and Dust.* New York: Dial Press, 1967.

Gass, William. *Fiction and the Figures of Life.* New York: Vintage, 1972.

Gaston, Karen Carmean. "The Theme of Female Self-Discovery in the Novels of Judith Rossner, Gail Godwin, Alice Walker, and Toni Morrison." Ph.D. dissertation, Auburn University, 1980.

————. "Women in the Lives of Grange Copeland." *CLA Journal* 24 (1981): 276–86.

Gates, Henry Louis, Jr. "Introduction: Criticism in de Jungle." *Black American Literature Forum* 15 (1981): 123–27.

————, ed. *Black Literature and Literary Theory.* New York: Methuen, 1984.

Gayle, Addison, Jr. *The Way of the New World: The Black Novel in America.* Garden City, N.Y.: Doubleday, Anchor Books, 1976.

————, ed. *The Black Aesthetic.* Garden City, N.Y.: Doubleday, 1971.

Genovese, Eugene. *Roll, Jordan, Roll: The World the Slaves Made.* New York: Random House, 1976.

Gervin, Mary A. "Developing a Sense of Self: The Androgynous Ideal in McPherson's 'Elbow Room.'" *CLA Journal* 26 (1982): 251–55.

Gibson, Donald B. "Individualism and Community in Black History and Ficton." *Black American Literature Forum* 11 (1977): 123–29.

Gover, Robert. "An Interview with Ishmael Reed." *Black American Literature Forum* 12 (1978): 12–19.

Greenway, John. "The Flight of the Gray Goose: Literary Symbolism in the Traditional Ballad." *Southern Folklore Quarterly* 18 (1954): 165–74.

Grimes, Johanna Lucille. "The Function of the Oral Tradition in Selected Afro-American Fiction." Ph.D. dissertation, Northwestern University, 1980.

Gutman, Herbert G. *The Black Family in Slavery and Freedom, 1750–1925.* New York: Random House, 1976.

Gysin, Fritz. *The Grotesque in American Negro Fiction: Jean Toomer, Richard Wright, and Ralph Ellison.* Basel, Switzerland: Francke Verlag Bern, 1975.

Harper, Michael S., and Robert B. Stepto, eds. *Chant of Saints: A Gathering of Afro-American Literature, Art, and Scholarship.* Urbana: University of Illinois Press, 1979.

Harris, A. Leslie. "Myth as Structure in Toni Morrison's *Song of Solomon.*" *MELUS* 7, no. 3 (1980): 69–76.

Harris, Charles B. *Contemporary American Novelists of the Absurd.* New Haven, Conn.: College and University Press, 1971.

Harris, Norman. "Politics as an Innovative Aspect of Literary Folklore: A Study of Ishmael Reed." *Obsidian* 5, nos. 1–2 (1979): 41–50.

Harris, Trudier. "Ellison's 'Peter Wheatstraw': His Basis in Black Folk Tradition." *Mississippi Folklore Register* 9 (1975): 117–26.

————. "Folklore in the Fiction of Alice Walker: A Perpetuation of Historical and Literary Traditions." *Black American Literature Forum* 11 (1977): 3–8.

————. *From Mammies to Militants: Domestics in Black American Literature.* Philadelphia: Temple University Press, 1982.

————. "A Spiritual Journey: Gayl Jones's *Song for Anninho.*" *Callaloo* 5 (1982): 105–11.

————. "Tiptoeing Through Taboo: Incest in 'The Child Who Favored Daughter.'" *Modern Fiction Studies* 28 (1982): 495–505.

————. "Violence in *The Third Life of Grange Copeland.*" *CLA Journal* 19 (1975): 238–47.

Hassan, Ihab. *Contemporary American Literature, 1945–1972: An Introduction.* New York: Frederick Ungar, 1973.

Hays, Peter. "The Incest Theme in *Invisible Man.*" *Western Humanities Review* 23 (1969): 335–39.

Hemenway, Robert, ed. *The Black Novelist.* Columbus: Charles Merrill, 1970.

Henderson, Stephen. *Understanding the New Black Poetry: Black Speech and Black Music as Poetic References.* New York: William Morrow, 1973.

Hersey, John, ed. *Ralph Ellison: A Collection of Critical Essays.* Englewood Cliffs, N.J.: Prentice-Hall, 1974.

Hicks, Jack. *In the Singer's Temple: Prose Fictions of Barthelme, Gaines, Brautigan, Piercy, Kesey, and Kosinski.* Chapel Hill: University of North Carolina, 1981.

————. "To Make These Bones Live: History and Community in Ernest Gaines's Fiction." *Black American Literature Forum* 11 (1977): 9–19.

Horowitz, Floyd R. "Ralph Ellison's Modern Version of Brer Bear and Brer Rabbit in *Invisible Man.*" *Midcontinent American Studies Journal* 4, no. 2 (1963): 21–27.

House, Elizabeth B. "The 'Sweet Life' in Toni Morrison's Fiction." *American Literature* 56 (1984): 181–202.

Hughes, Langston, and Arna Bontemps, eds. *The Book of Negro Folklore.* New York: Dodd, Mead, 1958.

Hurston, Zora Neale. *Mules and Men.* Philadelphia: J. P. Lippincott, 1935.

————. *Tell My Horse.* 1938. Reprint. Berkeley: Turtle Island, 1981.

"If He Changed My Name: An Interview with Leon Forrest." In *Chant of Saints: A Gathering of Afro-American Literature, Art, and Scholarship,* edited by Michael S. Harper and Robert B. Stepto. Urbana: University of Illinois Press, 1979.

Ingram, Forrest, and Barbara Steinberg. "On the Verge: An Interview with Ernest J. Gaines." *New Orleans Review* 1 (1969): 339–44.

"An Interview: Ernest Gaines." *New Orleans Review* 1 (1969): 331–35.

Israel, Joachim. *The Language of Dialectics and the Dialectics of Language.* Copenhagen: Munksgaard, 1979.

Jahn, Janheinz. *Muntu: An Outline of Neo-African Culture.* Translated by Marjorie Grene. London: Faber and Faber, 1961.

————. *Neo-African Literature: A History of Black Writing.* Translated by Oliver Coburn and Ursula Lehrburger. New York: Grove Press, 1968.

————. "Residual African Elements in the Blues." In *Mother Wit from the Laughing Barrel: Readings in the Interpretation of Afro-American Folklore,* edited by Alan Dundes. Englewood Cliffs, N.J.: Prentice-Hall, 1973.

Jameson, Frederic. *Marxism and Form.* Princeton, N.J.: Princeton University Press, 1976.

————. *The Prison-House of Language: A Critical Account of Structuralism and Russian Formalism.* Princeton, N.J.: Princeton University Press, 1972.

Jay, Martin. *The Dialectical Imagination.* Boston: Little, Brown, 1973.

Johnson, Diane. Review of *White Rat* by Gayl Jones and *Elbow Room* by James Alan McPherson. *New York Review of Books,* 10 November 1977, 6.

Jones, Gayl. *Corregidora.* New York: Random House, 1975.

————. *Eva's Man.* New York: Random House, 1976.

————. *White Rat.* New York: Random House, 1977.

Jones, LeRoi. *Home: Social Essays.* New York: William Morrow, 1966.

Jones, Robert W. "Language and Structure in Ishmael Reed's *Yellow Back Radio Broke-Down." Notes on Contemporary Literature* 8 (1978): 2–3.

Jordan, June. Review of *Eva's Man* by Gayl Jones. *New York Times Book Review,* 17 May 1976, 36.

Kaiser, Ernest. "A Critical Look at Ellison's Fiction and at Social and Literary Criticism About the Author." *Black World* 20 (1970): 53–59, 81.

Keil, Charles. *Urban Blues.* Chicago: University of Chicago Press, 1966.

Kent, George E. *Blackness and the Adventure of Western Culture.* Chicago: Third World Press, 1972.

————. "Ralph Ellison and Afro-American Folk and Cultural Tradition." *CLA Journal* 8 (1970): 265–76.

Klein, Marcus. *After Alienation.* Cleveland: World Publishing, 1964.

Klinkowitz, Jerome. "Clarence Major: An Interview with a Post-Contemporary Author." *Black American Literature Forum* 12 (1978): 32–37.

————. *Literary Disruptions: The Making of a Post-Contemporary American Fiction.* Urbana: University of Illinois Press, 1975.

————. "Notes on a Novel-in-Progress: Clarence Major's *Emergency Exit." Black American Literature Forum* 13 (1979): 46–50.

Klotman, Phyllis Rauch. *Another Man Gone: The Black Runner in Contemporary Afro-American Literature.* Port Washington, N.Y.: Kennikat Press, 1977.

————. "Dick-and-Jane and the Shirley Temple Sensibility in *The Bluest Eye." Black American Literature Forum* 13 (1979): 123–25.

Kohl, Ingrid Marja. "Ishmael Reed: Neo Hoodoo and Politics." M.A. thesis, University of Texas at Austin, 1981.

Kostelantez, Richard. "Politics of Ellison's Booker: *Invisible Man* as Symbolic History." *Chicago Review* 19, no. 2 (1967): 5–26.

Laney, Ruth. "A Conversation with Ernest Gaines." *Southern Review* 10 (1974): 1–14.

Lardner, Susan. Review of *The Salt Eaters* by Toni Cade Bambara. *New Yorker,* 5 May 1980, 169.

Laughlin, Rosemary M. "Attention, American Folklore: Doc Craft Comes Marching In." *Studies in American Fiction* 1 (1973): 220–27.

Lee, A. Robert, ed. *Black Fiction: New Studies in the Afro-American Novel Since 1945.* New York: Barnes and Noble, 1980.

Lee, Valerie Gray. "The Use of Folktalk in Novels by Black Women Writers." *CLA Journal* 23 (1980): 266–72.

Lemon, Lee T., and Marion J. Reis, eds. *Russian Formalist Criticism: Four Essays.* Lincoln: University of Nebraska Press, 1965.

Lentricchia, Frank. *After the New Criticism.* Chicago: University of Chicago Press, 1980.

Lester, Julius. *Black Folktales.* New York: Grove Press, 1969.

Levine, Lawrence. *Black Culture and Black Consciousness: Afro-American Folk Thought from Slavery to Freedom.* Oxford: Oxford University Press, 1977.

Lewald H. Ernest, ed. *The Cry of Home: Cultural Nationalism and the Modern Writer.* Knoxville: University of Tennessee Press, 1972.

Liebow, Elliot. *Tally's Corner: A Study of Negro Streetcorner Men.* Boston: Little, Brown, 1967.

Lounsberry, Barbara, and Grace Ann Hovet. "Flying as Symbol and Legend in Toni Morrison's *The Bluest Eye, Sula, Song of Solomon.*" *CLA Journal* 27 (1984): 119–40.

———. "Principles of Perception in Toni Morrison's *Sula.*" *Black American Literature Forum* 13 (1979): 126–29.

McCaffery, Larry, and Sinda Gregory. "Major's *Reflex and Bone Structure* and the Anti-Detective Tradition." *Black American Literature Forum* 13 (1979): 39–45.

McDowell, Deborah E. "The Self in Bloom: Alice Walker's *Meridian.*" *CLA Journal* 24 (1981): 262–75.

McGowan, Martha J. "Atonement and Release in Alice Walker's *Meridian.*" *CLA Journal* 23 (1981): 25–36.

Mackey, Nathaniel. "Ishmael Reed and the Black Aesthetic." *CLA Journal* 21 (1978): 355–66.

McPherson, James Alan. *Elbow Room.* Boston: Little, Brown, 1977.

———. *Hue and Cry.* Boston: Little, Brown, 1969.

Major, Clarence. *All Night Visitors.* New York: Olympia Press, 1969.

———. *The Dark and Feeling: Black American Writers and Their Work.* New York: Third Press, 1974.

———. *Emergency Exit.* New York: Fiction Collective, 1979.

———. *No.* New York: Emerson Hall, 1973.

———. "Reality, Fiction and Criticism: An Interview/Essay." *Par Rapport* 2 (1979): 67–73.

———. *Reflex and Bone Structure.* New York: Fiction Collective, 1975.

———. Review of *Bloodworth Orphans* by Leon Forrest. *Library Journal,* 1 May 1977, 1043.

———. Review of *Eva's Man* by Gayl Jones. *Library Journal,* 15 March 1976, 834.

Malone, Gloria S. "The Nature and Causes of Suffering in the Fiction of Paule Marshall, Kristen Hunter, Toni Morrison, and Alice Walker." Ph.D. dissertation, Kent State University, 1979.

Marcuse, Herbert. *One-Dimensional Man: Studies in the Ideology of Advanced Industrial Society.* Boston: Beacon Press, 1964.

Miller, R. Baxter, ed. *Black American Literature and Humanism*. Lexington: University Press of Kentucky, 1981.

Mitchell-Kernan, Claudia. "Signifying." In *Mother Wit from the Laughing Barrel: Readings in the Interpretation of Afro-American Folklore,* edited by Alan Dundes. Englewood Cliffs, N.J.: Prentice-Hall, 1973.

Moore, Judith. "So I'm Speakin' Out . . .: A Conversation with Ishmael Reed." *Express: The East Bay's Free Weekley* [Berkeley], 18 February 1983, 1, 11–14.

Morrison, Toni. *The Bluest Eye*. New York: Holt, Rinehart, Winston, 1970. Reprint. New York: Pocket Books, 1972.

———. *Song of Solomon*. New York: Knopf, 1977.

———. *Sula*. New York: Knopf, 1973.

———. *Tar Baby*. New York: Knopf, 1981.

Murray, Albert. *The Omni-Americans: New Perspectives on Black Experience and American Culture*. New York: Avon, 1970.

Musgrave, Marian E. "Sexual Excess and Deviation as Structural Devices in Gunter Grass's *Blechtrommel* and Ishmael Reed's *Free-Lance Pallbearers*." *CLA Journal* 22 (1979): 229–39.

Norris, Christopher. *Deconstruction: Theory and Practice*. London: Methuen, 1982.

Oakley, Giles. *The Devil's Music: A History of the Blues*. New York: Harcourt, Brace, Jovanovich, 1976.

O'Brien, John. *Interviews with Black Writers*. New York: Liveright, 1973.

O'Connor, Flannery. *Mystery and Manners*. Edited by Sally and Robert Fitzgerald. New York: Farrar, Strauss, and Giroux, 1961.

Ogunyemi, Chikwenge Okonjo. "Order and Disorder in Toni Morrison's *The Bluest Eye*." *Critique* 19 (1977): 112–20.

———. "*Sula*: 'A Nigger Joke.'" *Black American Literature Forum* 13 (1979): 130–33.

Olderman, Raymond M. *Beyond the Wasteland: A Study of the American Novel of the Nineteen-Sixties*. New Haven, Conn.: Yale University Press, 1972.

———. "Ralph Ellison's Blues and *Invisible Man*." *Wisconsin Studies in Literature* 7 (1966): 142–59.

O'Meally, Robert G. *The Craft of Ralph Ellison*. Cambridge: Harvard University Press, 1980.

Payne, Ladell. *Black Novelists and the Southern Literary Tradition*. Athens: University of Georgia Press, 1981.

Peden, William. *The American Short Story: Continuity and Change, 1940–1975*. 2d ed. Boston: Houghton Mifflin, 1975.

Perry, J. Douglas. "Gothic Vortex: The Form of Horror in Capote, Faulkner, and Styron." *Modern Fiction Studies* 19 (1973): 153–67.

"Person to Person." *Black Seeds* (London) 1, no. 1 (1980): 28–29. (Interview with Toni Morrison.)

Propp, Vladimir. *Morphology of the Folktale*. 2d ed. Translated by Laurence Scott. Austin: University of Texas Press, 1977.

Puckett, Newbill N. *Folk Beliefs of the Southern Negro*. Chapel Hill: University of North Carolina Press, 1926.

Redmond, Eugene B. *Drumvoices: The Mission of Afro-American Poetry—A Critical History*. Garden City, N.Y.: Doubleday, Anchor Books, 1976.

Reed, Ishmael. *Conjure: Selected Poems, 1963–1970*. Amherst: University of Massachusetts Press, 1972.

————. *Flight to Canada*. New York: Random House, 1976.

————. *The Free-Lance Pallbearers*. Garden City, N.Y.: Doubleday, 1967.

————. *The Last Days of Louisiana Red*. New York: Random House, 1974.

————. *Mumbo Jumbo*. Garden City, N.Y.: Doubleday, 1972.

————. *Shrovetide in Old New Orleans*. Garden City, N.Y.: Doubleday, 1978.

————. *The Terrible Twos*. New York: St. Martin's Press, 1982.

————. *Yellow Back Radio Broke-Down*. Garden City, N.Y.: Doubleday, 1969.

Reilly, John M. "The Reconstruction of Genre as Entry into Conscious History." *Black American Literature Forum* 13 (1979): 3–6.

————, ed. *Twentieth Century Interpretations of "Invisible Man."* Englewood Cliffs, N.J.: Prentice-Hall, 1970.

Rhodes, Jewell Parker. "*Mumbo Jumbo* and a Somewhat Private Literary Response." *American Humor* 6, no. 2 (1979): 11–13.

Rosenblatt, Roger. *Black Fiction*. Cambridge, Mass.: Harvard University Press, 1974.

Rowell, Charles H. "Ernest J. Gaines: A Checklist, 1964–1978." *Callaloo* 1, no. 3 (1978): 125–31.

————. "An Interview with Gayl Jones." *Callaloo* 5 (1982): 32–53.

Royster, Philip M. "A Priest and a Witch Against the Spiders and Snakes: Scapegoating in Toni Morrison's *Sula*." *Umoja* 2 (1978): 149–68.

Rubin, Louis D., Jr. *The American South*. Baton Rouge: Louisiana State University Press, 1980.

Saunders, Archie D. "Odysseus in Black: An Analysis of the Structure of *Invisible Man*." *CLA Journal* 13 (1970): 217–28.

Schmitz, Neil. "Neo-HooDoo: The Experimental Fiction of Ishmael Reed." *Twentieth Century Literature* 20 (1974): 126–40.

Scholes, Robert. *The Fabulators*. New York: Oxford University Press, 1967.

Schraufuagel, Noel. *From Apology to Protest: The Black American Novel*. Deland, Fla.: Everett/Edwards, 1973.

Schultz, Elizabeth A. "African and Afro-American Roots in Contemporary Afro-American Literature: The Difficult Search for Family Origins." *Studies in American Fiction* 8 (1980): 127–45.

————. "The Heirs of Ralph Ellison: Patterns of Individualism in the Contemporary Afro-American Novel." *CLA Journal* 22 (1978): 101–22.

————. "The Insistence upon Community in the Contemporary Afro-American Novel." *College English* 41 (1979): 170–84.

Sekora, John, and Darwin T. Turner, eds. *The Art of Slave Narrative*. Macomb: Western Illinois University Press, 1982.

"A Selected Checklist of Materials by and About Ralph Ellison." *Black World* 19 (1970): 126–30.

Sequeira, Isaac. "The Uncompleted Initiation of the Invisible Man." *Studies in Black Literature* 6, no. 1 (1975): 9–13.

Settle, Elizabeth A., and Thomas A. Settle, eds. *Ishmael Reed: A Primary and Secondary Bibliography*. Boston: Hall, 1982.

Shelton, Frank W. "Ambiguous Manhood in Ernest J. Gaines' *Bloodline*." *CLA Journal* 19 (1975): 200–209.

Snead, James A. "On Repetition in Black Culture." *Black American Literature Forum* 15 (1981): 146–53.

Spillers, Hortense. "Ellison's 'Usable Past': Toward a Theory of Myth." *Interpretations* 9 (1977): 53–69.

Steinbrink, Jeffrey. "Toward a Vision of Infinite Possibility: A Reading of *Invisible Man*." *Studies in Black Literature* 7, no. 3 (1976): 1–5.

Stepto, Robert B. *From Behind the Veil: A Study of Afro-American Narrative*. Urbana: University of Illinois Press, 1979.

———, and Dexter Fisher, eds. *Afro-American Literature: The Reconstruction of Instruction*. New York: Modern Language Association, 1979.

Stern, Richard G. "That Same Pain, That Same Pleasure." *December* 3 (1961): 30–46. (Interview with Ralph Ellison.)

Sternburg, Janet, ed. *The Writer on Her Work*. New York: Norton, 1981.

Stoelting, Winifred L. "Human Dignity and Pride in the Novels of Ernest Gaines." *CLA Journal* 14 (1970): 340–58.

Sullivan, Walter. "Where Have All the Flowers Gone: The Short Story in Search of Itself." *Sewanee Review* 8 (1970): 531–42.

Tanner, Tony. *City of Words: American Fiction, 1950–1970*. New York: Harper and Row, 1971.

Tate, Claudia C. "*Corregidora*: Ursa's Blues Medley." *Black American Literature Forum* 13 (1979): 139–41.

———. "An Interview with Gayl Jones." *Black American Literature Forum* 13 (1979): 142–48.

———, ed. *Black Women Writers at Work*. New York: Continuum, 1983.

Thomas, Lorenzo. "Two Crowns of Thoth: A Study of Ishmael Reed's *The Last Days of Louisiana Red*." *Obsidian* 2, no. 3 (1976): 5–25.

Todorov, Tzvetan. *The Poetics of Prose*. Translated by Richard Howard. Ithaca, N.Y.: Cornell University Press, 1977.

Tomashevsky, Boris. "Thematics." In *Russian Formalist Criticism: Four Essays*, edited by Lee T. Lemon and Marion J. Reis. Lincoln: University of Nebraska Press, 1965.

Traylor, Eleanor. "*The Salt Eaters:* My Soul Looks Back in Wonder." *First World* 2, no. 4 (1980): 44–47, 64.

Trimmer, Joseph F., ed. *A Casebook on Ralph Ellison's "Invisible Man."* New York: Thomas Y. Crowell, 1972.

Turner, Darwin T. "Black Fiction: History and Myth." *Studies in American Fiction* 5 (1977): 109–26.

Turner, Victor. *The Ritual Process: Structure and Anti-Structure.* Chicago: Aldine, 1969.

Updike, John. Review of *Eva's Man* by Gayl Jones. *New Yorker,* 9 August 1976, 74.

Uphaus, Suzanne Henning. "Ishmael Reed's Canada." *Canadian Review of American Studies* 8 (1977): 95–99.

"A Very Stern Discipline." *Harper's,* March 1967, 76–95. (Interview with Ralph Ellison.)

Walker, Alice. *The Color Purple.* New York: Harcourt, Brace, Jovanovich, 1982.

———. *In Love and Trouble.* New York: Harcourt, Brace, Jovanovich, 1973.

———. "In Search of Our Mothers' Gardens." *Ms.,* May 1974, 64–70, 105.

———. *Meridian.* New York: Harcourt, Brace, Jovanovich, 1976.

———. *The Third Life of Grange Copeland.* New York: Harcourt, Brace, Jovanovich, 1970.

———. *You Can't Keep a Good Woman Down.* New York: Harcourt, Brace, Jovanovich, 1981.

Walker, Cam. Review of *The Third Life of Grange Copeland* and *Meridian* by Alice Walker. *Southern Exposure* 5 (1977): 102–3.

Ward, Jerry W. "Escape from Trublem: The Fiction of Gayl Jones." *Callaloo* 5 (1982): 95–104.

Washington, Booker T. *Up from Slavery.* 1901. Reprint. New York: Bantam, 1963.

Washington, Mary Helen. "Black Women: Myth and Image Makers." *Black World* 23 (August 1974): 10–18.

———. Review of *A Gathering of Old Men* by Ernest Gaines. *Nation,* 14 January 1984, 22.

Weever, Jacquline de. "The Inverted World of Toni Morrison's *The Bluest Eye* and *Sula.*" *CLA Journal* 22 (1979): 402–14.

Weixlmann, Joe. "Clarence Major: A Checklist of Criticism." *Obsidian* 4, no. 2 (1978): 101–13.

———. "Politics, Piracy, and Other Games: Slavery and Liberation in *Flight to Canada.*" *MELUS* 6, no. 3 (1979): 41–50.

———, and Clarence Major. "Toward a Primary Bibliography of Clarence Major." *Black American Literature Forum* 13 (1979): 70–72.

———, and John O'Banion. "A Checklist of Ellison Criticism, 1972–1978." *Black American Literature Forum* 12 (1978): 51–55.

———, Robert Fikes, Jr., and Ishmael Reed, eds. "Mapping Out the Gumbo

Works: An Ishmael Reed Bibliography." *Black American Literature Forum* 12 (1978): 24–29.

Whitlow, Roger. *Black American Literature: A Critical History.* Chicago: Nelson Hall, 1973.

Wideman, John. "Defining the Black Voice in Fiction." *Black American Literature Forum* 11 (1977): 79–82.

——. "*Of Love and Dust:* A Reconsideration." *Callaloo* 1, no. 3 (1978): 76–84.

——. Review of *The Salt Eaters* by Toni Cade Bambara. *New York Times Book Review,* 1 June 1980, 14.

Williams, Sherley Anne. *Give Birth to Brightness: A Thematic Study in Neo-Black Literature.* New York: Dial Press, 1972.

Willis, Susan. "Eruptions of Funk: Historicizing Toni Morrison." *Black American Literature Forum* 16 (1982): 34–42.

Wilner, Eleanor R. "The Invisible Black Thread: Identity and Nonentity in *Invisible Man.*" *CLA Journal* 13 (1970): 242–57.

Winther, Per. "Imagery of Imprisonment in Ralph Ellison's *Invisible Man.*" *Black American Literature Forum* 17 (1983): 115–19.

Index

303